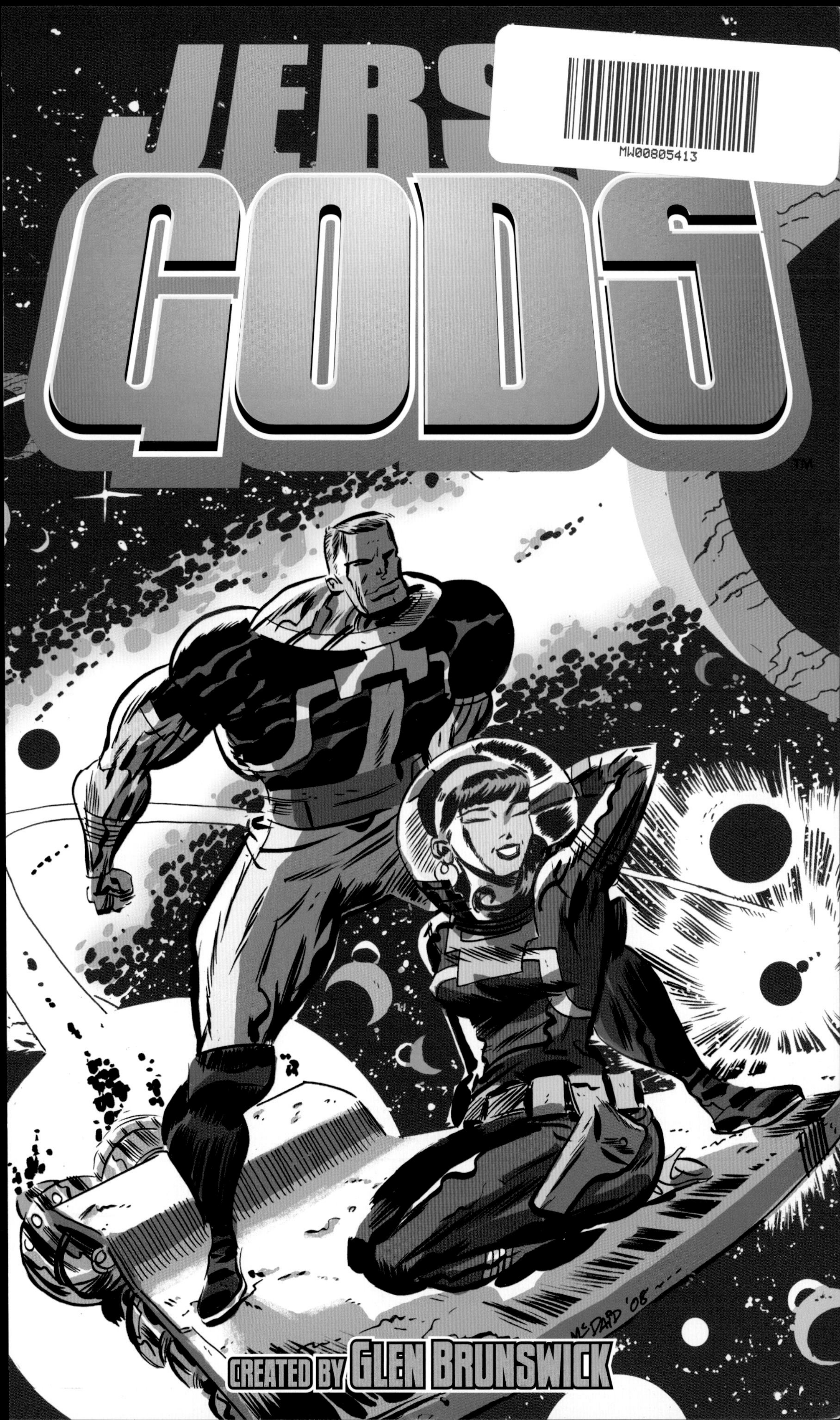
JERS
GODS
™
McDAID '08
CREATED BY GLEN BRUNSWICK

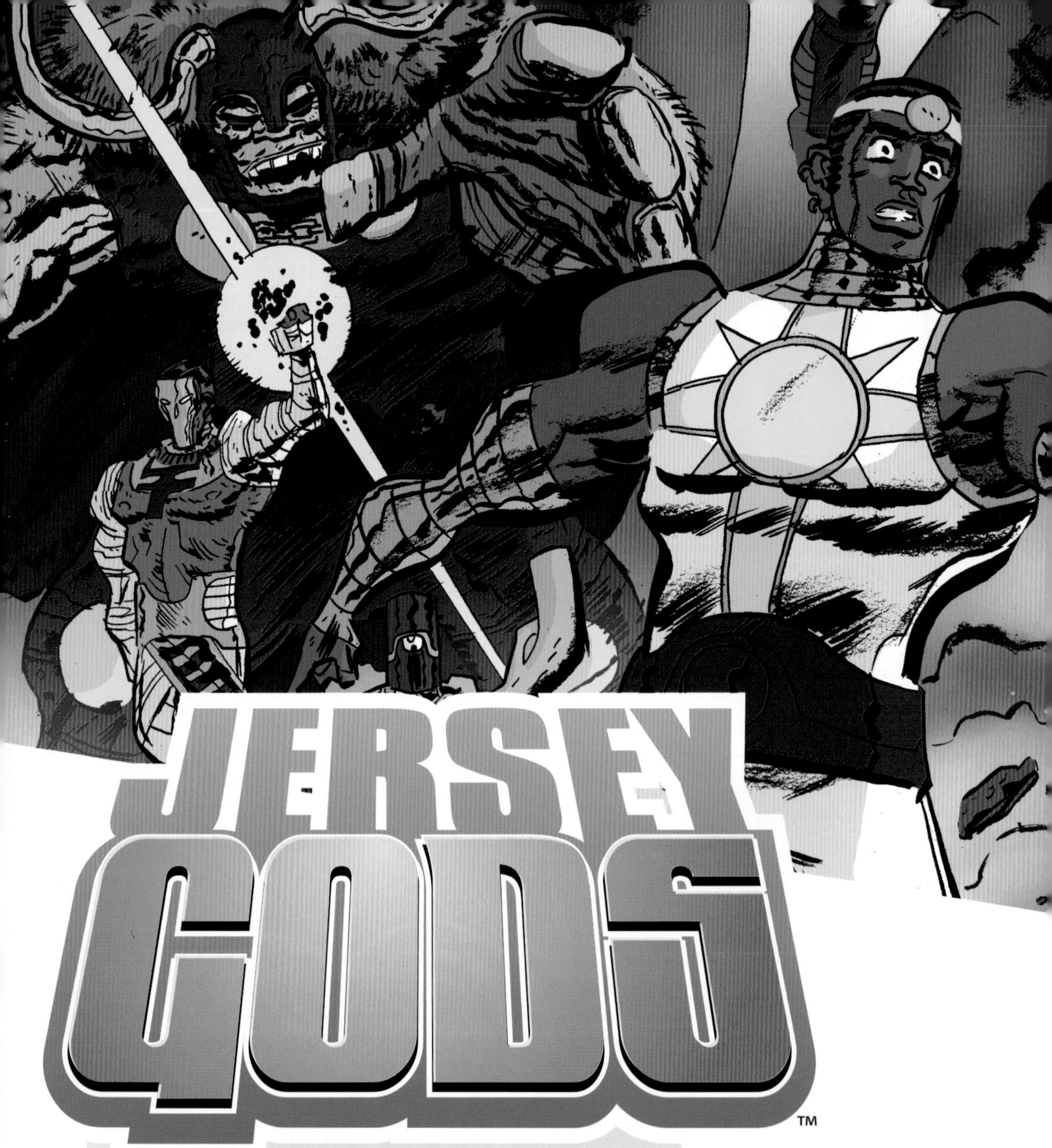

JERSEY GODS™

WRITTEN BY GLEN BRUNSWICK

ART BY DAN MCDAID

COLORS BY RACHELLE ROSENBERG

LETTERING BY RUS WOOTON

COVER BY DAN MCDAID & RICO RENZI

BOOK DESIGN & PRODUCTION BY JONATHAN CHAN

JERSEYGODS.BLOGSPOT.COM

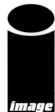

IMAGE COMICS, INC.

Robert Kirkman - chief operating officer
Erik Larsen - chief financial officer
Todd McFarlane - president
Marc Silvestri - chief executive officer
Jim Valentino - vice-president

ericstephenson - publisher
Joe Keatinge - pr & marketing coordinator
Branwyn Bigglestone - accounts manager
Tyler Shainline - traffic manager
Allen Hui - production manager
Drew Gill - production artist
Jonathan Chan - production artist
Monica Howard - production artist

www.imagecomics.com

JERSEY GODS, VOL. 1: I'D LIVE AND I'D DIE FOR YOU
ISBN: 978-1-60706-063-5
First Printing

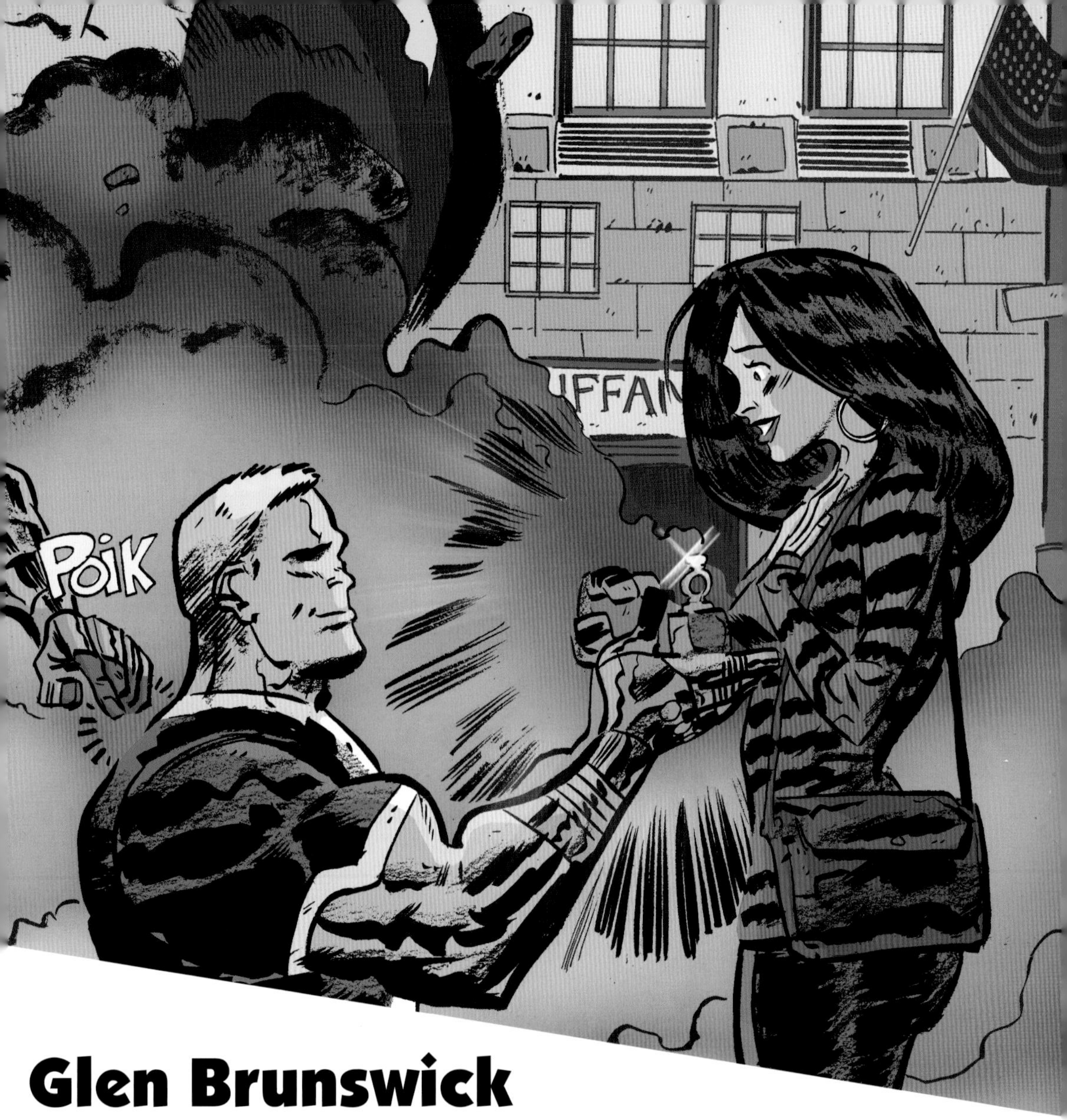
POIK

Glen Brunswick is a braver man than am I.

Seriously, I've made my career out of writing larger-than-life heroes, but the bigger and more cosmic they get, the harder it is for me to wrestle them into any sort of story I might be comfortable writing. All other things being equal, I'd much rather write small moments than big, godly, planet-smashing ones.

Glen's got the courage to take on both and not only do them both justice, but tie the earthbound and the cosmic together into a tapestry that is beyond my own ambition. And that he does it so expertly is that much more impressive.

Glen's story is about finding the humanity within gods and the godlike qualities in humans and showing us that everyone's struggle, from the most pyrotechnic to the most mundane, is a story worth telling whether they be princes to some galactic throne or princesses of some suburban mall. JERSEY GODS isn't the first attempt in comics to build some sort of narrative between the earth and the skies, but it's one of the most successful in that each venue is of equal importance and equal interest.

In Dan McDaid, your author has found a beautifully simpatico spirit, someone who can realize Brunswick's vision with a power that makes characters leap off the page without ever sacrificing storytelling clarity. Together, McDaid and Brunswick have created a world that has unusual breadth and depth, and I want to go there every issue to see what's new. I think you will, too.

Mark Waid
Midgard, 2009

CHAPTER ONE

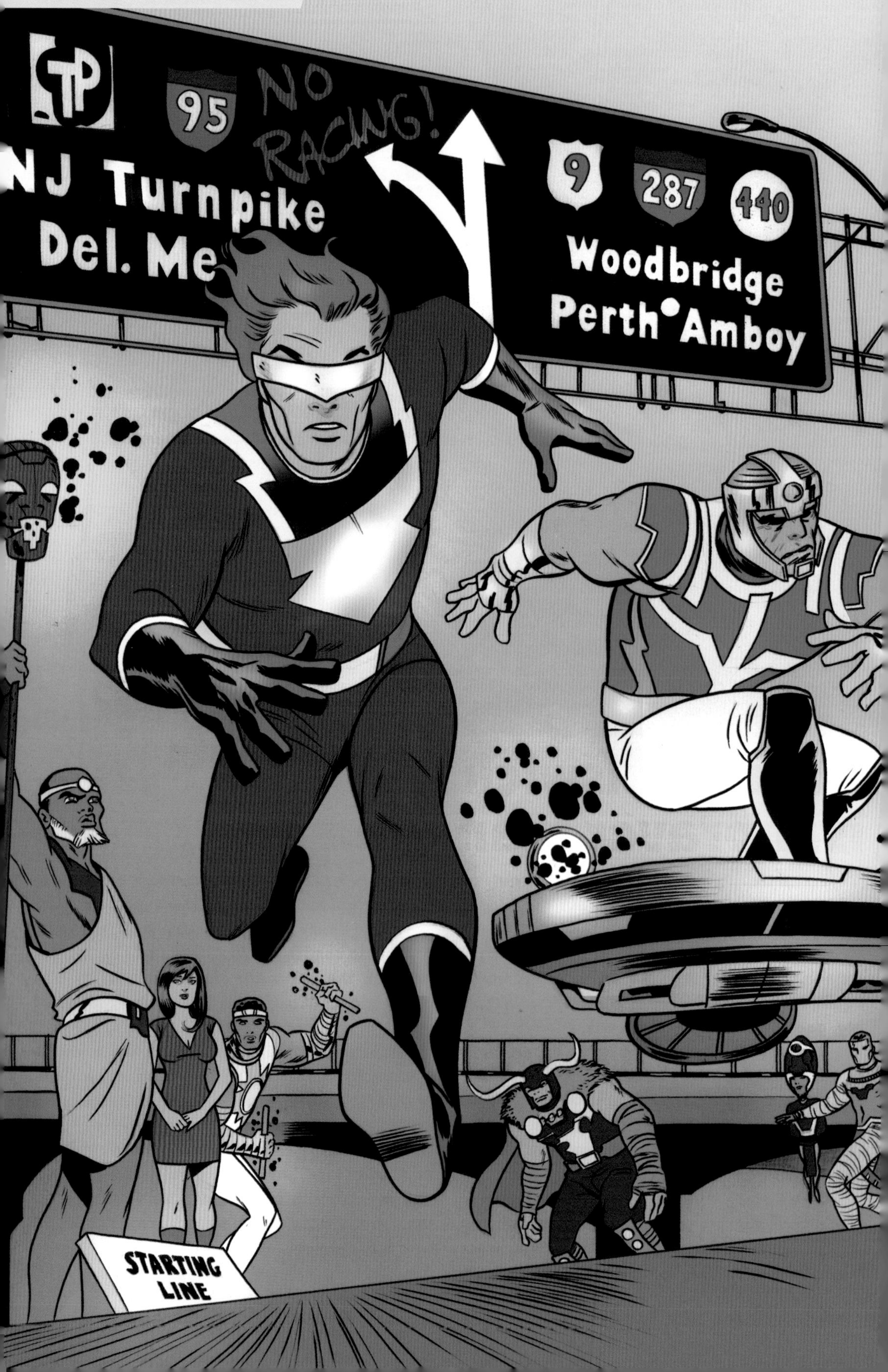
TP
95
NO RACING!
NJ Turnpike
Del. Me
9
287
440
Woodbridge
Perth Amboy
STARTING LINE

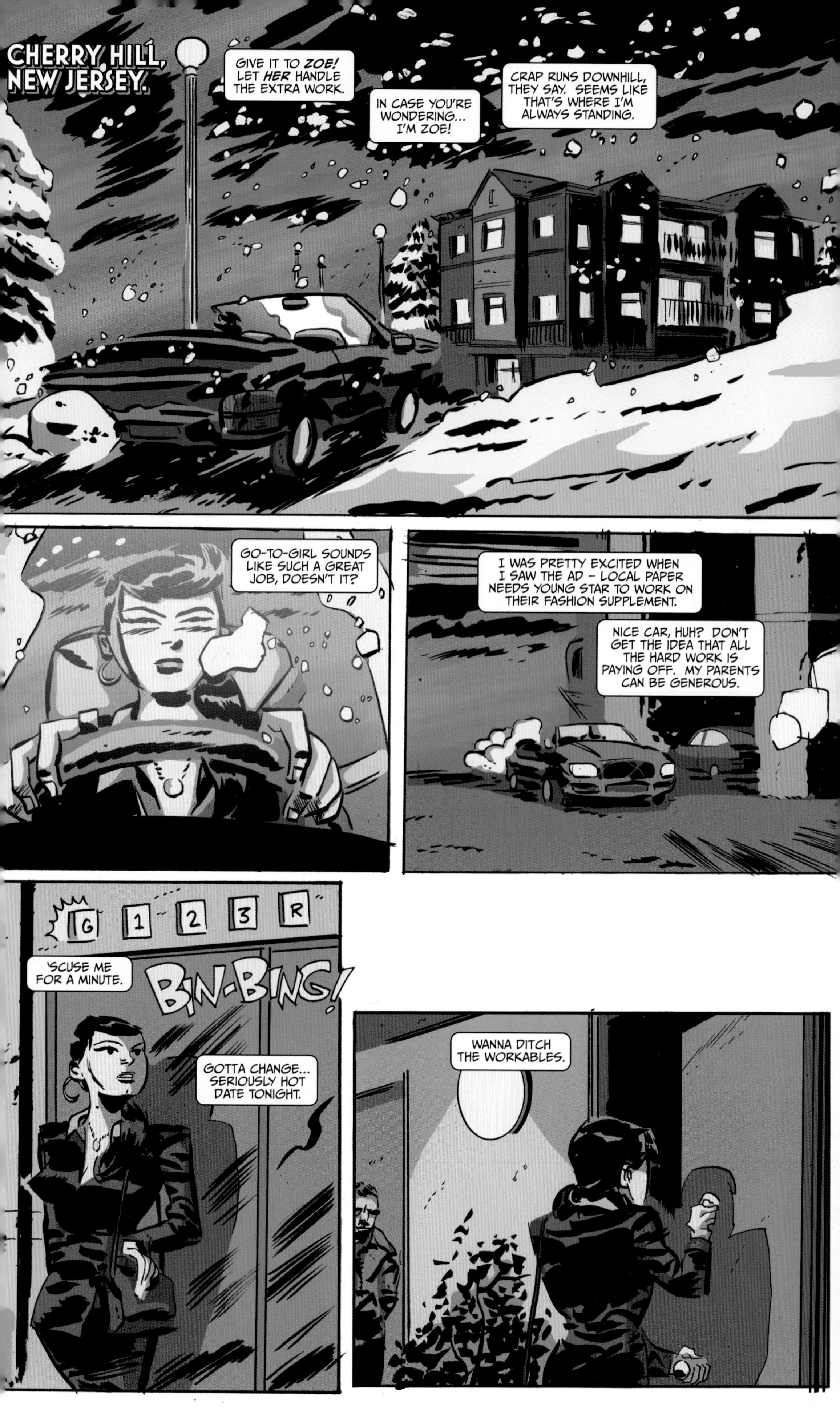
CHERRY HILL, NEW JERSEY.
GIVE IT TO ZOE! LET HER HANDLE THE EXTRA WORK.
IN CASE YOU'RE WONDERING... I'M ZOE!
CRAP RUNS DOWNHILL, THEY SAY. SEEMS LIKE THAT'S WHERE I'M ALWAYS STANDING.
GO-TO-GIRL SOUNDS LIKE SUCH A GREAT JOB, DOESN'T IT?
I WAS PRETTY EXCITED WHEN I SAW THE AD – LOCAL PAPER NEEDS YOUNG STAR TO WORK ON THEIR FASHION SUPPLEMENT.
NICE CAR, HUH? DON'T GET THE IDEA THAT ALL THE HARD WORK IS PAYING OFF. MY PARENTS CAN BE GENEROUS.
G 1 2 3 R
'SCUSE ME FOR A MINUTE.
BIN-BING!
GOTTA CHANGE... SERIOUSLY HOT DATE TONIGHT.
WANNA DITCH THE WORKABLES.

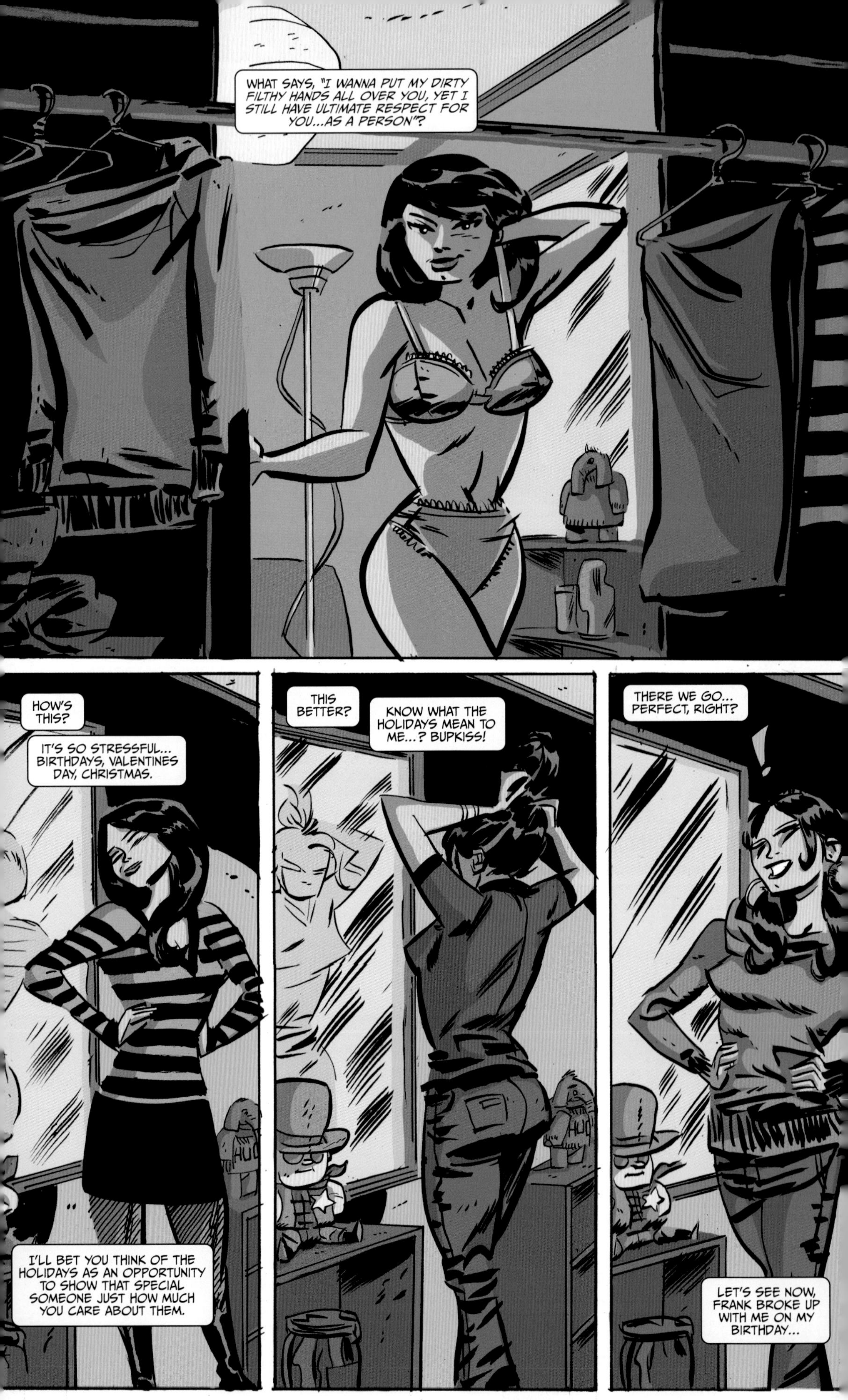

WHAT SAYS, "I WANNA PUT MY DIRTY FILTHY HANDS ALL OVER YOU, YET I STILL HAVE ULTIMATE RESPECT FOR YOU...AS A PERSON"?
HOW'S THIS?
IT'S SO STRESSFUL... BIRTHDAYS, VALENTINES DAY, CHRISTMAS.
I'LL BET YOU THINK OF THE HOLIDAYS AS AN OPPORTUNITY TO SHOW THAT SPECIAL SOMEONE JUST HOW MUCH YOU CARE ABOUT THEM.
THIS BETTER?
KNOW WHAT THE HOLIDAYS MEAN TO ME...? BUPKISS!
THERE WE GO... PERFECT, RIGHT?
!
LET'S SEE NOW, FRANK BROKE UP WITH ME ON MY BIRTHDAY...

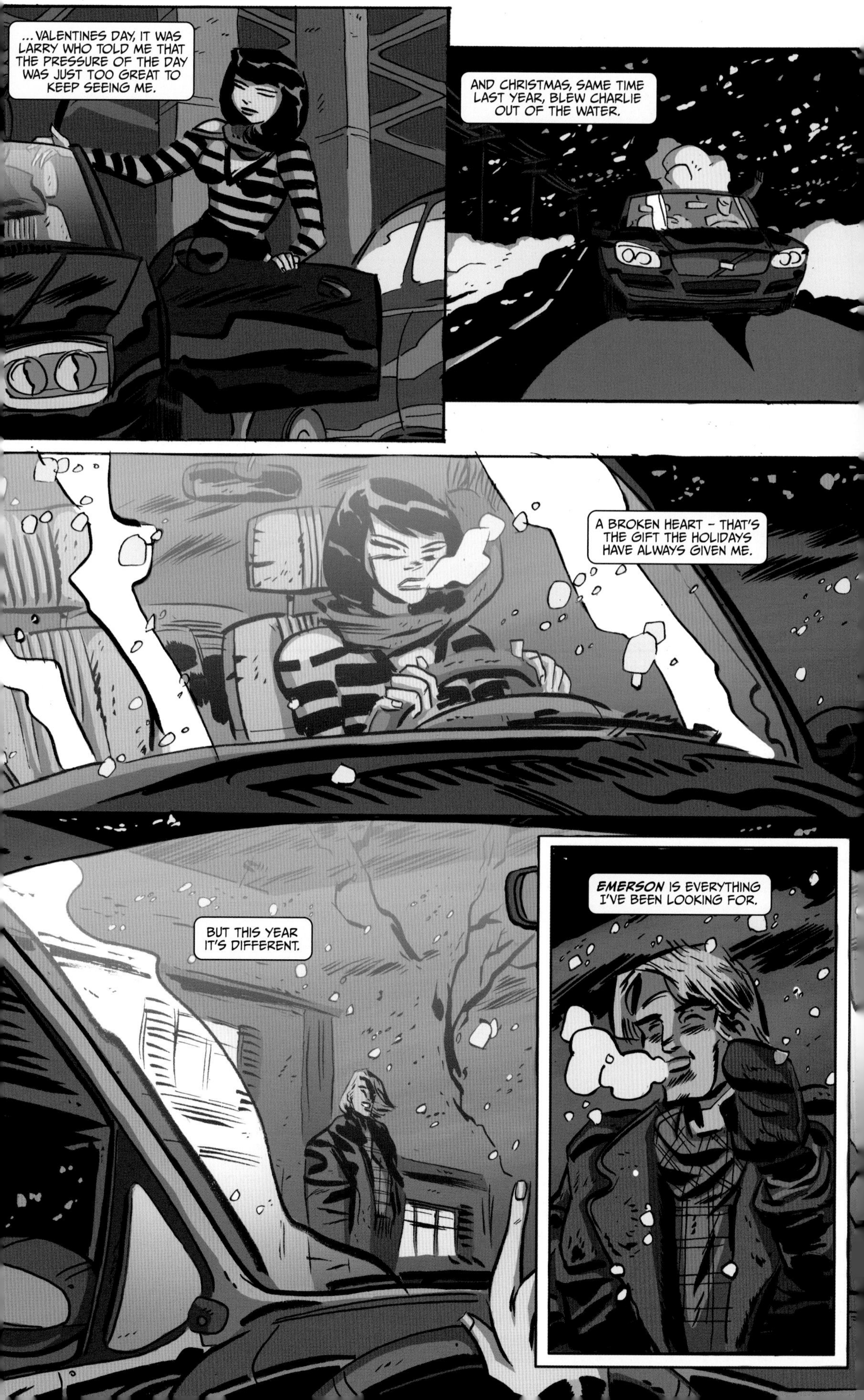
...VALENTINES DAY, IT WAS LARRY WHO TOLD ME THAT THE PRESSURE OF THE DAY WAS JUST TOO GREAT TO KEEP SEEING ME.
AND CHRISTMAS, SAME TIME LAST YEAR, BLEW CHARLIE OUT OF THE WATER.
A BROKEN HEART - THAT'S THE GIFT THE HOLIDAYS HAVE ALWAYS GIVEN ME.
BUT THIS YEAR IT'S DIFFERENT.
EMERSON IS EVERYTHING I'VE BEEN LOOKING FOR.

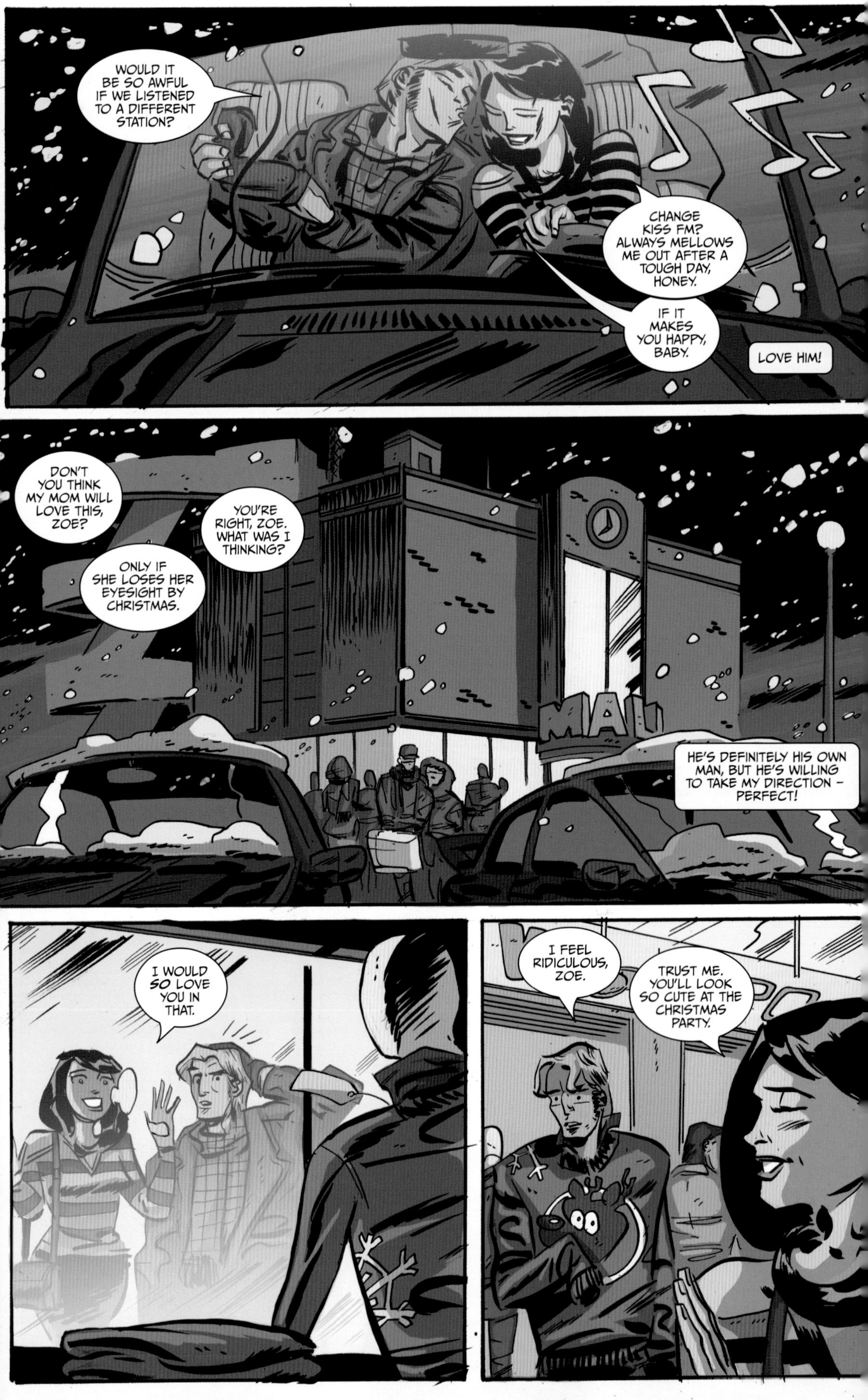
WOULD IT BE SO AWFUL IF WE LISTENED TO A DIFFERENT STATION?
CHANGE KISS FM? ALWAYS MELLOWS ME OUT AFTER A TOUGH DAY, HONEY.
IF IT MAKES YOU HAPPY, BABY.
LOVE HIM!
DON'T YOU THINK MY MOM WILL LOVE THIS, ZOE?
ONLY IF SHE LOSES HER EYESIGHT BY CHRISTMAS.
YOU'RE RIGHT, ZOE. WHAT WAS I THINKING?
HE'S DEFINITELY HIS OWN MAN, BUT HE'S WILLING TO TAKE MY DIRECTION – PERFECT!
I WOULD *SO* LOVE YOU IN THAT.
I FEEL RIDICULOUS, ZOE.
TRUST ME. YOU'LL LOOK SO CUTE AT THE CHRISTMAS PARTY.

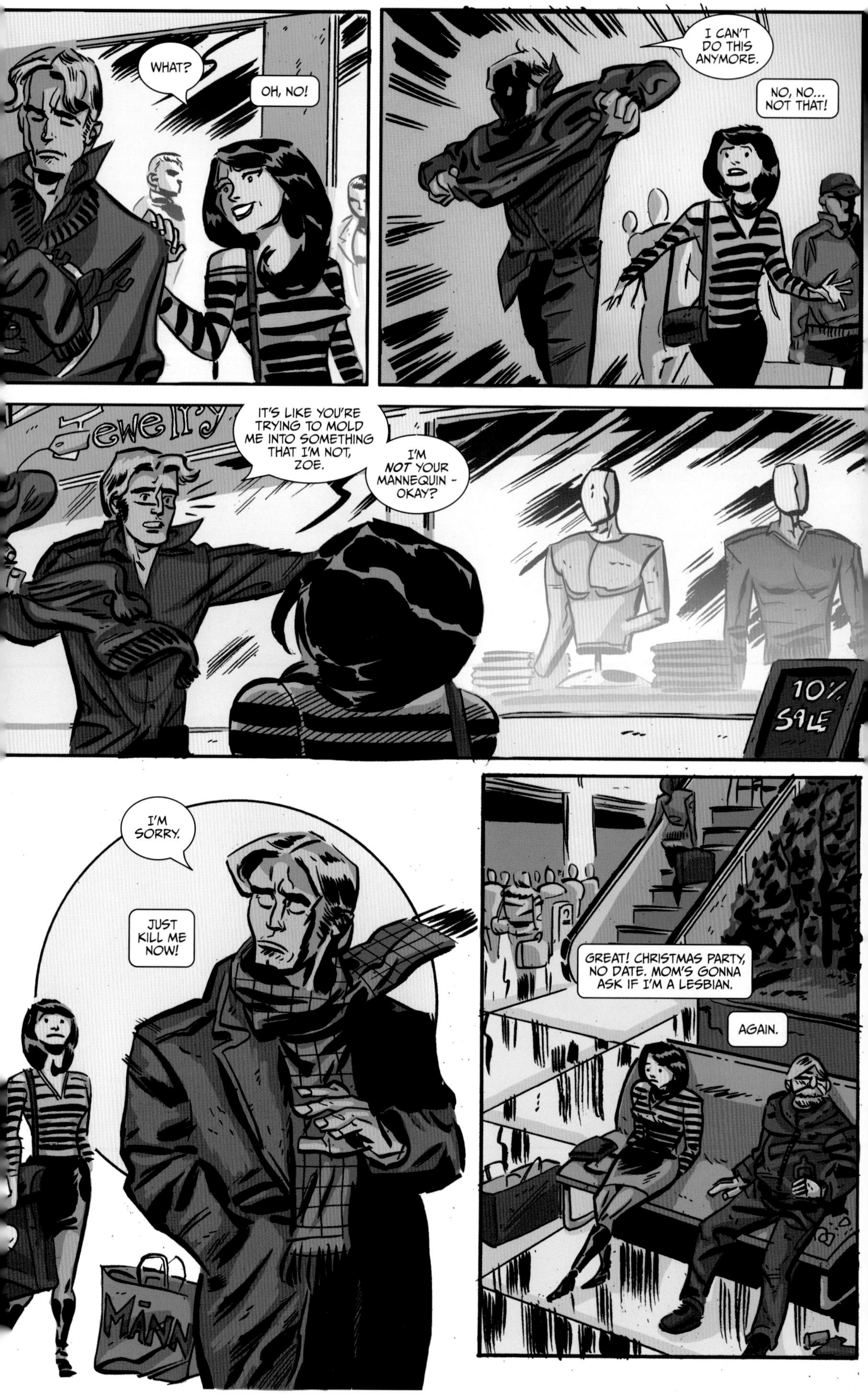
WHAT?
OH, NO!
I CAN'T DO THIS ANYMORE.
NO, NO... NOT THAT!
Jewelry
IT'S LIKE YOU'RE TRYING TO MOLD ME INTO SOMETHING THAT I'M NOT, ZOE.
I'M *NOT* YOUR MANNEQUIN - OKAY?
10% SALE
I'M SORRY.
JUST KILL ME NOW!
MANN
GREAT! CHRISTMAS PARTY, NO DATE. MOM'S GONNA ASK IF I'M A LESBIAN.
AGAIN.

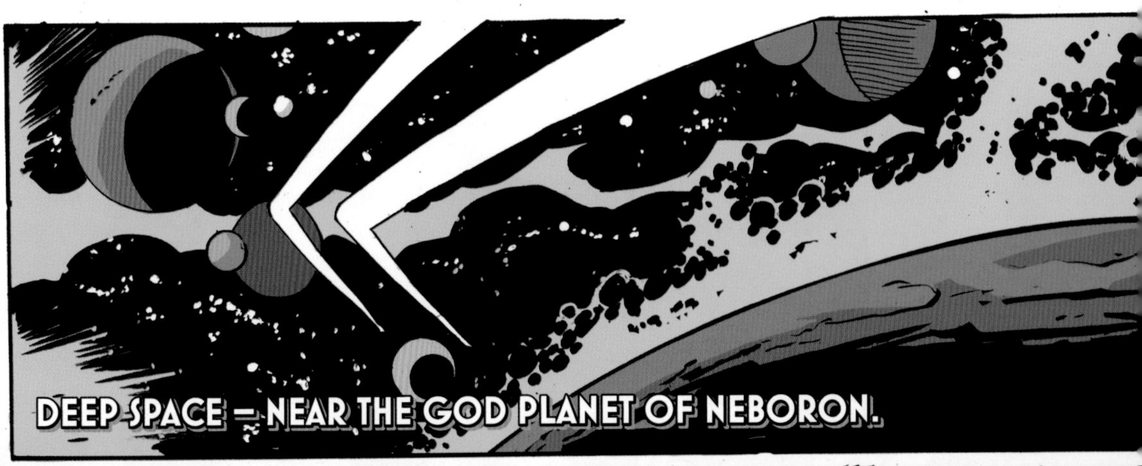
DEEP SPACE — NEAR THE GOD PLANET OF NEBORON.

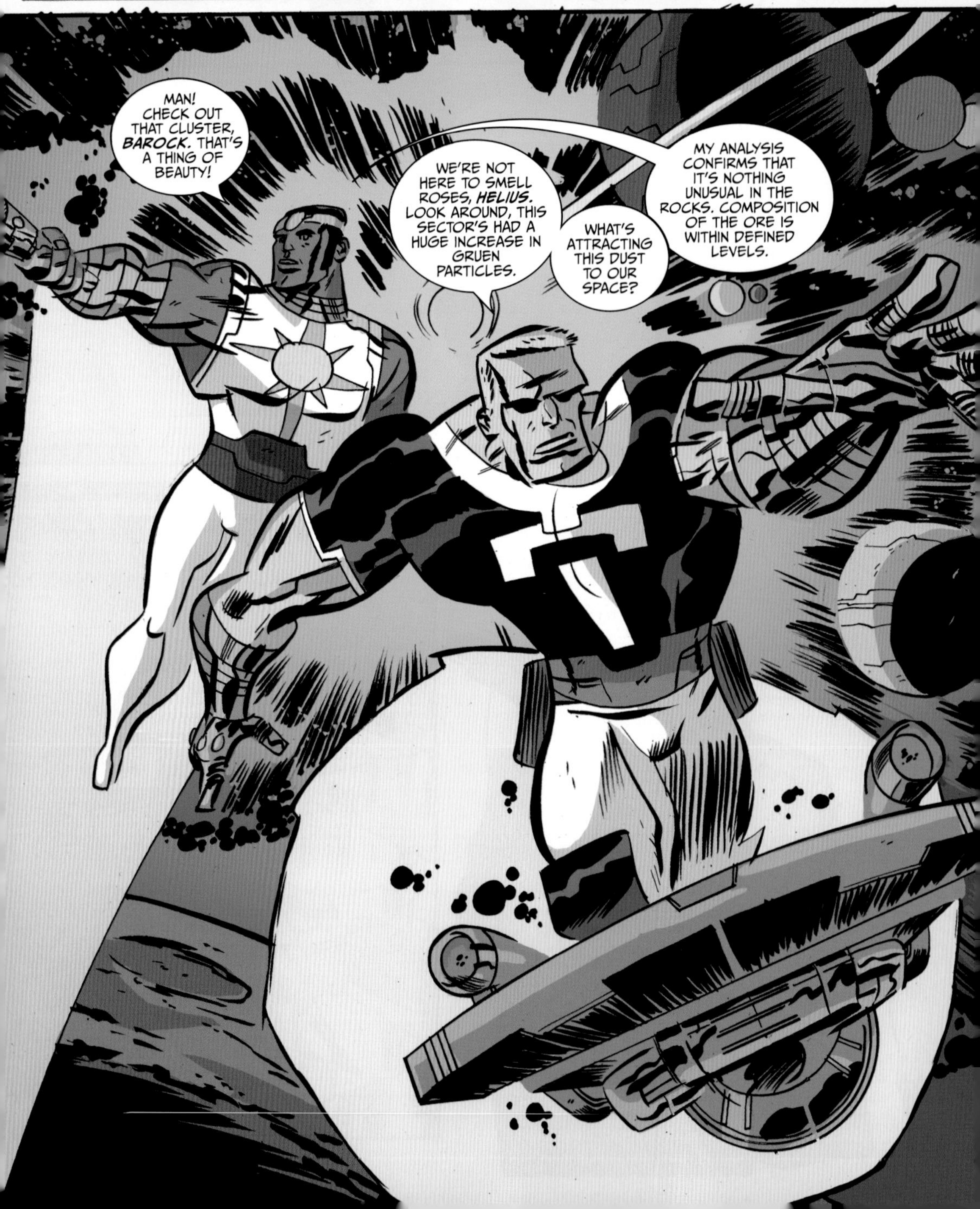
MAN! CHECK OUT THAT CLUSTER, BAROCK. THAT'S A THING OF BEAUTY!
WE'RE NOT HERE TO SMELL ROSES, HELIUS. LOOK AROUND, THIS SECTOR'S HAD A HUGE INCREASE IN GRUEN PARTICLES.
WHAT'S ATTRACTING THIS DUST TO OUR SPACE?
MY ANALYSIS CONFIRMS THAT IT'S NOTHING UNUSUAL IN THE ROCKS. COMPOSITION OF THE ORE IS WITHIN DEFINED LEVELS.

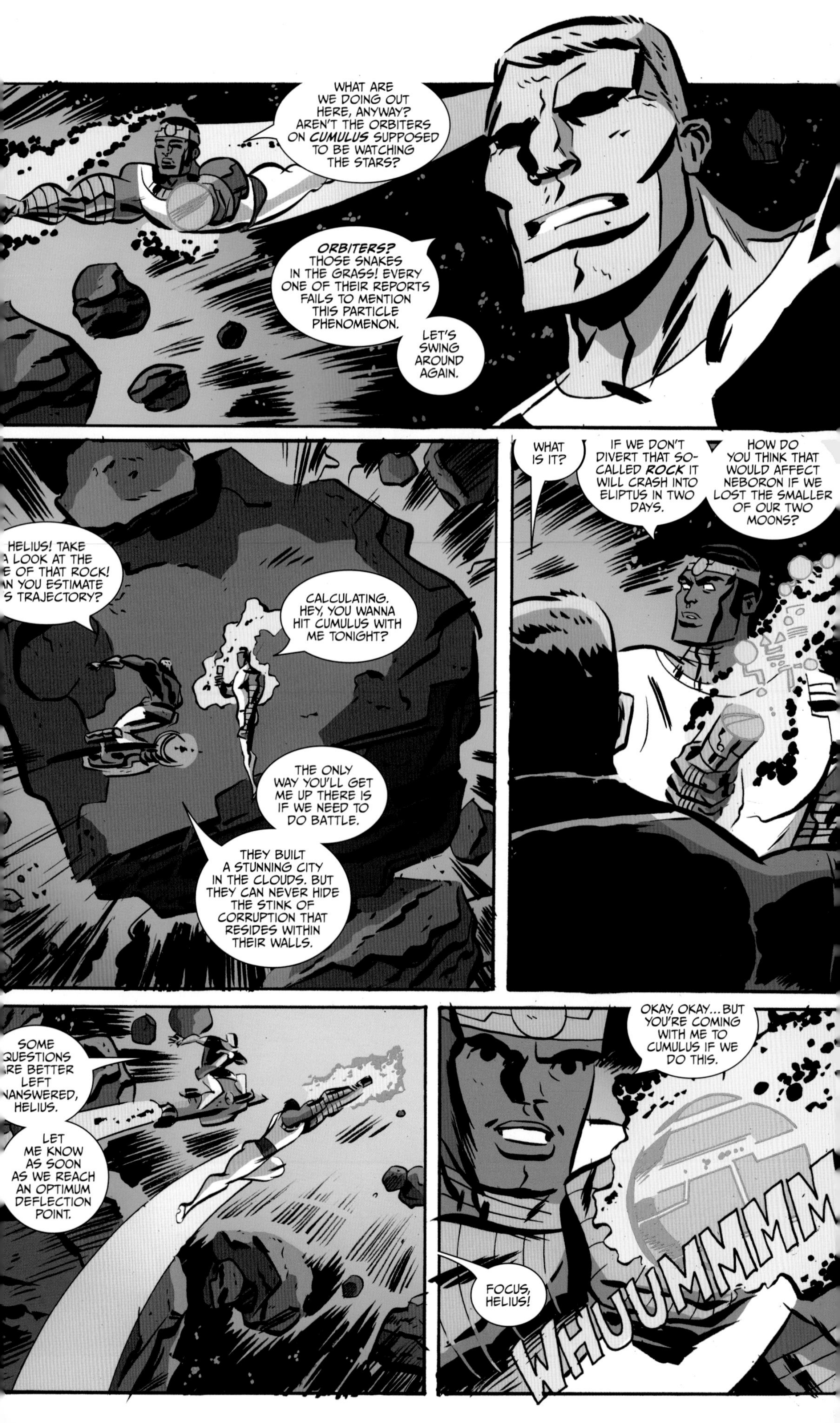
WHAT ARE WE DOING OUT HERE, ANYWAY? AREN'T THE ORBITERS ON CUMULUS SUPPOSED TO BE WATCHING THE STARS?
ORBITERS? THOSE SNAKES IN THE GRASS! EVERY ONE OF THEIR REPORTS FAILS TO MENTION THIS PARTICLE PHENOMENON.
LET'S SWING AROUND AGAIN.
HELIUS! TAKE A LOOK AT THE E OF THAT ROCK! AN YOU ESTIMATE S TRAJECTORY?
CALCULATING. HEY, YOU WANNA HIT CUMULUS WITH ME TONIGHT?
THE ONLY WAY YOU'LL GET ME UP THERE IS IF WE NEED TO DO BATTLE.
THEY BUILT A STUNNING CITY IN THE CLOUDS. BUT THEY CAN NEVER HIDE THE STINK OF CORRUPTION THAT RESIDES WITHIN THEIR WALLS.
WHAT IS IT?
IF WE DON'T DIVERT THAT SO-CALLED ROCK IT WILL CRASH INTO ELIPTUS IN TWO DAYS.
HOW DO YOU THINK THAT WOULD AFFECT NEBORON IF WE LOST THE SMALLER OF OUR TWO MOONS?
SOME QUESTIONS ARE BETTER LEFT NANSWERED, HELIUS.
LET ME KNOW AS SOON AS WE REACH AN OPTIMUM DEFLECTION POINT.
OKAY, OKAY... BUT YOU'RE COMING WITH ME TO CUMULUS IF WE DO THIS.
FOCUS, HELIUS!
WHUUMMMM

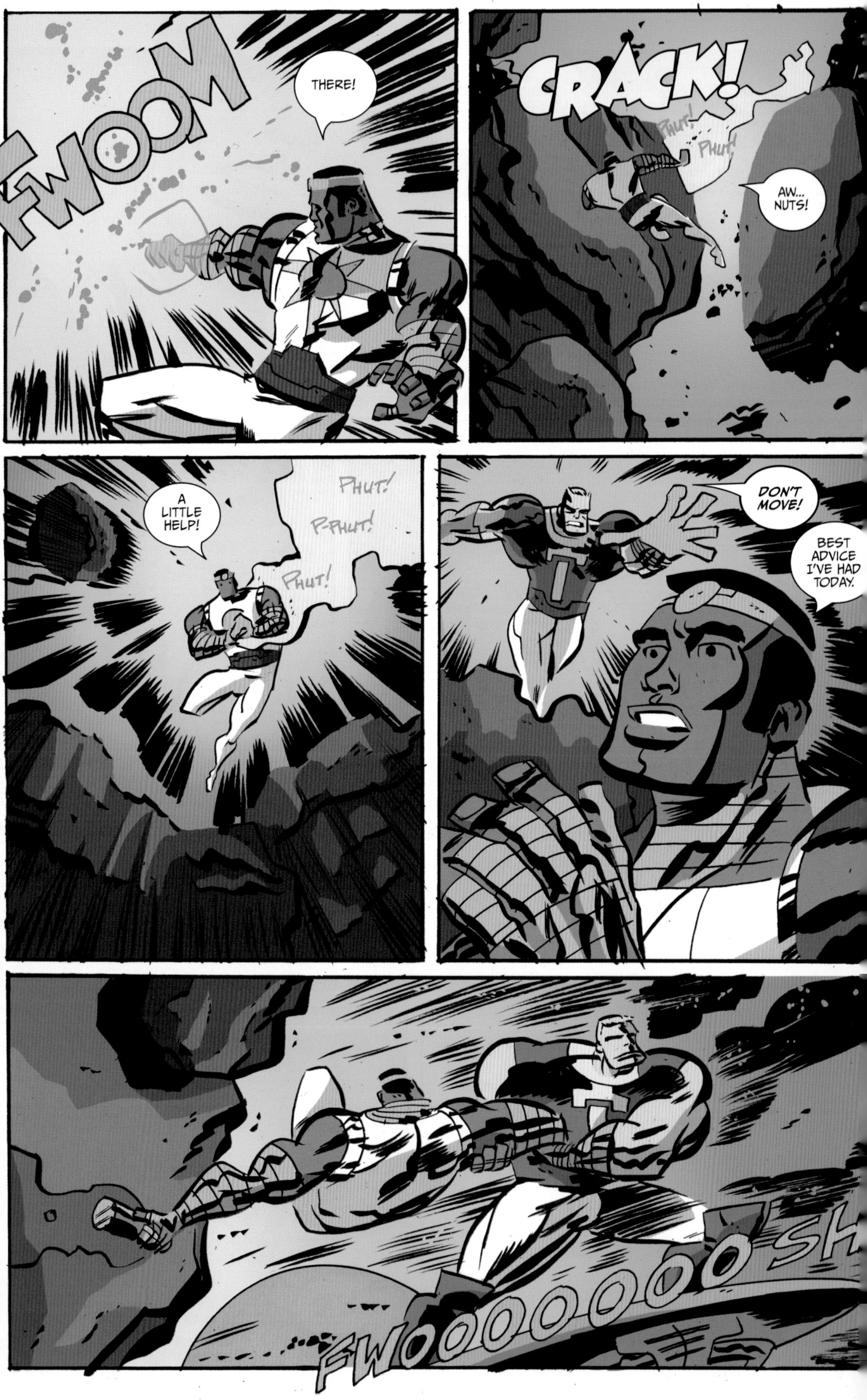

FWOOM
THERE!
CRACK!
PHUT!
PHUT!
AW... NUTS!
A LITTLE HELP!
PHUT!
P-PHUT!
PHUT!
DON'T MOVE!
BEST ADVICE I'VE HAD TODAY.
FWOOOOOOOOSH

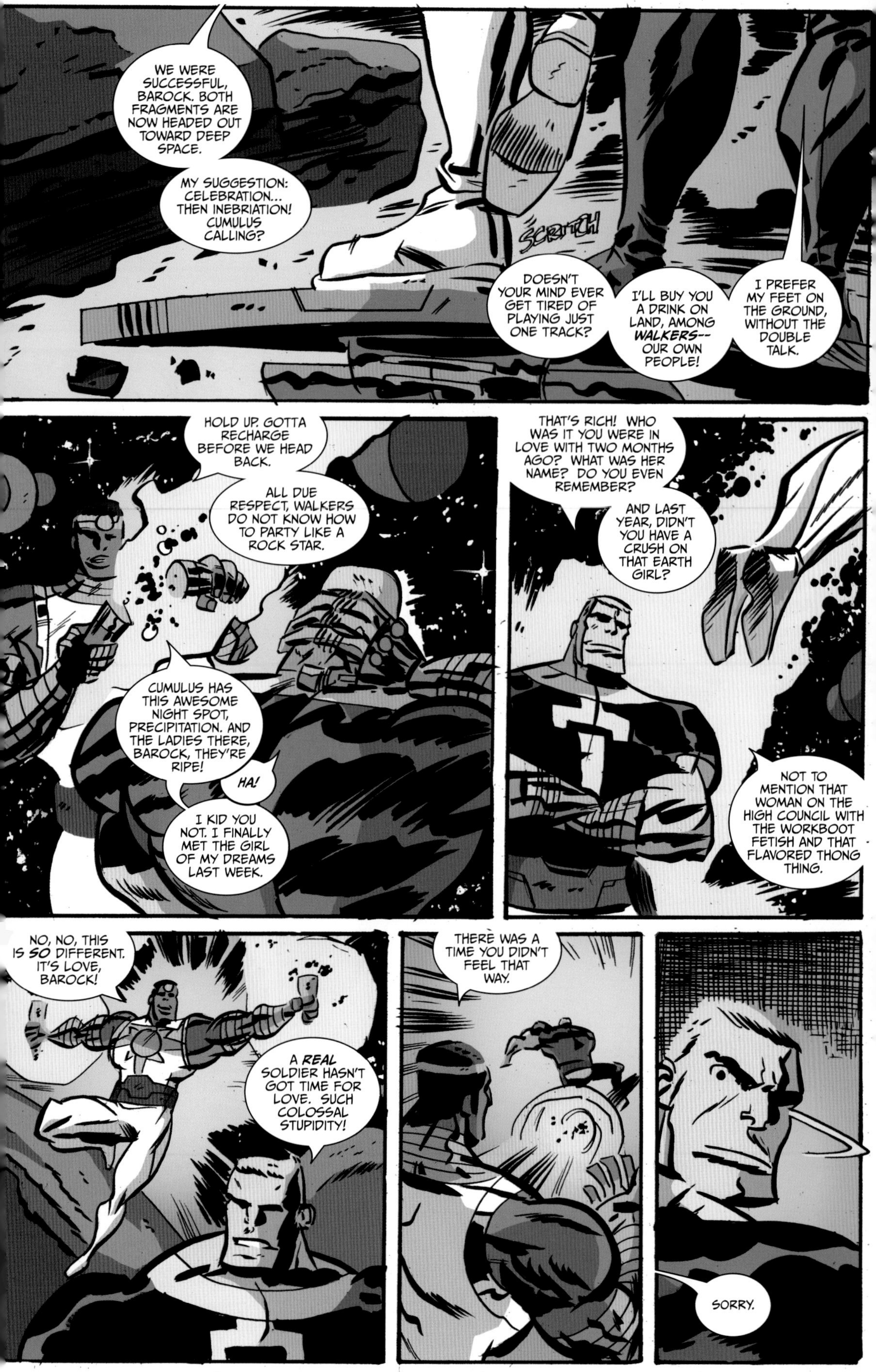
WE WERE SUCCESSFUL, BAROCK. BOTH FRAGMENTS ARE NOW HEADED OUT TOWARD DEEP SPACE.
MY SUGGESTION: CELEBRATION... THEN INEBRIATION! CUMULUS CALLING?
SCRITCH
DOESN'T YOUR MIND EVER GET TIRED OF PLAYING JUST ONE TRACK?
I'LL BUY YOU A DRINK ON LAND, AMONG *WALKERS*-- OUR OWN PEOPLE!
I PREFER MY FEET ON THE GROUND, WITHOUT THE DOUBLE TALK.
HOLD UP. GOTTA RECHARGE BEFORE WE HEAD BACK.
ALL DUE RESPECT, WALKERS DO NOT KNOW HOW TO PARTY LIKE A ROCK STAR.
CUMULUS HAS THIS AWESOME NIGHT SPOT, PRECIPITATION. AND THE LADIES THERE, BAROCK, THEY'RE RIPE!
HA!
I KID YOU NOT. I FINALLY MET THE GIRL OF MY DREAMS LAST WEEK.
THAT'S RICH! WHO WAS IT YOU WERE IN LOVE WITH TWO MONTHS AGO? WHAT WAS HER NAME? DO YOU EVEN REMEMBER?
AND LAST YEAR, DIDN'T YOU HAVE A CRUSH ON THAT EARTH GIRL?
NOT TO MENTION THAT WOMAN ON THE HIGH COUNCIL WITH THE WORKBOOT FETISH AND THAT FLAVORED THONG THING.
NO, NO, THIS IS *SO* DIFFERENT. IT'S LOVE, BAROCK!
A *REAL* SOLDIER HASN'T GOT TIME FOR LOVE. SUCH COLOSSAL STUPIDITY!
THERE WAS A TIME YOU DIDN'T FEEL THAT WAY.
SORRY.

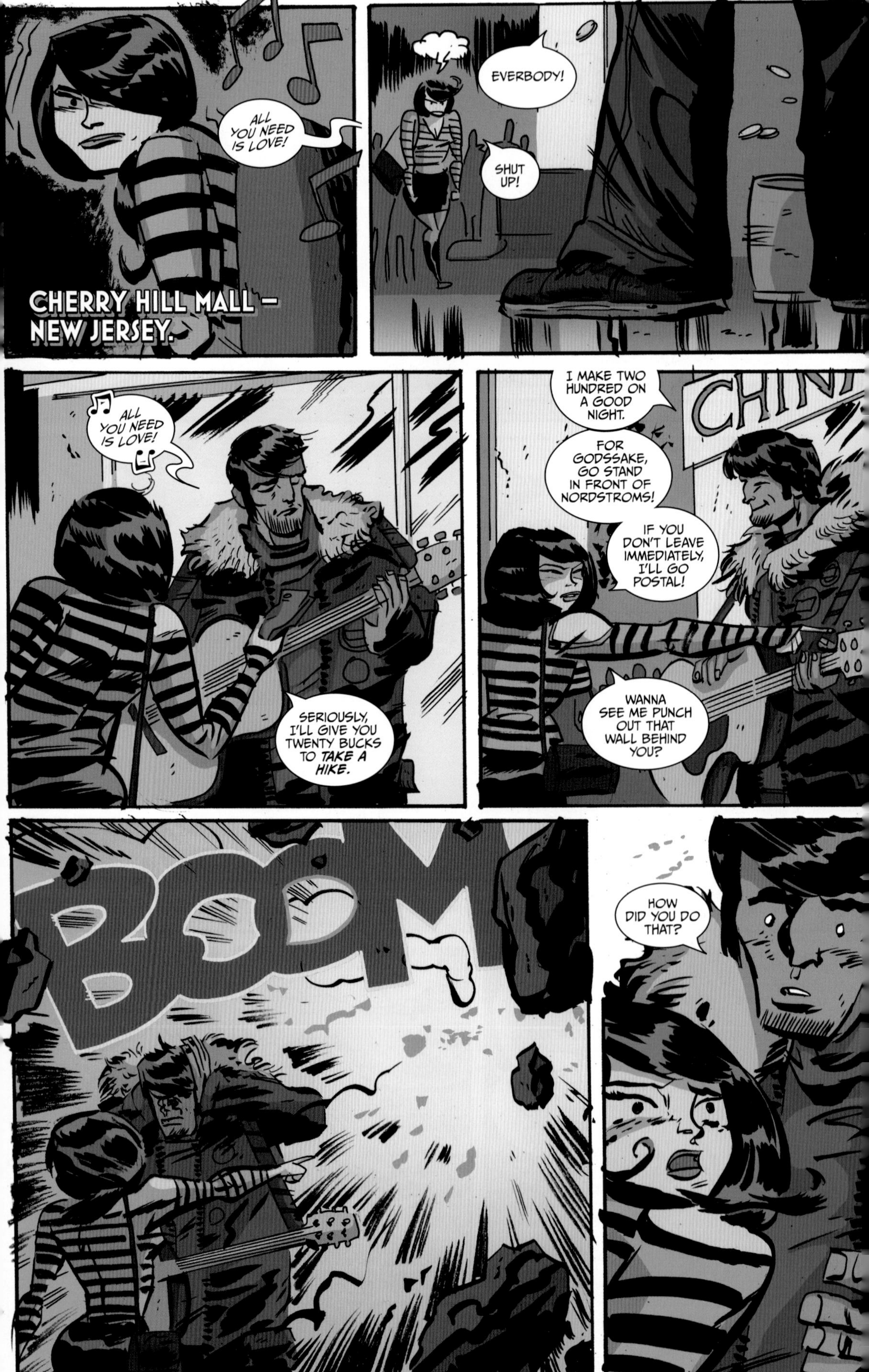
CHERRY HILL MALL – NEW JERSEY.
ALL YOU NEED IS LOVE!
EVERBODY!
SHUT UP!
ALL YOU NEED IS LOVE!
SERIOUSLY, I'LL GIVE YOU TWENTY BUCKS TO TAKE A HIKE.
I MAKE TWO HUNDRED ON A GOOD NIGHT.
FOR GODSSAKE, GO STAND IN FRONT OF NORDSTROMS!
IF YOU DON'T LEAVE IMMEDIATELY, I'LL GO POSTAL!
WANNA SEE ME PUNCH OUT THAT WALL BEHIND YOU?
BOOM
HOW DID YOU DO THAT?

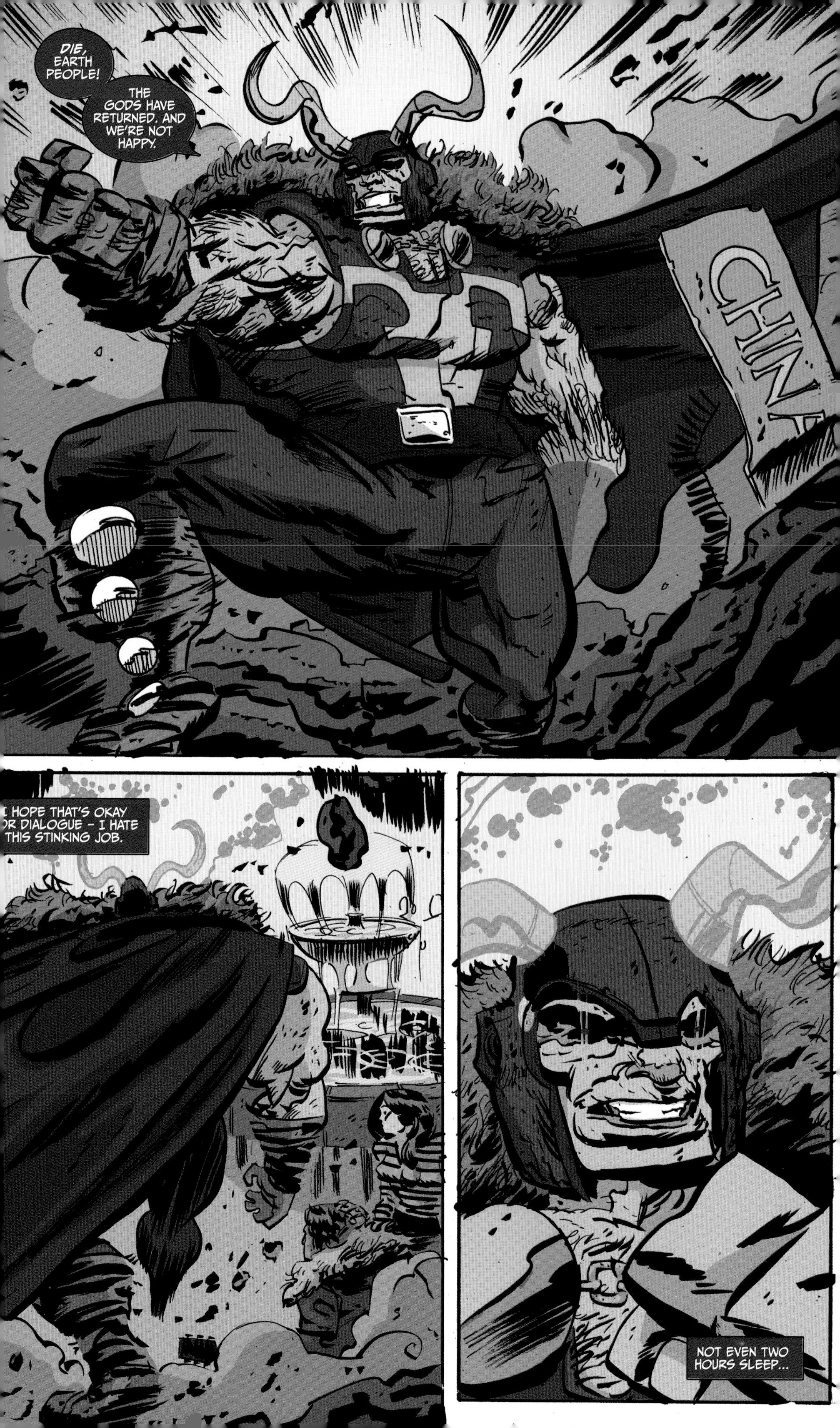
DIE, EARTH PEOPLE!
THE GODS HAVE RETURNED. AND WE'RE NOT HAPPY.
I HOPE THAT'S OKAY OR DIALOGUE – I HATE THIS STINKING JOB.
NOT EVEN TWO HOURS SLEEP...

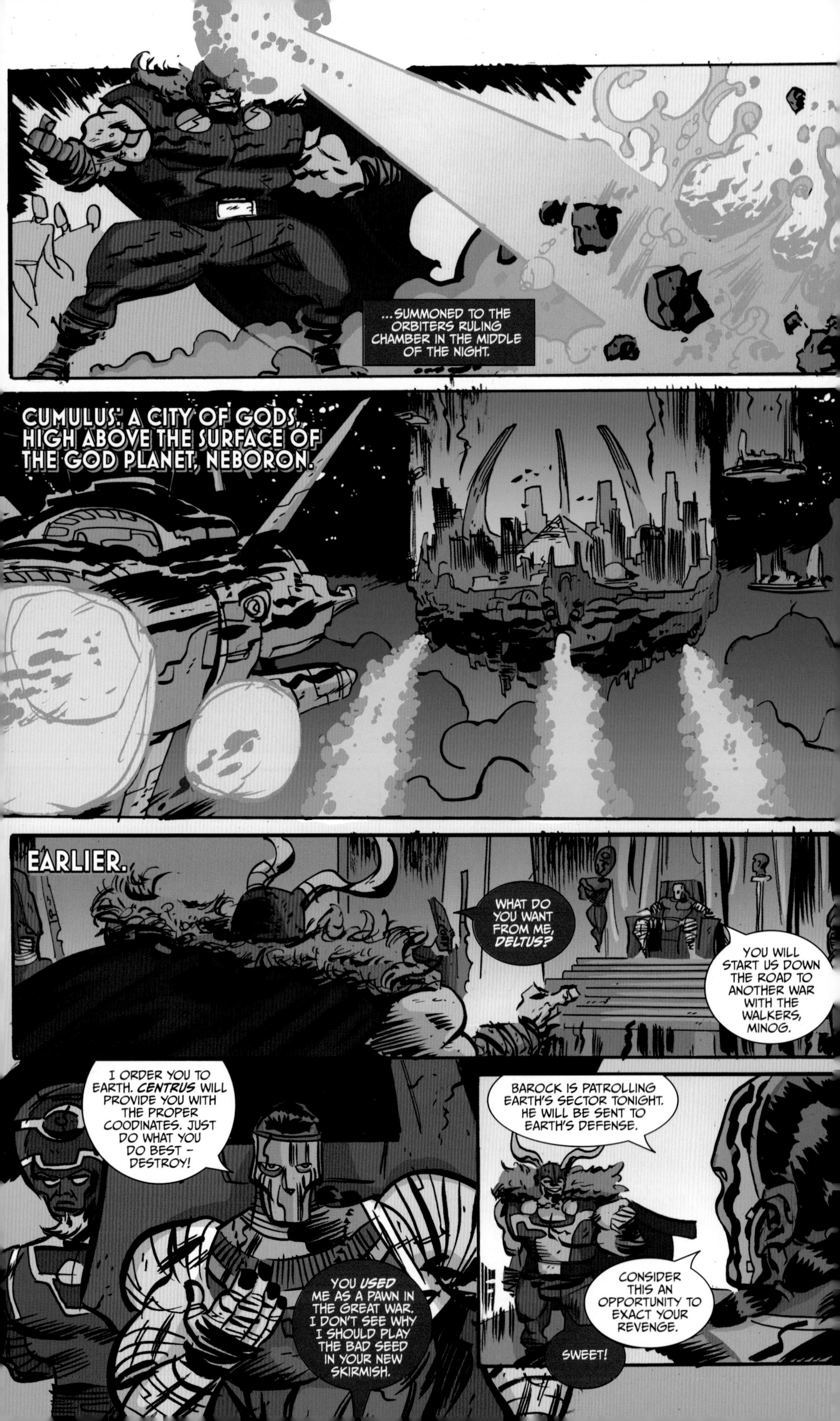
...SUMMONED TO THE ORBITERS RULING CHAMBER IN THE MIDDLE OF THE NIGHT.
CUMULUS: A CITY OF GODS, HIGH ABOVE THE SURFACE OF THE GOD PLANET, NEBORON.
EARLIER.
WHAT DO YOU WANT FROM ME, DELTUS?
YOU WILL START US DOWN THE ROAD TO ANOTHER WAR WITH THE WALKERS, MINOG.
I ORDER YOU TO EARTH. CENTRUS WILL PROVIDE YOU WITH THE PROPER COODINATES. JUST DO WHAT YOU DO BEST - DESTROY!
YOU USED ME AS A PAWN IN THE GREAT WAR. I DON'T SEE WHY I SHOULD PLAY THE BAD SEED IN YOUR NEW SKIRMISH.
BAROCK IS PATROLLING EARTH'S SECTOR TONIGHT. HE WILL BE SENT TO EARTH'S DEFENSE.
CONSIDER THIS AN OPPORTUNITY TO EXACT YOUR REVENGE.
SWEET!

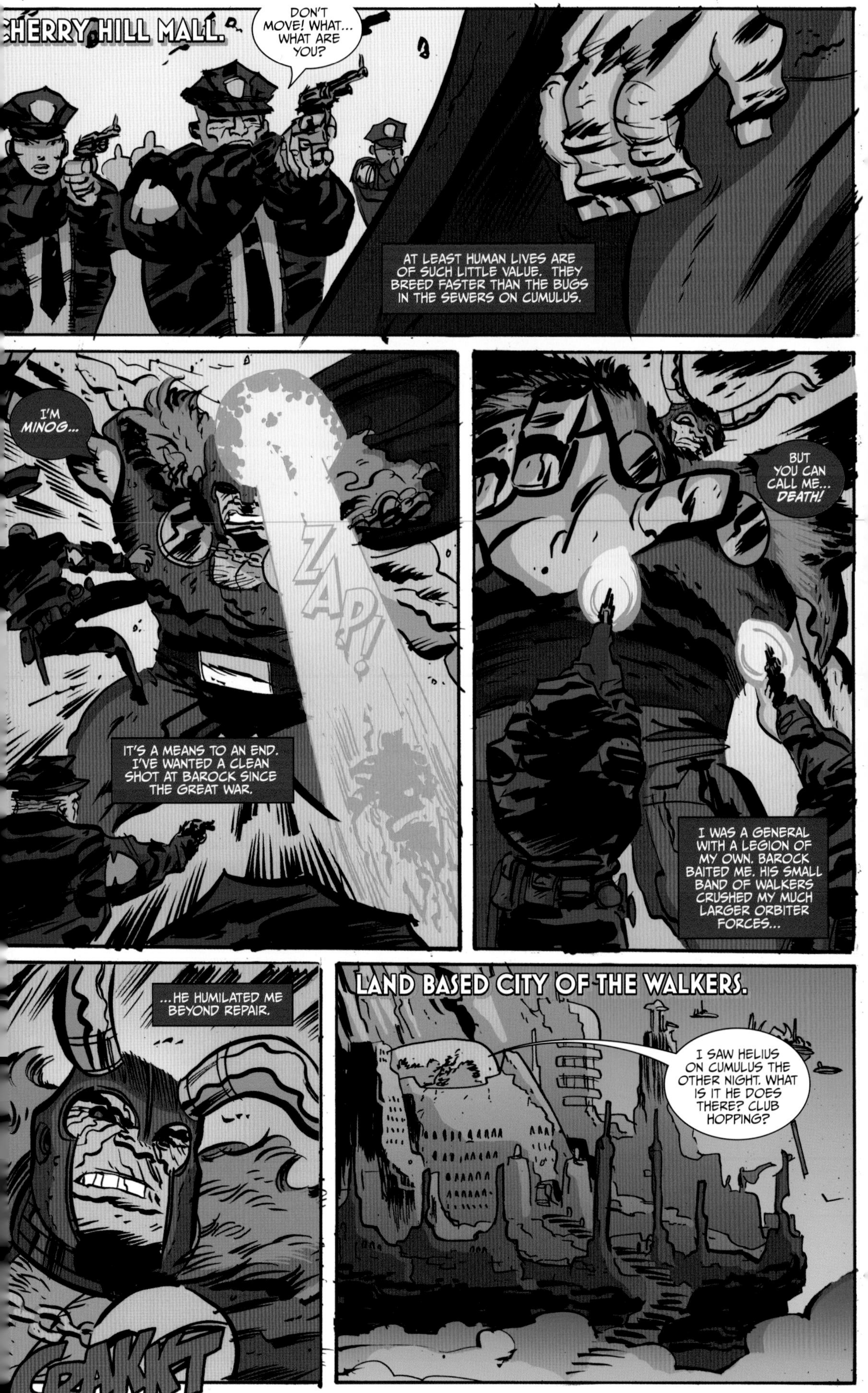
CHERRY HILL MALL.
DON'T MOVE! WHAT... WHAT ARE YOU?
AT LEAST HUMAN LIVES ARE OF SUCH LITTLE VALUE. THEY BREED FASTER THAN THE BUGS IN THE SEWERS ON CUMULUS.
I'M MINOG...
ZAP!
IT'S A MEANS TO AN END. I'VE WANTED A CLEAN SHOT AT BAROCK SINCE THE GREAT WAR.
BUT YOU CAN CALL ME... DEATH!
I WAS A GENERAL WITH A LEGION OF MY OWN. BAROCK BAITED ME. HIS SMALL BAND OF WALKERS CRUSHED MY MUCH LARGER ORBITER FORCES...
...HE HUMILATED ME BEYOND REPAIR.
CRAKKT
LAND BASED CITY OF THE WALKERS.
I SAW HELIUS ON CUMULUS THE OTHER NIGHT. WHAT IS IT HE DOES THERE? CLUB HOPPING?

FOR A BLIND MAN YOU HAVE INCREDIBLE EYESIGHT, *RUSHMORE*.

HOW IS IT YOU'RE ALWAYS AT THE RIGHT PLACE AT THE RIGHT TIME?

MY LENSES ALLOW ME TO SEE AT THE SUBATOMIC LEVEL. I ASSURE YOU THE ACCURACY OF MY EYES IS FAR SUPERIOR TO YOURS.

MY SON, HELIUS, DOESN'T LISTEN TO THE WORDS OF HIS FATHER. I REALLY DON'T KNOW WHAT TO DO ABOUT HIM.

I SENT HIM ON PATROL WITH BAROCK TODAY. I THOUGHT IT MIGHT TEACH HIM SOMETHING ABOUT RESPONSIBILITY.

SO THAT'S WHY YOU'RE TAKING CARE OF HIS DOG TODAY?

HA! YES, INDEED! I ALWAYS SEEM TO WIND UP WALKING DOGSTAR, DON'T I BOY. I DON'T MIND.

HE'S YOUNG, *SERIUS*. I'VE HEARD SOME WILD STORIES OF YOU AS A YOUNG MAN.

THERE APPEARS TO BE SOME KIND OF UNEXPECTED ACTIVITY ON EARTH.

ON THE MONITOR, RUSHMORE. LET ME HAVE A LOOK.

MINOG! WHY WOULD *HE* BE ON EARTH?

TRANSMISSION COMING IN FROM YOUR FATHER.

PROBA... WANTS TO CO... STRAIG... HOME

VDEEP!

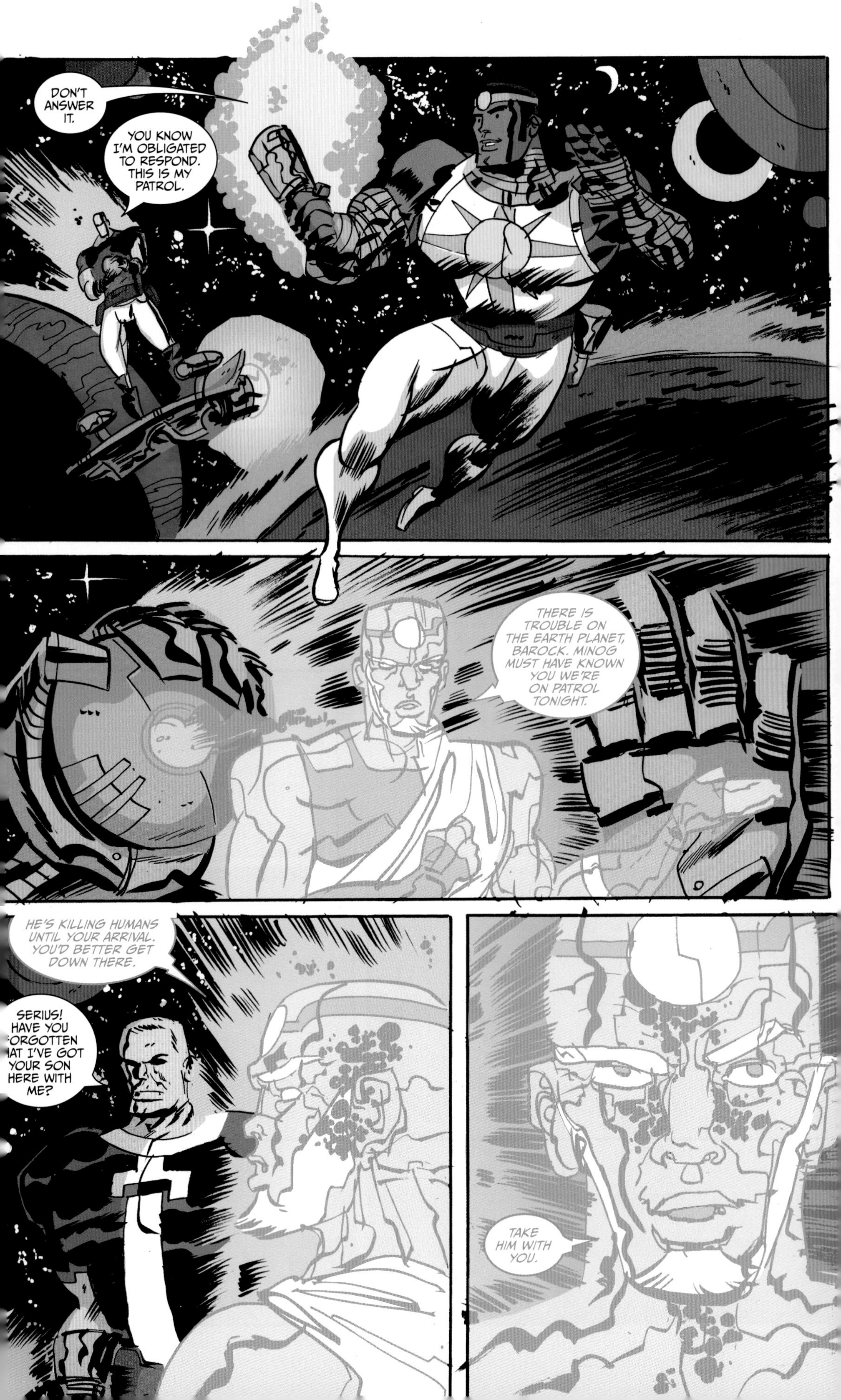
DON'T ANSWER IT.
YOU KNOW I'M OBLIGATED TO RESPOND. THIS IS MY PATROL.
THERE IS TROUBLE ON THE EARTH PLANET, BAROCK. MINOG MUST HAVE KNOWN YOU WE'RE ON PATROL TONIGHT.
HE'S KILLING HUMANS UNTIL YOUR ARRIVAL. YOU'D BETTER GET DOWN THERE.
SERIUS! HAVE YOU FORGOTTEN HAT I'VE GOT YOUR SON HERE WITH ME?
TAKE HIM WITH YOU.

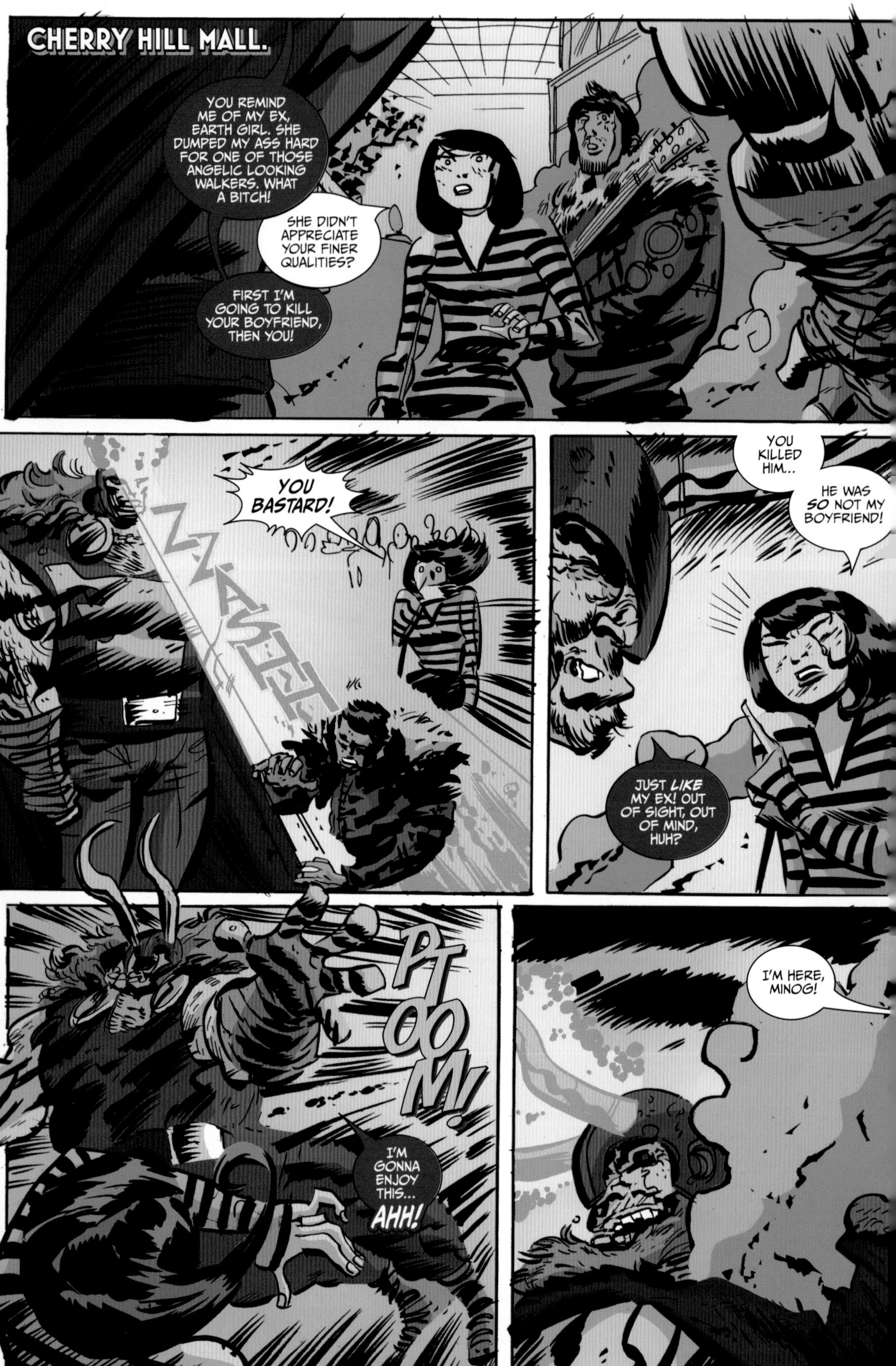
CHERRY HILL MALL.
YOU REMIND ME OF MY EX, EARTH GIRL. SHE DUMPED MY ASS HARD FOR ONE OF THOSE ANGELIC LOOKING WALKERS. WHAT A BITCH!
SHE DIDN'T APPRECIATE YOUR FINER QUALITIES?
FIRST I'M GOING TO KILL YOUR BOYFRIEND, THEN YOU!
YOU BASTARD!
ZZASHH
YOU KILLED HIM...
HE WAS SO NOT MY BOYFRIEND!
JUST LIKE MY EX! OUT OF SIGHT, OUT OF MIND, HUH?
PTOOM!
I'M GONNA ENJOY THIS... AHH!
I'M HERE, MINOG!

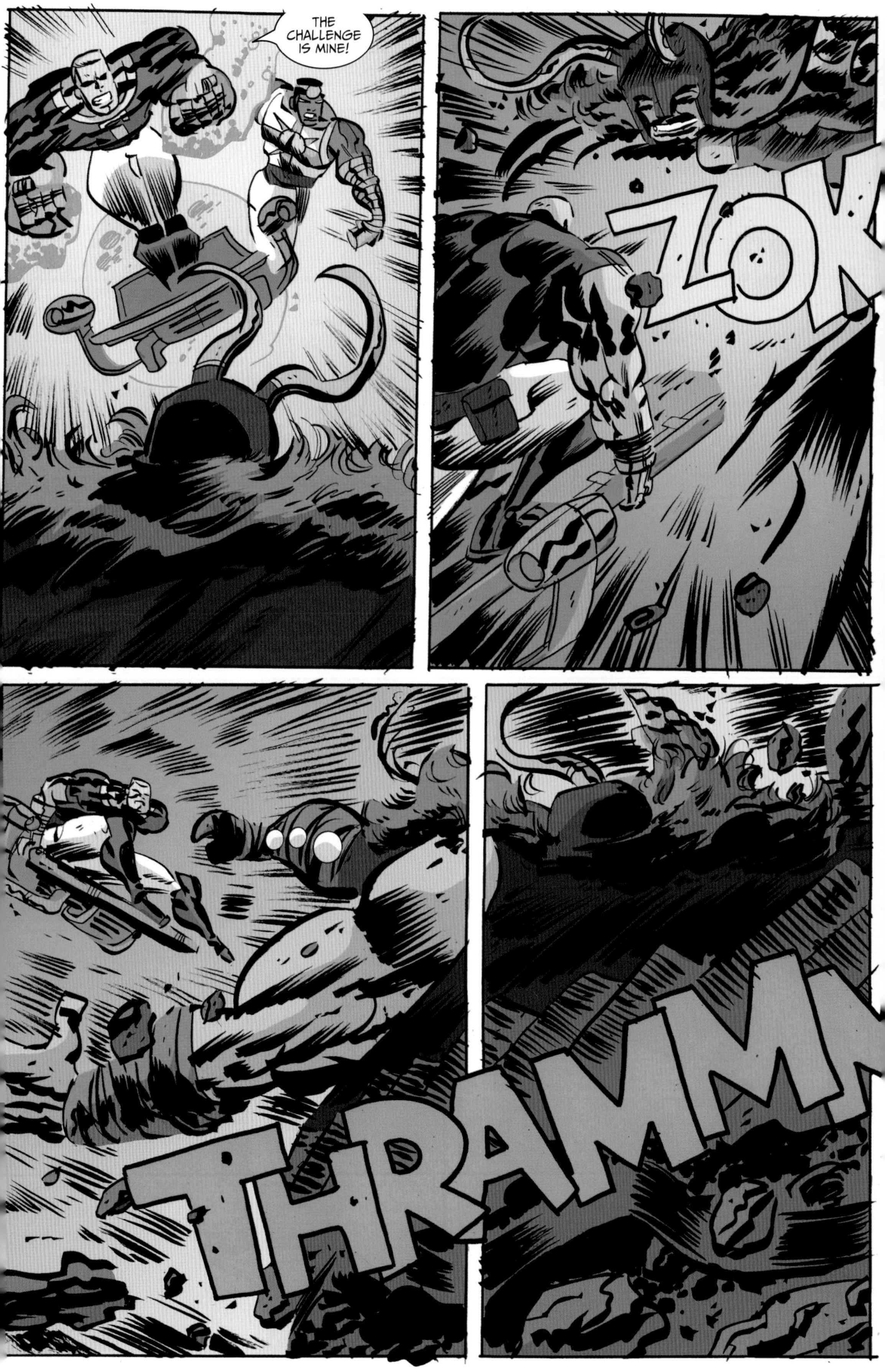
THE CHALLENGE IS MINE!
ZOK
THRAMM

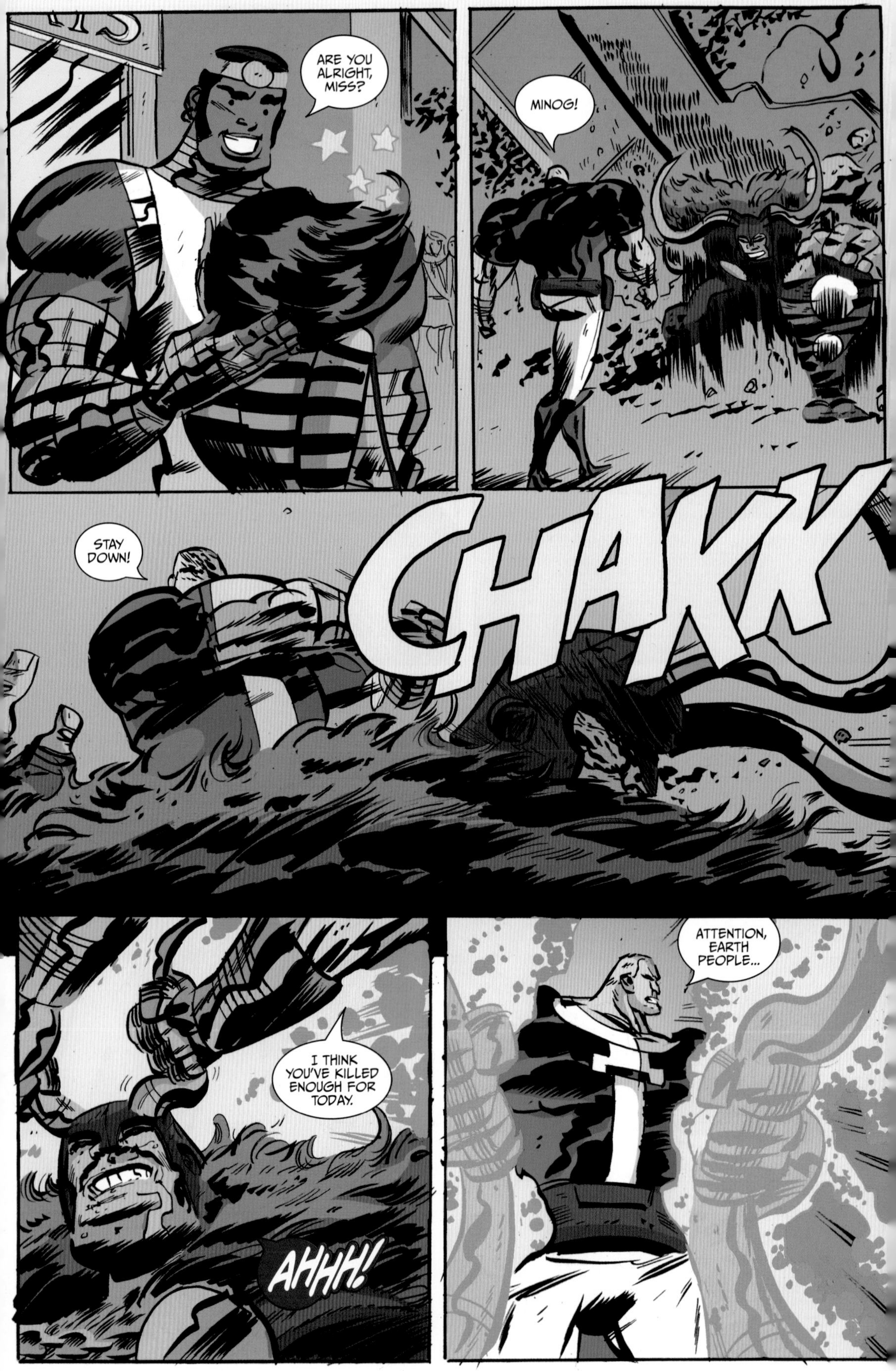
ARE YOU ALRIGHT, MISS?
MINOG!
STAY DOWN!
CHAKK
I THINK YOU'VE KILLED ENOUGH FOR TODAY.
AHHH!
ATTENTION, EARTH PEOPLE...

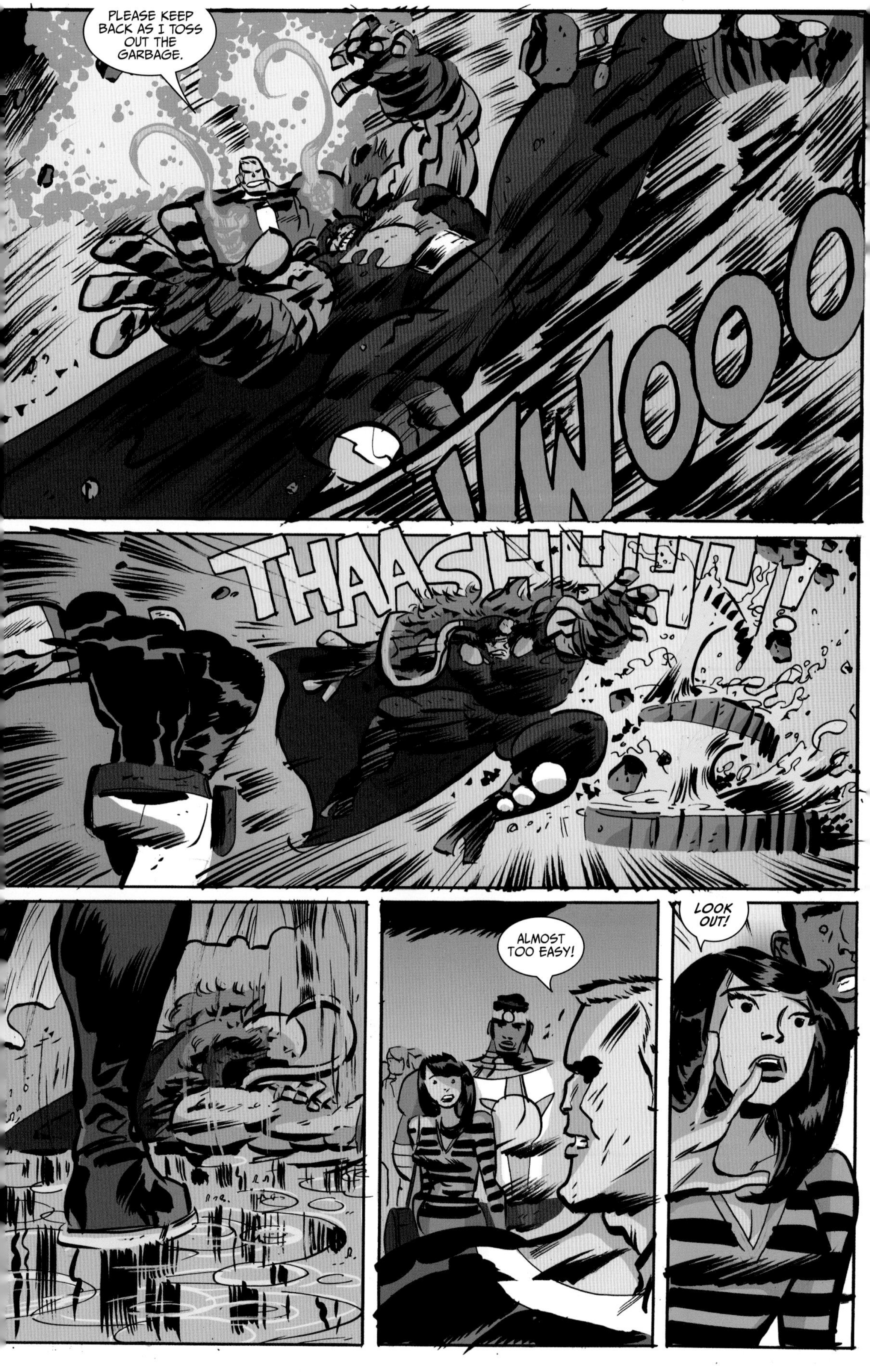
PLEASE KEEP BACK AS I TOSS OUT THE GARBAGE.
WOOOO
THAASHHHHT!
ALMOST TOO EASY!
LOOK OUT!

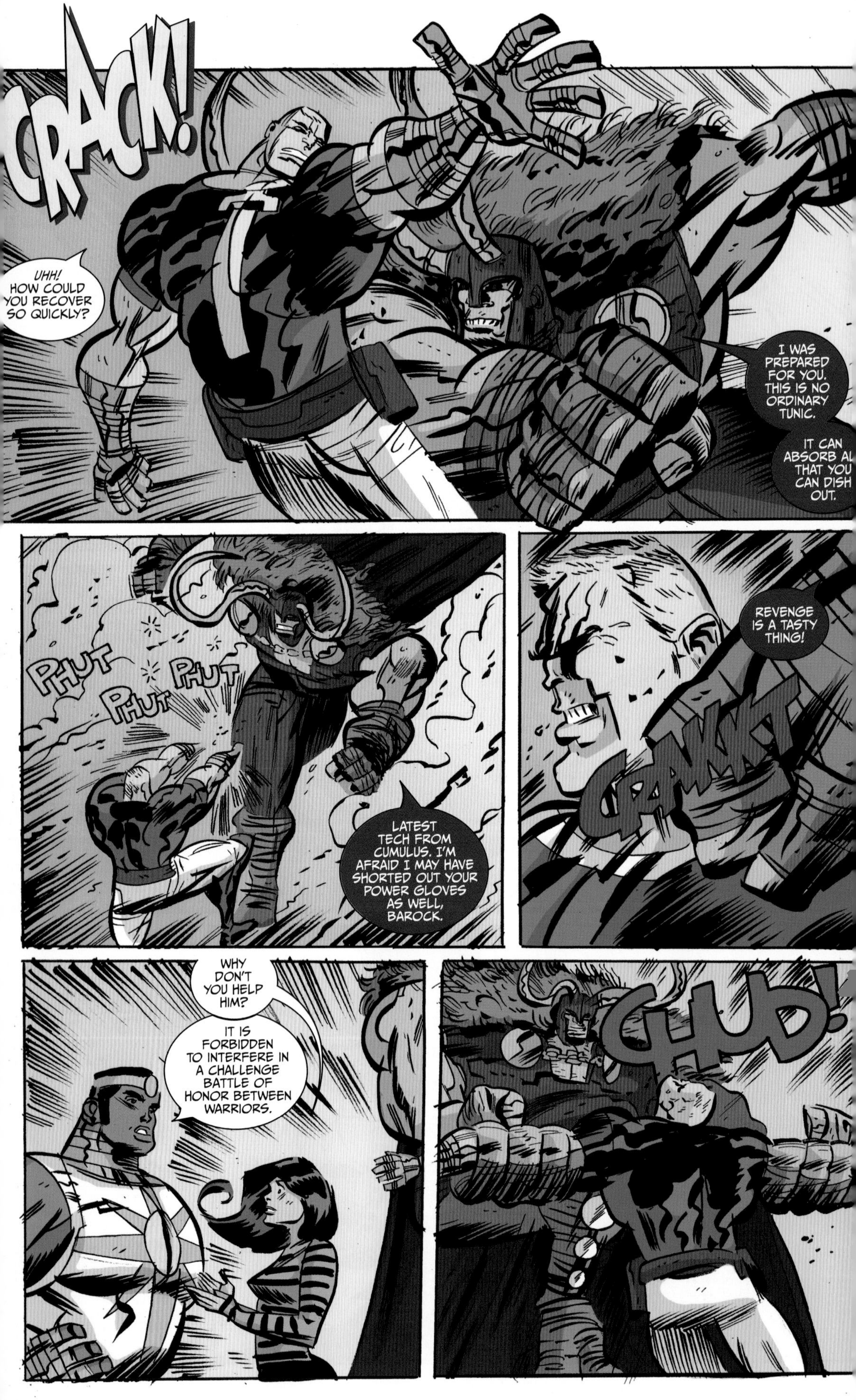
CRACK!
UHH! HOW COULD YOU RECOVER SO QUICKLY?
I WAS PREPARED FOR YOU. THIS IS NO ORDINARY TUNIC.
IT CAN ABSORB AL THAT YOU CAN DISH OUT.
PHUT PHUT PHUT
LATEST TECH FROM CUMULUS. I'M AFRAID I MAY HAVE SHORTED OUT YOUR POWER GLOVES AS WELL, BAROCK.
REVENGE IS A TASTY THING!
WHY DON'T YOU HELP HIM?
IT IS FORBIDDEN TO INTERFERE IN A CHALLENGE BATTLE OF HONOR BETWEEN WARRIORS.
CHUD!

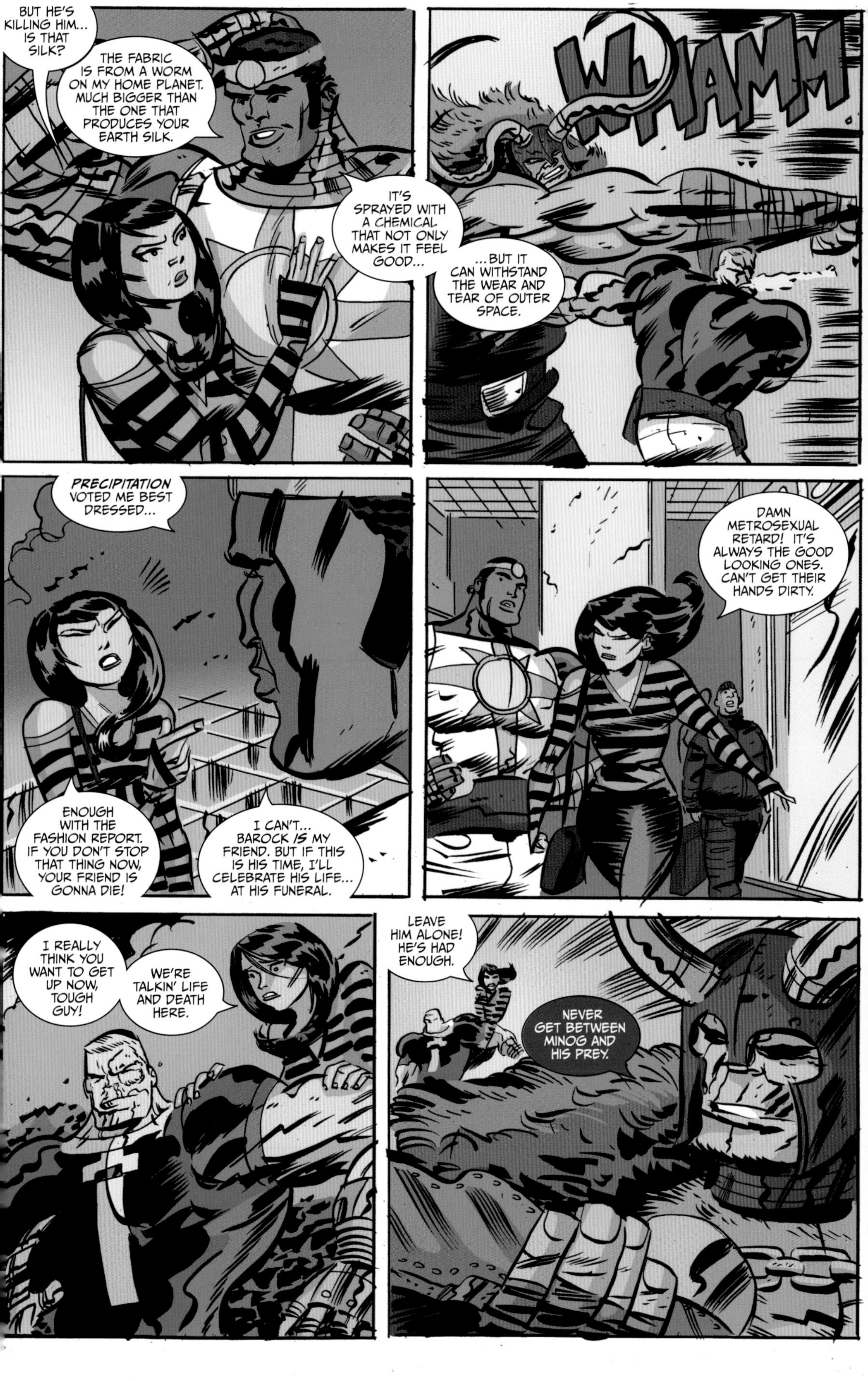
BUT HE'S KILLING HIM... IS THAT SILK?
THE FABRIC IS FROM A WORM ON MY HOME PLANET. MUCH BIGGER THAN THE ONE THAT PRODUCES YOUR EARTH SILK.
IT'S SPRAYED WITH A CHEMICAL THAT NOT ONLY MAKES IT FEEL GOOD...
...BUT IT CAN WITHSTAND THE WEAR AND TEAR OF OUTER SPACE.
WHAMM
PRECIPITATION VOTED ME BEST DRESSED...
ENOUGH WITH THE FASHION REPORT. IF YOU DON'T STOP THAT THING NOW, YOUR FRIEND IS GONNA DIE!
I CAN'T... BAROCK IS MY FRIEND. BUT IF THIS IS HIS TIME, I'LL CELEBRATE HIS LIFE... AT HIS FUNERAL.
DAMN METROSEXUAL RETARD! IT'S ALWAYS THE GOOD LOOKING ONES. CAN'T GET THEIR HANDS DIRTY.
I REALLY THINK YOU WANT TO GET UP NOW, TOUGH GUY!
WE'RE TALKIN' LIFE AND DEATH HERE.
LEAVE HIM ALONE! HE'S HAD ENOUGH.
NEVER GET BETWEEN MINOG AND HIS PREY.

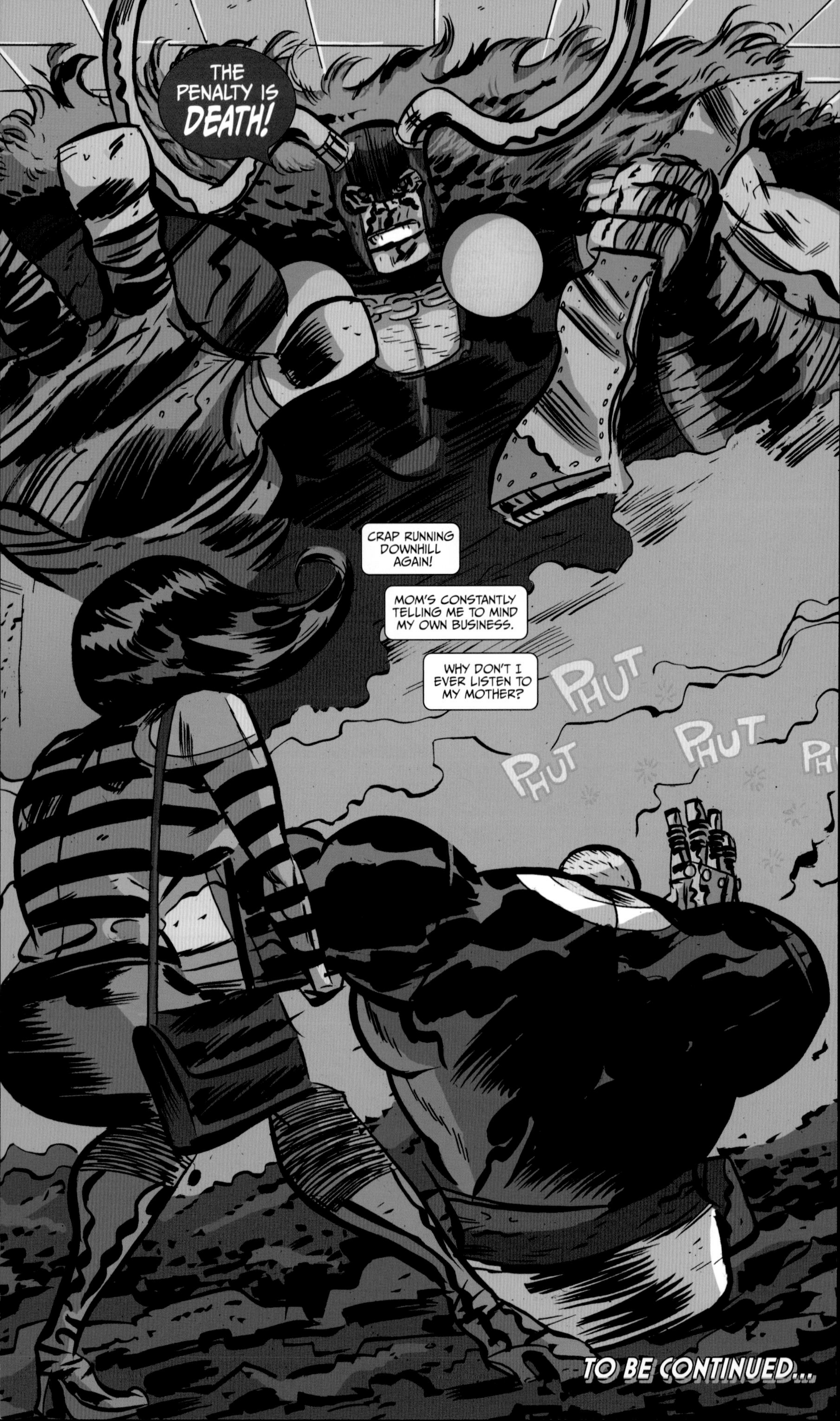
THE PENALTY IS DEATH!
CRAP RUNNING DOWNHILL AGAIN!
MOM'S CONSTANTLY TELLING ME TO MIND MY OWN BUSINESS.
WHY DON'T I EVER LISTEN TO MY MOTHER?
PHUT
PHUT
PHUT
TO BE CONTINUED...

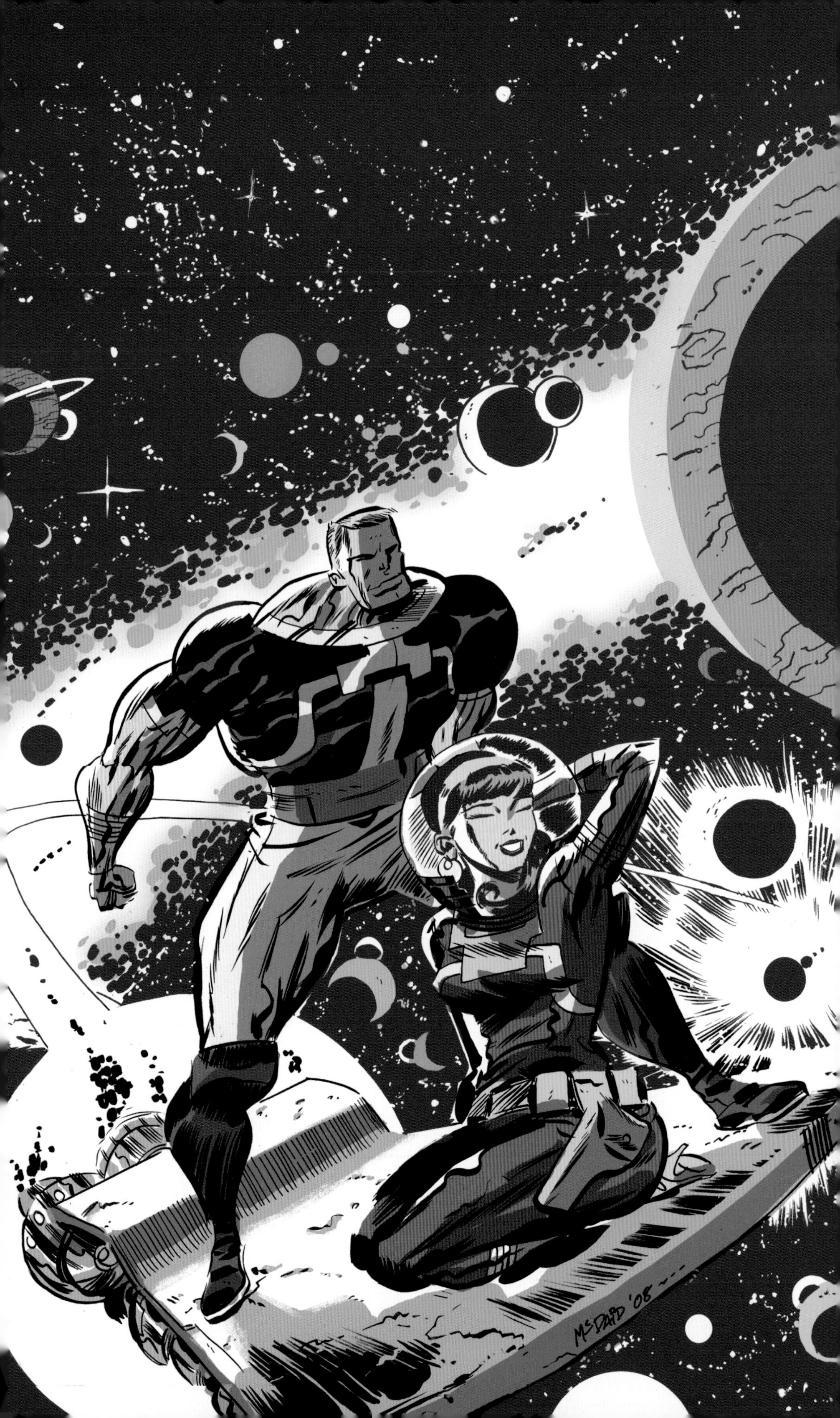
McDAID '08

CHAPTER TWO

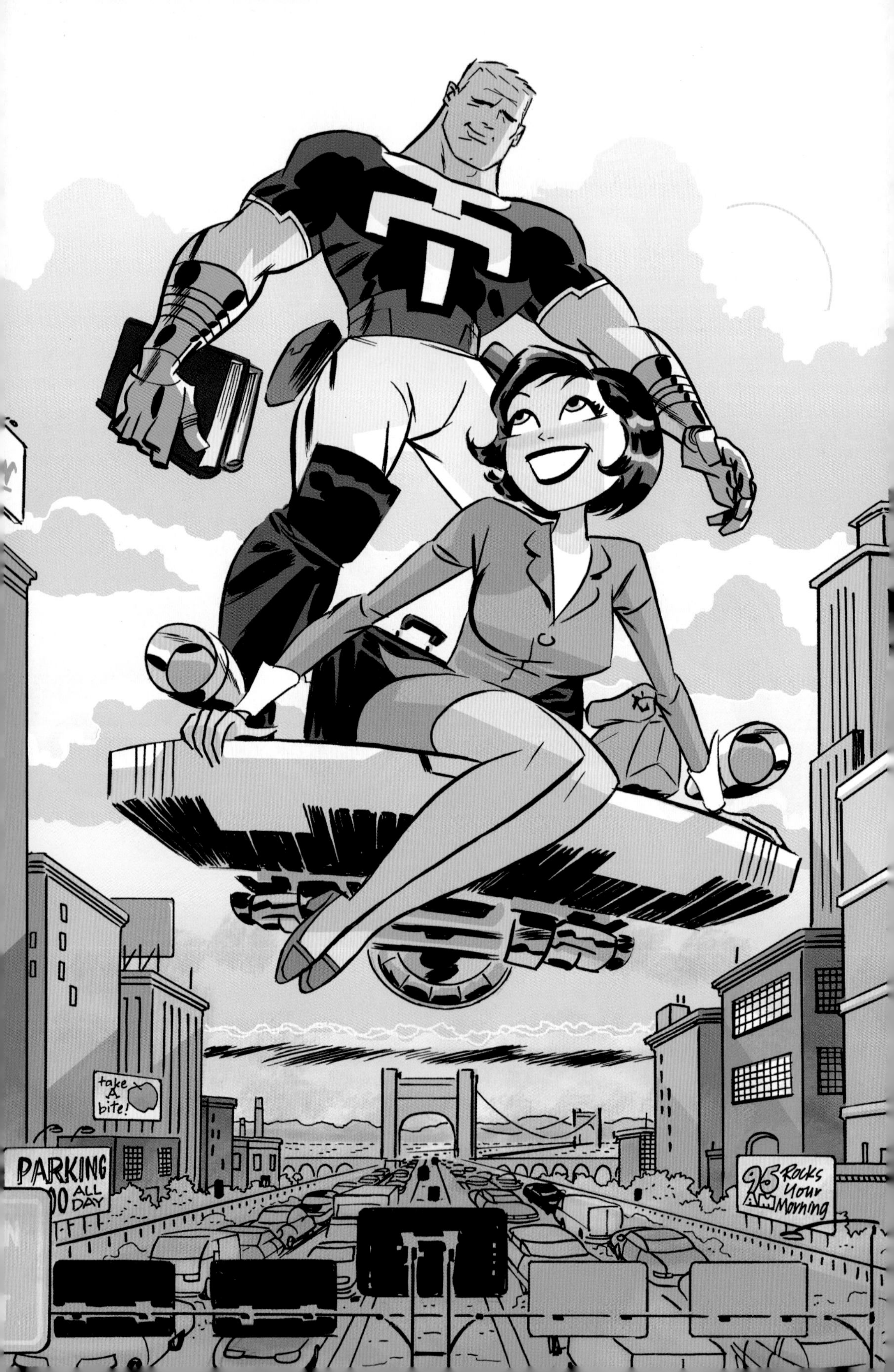
take A bite!
PARKING
ALL DAY
95 AM Rocks Your Morning

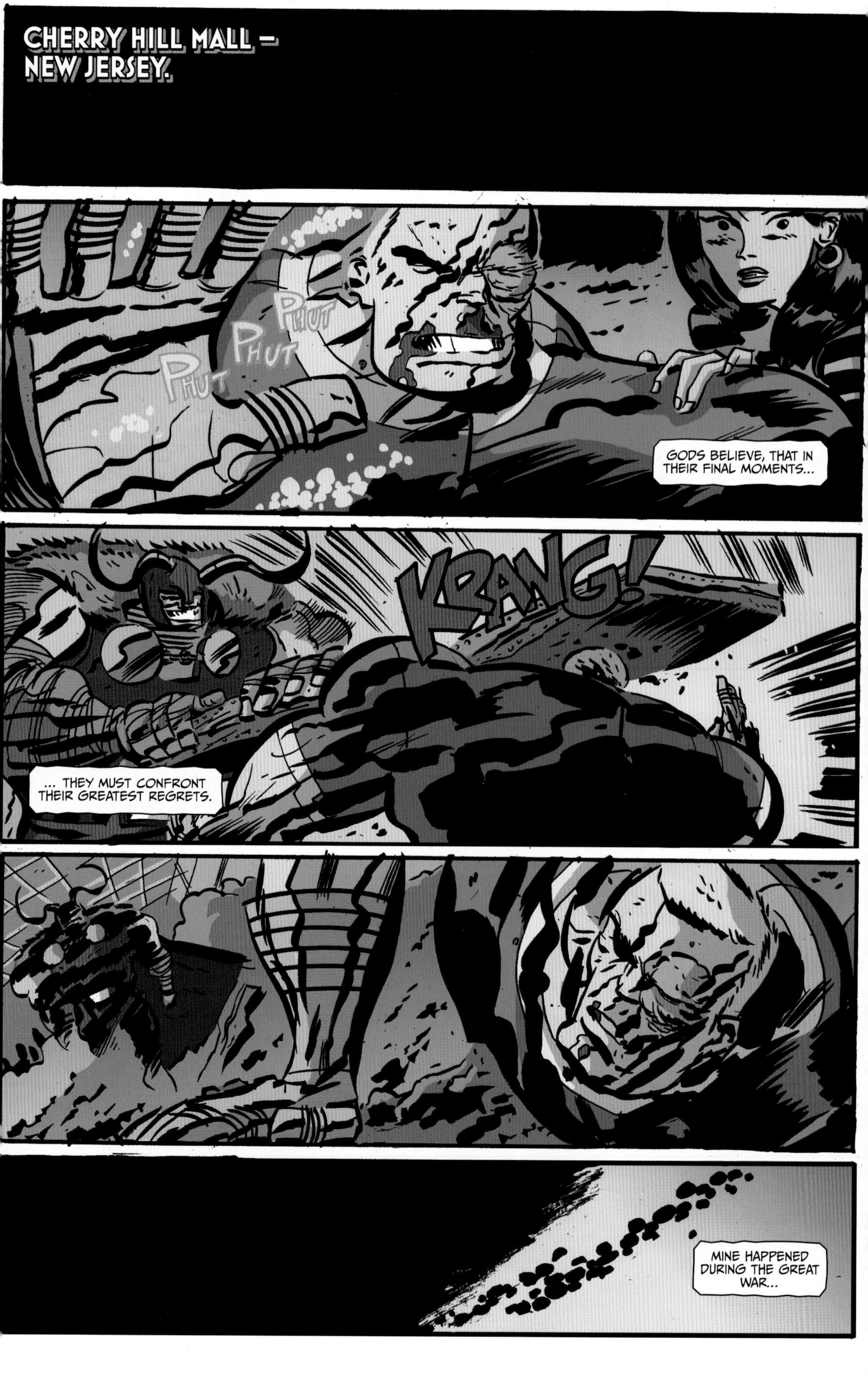
CHERRY HILL MALL –
NEW JERSEY.
PHUT PHUT PHUT
GODS BELIEVE, THAT IN THEIR FINAL MOMENTS...
KRANG!
... THEY MUST CONFRONT THEIR GREATEST REGRETS.
MINE HAPPENED DURING THE GREAT WAR...

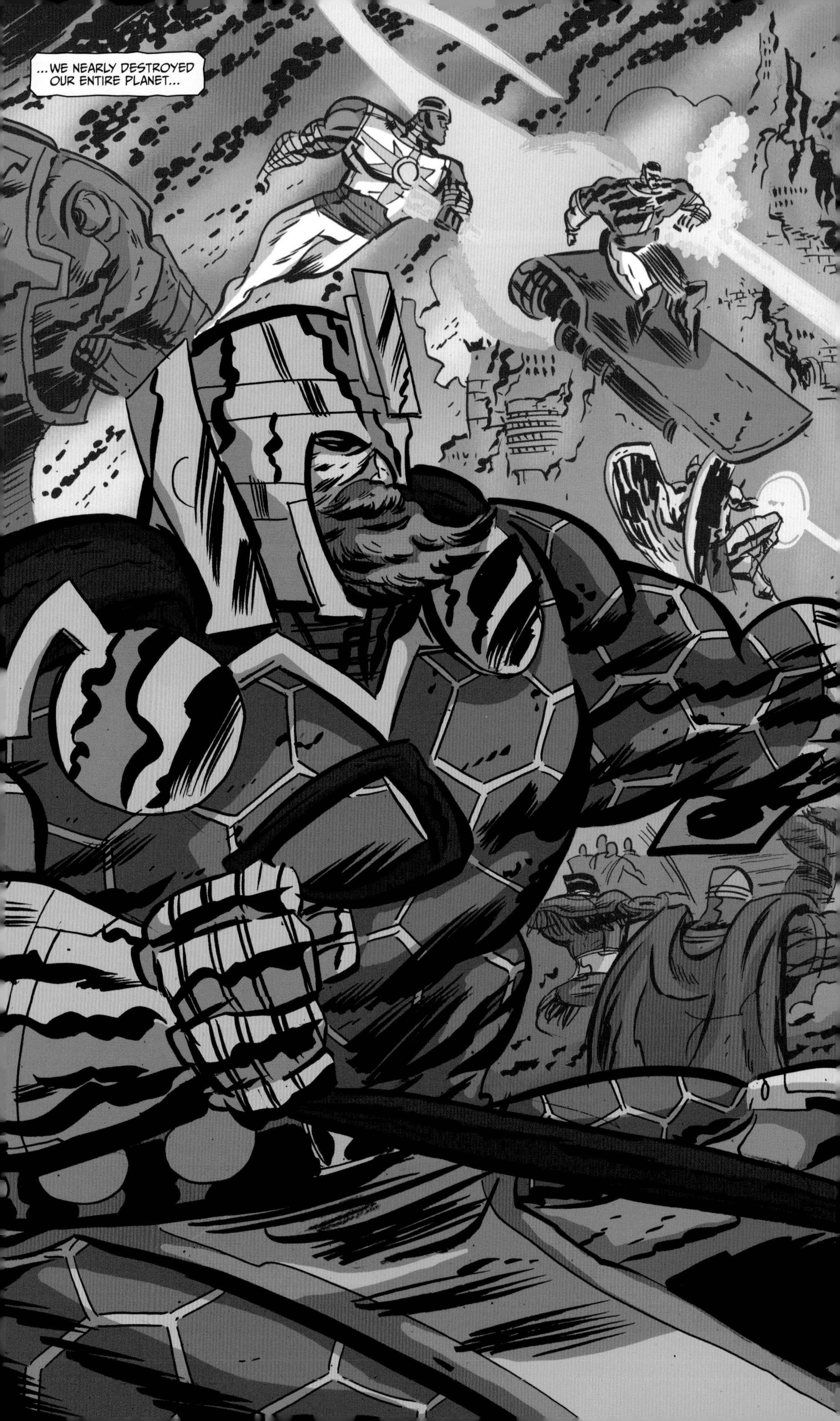
...WE NEARLY DESTROYED OUR ENTIRE PLANET...

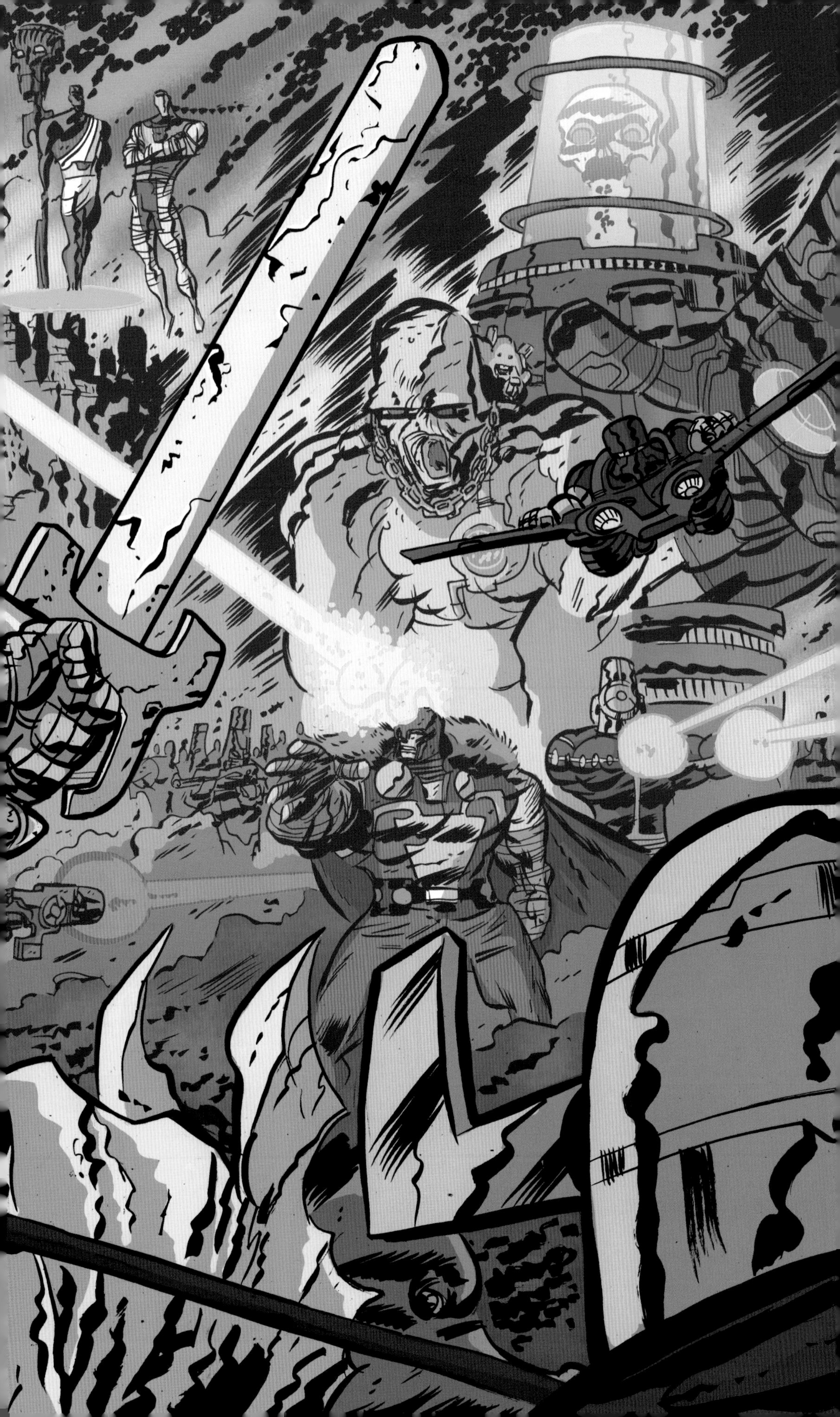

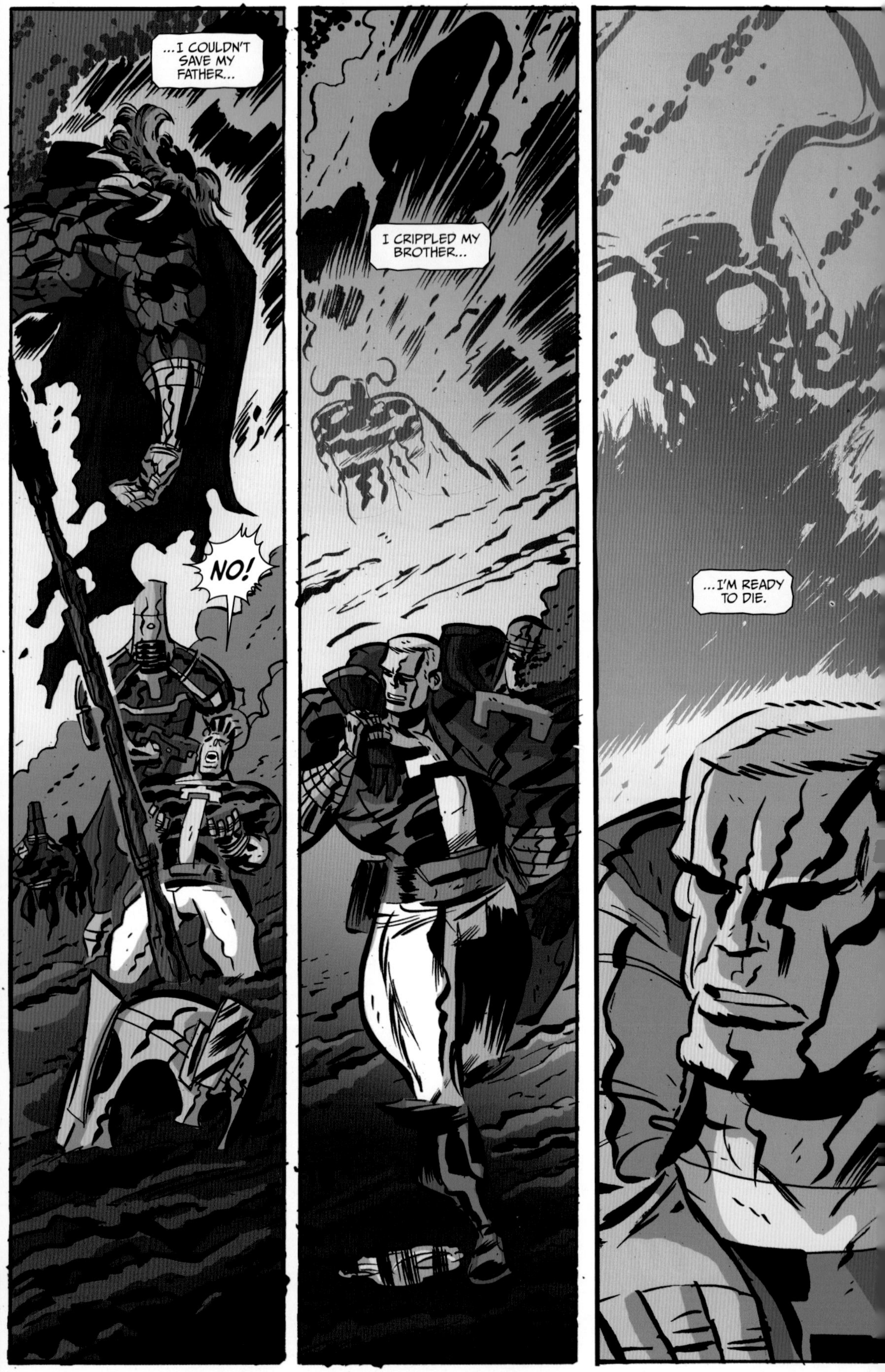
...I COULDN'T SAVE MY FATHER...
NO!
I CRIPPLED MY BROTHER...
...I'M READY TO DIE.

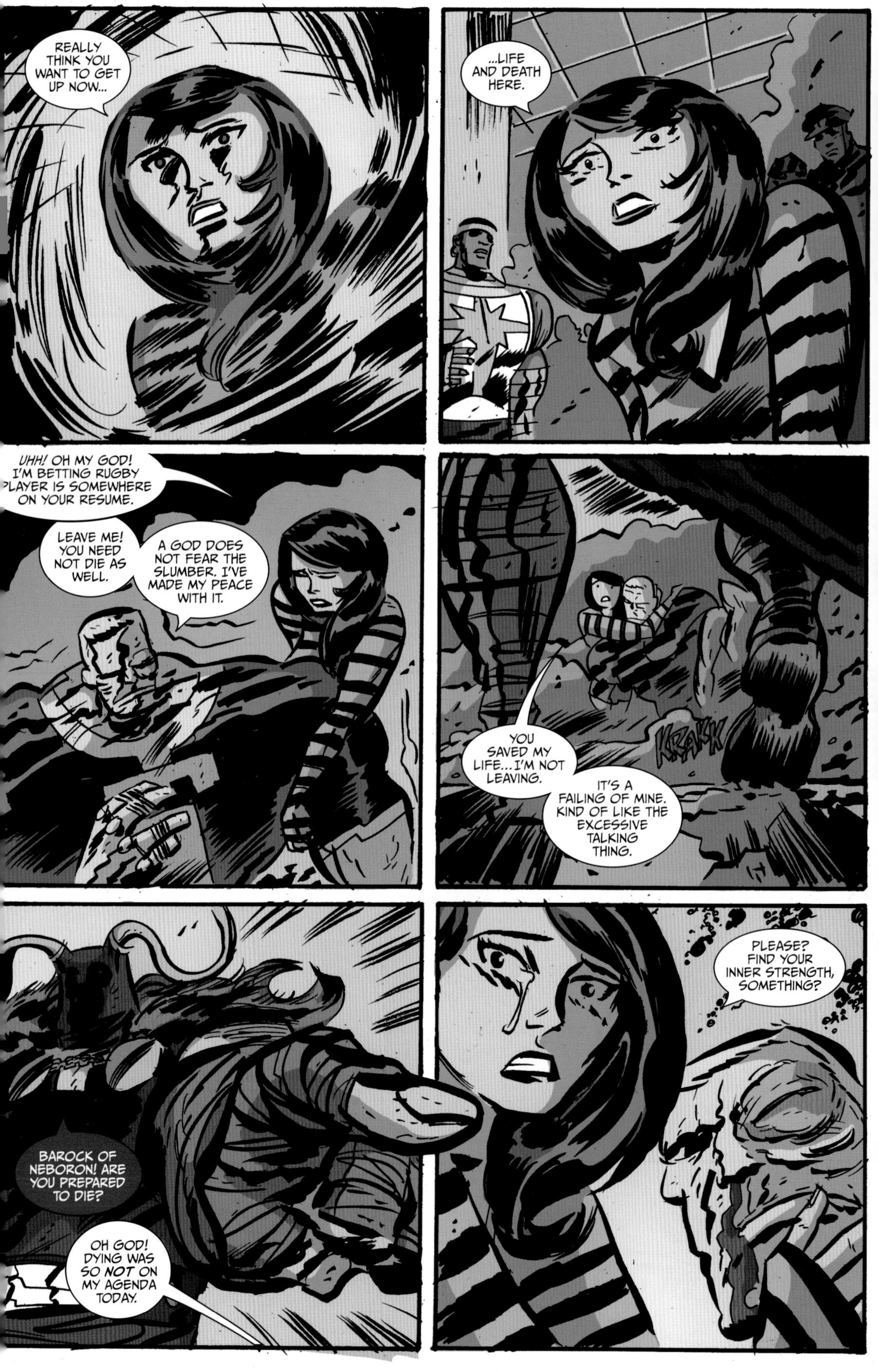
REALLY THINK YOU WANT TO GET UP NOW...
...LIFE AND DEATH HERE.
UHH! OH MY GOD! I'M BETTING RUGBY PLAYER IS SOMEWHERE ON YOUR RESUME.
LEAVE ME! YOU NEED NOT DIE AS WELL.
A GOD DOES NOT FEAR THE SLUMBER. I'VE MADE MY PEACE WITH IT.
YOU SAVED MY LIFE...I'M NOT LEAVING.
IT'S A FAILING OF MINE. KIND OF LIKE THE EXCESSIVE TALKING THING.
KRAKK
BAROCK OF NEBORON! ARE YOU PREPARED TO DIE?
OH GOD! DYING WAS SO NOT ON MY AGENDA TODAY.
PLEASE? FIND YOUR INNER STRENGTH, SOMETHING?

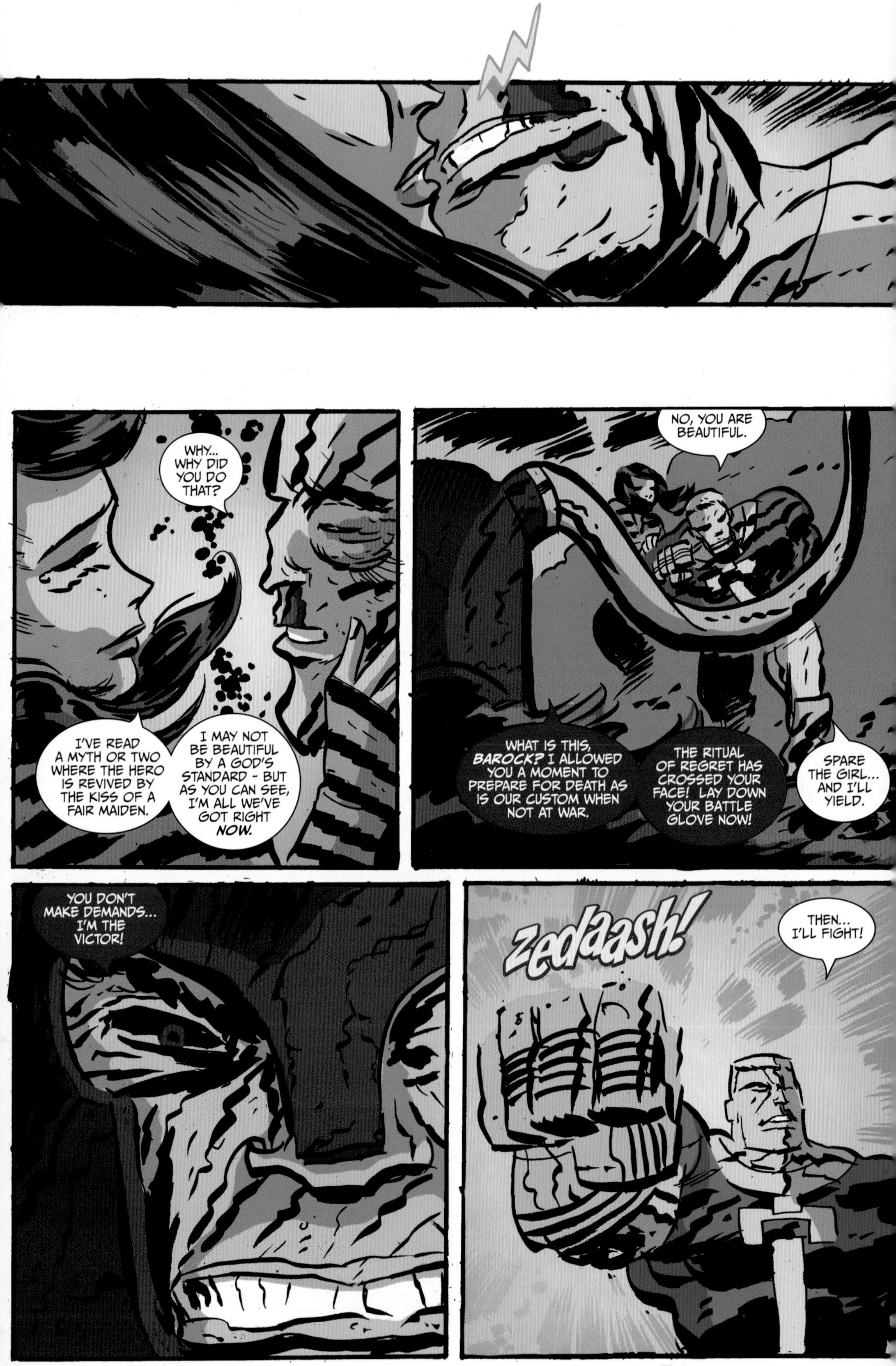
WHY... WHY DID YOU DO THAT?
I'VE READ A MYTH OR TWO WHERE THE HERO IS REVIVED BY THE KISS OF A FAIR MAIDEN.
I MAY NOT BE BEAUTIFUL BY A GOD'S STANDARD - BUT AS YOU CAN SEE, I'M ALL WE'VE GOT RIGHT NOW.
NO, YOU ARE BEAUTIFUL.
WHAT IS THIS, BAROCK? I ALLOWED YOU A MOMENT TO PREPARE FOR DEATH AS IS OUR CUSTOM WHEN NOT AT WAR.
THE RITUAL OF REGRET HAS CROSSED YOUR FACE! LAY DOWN YOUR BATTLE GLOVE NOW!
SPARE THE GIRL... AND I'LL YIELD.
YOU DON'T MAKE DEMANDS... I'M THE VICTOR!
ZEDAASH!
THEN... I'LL FIGHT!

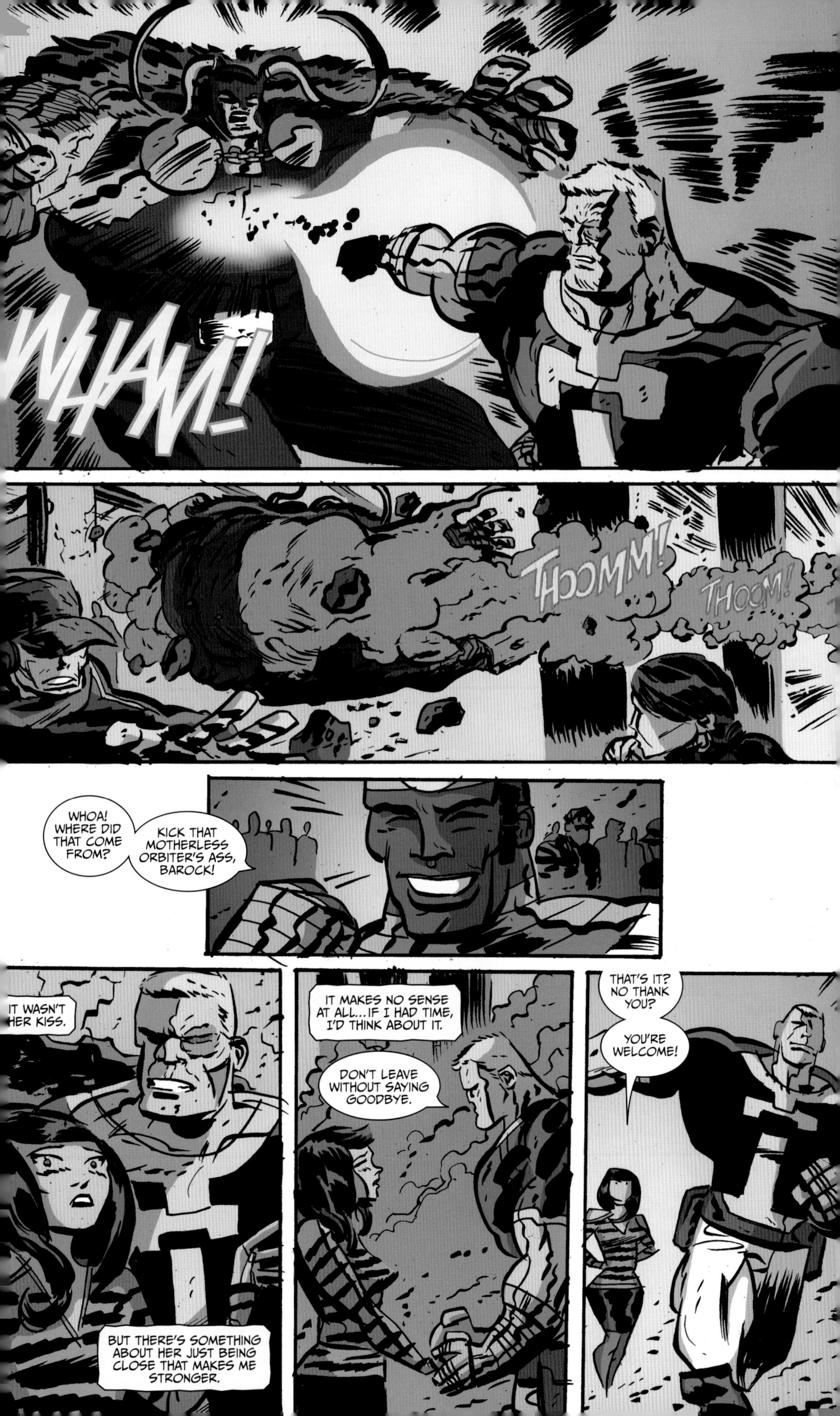
WHAM!
THOOMM!
THOOM!
WHOA! WHERE DID THAT COME FROM?
KICK THAT MOTHERLESS ORBITER'S ASS, BAROCK!
IT WASN'T HER KISS.
BUT THERE'S SOMETHING ABOUT HER JUST BEING CLOSE THAT MAKES ME STRONGER.
IT MAKES NO SENSE AT ALL... IF I HAD TIME, I'D THINK ABOUT IT.
DON'T LEAVE WITHOUT SAYING GOODBYE.
THAT'S IT? NO THANK YOU?
YOU'RE WELCOME!

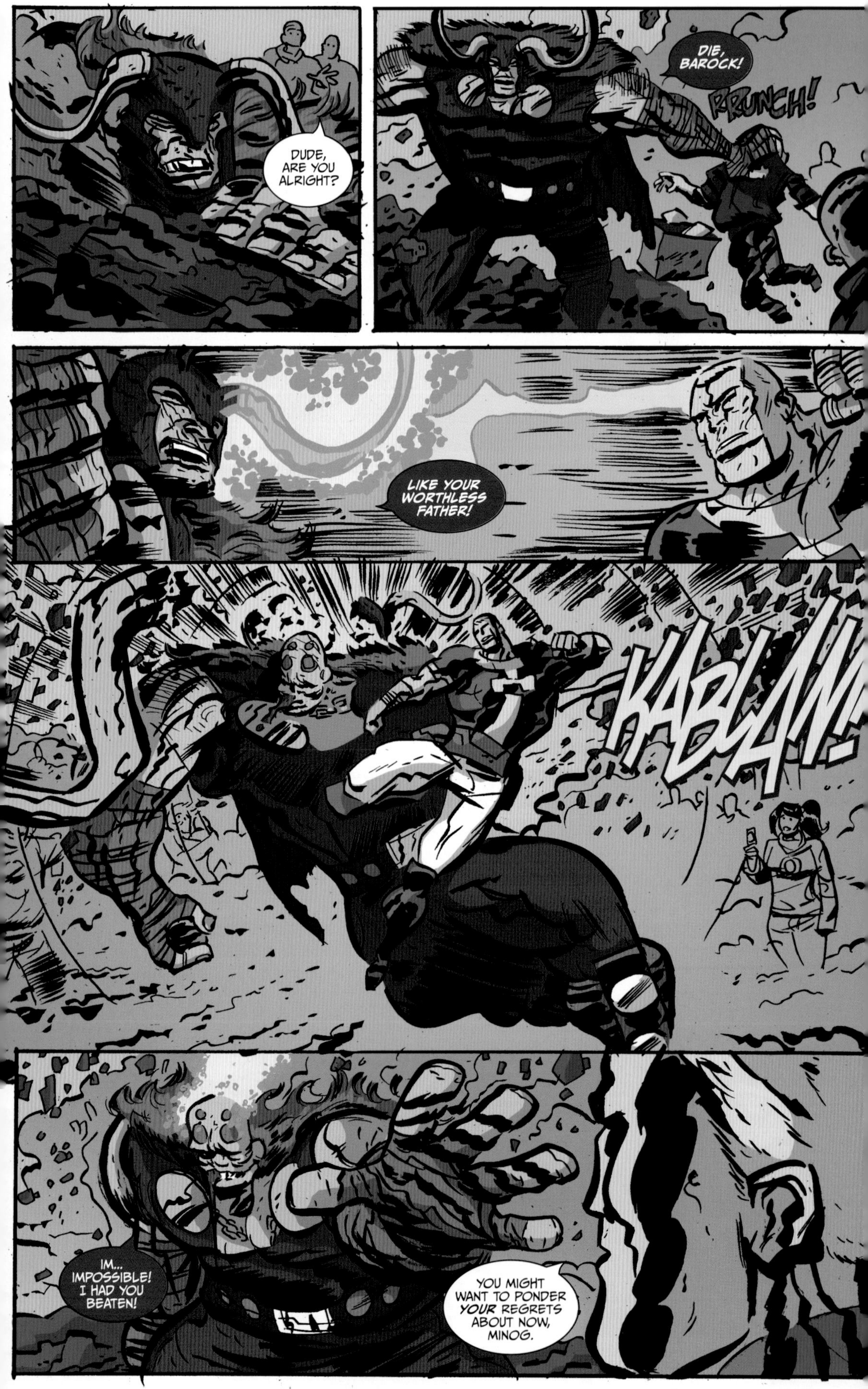
DUDE, ARE YOU ALRIGHT?
DIE, BAROCK!
KRUNCH!
LIKE YOUR WORTHLESS FATHER!
KABLAM!
IM... IMPOSSIBLE! I HAD YOU BEATEN!
YOU MIGHT WANT TO PONDER YOUR REGRETS ABOUT NOW, MINOG.

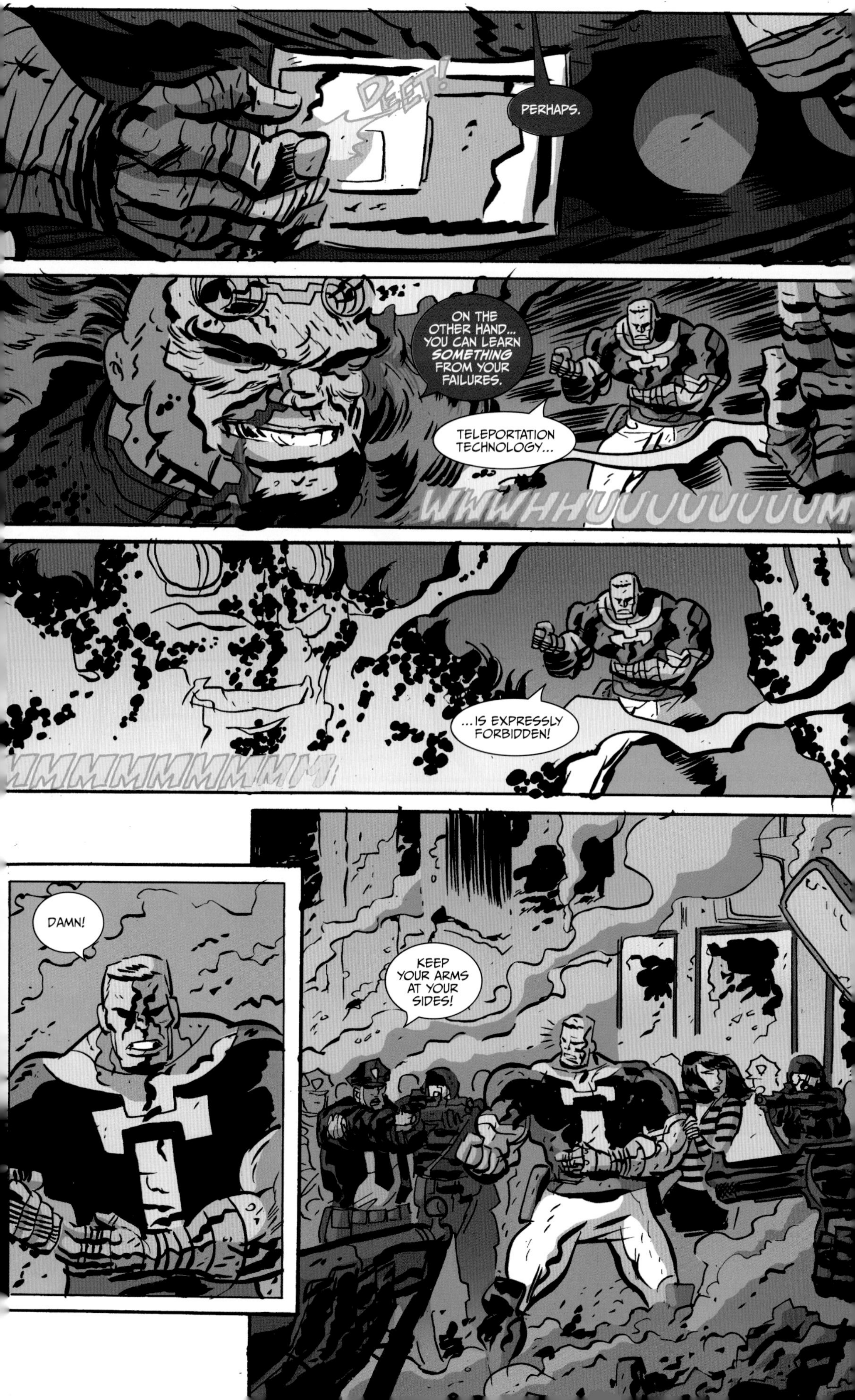
DEET!
PERHAPS.
ON THE OTHER HAND... YOU CAN LEARN *SOMETHING* FROM YOUR FAILURES.
TELEPORTATION TECHNOLOGY...
WWWHHUUUUUUUUUM
...IS EXPRESSLY FORBIDDEN!
MMMMMMMMMMM
DAMN!
KEEP YOUR ARMS AT YOUR SIDES!

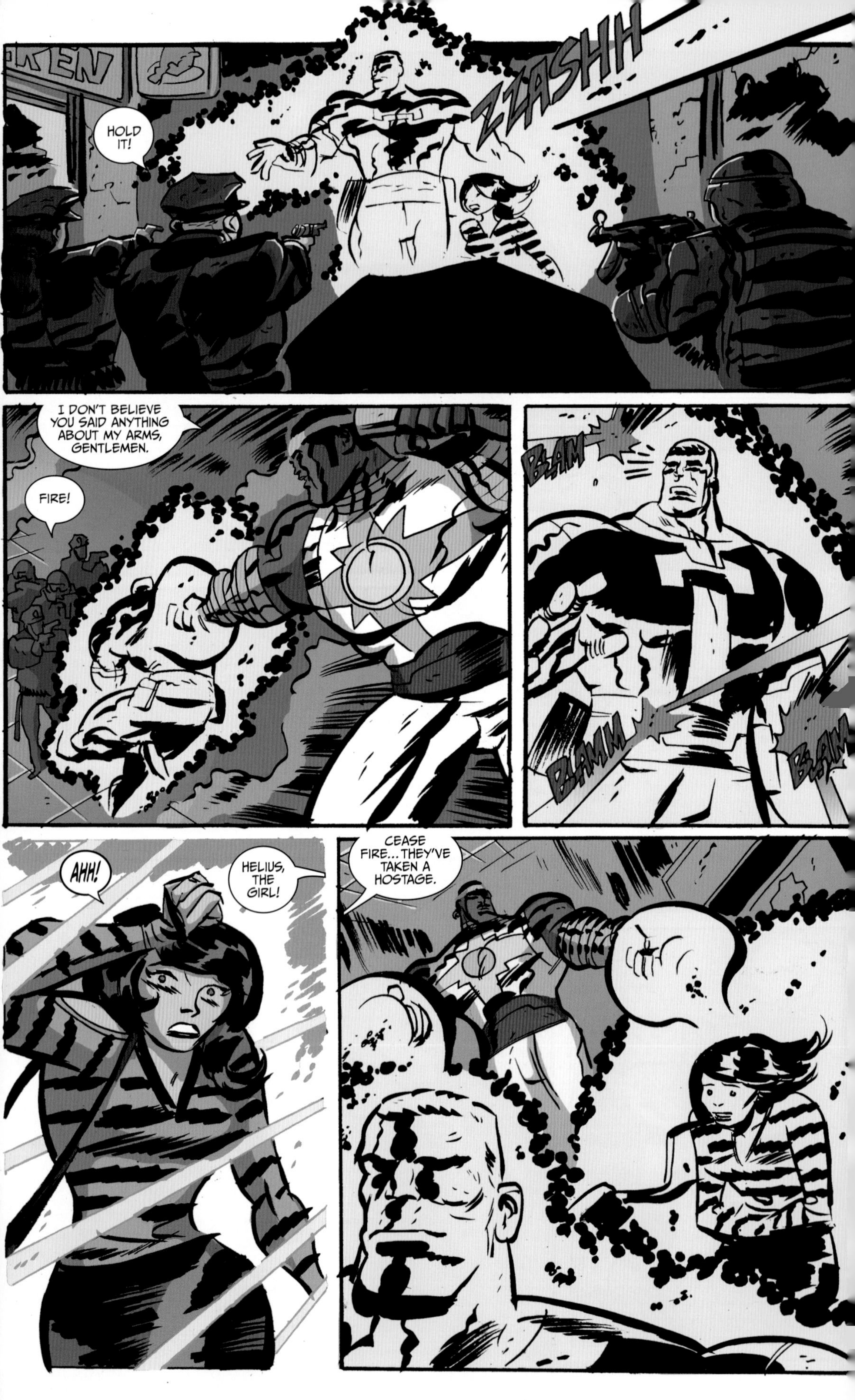
KEN
ZZASHH
HOLD IT!
I DON'T BELIEVE YOU SAID ANYTHING ABOUT MY ARMS, GENTLEMEN.
FIRE!
BLAM
BLAMM
BLAM
AHH!
HELIUS, THE GIRL!
CEASE FIRE... THEY'VE TAKEN A HOSTAGE.

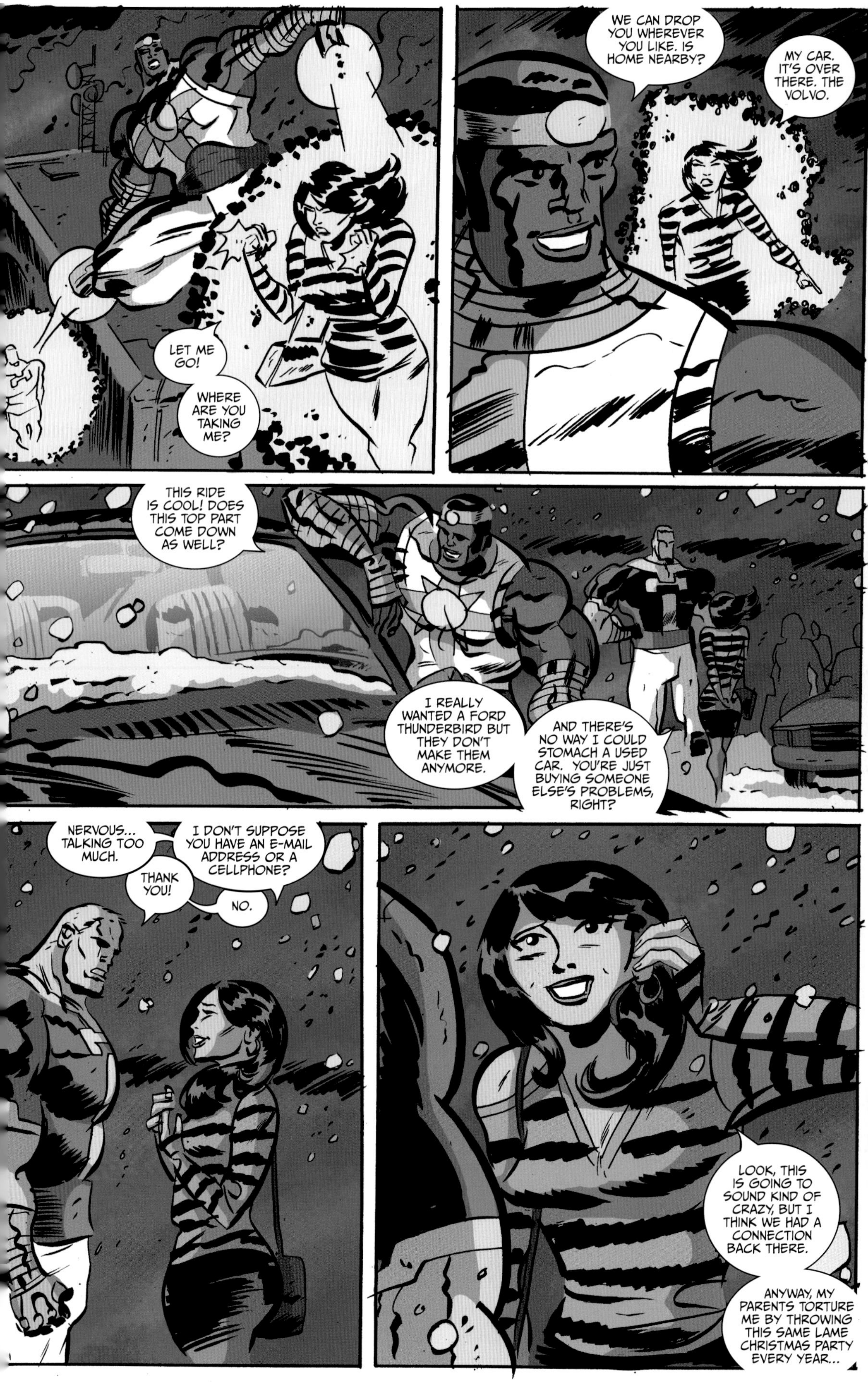
LET ME GO!
WHERE ARE YOU TAKING ME?
WE CAN DROP YOU WHEREVER YOU LIKE. IS HOME NEARBY?
MY CAR. IT'S OVER THERE. THE VOLVO.
THIS RIDE IS COOL! DOES THIS TOP PART COME DOWN AS WELL?
I REALLY WANTED A FORD THUNDERBIRD BUT THEY DON'T MAKE THEM ANYMORE.
AND THERE'S NO WAY I COULD STOMACH A USED CAR. YOU'RE JUST BUYING SOMEONE ELSE'S PROBLEMS, RIGHT?
NERVOUS... TALKING TOO MUCH.
THANK YOU!
I DON'T SUPPOSE YOU HAVE AN E-MAIL ADDRESS OR A CELLPHONE?
NO.
LOOK, THIS IS GOING TO SOUND KIND OF CRAZY, BUT I THINK WE HAD A CONNECTION BACK THERE.
ANYWAY, MY PARENTS TORTURE ME BY THROWING THIS SAME LAME CHRISTMAS PARTY EVERY YEAR...

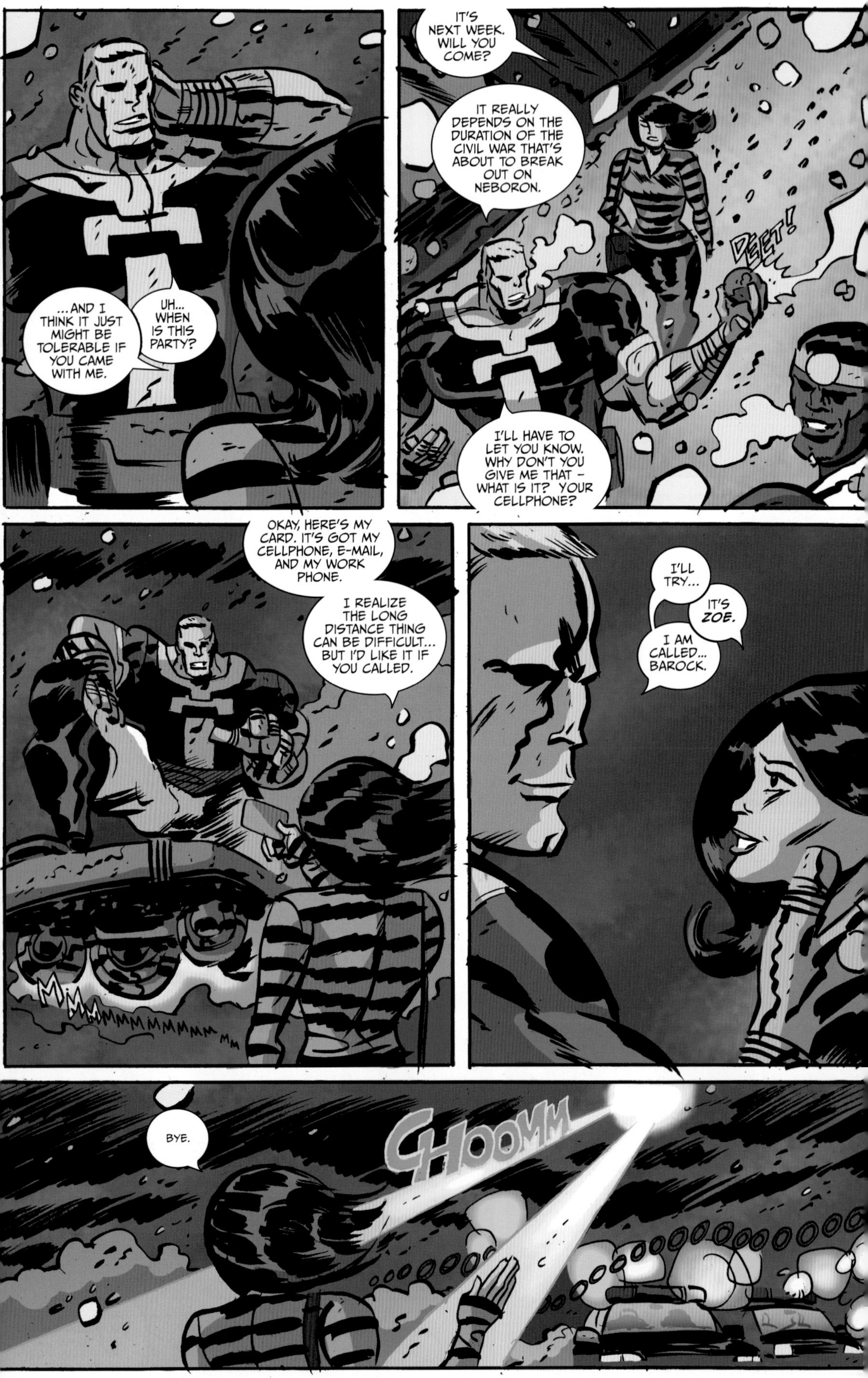
UH... WHEN IS THIS PARTY?
...AND I THINK IT JUST MIGHT BE TOLERABLE IF YOU CAME WITH ME.
IT'S NEXT WEEK. WILL YOU COME?
IT REALLY DEPENDS ON THE DURATION OF THE CIVIL WAR THAT'S ABOUT TO BREAK OUT ON NEBORON.
DEET!
I'LL HAVE TO LET YOU KNOW. WHY DON'T YOU GIVE ME THAT – WHAT IS IT? YOUR CELLPHONE?
OKAY, HERE'S MY CARD. IT'S GOT MY CELLPHONE, E-MAIL, AND MY WORK PHONE.
I REALIZE THE LONG DISTANCE THING CAN BE DIFFICULT... BUT I'D LIKE IT IF YOU CALLED.
MMMMMMMMMMMMMMM MM
I'LL TRY...
IT'S *ZOE.*
I AM CALLED... BAROCK.
BYE.
CHOOMM

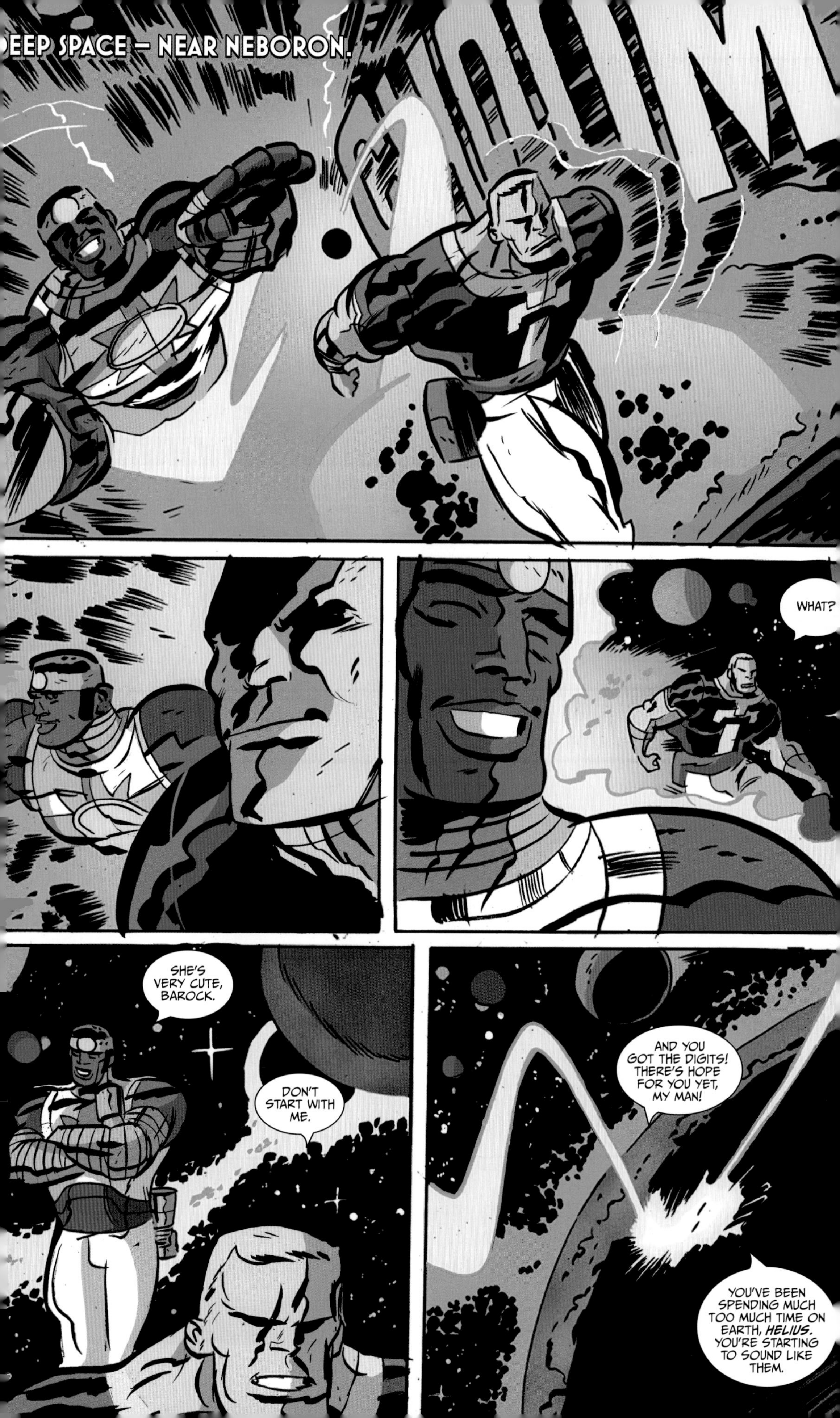
EEP SPACE – NEAR NEBORON.
WHAT?
SHE'S VERY CUTE, BAROCK.
DON'T START WITH ME.
AND YOU GOT THE DIGITS! THERE'S HOPE FOR YOU YET, MY MAN!
YOU'VE BEEN SPENDING MUCH TOO MUCH TIME ON EARTH, HELIUS. YOU'RE STARTING TO SOUND LIKE THEM.

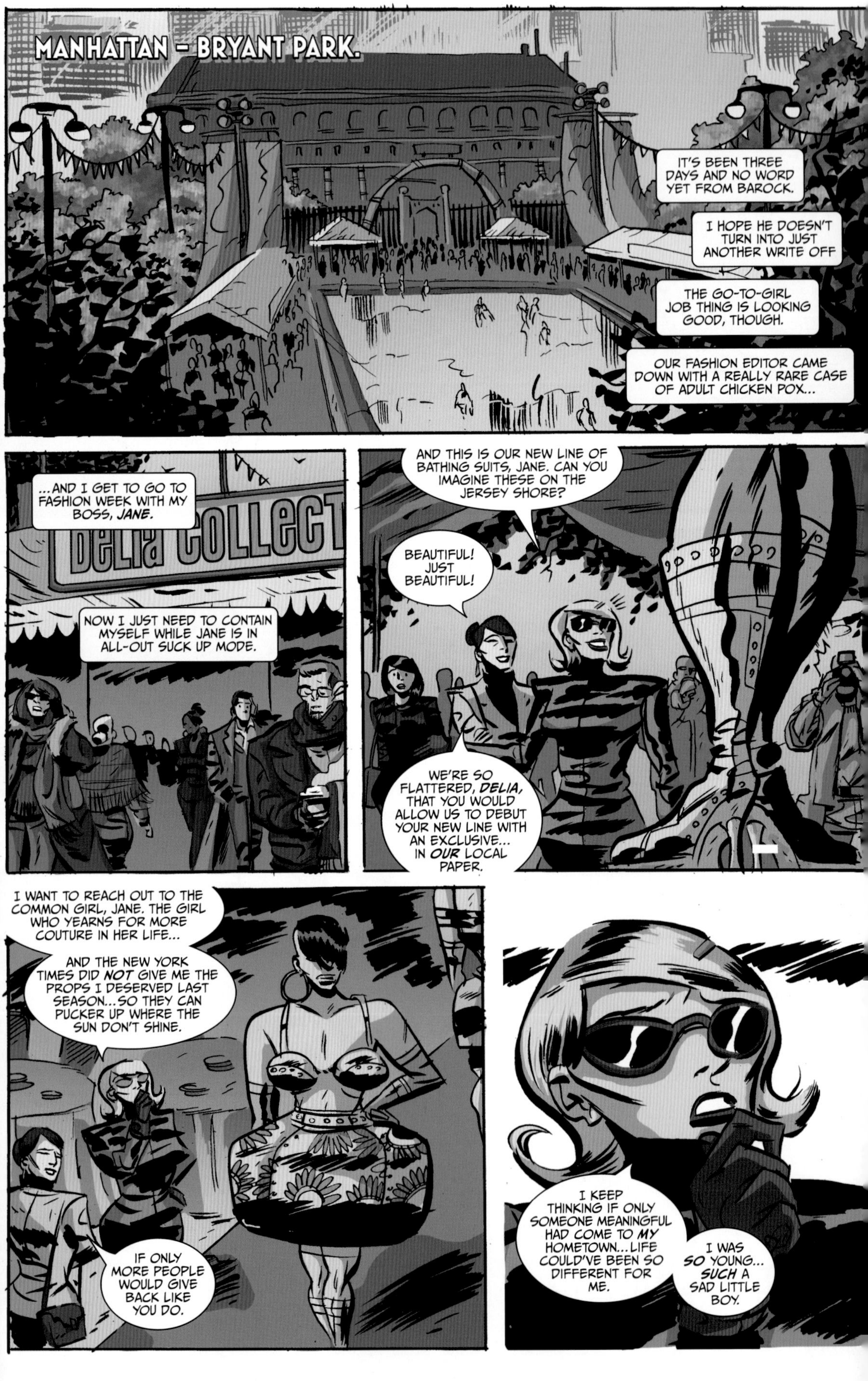
MANHATTAN – BRYANT PARK.
IT'S BEEN THREE DAYS AND NO WORD YET FROM BAROCK.
I HOPE HE DOESN'T TURN INTO JUST ANOTHER WRITE OFF
THE GO-TO-GIRL JOB THING IS LOOKING GOOD, THOUGH.
OUR FASHION EDITOR CAME DOWN WITH A REALLY RARE CASE OF ADULT CHICKEN POX...
...AND I GET TO GO TO FASHION WEEK WITH MY BOSS, JANE.
DELIA COLLECT
NOW I JUST NEED TO CONTAIN MYSELF WHILE JANE IS IN ALL-OUT SUCK UP MODE.
AND THIS IS OUR NEW LINE OF BATHING SUITS, JANE. CAN YOU IMAGINE THESE ON THE JERSEY SHORE?
BEAUTIFUL! JUST BEAUTIFUL!
WE'RE SO FLATTERED, DELIA, THAT YOU WOULD ALLOW US TO DEBUT YOUR NEW LINE WITH AN EXCLUSIVE... IN OUR LOCAL PAPER.
I WANT TO REACH OUT TO THE COMMON GIRL, JANE. THE GIRL WHO YEARNS FOR MORE COUTURE IN HER LIFE...
AND THE NEW YORK TIMES DID NOT GIVE ME THE PROPS I DESERVED LAST SEASON...SO THEY CAN PUCKER UP WHERE THE SUN DON'T SHINE.
IF ONLY MORE PEOPLE WOULD GIVE BACK LIKE YOU DO.
I KEEP THINKING IF ONLY SOMEONE MEANINGFUL HAD COME TO MY HOMETOWN...LIFE COULD'VE BEEN SO DIFFERENT FOR ME.
I WAS SO YOUNG... SUCH A SAD LITTLE BOY.

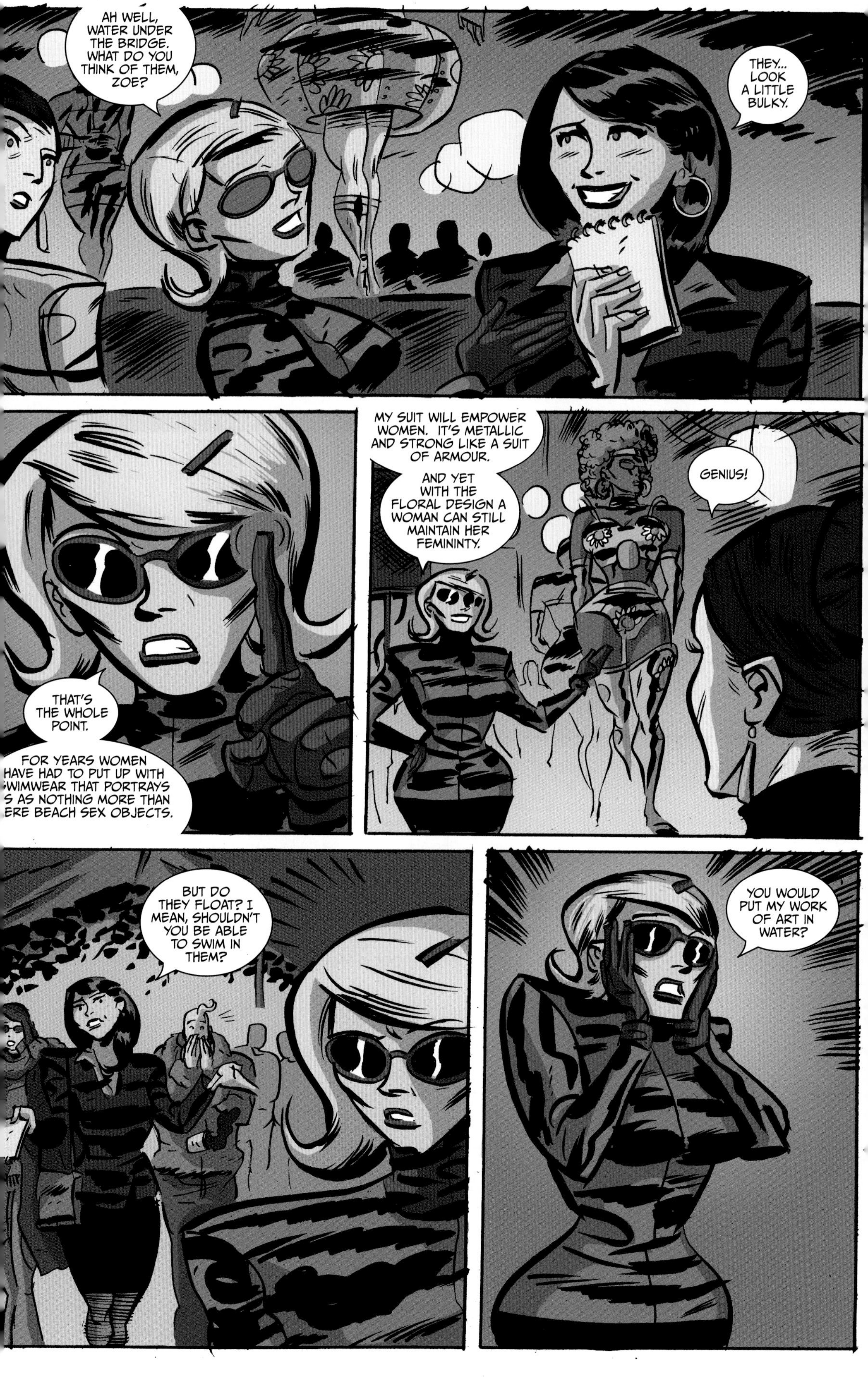
AH WELL, WATER UNDER THE BRIDGE. WHAT DO YOU THINK OF THEM, ZOE?
THEY... LOOK A LITTLE BULKY.
THAT'S THE WHOLE POINT.
FOR YEARS WOMEN HAVE HAD TO PUT UP WITH SWIMWEAR THAT PORTRAYS US AS NOTHING MORE THAN MERE BEACH SEX OBJECTS.
MY SUIT WILL EMPOWER WOMEN. IT'S METALLIC AND STRONG LIKE A SUIT OF ARMOUR.
AND YET WITH THE FLORAL DESIGN A WOMAN CAN STILL MAINTAIN HER FEMININTY.
GENIUS!
BUT DO THEY FLOAT? I MEAN, SHOULDN'T YOU BE ABLE TO SWIM IN THEM?
YOU WOULD PUT MY WORK OF ART IN WATER?

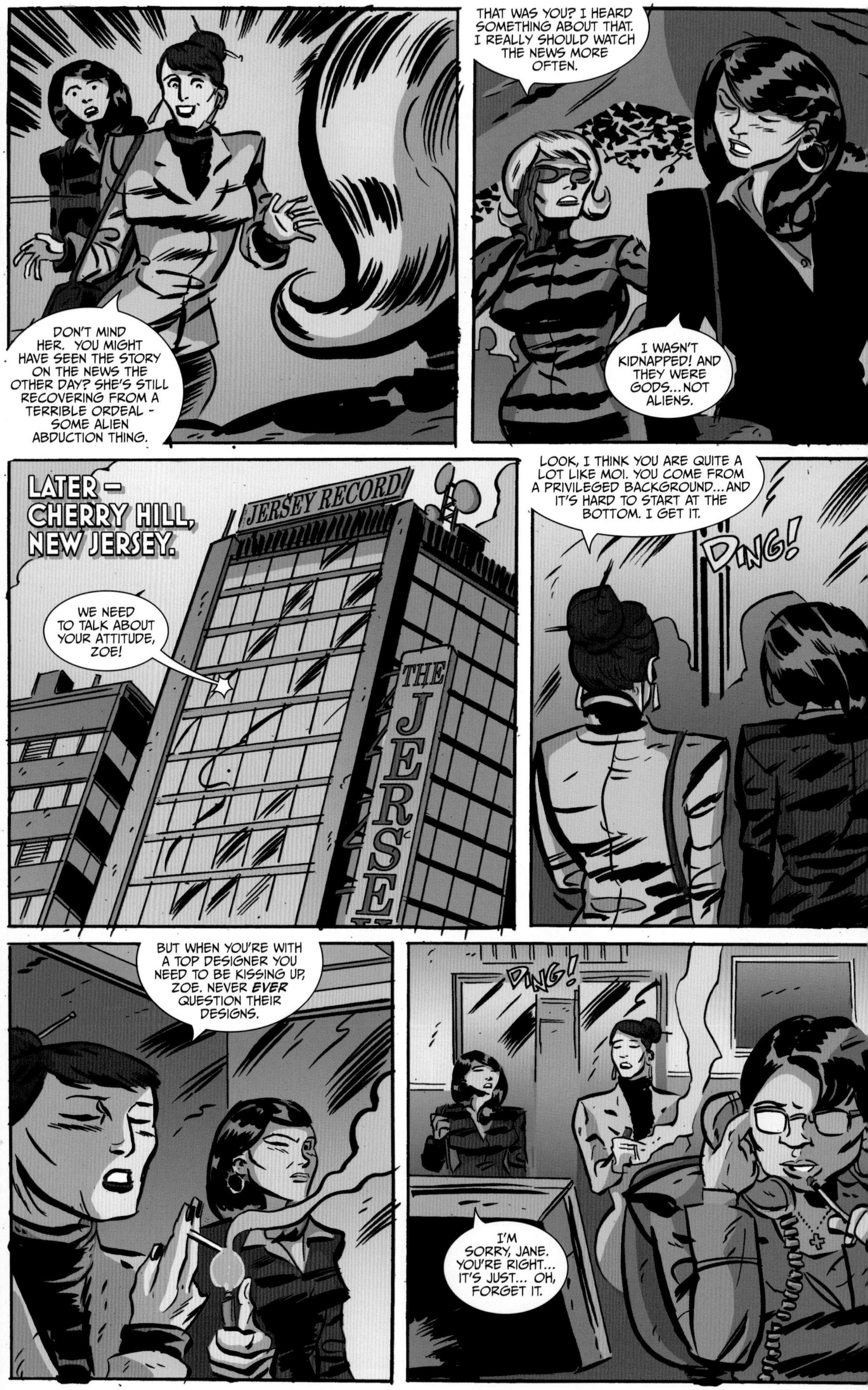

DON'T MIND HER. YOU MIGHT HAVE SEEN THE STORY ON THE NEWS THE OTHER DAY? SHE'S STILL RECOVERING FROM A TERRIBLE ORDEAL - SOME ALIEN ABDUCTION THING.
THAT WAS YOU? I HEARD SOMETHING ABOUT THAT. I REALLY SHOULD WATCH THE NEWS MORE OFTEN.
I WASN'T KIDNAPPED! AND THEY WERE GODS...NOT ALIENS.
LATER - CHERRY HILL, NEW JERSEY.
JERSEY RECORD
THE JERSE
WE NEED TO TALK ABOUT YOUR ATTITUDE, ZOE!
LOOK, I THINK YOU ARE QUITE A LOT LIKE MOI. YOU COME FROM A PRIVILEGED BACKGROUND...AND IT'S HARD TO START AT THE BOTTOM. I GET IT.
DING!
BUT WHEN YOU'RE WITH A TOP DESIGNER YOU NEED TO BE KISSING UP, ZOE. NEVER EVER QUESTION THEIR DESIGNS.
DING!
I'M SORRY, JANE. YOU'RE RIGHT... IT'S JUST... OH, FORGET IT.

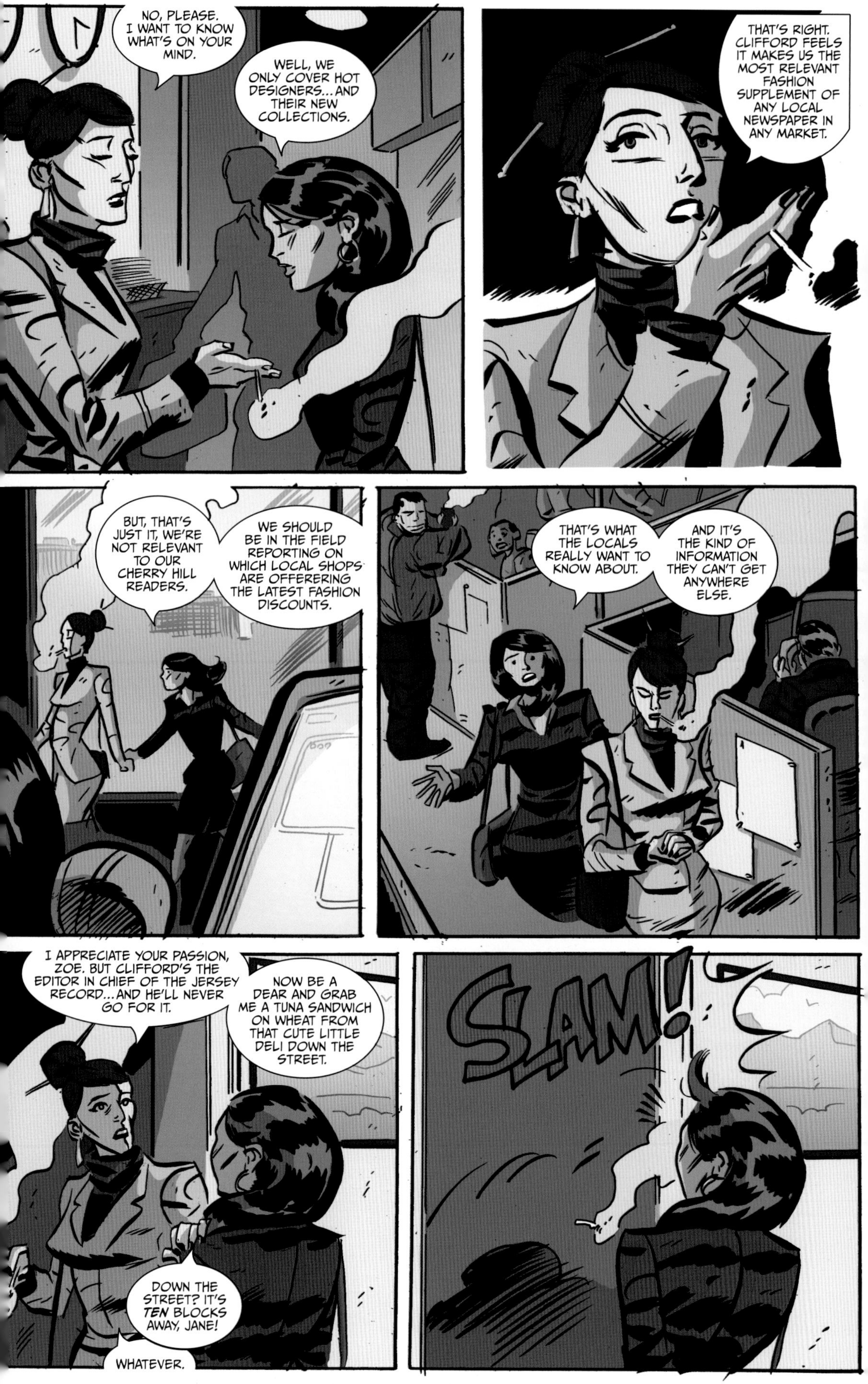

NO, PLEASE. I WANT TO KNOW WHAT'S ON YOUR MIND.
WELL, WE ONLY COVER HOT DESIGNERS... AND THEIR NEW COLLECTIONS.
THAT'S RIGHT. CLIFFORD FEELS IT MAKES US THE MOST RELEVANT FASHION SUPPLEMENT OF ANY LOCAL NEWSPAPER IN ANY MARKET.
BUT, THAT'S JUST IT, WE'RE NOT RELEVANT TO OUR CHERRY HILL READERS.
WE SHOULD BE IN THE FIELD REPORTING ON WHICH LOCAL SHOPS ARE OFFERERING THE LATEST FASHION DISCOUNTS.
THAT'S WHAT THE LOCALS REALLY WANT TO KNOW ABOUT.
AND IT'S THE KIND OF INFORMATION THEY CAN'T GET ANYWHERE ELSE.
I APPRECIATE YOUR PASSION, ZOE. BUT CLIFFORD'S THE EDITOR IN CHIEF OF THE JERSEY RECORD... AND HE'LL NEVER GO FOR IT.
NOW BE A DEAR AND GRAB ME A TUNA SANDWICH ON WHEAT FROM THAT CUTE LITTLE DELI DOWN THE STREET.
DOWN THE STREET? IT'S *TEN* BLOCKS AWAY, JANE!
WHATEVER.
SLAM!

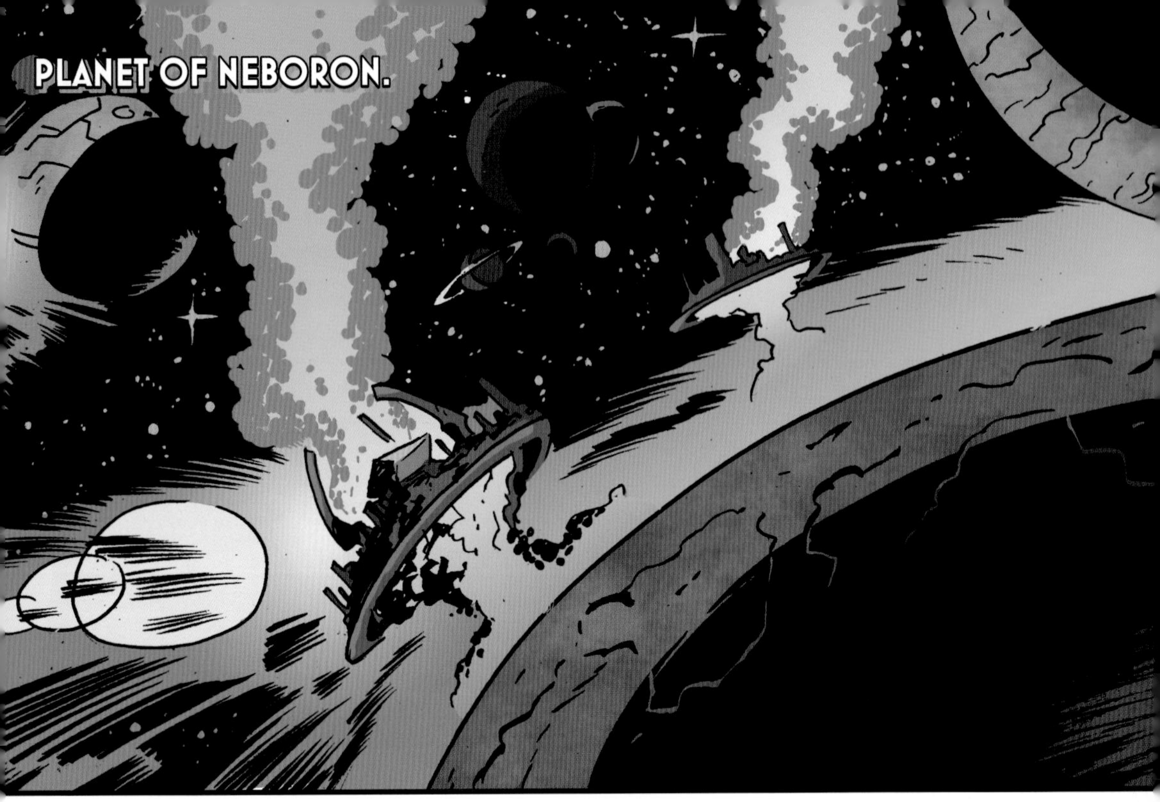
PLANET OF NEBORON.

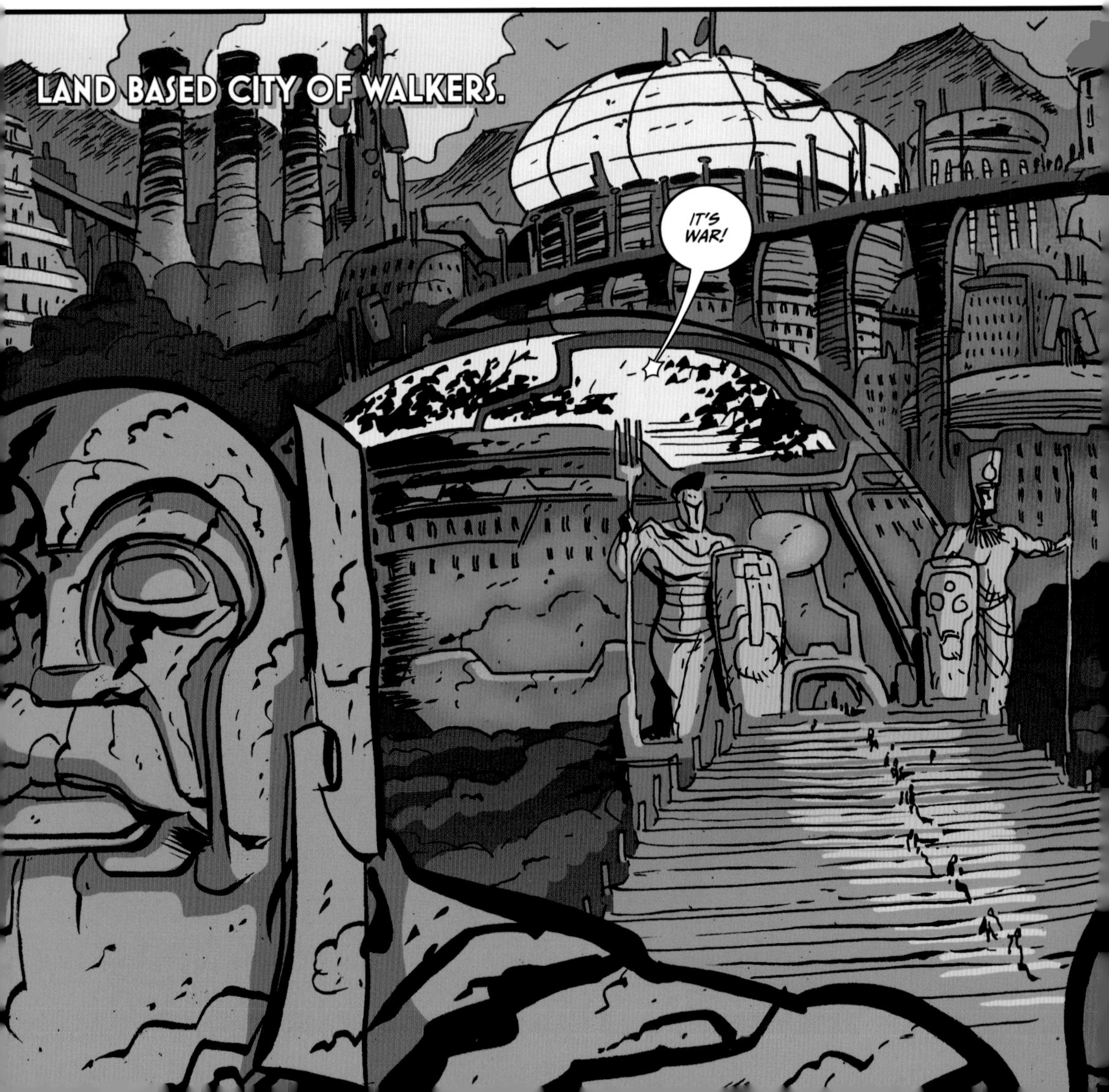
LAND BASED CITY OF WALKERS.
IT'S WAR!

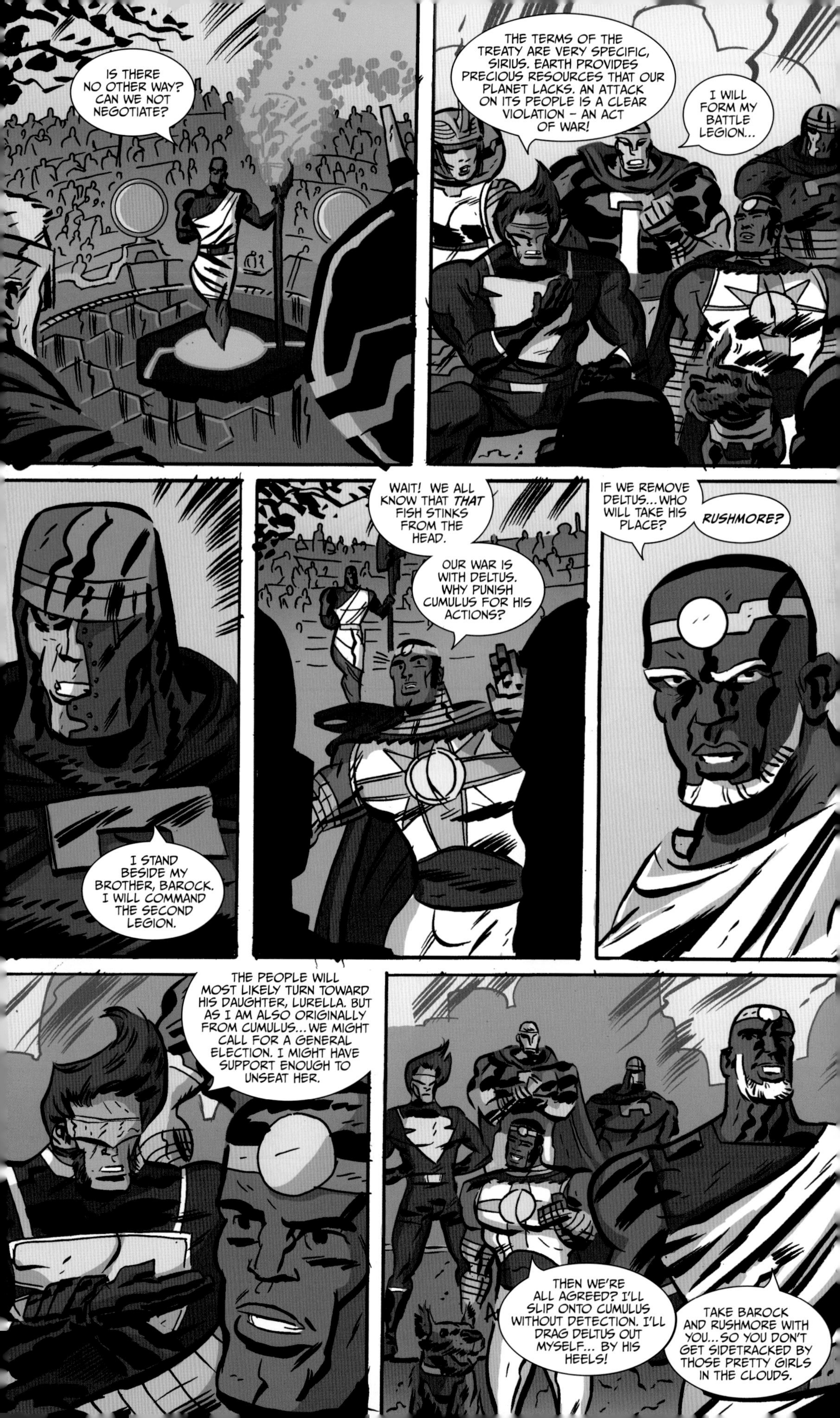
IS THERE NO OTHER WAY? CAN WE NOT NEGOTIATE?
THE TERMS OF THE TREATY ARE VERY SPECIFIC, SIRIUS. EARTH PROVIDES PRECIOUS RESOURCES THAT OUR PLANET LACKS. AN ATTACK ON ITS PEOPLE IS A CLEAR VIOLATION - AN ACT OF WAR!
I WILL FORM MY BATTLE LEGION...
I STAND BESIDE MY BROTHER, BAROCK. I WILL COMMAND THE SECOND LEGION.
WAIT! WE ALL KNOW THAT *THAT* FISH STINKS FROM THE HEAD.
OUR WAR IS WITH DELTUS. WHY PUNISH CUMULUS FOR HIS ACTIONS?
IF WE REMOVE DELTUS...WHO WILL TAKE HIS PLACE?
RUSHMORE?
THE PEOPLE WILL MOST LIKELY TURN TOWARD HIS DAUGHTER, LURELLA. BUT AS I AM ALSO ORIGINALLY FROM CUMULUS...WE MIGHT CALL FOR A GENERAL ELECTION. I MIGHT HAVE SUPPORT ENOUGH TO UNSEAT HER.
THEN WE'RE ALL AGREED? I'LL SLIP ONTO CUMULUS WITHOUT DETECTION. I'LL DRAG DELTUS OUT MYSELF... BY HIS HEELS!
TAKE BAROCK AND RUSHMORE WITH YOU...SO YOU DON'T GET SIDETRACKED BY THOSE PRETTY GIRLS IN THE CLOUDS.

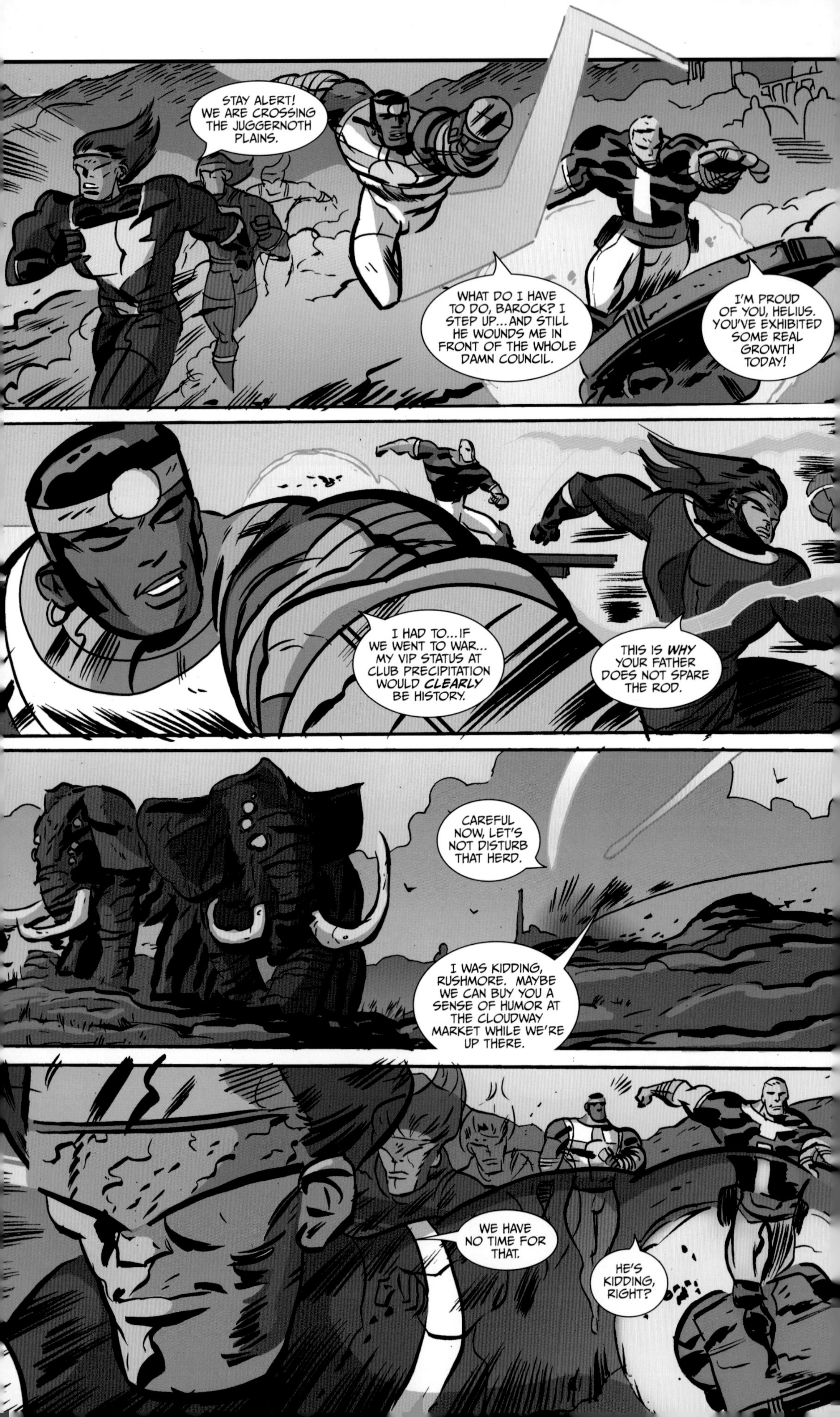
STAY ALERT! WE ARE CROSSING THE JUGGERNOTH PLAINS.
WHAT DO I HAVE TO DO, BAROCK? I STEP UP...AND STILL HE WOUNDS ME IN FRONT OF THE WHOLE DAMN COUNCIL.
I'M PROUD OF YOU, HELIUS. YOU'VE EXHIBITED SOME REAL GROWTH TODAY!
I HAD TO...IF WE WENT TO WAR... MY VIP STATUS AT CLUB PRECIPITATION WOULD *CLEARLY* BE HISTORY.
THIS IS *WHY* YOUR FATHER DOES NOT SPARE THE ROD.
CAREFUL NOW, LET'S NOT DISTURB THAT HERD.
I WAS KIDDING, RUSHMORE. MAYBE WE CAN BUY YOU A SENSE OF HUMOR AT THE CLOUDWAY MARKET WHILE WE'RE UP THERE.
WE HAVE NO TIME FOR THAT.
HE'S KIDDING, RIGHT?

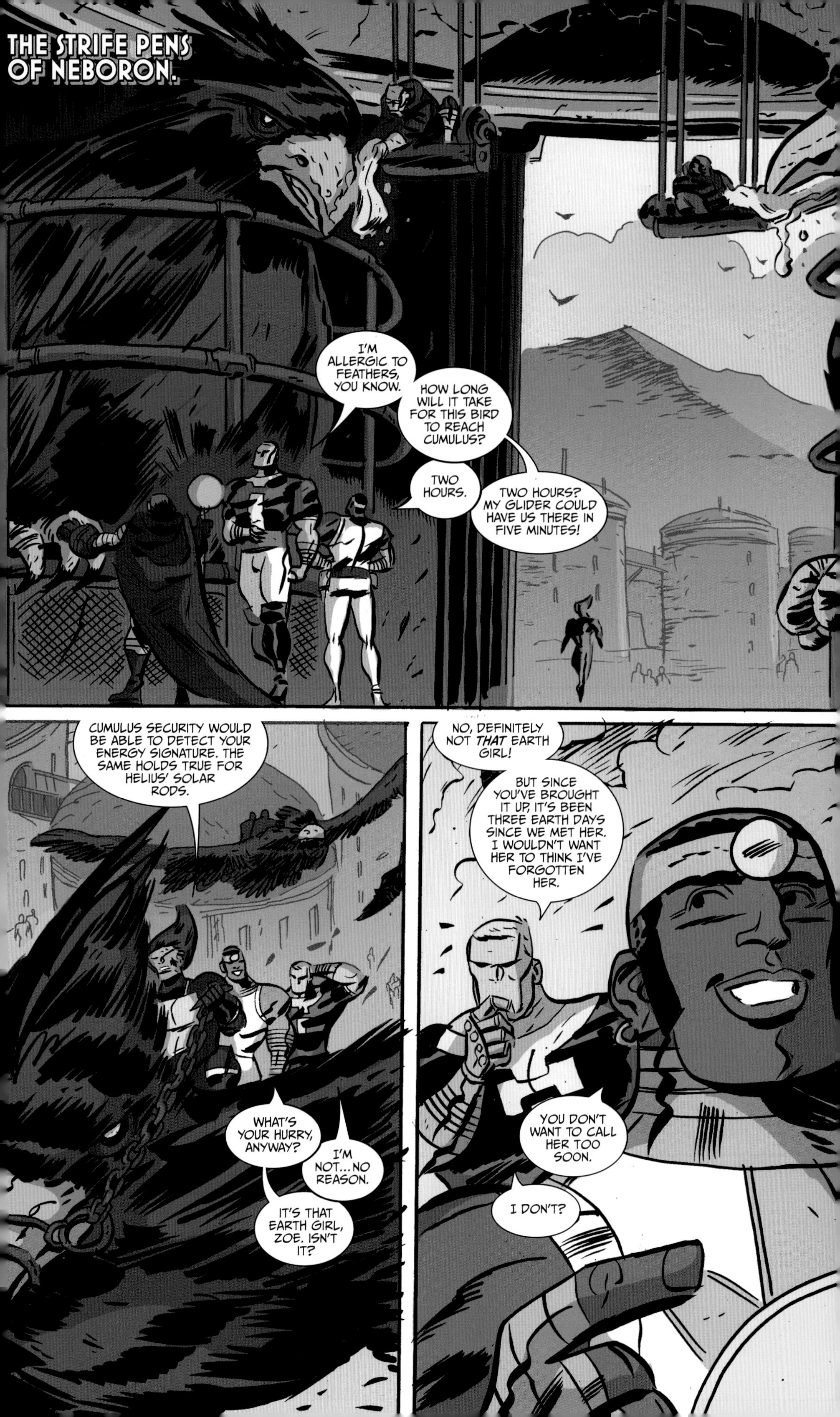
THE STRIFE PENS OF NEBORON.
I'M ALLERGIC TO FEATHERS, YOU KNOW.
HOW LONG WILL IT TAKE FOR THIS BIRD TO REACH CUMULUS?
TWO HOURS.
TWO HOURS? MY GLIDER COULD HAVE US THERE IN FIVE MINUTES!
CUMULUS SECURITY WOULD BE ABLE TO DETECT YOUR ENERGY SIGNATURE. THE SAME HOLDS TRUE FOR HELIUS' SOLAR RODS.
WHAT'S YOUR HURRY, ANYWAY?
I'M NOT...NO REASON.
IT'S THAT EARTH GIRL, ZOE. ISN'T IT?
NO, DEFINITELY NOT *THAT* EARTH GIRL!
BUT SINCE YOU'VE BROUGHT IT UP, IT'S BEEN THREE EARTH DAYS SINCE WE MET HER. I WOULDN'T WANT HER TO THINK I'VE FORGOTTEN HER.
YOU DON'T WANT TO CALL HER TOO SOON.
I DON'T?

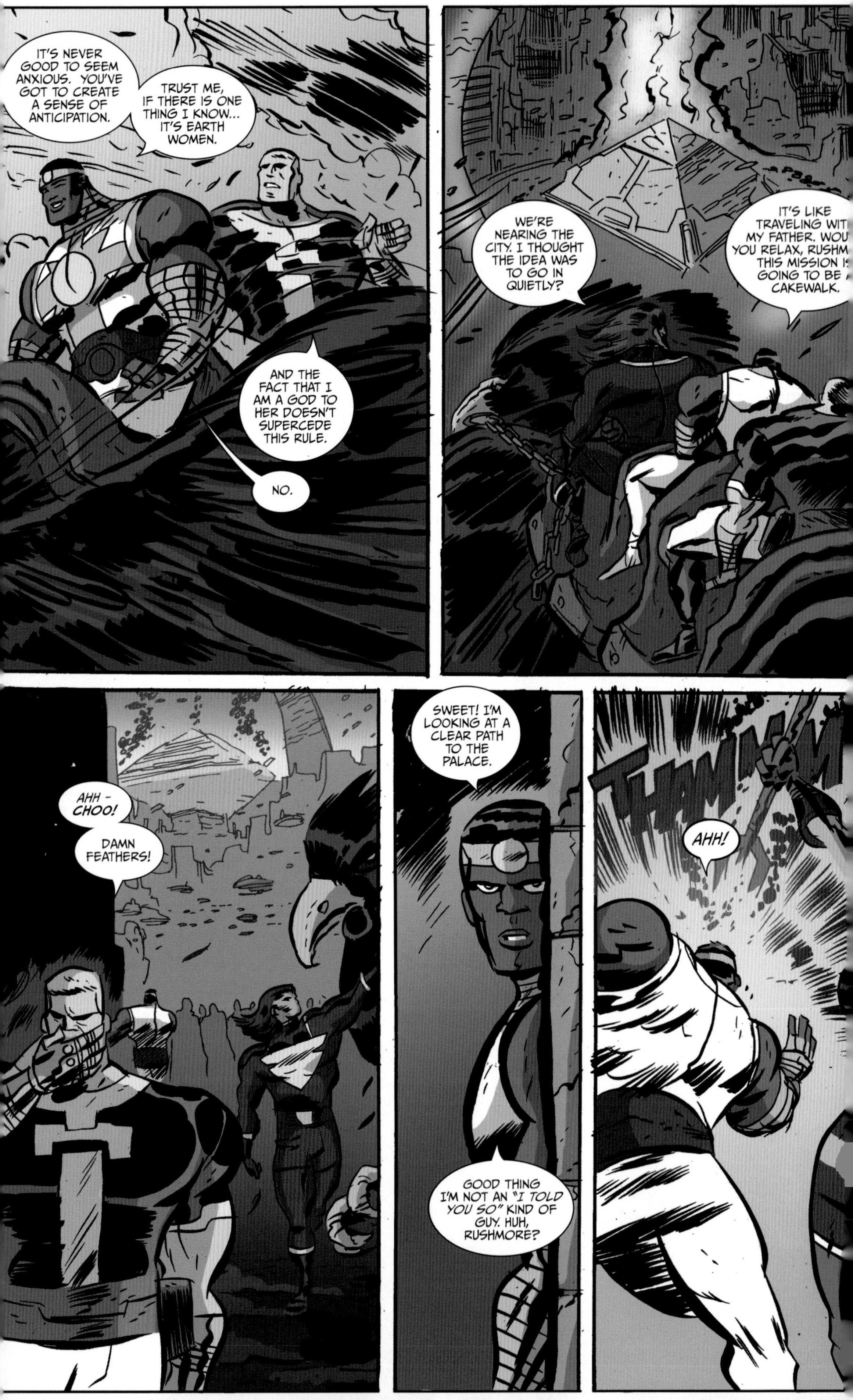
IT'S NEVER GOOD TO SEEM ANXIOUS. YOU'VE GOT TO CREATE A SENSE OF ANTICIPATION.
TRUST ME, IF THERE IS ONE THING I KNOW... IT'S EARTH WOMEN.
AND THE FACT THAT I AM A GOD TO HER DOESN'T SUPERCEDE THIS RULE.
NO.
WE'RE NEARING THE CITY. I THOUGHT THE IDEA WAS TO GO IN QUIETLY?
IT'S LIKE TRAVELING WIT MY FATHER. WOU YOU RELAX, RUSHM THIS MISSION IS GOING TO BE CAKEWALK.
AHH - CHOO!
DAMN FEATHERS!
SWEET! I'M LOOKING AT A CLEAR PATH TO THE PALACE.
GOOD THING I'M NOT AN "I TOLD YOU SO" KIND OF GUY. HUH, RUSHMORE?
THMMM
AHH!

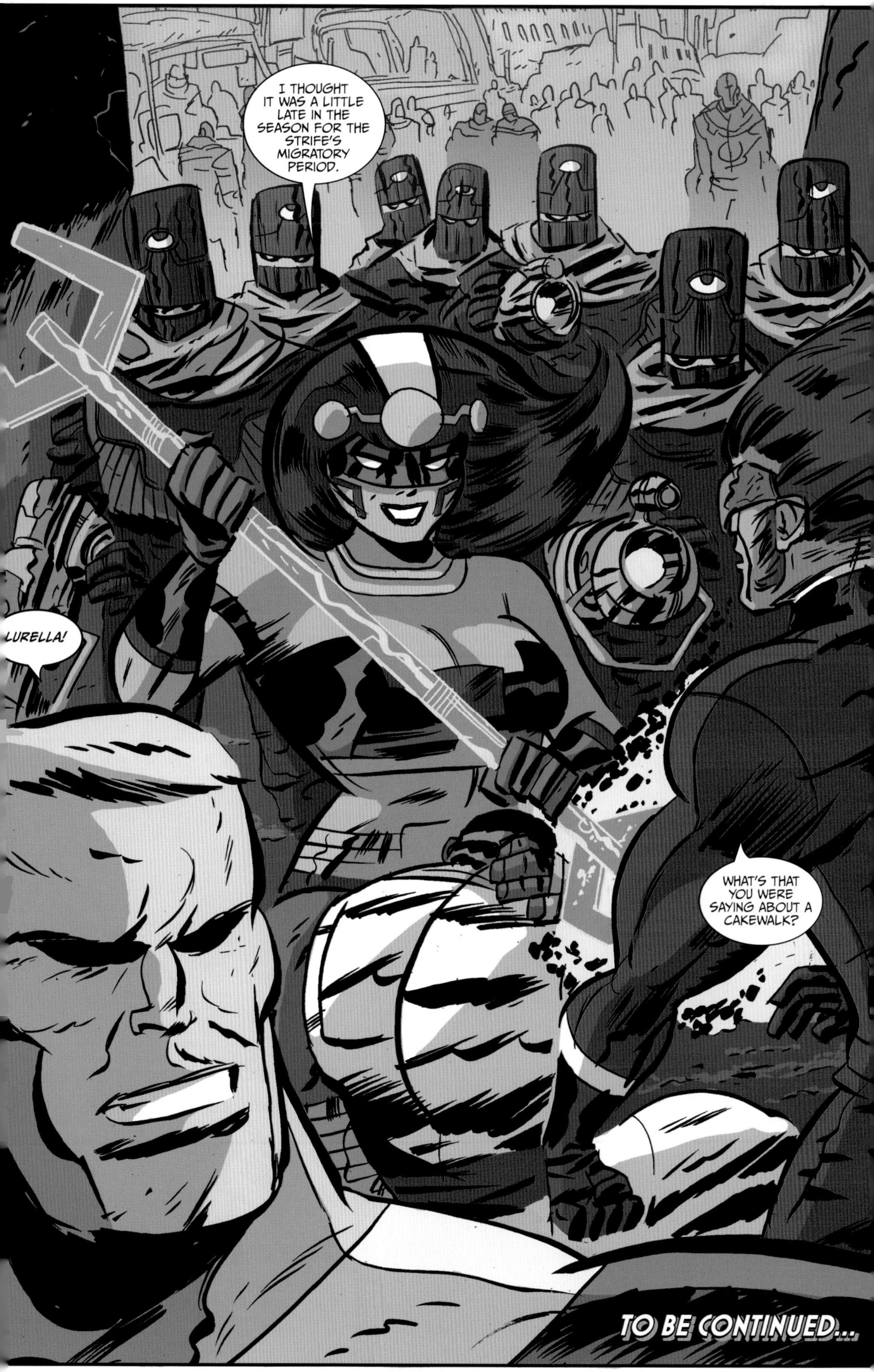
I THOUGHT IT WAS A LITTLE LATE IN THE SEASON FOR THE STRIFE'S MIGRATORY PERIOD.
LURELLA!
WHAT'S THAT YOU WERE SAYING ABOUT A CAKEWALK?
TO BE CONTINUED...

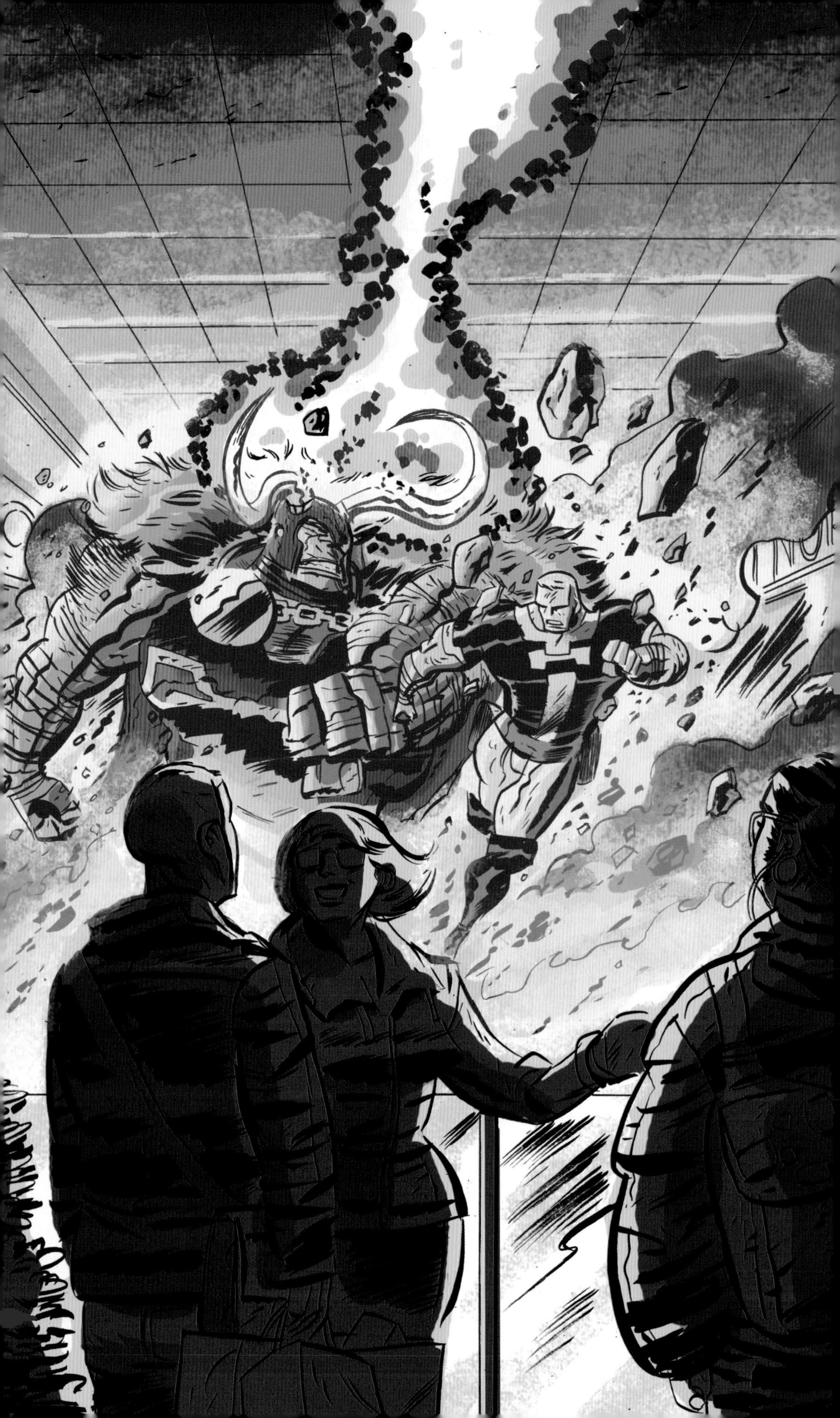

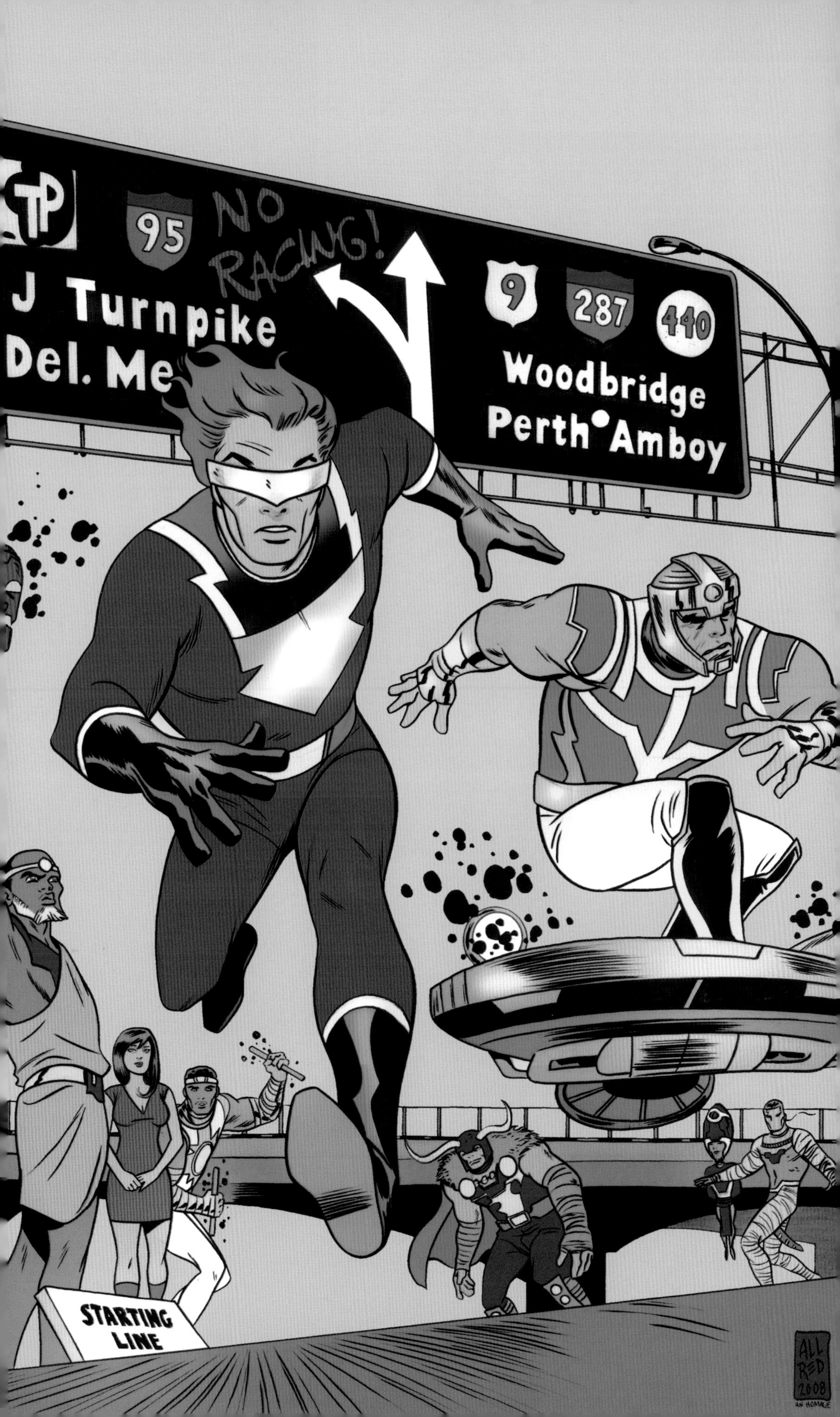
TP
95
NO RACING!
J Turnpike
Del. Me
9
287
440
Woodbridge
Perth Amboy
STARTING LINE
ALL RED 2008
AN HOMAGE

CHAPTER THREE

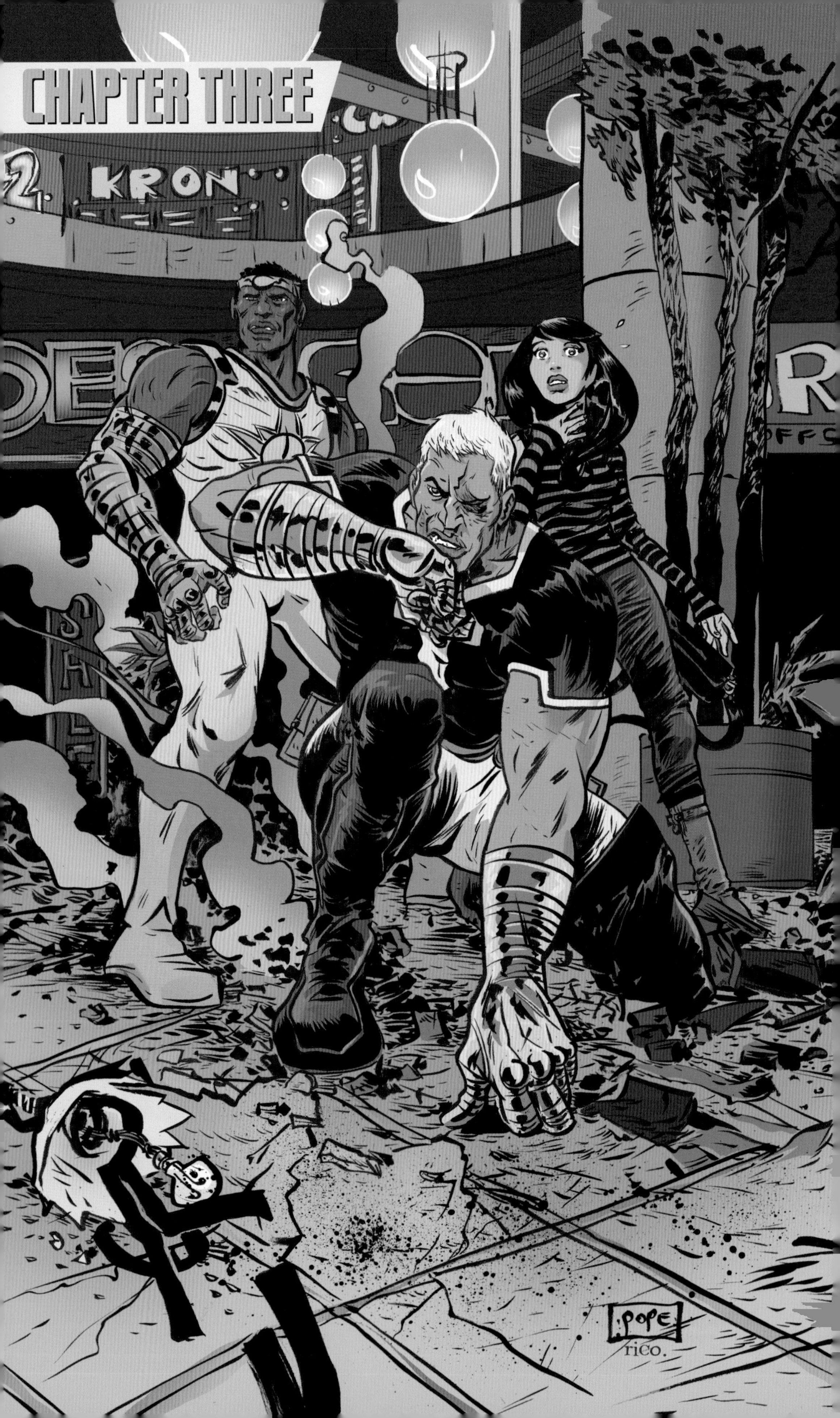
KRON
POPE
rico.

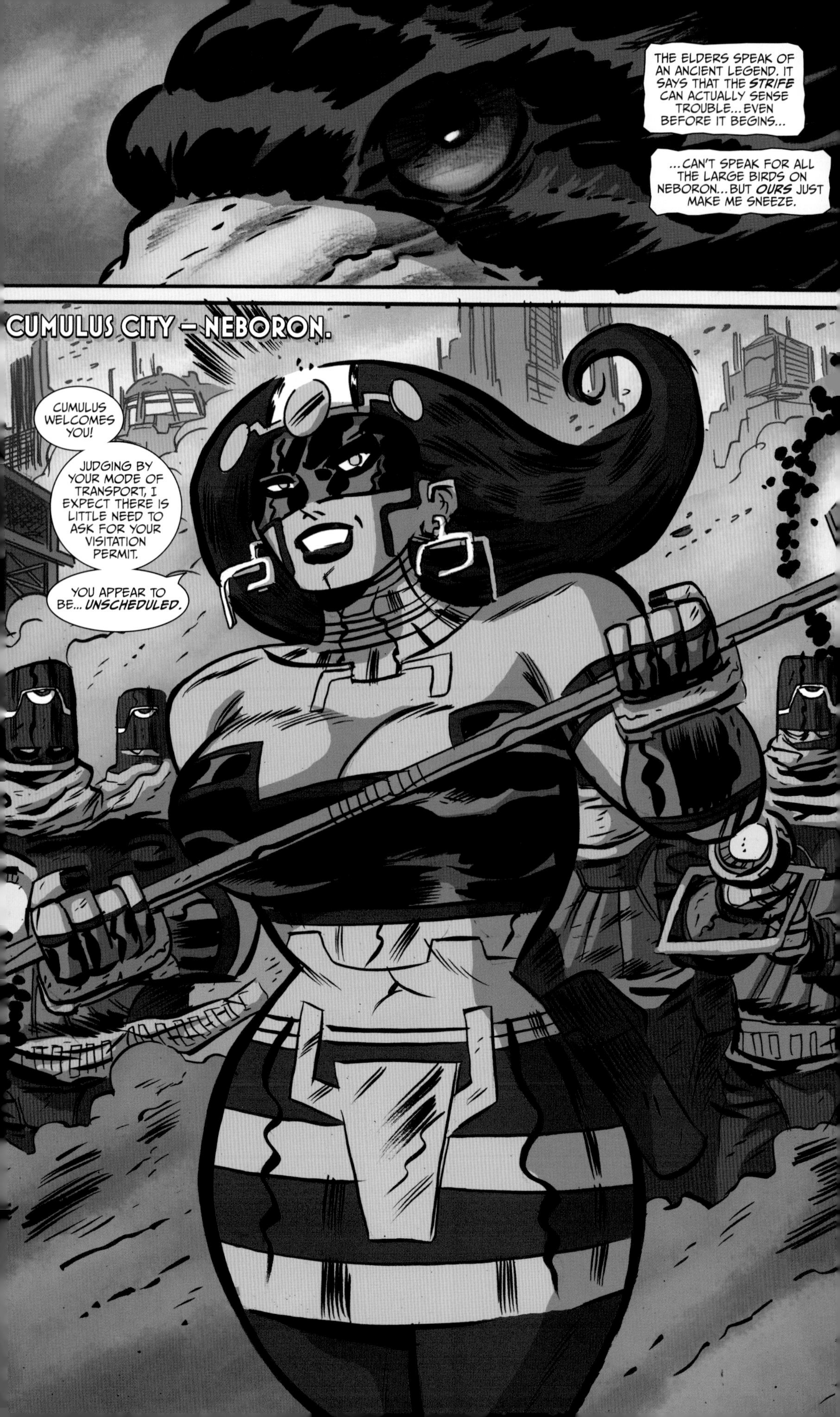
THE ELDERS SPEAK OF AN ANCIENT LEGEND. IT SAYS THAT THE STRIFE CAN ACTUALLY SENSE TROUBLE... EVEN BEFORE IT BEGINS...
...CAN'T SPEAK FOR ALL THE LARGE BIRDS ON NEBORON... BUT OURS JUST MAKE ME SNEEZE.
CUMULUS CITY — NEBORON.
CUMULUS WELCOMES YOU!
JUDGING BY YOUR MODE OF TRANSPORT, I EXPECT THERE IS LITTLE NEED TO ASK FOR YOUR VISITATION PERMIT.
YOU APPEAR TO BE... UNSCHEDULED.

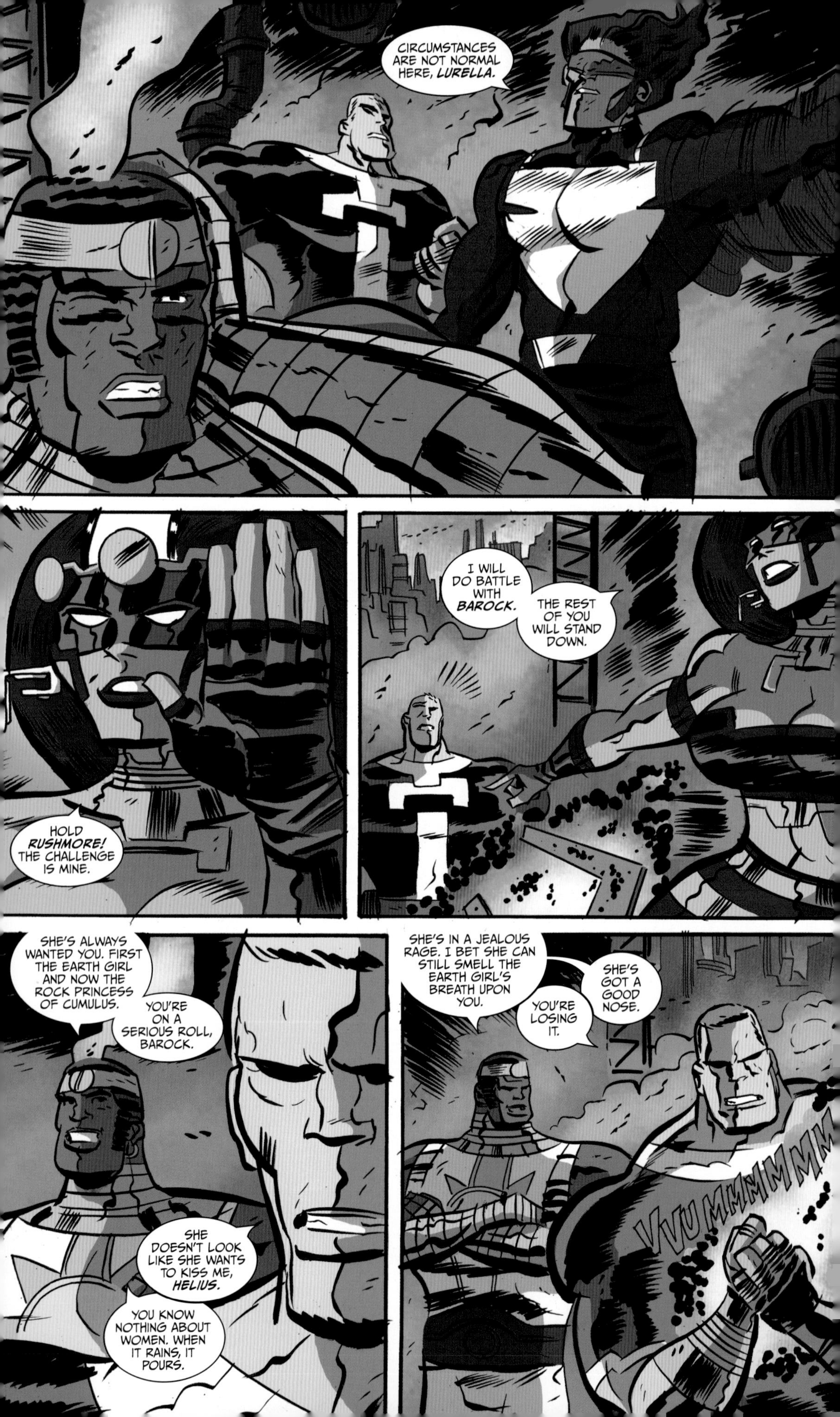
CIRCUMSTANCES ARE NOT NORMAL HERE, LURELLA.
HOLD RUSHMORE! THE CHALLENGE IS MINE.
I WILL DO BATTLE WITH BAROCK.
THE REST OF YOU WILL STAND DOWN.
SHE'S ALWAYS WANTED YOU. FIRST THE EARTH GIRL AND NOW THE ROCK PRINCESS OF CUMULUS.
YOU'RE ON A SERIOUS ROLL, BAROCK.
SHE DOESN'T LOOK LIKE SHE WANTS TO KISS ME, HELIUS.
YOU KNOW NOTHING ABOUT WOMEN. WHEN IT RAINS, IT POURS.
SHE'S IN A JEALOUS RAGE. I BET SHE CAN STILL SMELL THE EARTH GIRL'S BREATH UPON YOU.
YOU'RE LOSING IT.
SHE'S GOT A GOOD NOSE.
VVUMMMMMMMM

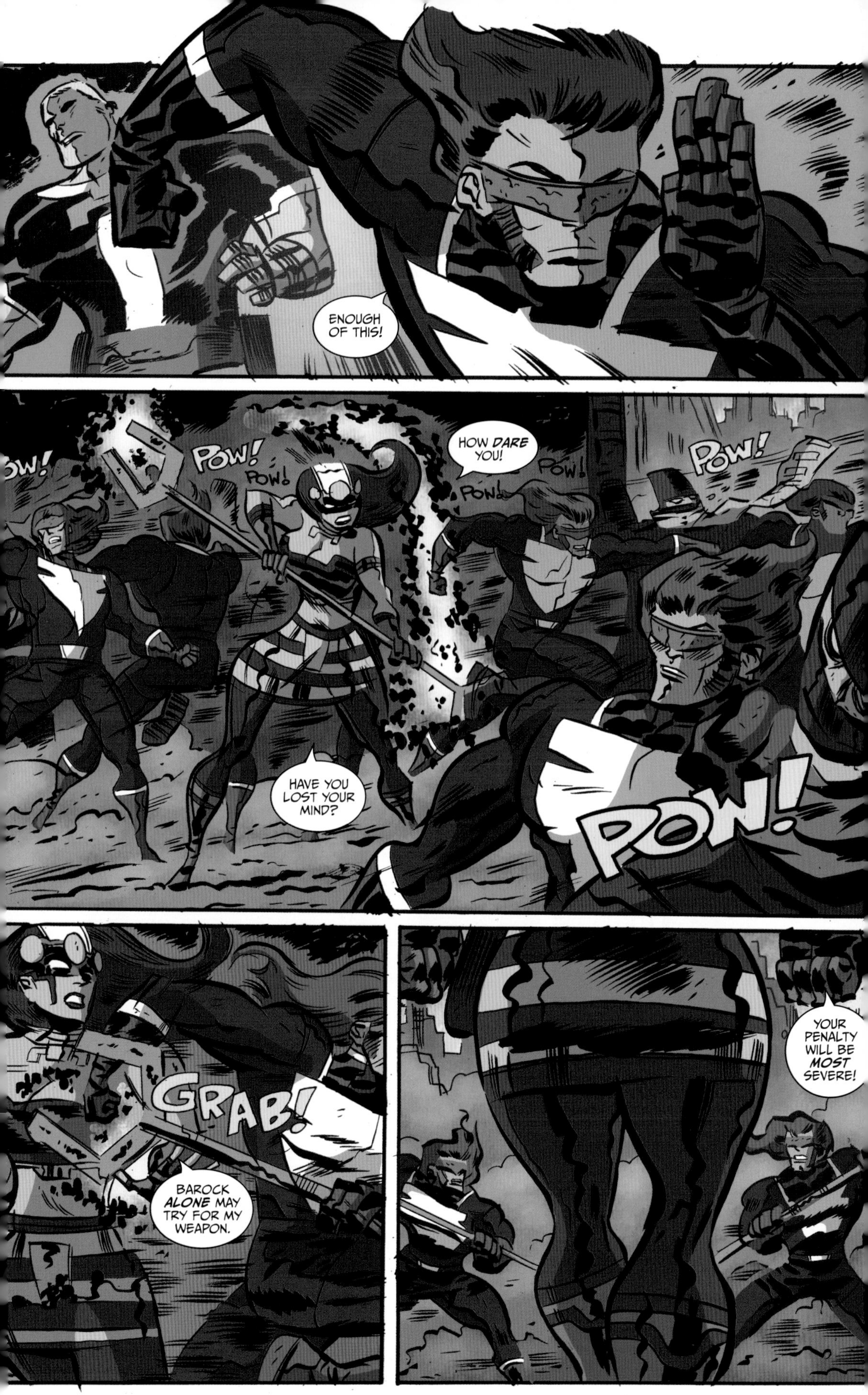
ENOUGH OF THIS!
POW!
POW!
HOW *DARE* YOU!
POW!
POW!
POW!
HAVE YOU LOST YOUR MIND?
POW!
GRAB!
BAROCK *ALONE* MAY TRY FOR MY WEAPON.
YOUR PENALTY WILL BE *MOST* SEVERE!

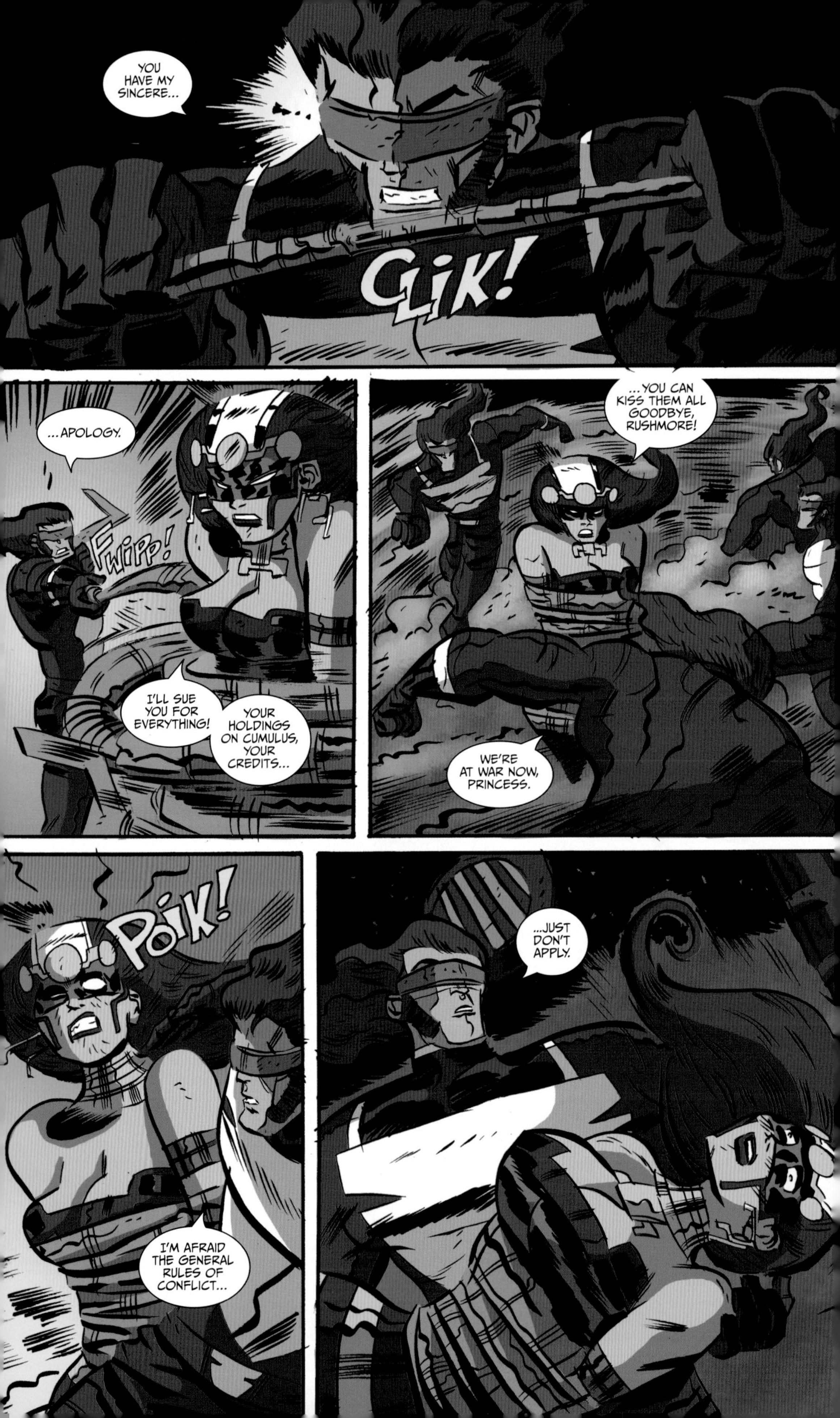
YOU HAVE MY SINCERE...
CLIK!
...APOLOGY.
FWIPP!
I'LL SUE YOU FOR EVERYTHING!
YOUR HOLDINGS ON CUMULUS, YOUR CREDITS...
...YOU CAN KISS THEM ALL GOODBYE, RUSHMORE!
WE'RE AT WAR NOW, PRINCESS.
POIK!
I'M AFRAID THE GENERAL RULES OF CONFLICT...
...JUST DON'T APPLY.

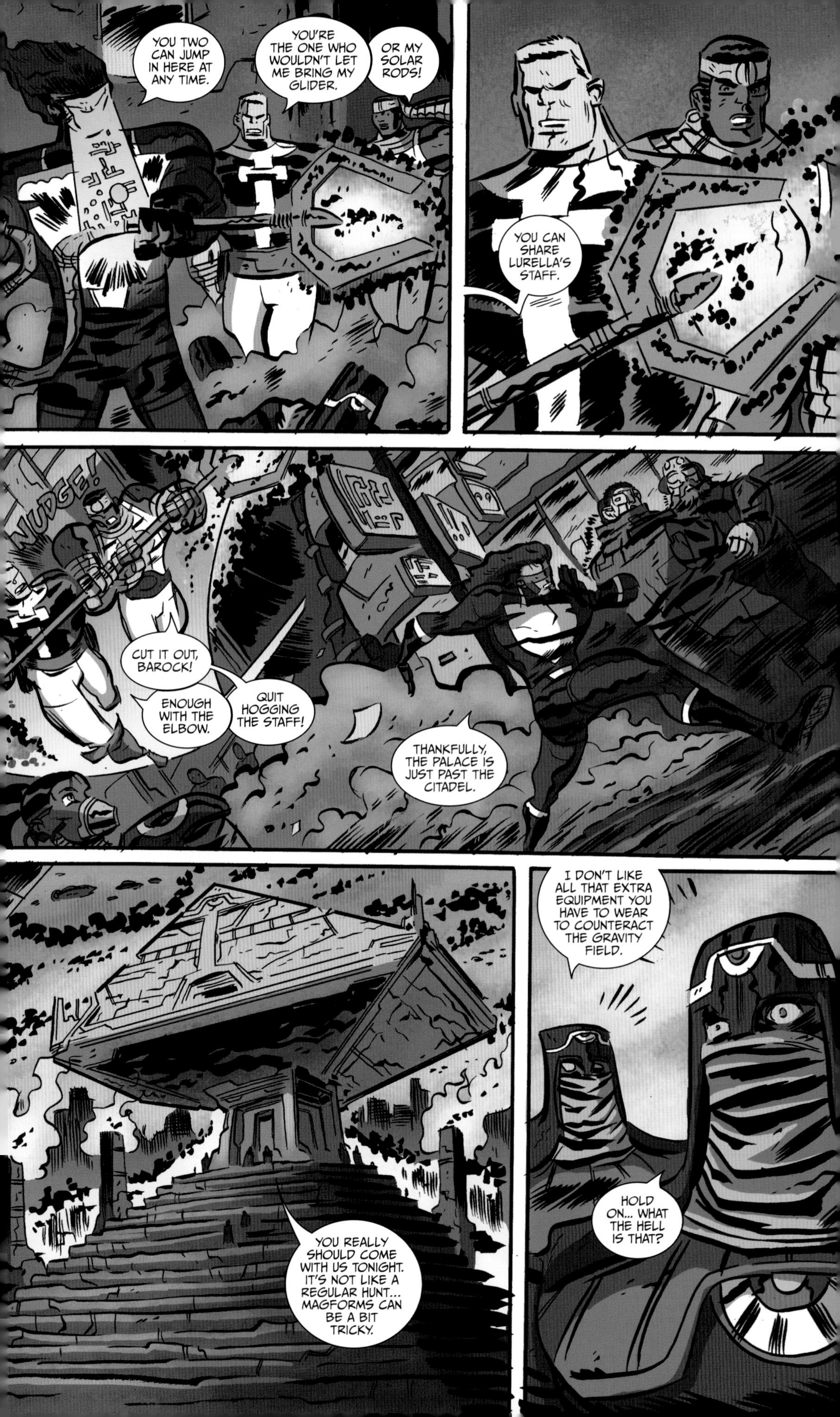
YOU TWO CAN JUMP IN HERE AT ANY TIME.
YOU'RE THE ONE WHO WOULDN'T LET ME BRING MY GLIDER.
OR MY SOLAR RODS!
YOU CAN SHARE LURELLA'S STAFF.
NUDGE!
CUT IT OUT, BAROCK!
ENOUGH WITH THE ELBOW.
QUIT HOGGING THE STAFF!
THANKFULLY, THE PALACE IS JUST PAST THE CITADEL.
YOU REALLY SHOULD COME WITH US TONIGHT. IT'S NOT LIKE A REGULAR HUNT... MAGFORMS CAN BE A BIT TRICKY.
I DON'T LIKE ALL THAT EXTRA EQUIPMENT YOU HAVE TO WEAR TO COUNTERACT THE GRAVITY FIELD.
HOLD ON... WHAT THE HELL IS THAT?

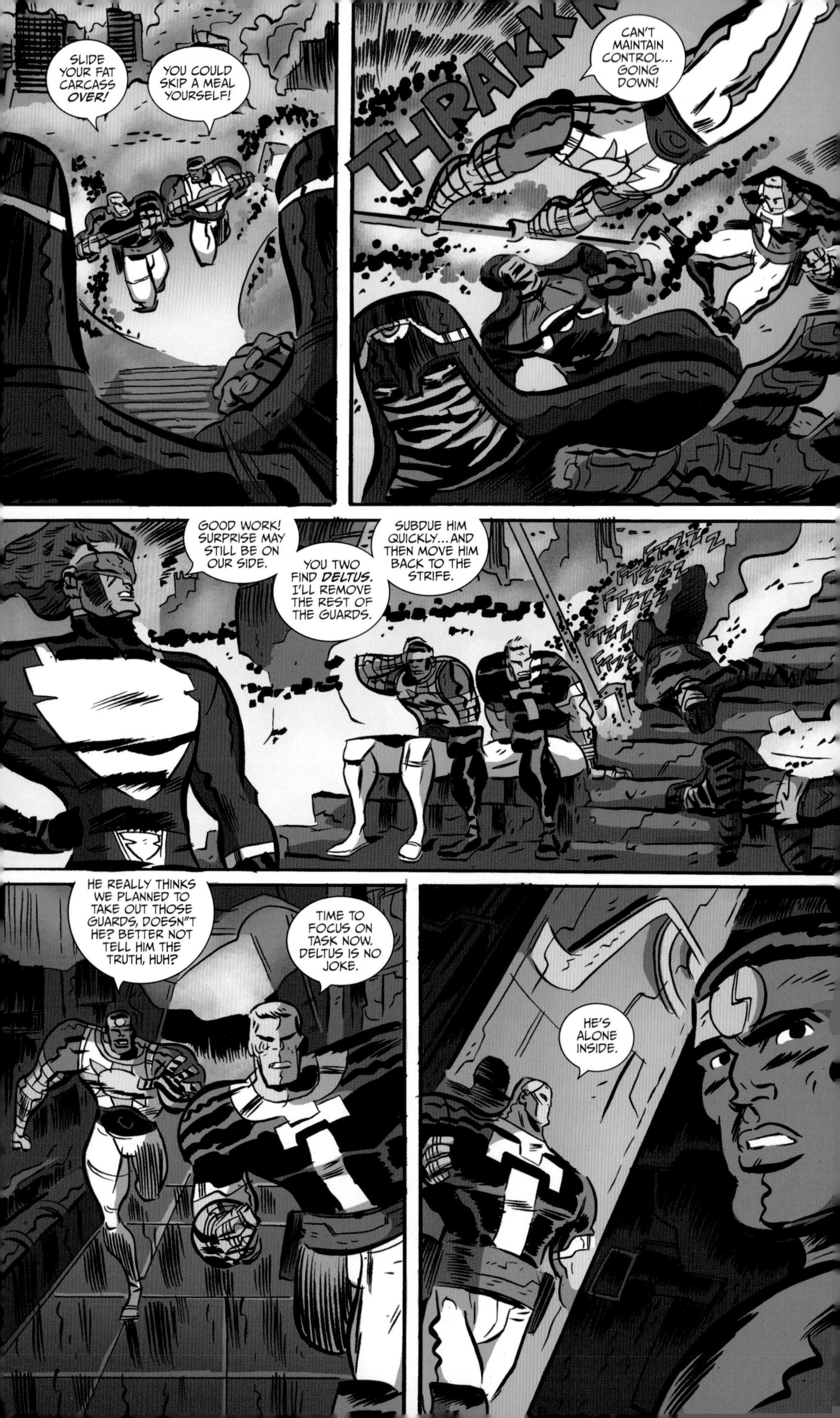
SLIDE YOUR FAT CARCASS OVER!
YOU COULD SKIP A MEAL YOURSELF!
THRAKK
CAN'T MAINTAIN CONTROL... GOING DOWN!
GOOD WORK! SURPRISE MAY STILL BE ON OUR SIDE.
YOU TWO FIND DELTUS. I'LL REMOVE THE REST OF THE GUARDS.
SUBDUE HIM QUICKLY...AND THEN MOVE HIM BACK TO THE STRIFE.
FTZZZZ
HE REALLY THINKS WE PLANNED TO TAKE OUT THOSE GUARDS, DOESN'T HE? BETTER NOT TELL HIM THE TRUTH, HUH?
TIME TO FOCUS ON TASK NOW. DELTUS IS NO JOKE.
HE'S ALONE INSIDE.

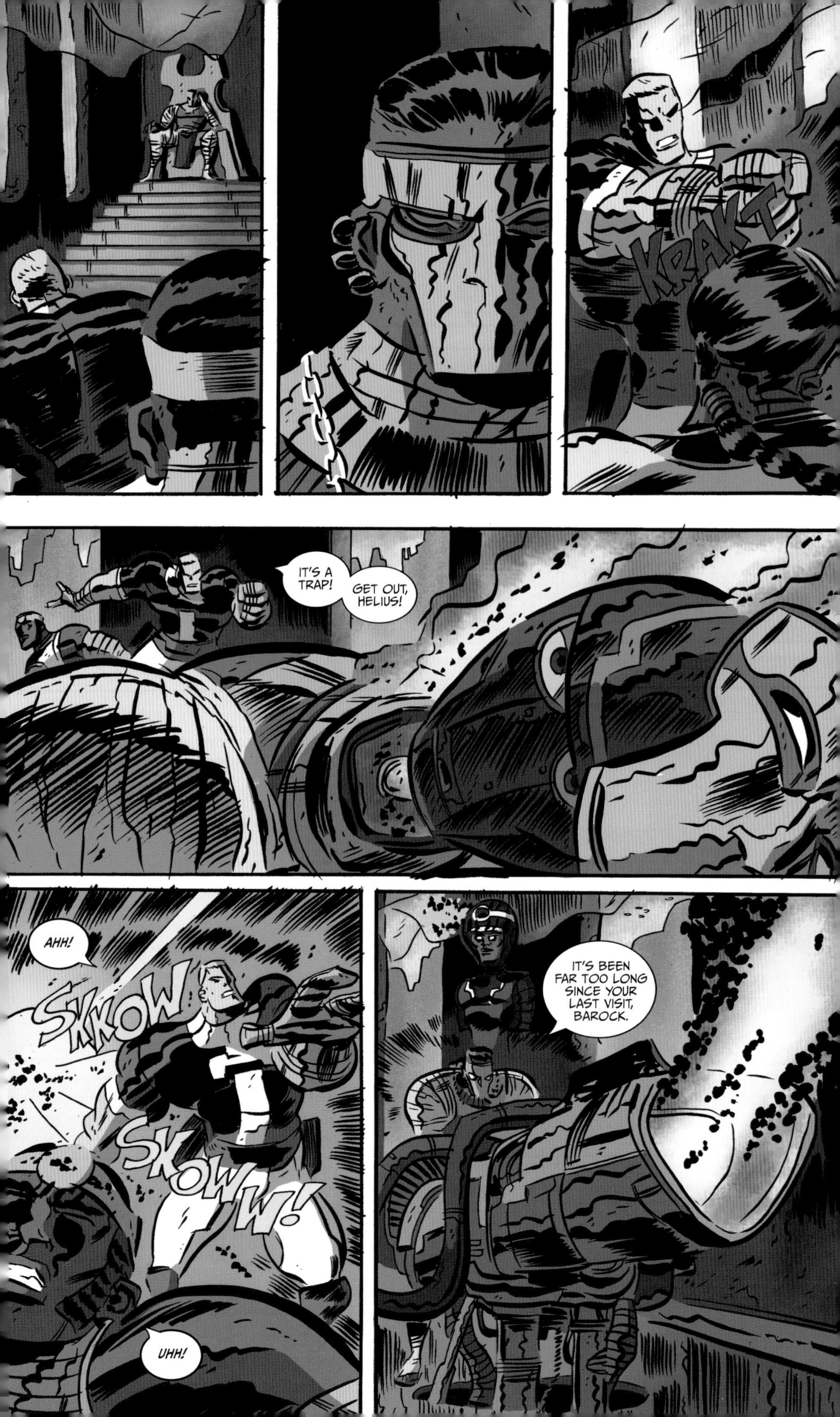
KRAKT
IT'S A TRAP!
GET OUT, HELIUS!
AHH!
SKKOW
SKOWW!
UHH!
IT'S BEEN FAR TOO LONG SINCE YOUR LAST VISIT, BAROCK.

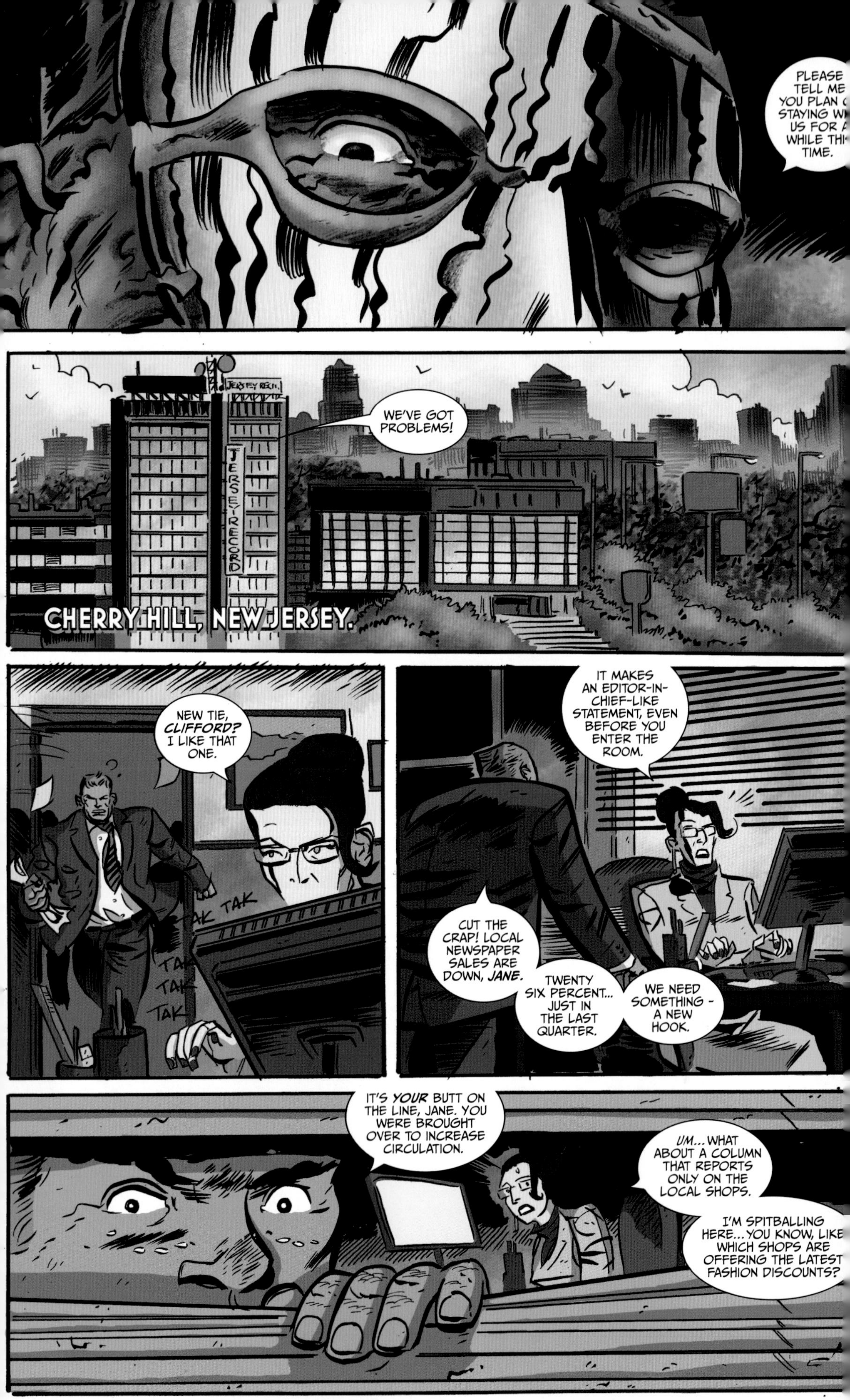
PLEASE TELL ME YOU PLAN O STAYING WI US FOR A WHILE THI TIME.
WE'VE GOT PROBLEMS!
JERSEY RECORD
CHERRY HILL, NEW JERSEY.
NEW TIE, *CLIFFORD?* I LIKE THAT ONE.
TAK TAK
TAK TAK TAK
IT MAKES AN EDITOR-IN-CHIEF-LIKE STATEMENT, EVEN BEFORE YOU ENTER THE ROOM.
CUT THE CRAP! LOCAL NEWSPAPER SALES ARE DOWN, *JANE.*
TWENTY SIX PERCENT... JUST IN THE LAST QUARTER.
WE NEED SOMETHING - A NEW HOOK.
IT'S *YOUR* BUTT ON THE LINE, JANE. YOU WERE BROUGHT OVER TO INCREASE CIRCULATION.
UM... WHAT ABOUT A COLUMN THAT REPORTS ONLY ON THE LOCAL SHOPS.
I'M SPITBALLING HERE... YOU KNOW, LIKE WHICH SHOPS ARE OFFERING THE LATEST FASHION DISCOUNTS?

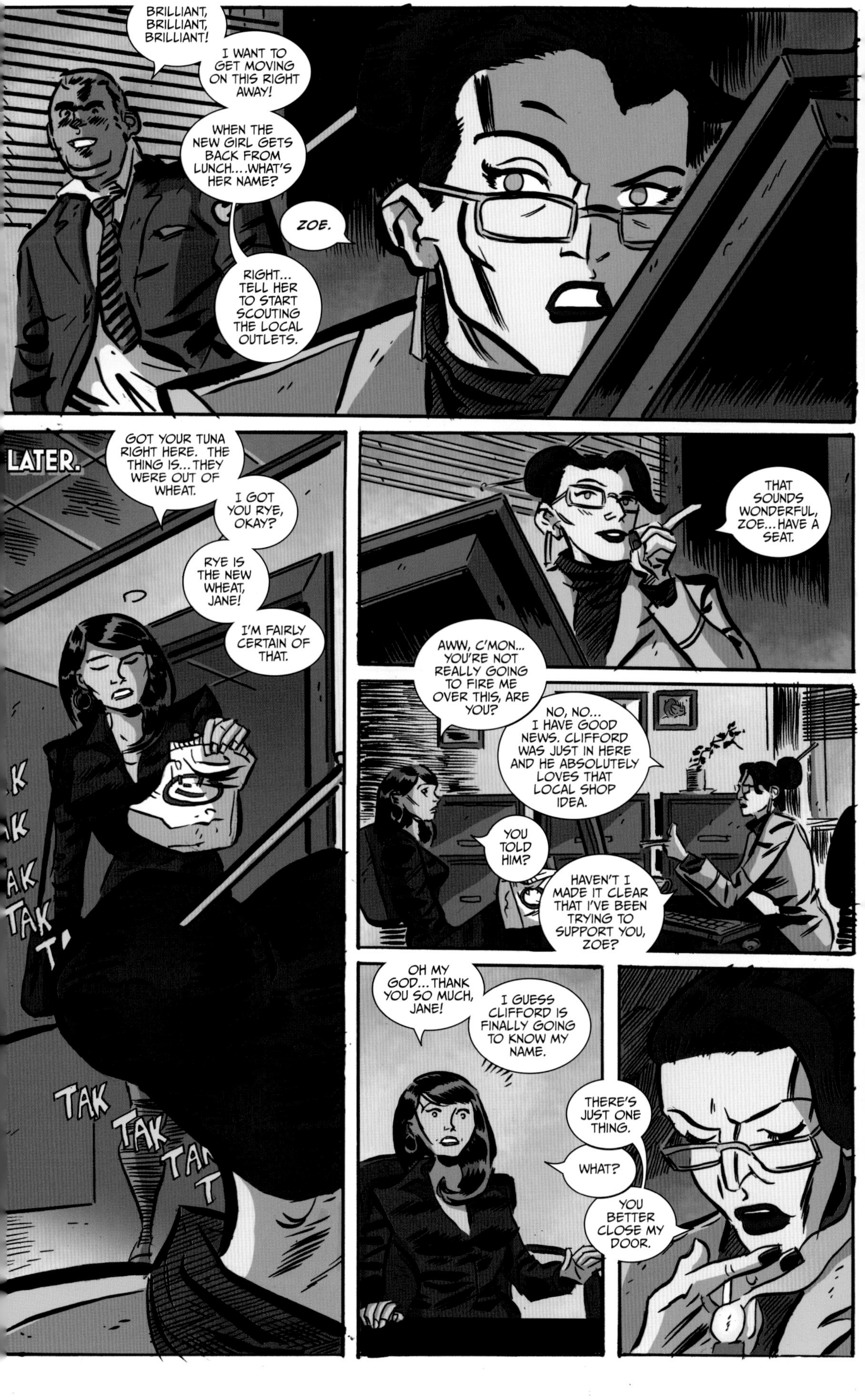
BRILLIANT, BRILLIANT, BRILLIANT!
I WANT TO GET MOVING ON THIS RIGHT AWAY!
WHEN THE NEW GIRL GETS BACK FROM LUNCH....WHAT'S HER NAME?
ZOE.
RIGHT... TELL HER TO START SCOUTING THE LOCAL OUTLETS.
LATER.
GOT YOUR TUNA RIGHT HERE. THE THING IS...THEY WERE OUT OF WHEAT.
I GOT YOU RYE, OKAY?
RYE IS THE NEW WHEAT, JANE!
I'M FAIRLY CERTAIN OF THAT.
TAK TAK TAK TAK
TAK TAK TAK
THAT SOUNDS WONDERFUL, ZOE...HAVE A SEAT.
AWW, C'MON... YOU'RE NOT REALLY GOING TO FIRE ME OVER THIS, ARE YOU?
NO, NO... I HAVE GOOD NEWS. CLIFFORD WAS JUST IN HERE AND HE ABSOLUTELY LOVES THAT LOCAL SHOP IDEA.
YOU TOLD HIM?
HAVEN'T I MADE IT CLEAR THAT I'VE BEEN TRYING TO SUPPORT YOU, ZOE?
OH MY GOD...THANK YOU SO MUCH, JANE!
I GUESS CLIFFORD IS FINALLY GOING TO KNOW MY NAME.
THERE'S JUST ONE THING.
WHAT?
YOU BETTER CLOSE MY DOOR.

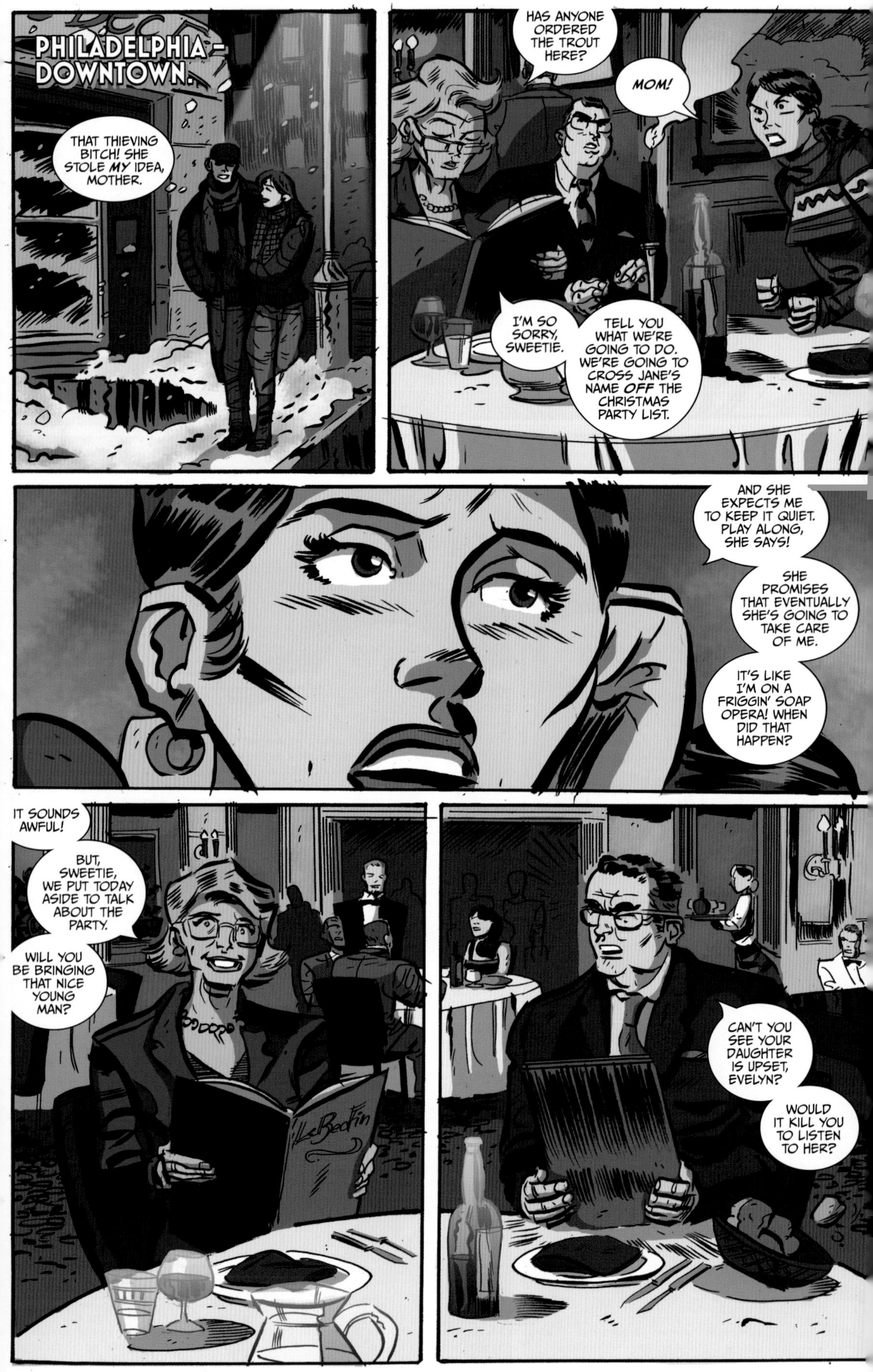
PHILADELPHIA - DOWNTOWN.
THAT THIEVING BITCH! SHE STOLE MY IDEA, MOTHER.
HAS ANYONE ORDERED THE TROUT HERE?
MOM!
I'M SO SORRY, SWEETIE.
TELL YOU WHAT WE'RE GOING TO DO. WE'RE GOING TO CROSS JANE'S NAME OFF THE CHRISTMAS PARTY LIST.
AND SHE EXPECTS ME TO KEEP IT QUIET. PLAY ALONG, SHE SAYS!
SHE PROMISES THAT EVENTUALLY SHE'S GOING TO TAKE CARE OF ME.
IT'S LIKE I'M ON A FRIGGIN' SOAP OPERA! WHEN DID THAT HAPPEN?
IT SOUNDS AWFUL!
BUT, SWEETIE, WE PUT TODAY ASIDE TO TALK ABOUT THE PARTY.
WILL YOU BE BRINGING THAT NICE YOUNG MAN?
Le Bec Fin
CAN'T YOU SEE YOUR DAUGHTER IS UPSET, EVELYN?
WOULD IT KILL YOU TO LISTEN TO HER?

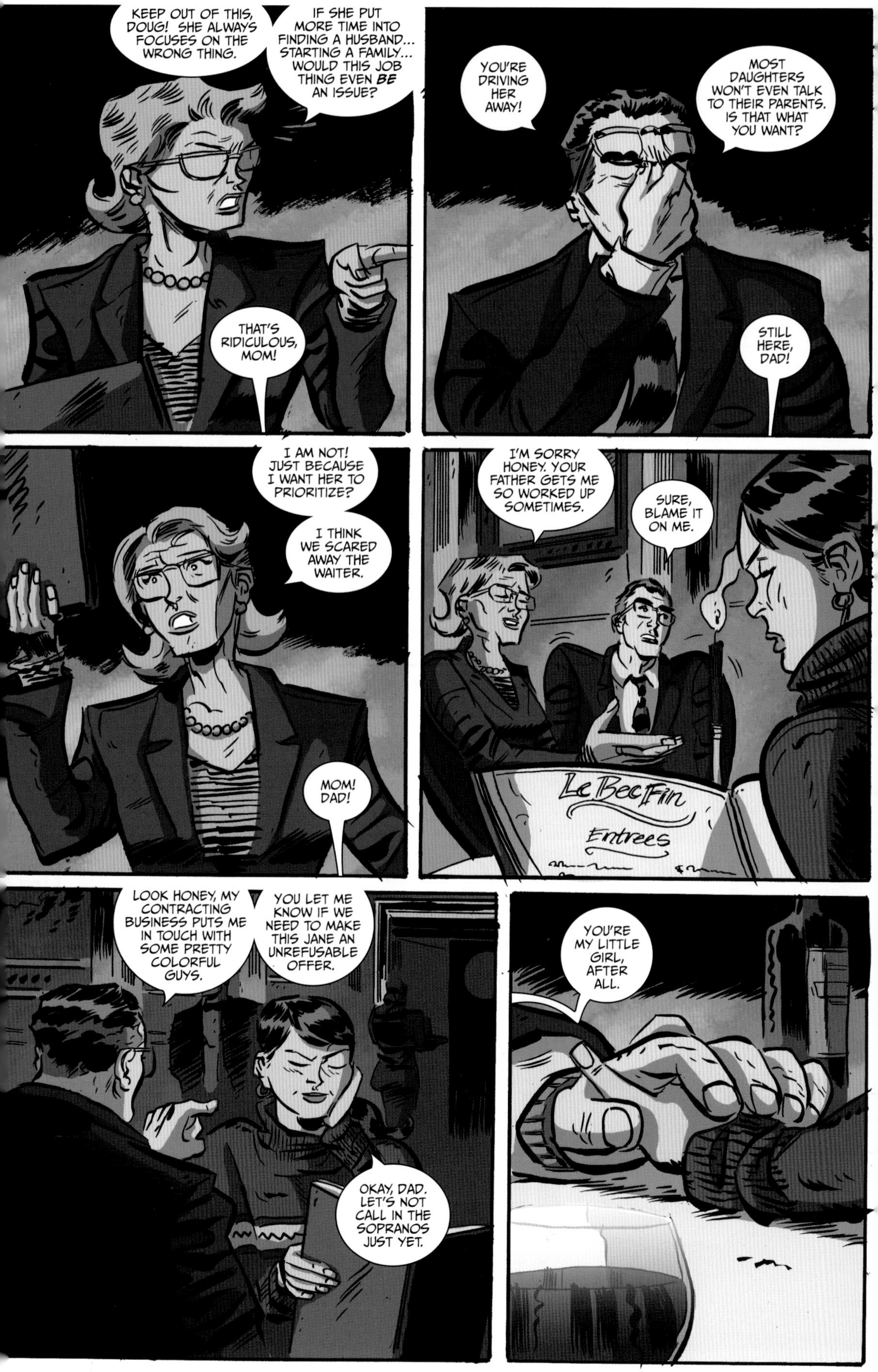
KEEP OUT OF THIS, DOUG! SHE ALWAYS FOCUSES ON THE WRONG THING.
IF SHE PUT MORE TIME INTO FINDING A HUSBAND... STARTING A FAMILY... WOULD THIS JOB THING EVEN **BE** AN ISSUE?
THAT'S RIDICULOUS, MOM!
YOU'RE DRIVING HER AWAY!
MOST DAUGHTERS WON'T EVEN TALK TO THEIR PARENTS. IS THAT WHAT YOU WANT?
STILL HERE, DAD!
I AM NOT! JUST BECAUSE I WANT HER TO PRIORITIZE?
I THINK WE SCARED AWAY THE WAITER.
MOM! DAD!
I'M SORRY HONEY. YOUR FATHER GETS ME SO WORKED UP SOMETIMES.
SURE, BLAME IT ON ME.
Le Bec Fin
Entrees
LOOK HONEY, MY CONTRACTING BUSINESS PUTS ME IN TOUCH WITH SOME PRETTY COLORFUL GUYS.
YOU LET ME KNOW IF WE NEED TO MAKE THIS JANE AN UNREFUSABLE OFFER.
OKAY, DAD. LET'S NOT CALL IN THE SOPRANOS JUST YET.
YOU'RE MY LITTLE GIRL, AFTER ALL.

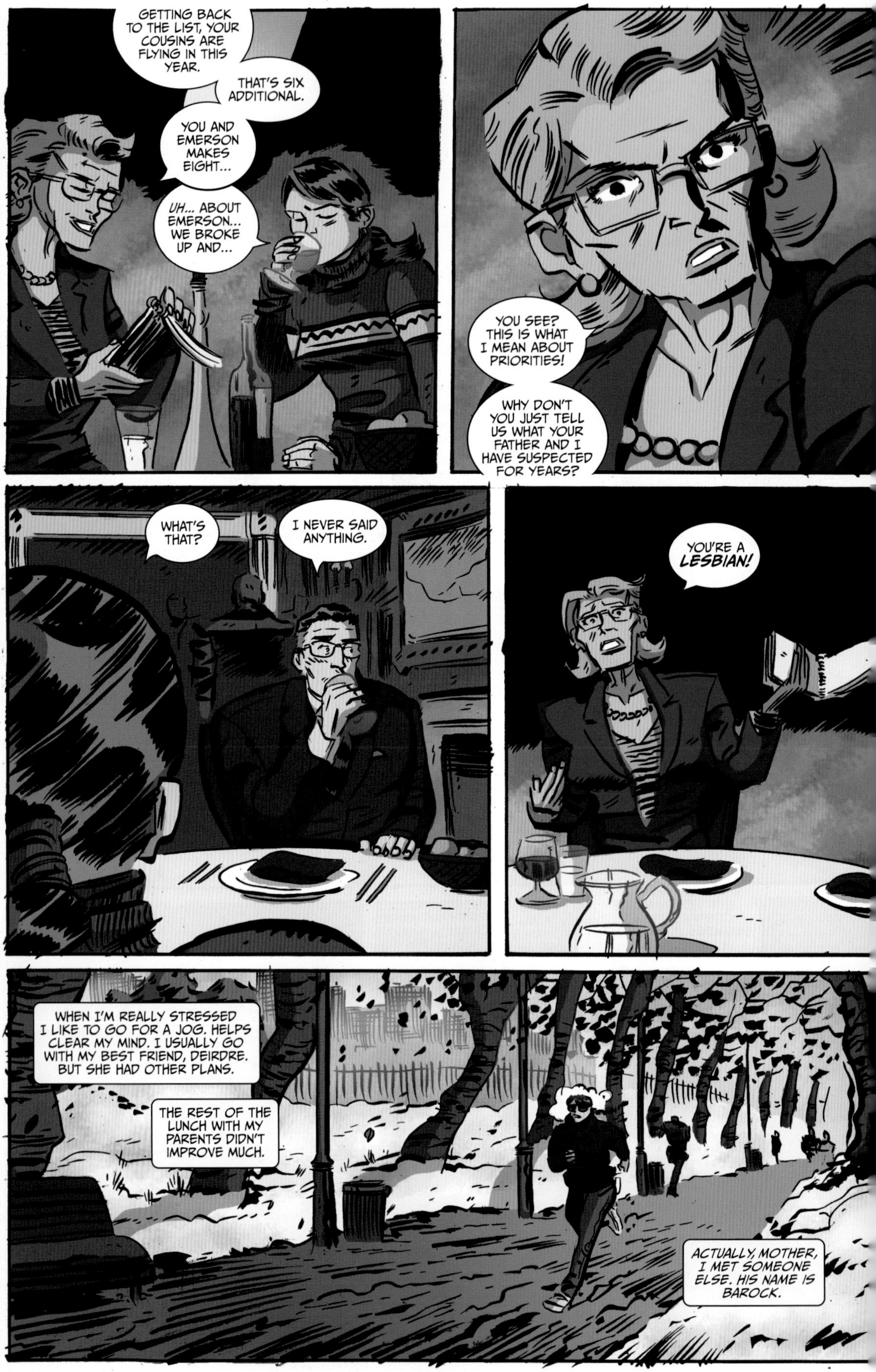
GETTING BACK TO THE LIST, YOUR COUSINS ARE FLYING IN THIS YEAR.
THAT'S SIX ADDITIONAL.
YOU AND EMERSON MAKES EIGHT...
UH... ABOUT EMERSON... WE BROKE UP AND...
YOU SEE? THIS IS WHAT I MEAN ABOUT PRIORITIES!
WHY DON'T YOU JUST TELL US WHAT YOUR FATHER AND I HAVE SUSPECTED FOR YEARS?
WHAT'S THAT?
I NEVER SAID ANYTHING.
YOU'RE A **LESBIAN!**
WHEN I'M REALLY STRESSED I LIKE TO GO FOR A JOG. HELPS CLEAR MY MIND. I USUALLY GO WITH MY BEST FRIEND, DEIRDRE. BUT SHE HAD OTHER PLANS.
THE REST OF THE LUNCH WITH MY PARENTS DIDN'T IMPROVE MUCH.
ACTUALLY, MOTHER, I MET SOMEONE ELSE. HIS NAME IS BAROCK.

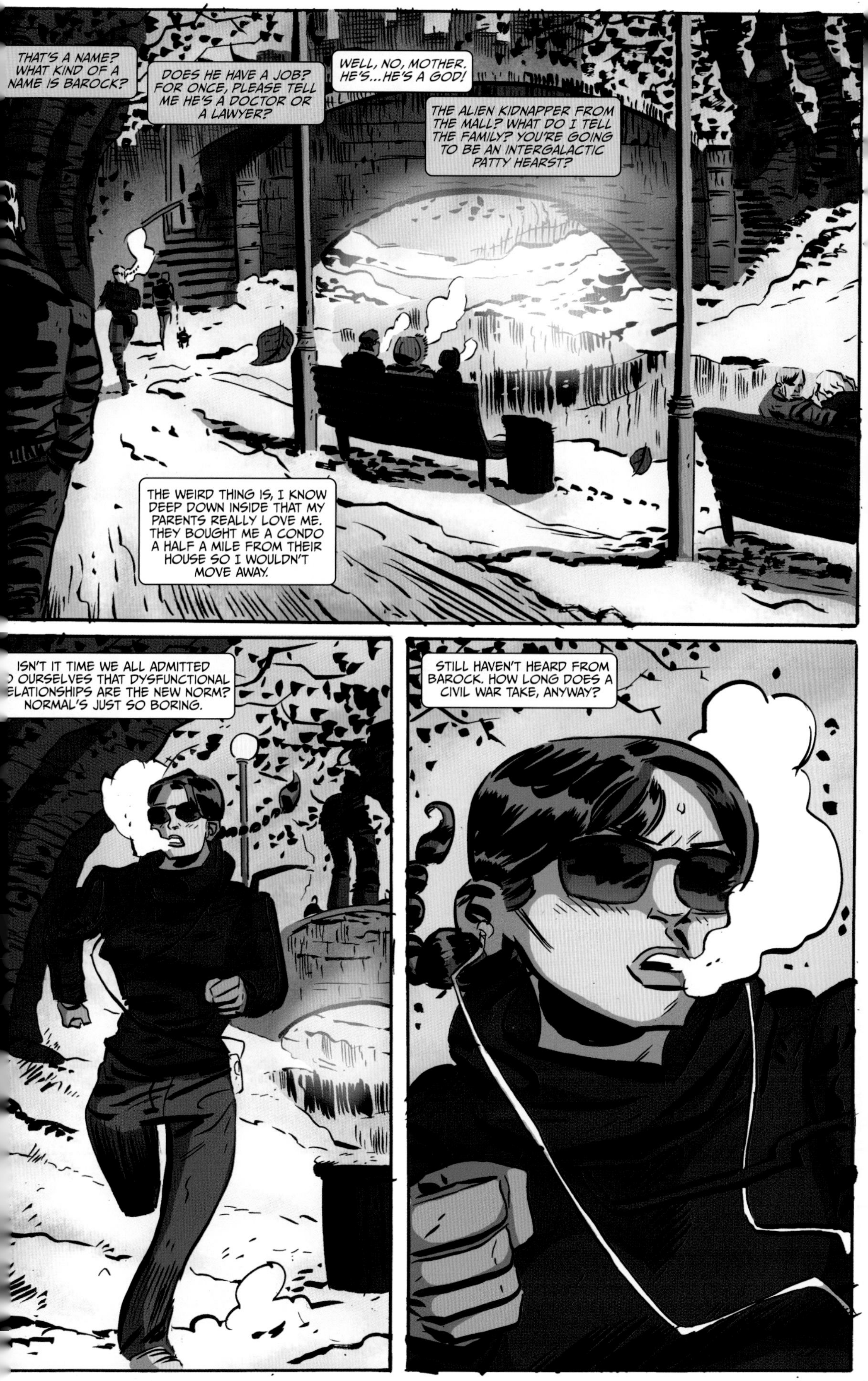
THAT'S A NAME? WHAT KIND OF A NAME IS BAROCK?
DOES HE HAVE A JOB? FOR ONCE, PLEASE TELL ME HE'S A DOCTOR OR A LAWYER?
WELL, NO, MOTHER. HE'S...HE'S A GOD!
THE ALIEN KIDNAPPER FROM THE MALL? WHAT DO I TELL THE FAMILY? YOU'RE GOING TO BE AN INTERGALACTIC PATTY HEARST?
THE WEIRD THING IS, I KNOW DEEP DOWN INSIDE THAT MY PARENTS REALLY LOVE ME. THEY BOUGHT ME A CONDO A HALF A MILE FROM THEIR HOUSE SO I WOULDN'T MOVE AWAY.
ISN'T IT TIME WE ALL ADMITTED O OURSELVES THAT DYSFUNCTIONAL ELATIONSHIPS ARE THE NEW NORM? NORMAL'S JUST SO BORING.
STILL HAVEN'T HEARD FROM BAROCK. HOW LONG DOES A CIVIL WAR TAKE, ANYWAY?

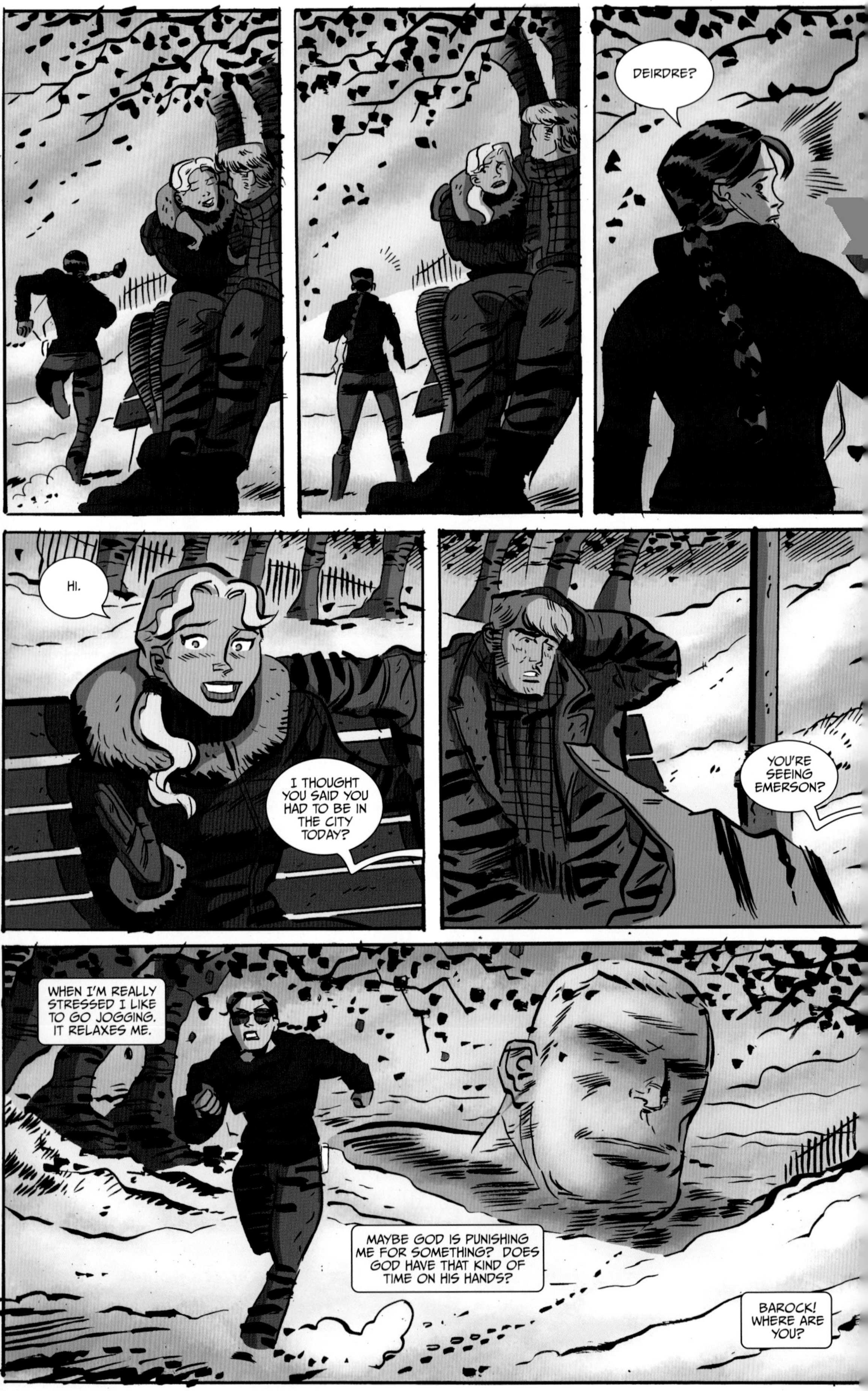
DEIRDRE?
HI.
I THOUGHT YOU SAID YOU HAD TO BE IN THE CITY TODAY?
YOU'RE SEEING EMERSON?
WHEN I'M REALLY STRESSED I LIKE TO GO JOGGING. IT RELAXES ME.
MAYBE GOD IS PUNISHING ME FOR SOMETHING? DOES GOD HAVE THAT KIND OF TIME ON HIS HANDS?
BAROCK! WHERE ARE YOU?

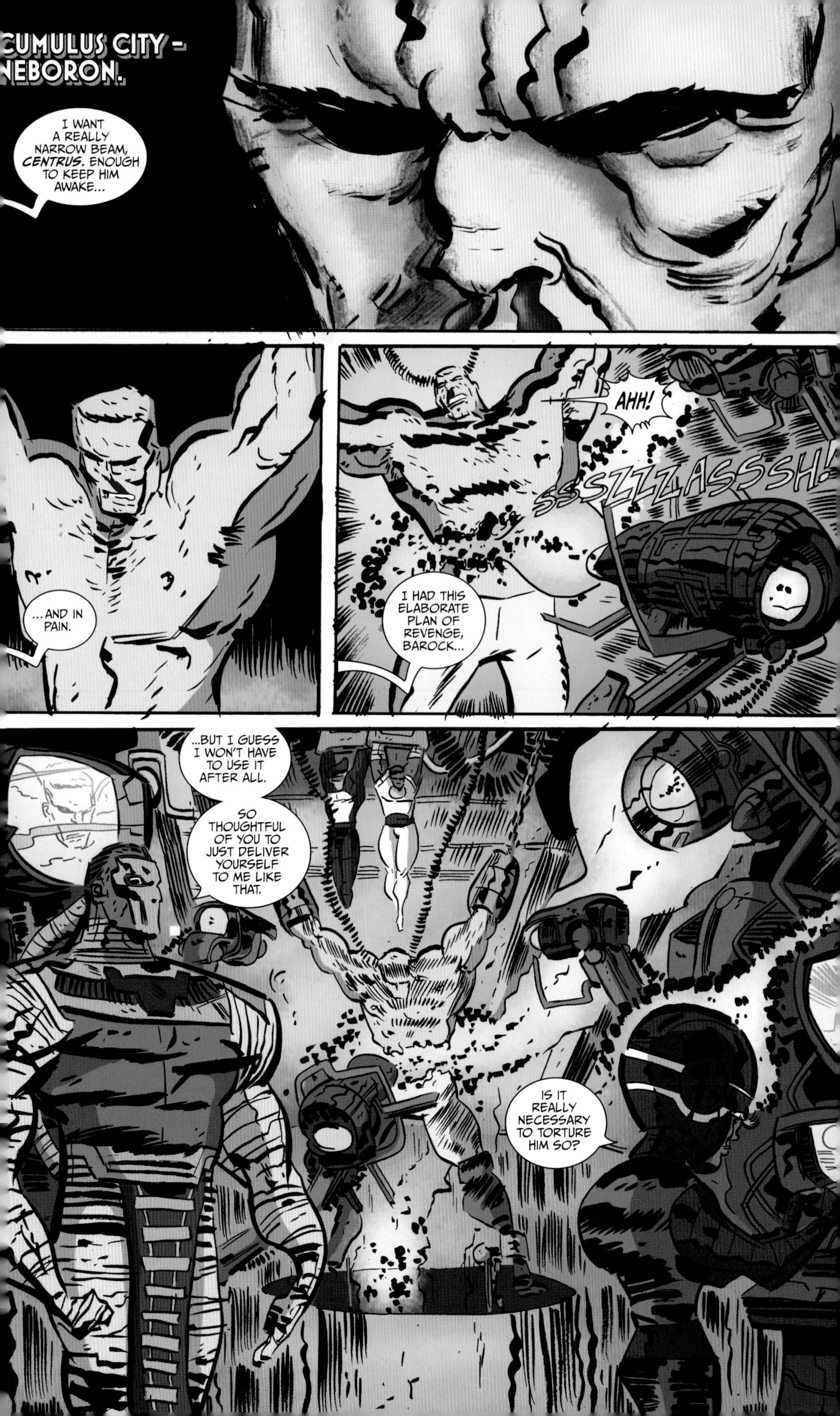
CUMULUS CITY – NEBORON.
I WANT A REALLY NARROW BEAM, CENTRUS. ENOUGH TO KEEP HIM AWAKE...
...AND IN PAIN.
AHH!
SSSZZZZASSSSH!
I HAD THIS ELABORATE PLAN OF REVENGE, BAROCK...
...BUT I GUESS I WON'T HAVE TO USE IT AFTER ALL.
SO THOUGHTFUL OF YOU TO JUST DELIVER YOURSELF TO ME LIKE THAT.
IS IT REALLY NECESSARY TO TORTURE HIM SO?

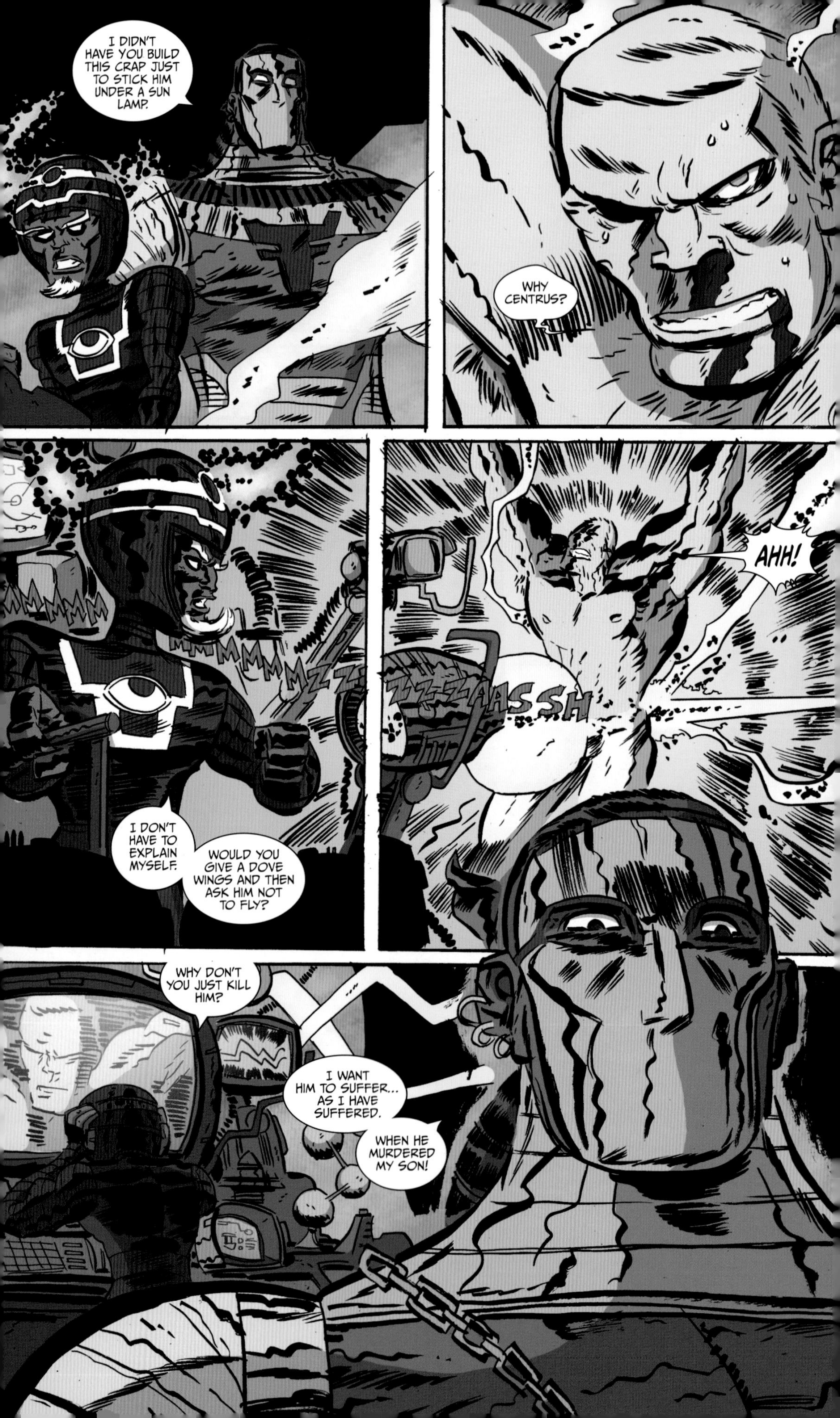
I DIDN'T HAVE YOU BUILD THIS CRAP JUST TO STICK HIM UNDER A SUN LAMP.
WHY CENTRUS?
MMMMMM
MMMMMMZZZ
ZZZZAASSH
AHH!
I DON'T HAVE TO EXPLAIN MYSELF.
WOULD YOU GIVE A DOVE WINGS AND THEN ASK HIM NOT TO FLY?
WHY DON'T YOU JUST KILL HIM?
I WANT HIM TO SUFFER... AS I HAVE SUFFERED.
WHEN HE MURDERED MY SON!

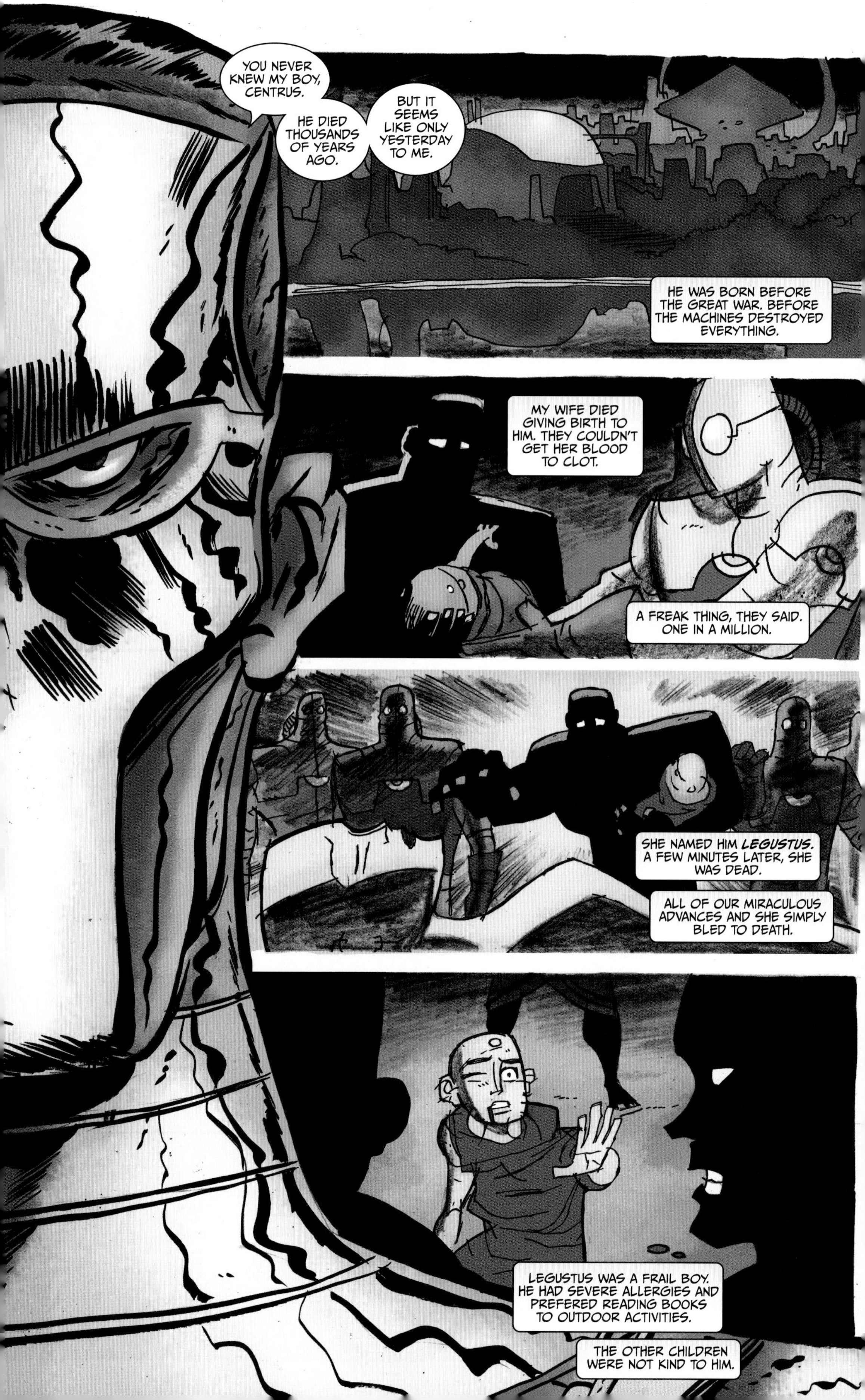
YOU NEVER KNEW MY BOY, CENTRUS.
HE DIED THOUSANDS OF YEARS AGO.
BUT IT SEEMS LIKE ONLY YESTERDAY TO ME.
HE WAS BORN BEFORE THE GREAT WAR. BEFORE THE MACHINES DESTROYED EVERYTHING.
MY WIFE DIED GIVING BIRTH TO HIM. THEY COULDN'T GET HER BLOOD TO CLOT.
A FREAK THING, THEY SAID. ONE IN A MILLION.
SHE NAMED HIM LEGUSTUS. A FEW MINUTES LATER, SHE WAS DEAD.
ALL OF OUR MIRACULOUS ADVANCES AND SHE SIMPLY BLED TO DEATH.
LEGUSTUS WAS A FRAIL BOY. HE HAD SEVERE ALLERGIES AND PREFERED READING BOOKS TO OUTDOOR ACTIVITIES.
THE OTHER CHILDREN WERE NOT KIND TO HIM.

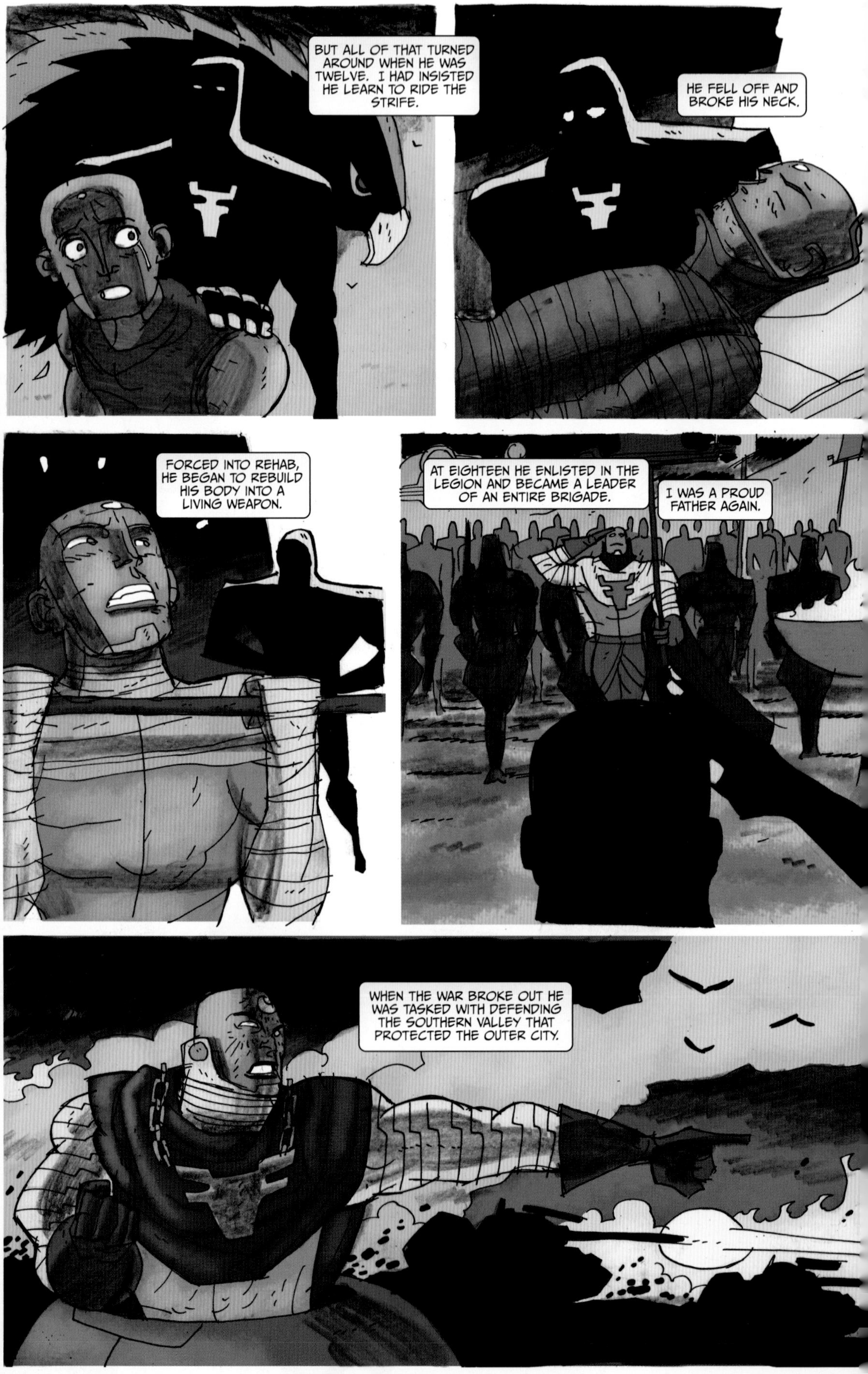
BUT ALL OF THAT TURNED AROUND WHEN HE WAS TWELVE. I HAD INSISTED HE LEARN TO RIDE THE STRIFE.
HE FELL OFF AND BROKE HIS NECK.
FORCED INTO REHAB, HE BEGAN TO REBUILD HIS BODY INTO A LIVING WEAPON.
AT EIGHTEEN HE ENLISTED IN THE LEGION AND BECAME A LEADER OF AN ENTIRE BRIGADE.
I WAS A PROUD FATHER AGAIN.
WHEN THE WAR BROKE OUT HE WAS TASKED WITH DEFENDING THE SOUTHERN VALLEY THAT PROTECTED THE OUTER CITY.

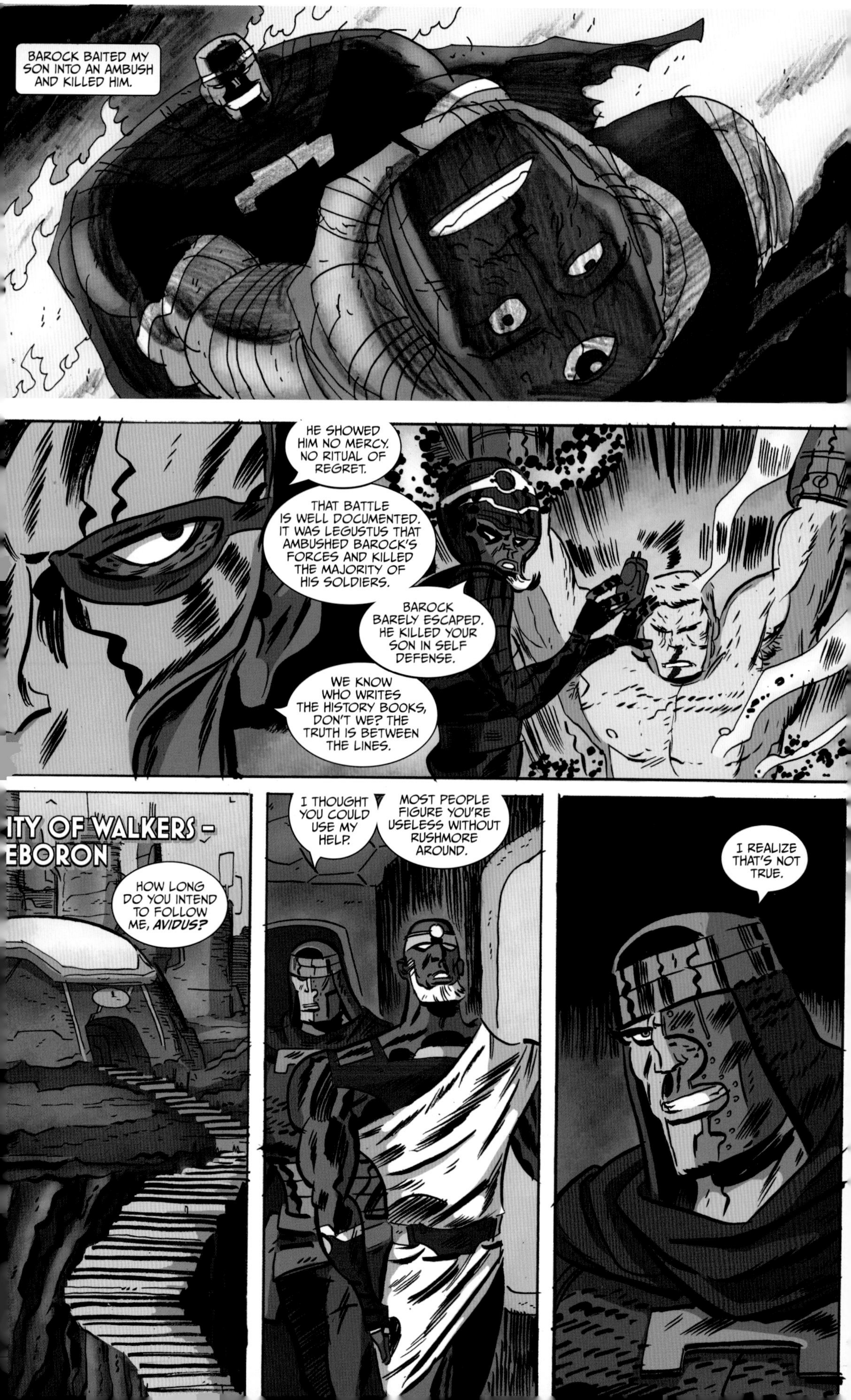

BAROCK BAITED MY SON INTO AN AMBUSH AND KILLED HIM.
HE SHOWED HIM NO MERCY. NO RITUAL OF REGRET.
THAT BATTLE IS WELL DOCUMENTED. IT WAS LEGUSTUS THAT AMBUSHED BAROCK'S FORCES AND KILLED THE MAJORITY OF HIS SOLDIERS.
BAROCK BARELY ESCAPED. HE KILLED YOUR SON IN SELF DEFENSE.
WE KNOW WHO WRITES THE HISTORY BOOKS, DON'T WE? THE TRUTH IS BETWEEN THE LINES.
ITY OF WALKERS - EBORON
HOW LONG DO YOU INTEND TO FOLLOW ME, *AVIDUS?*
I THOUGHT YOU COULD USE MY HELP.
MOST PEOPLE FIGURE YOU'RE USELESS WITHOUT RUSHMORE AROUND.
I REALIZE THAT'S NOT TRUE.

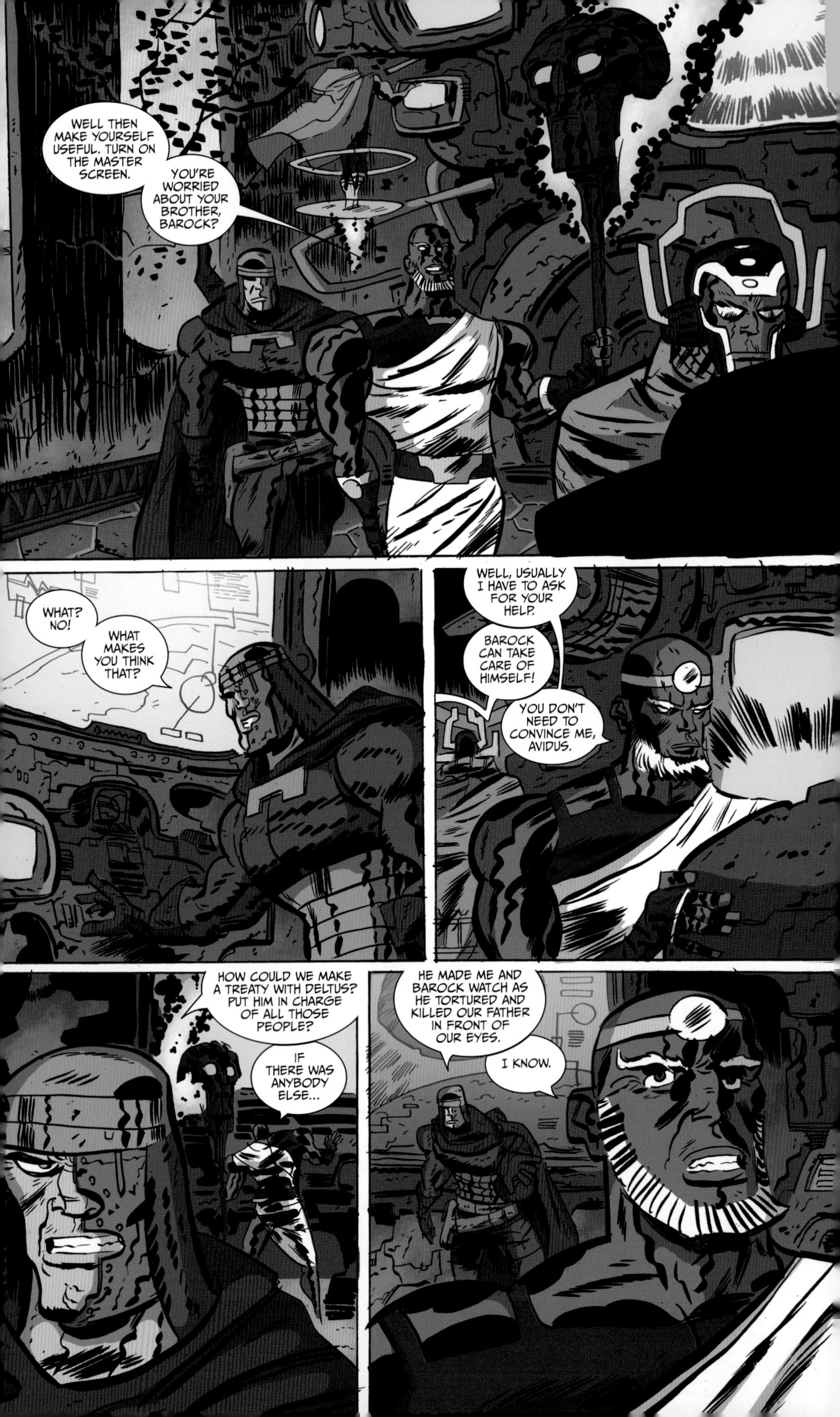
WELL THEN MAKE YOURSELF USEFUL. TURN ON THE MASTER SCREEN.
YOU'RE WORRIED ABOUT YOUR BROTHER, BAROCK?
WHAT? NO!
WHAT MAKES YOU THINK THAT?
WELL, USUALLY I HAVE TO ASK FOR YOUR HELP.
BAROCK CAN TAKE CARE OF HIMSELF!
YOU DON'T NEED TO CONVINCE ME, AVIDUS.
HOW COULD WE MAKE A TREATY WITH DELTUS? PUT HIM IN CHARGE OF ALL THOSE PEOPLE?
IF THERE WAS ANYBODY ELSE...
HE MADE ME AND BAROCK WATCH AS HE TORTURED AND KILLED OUR FATHER IN FRONT OF OUR EYES.
I KNOW.

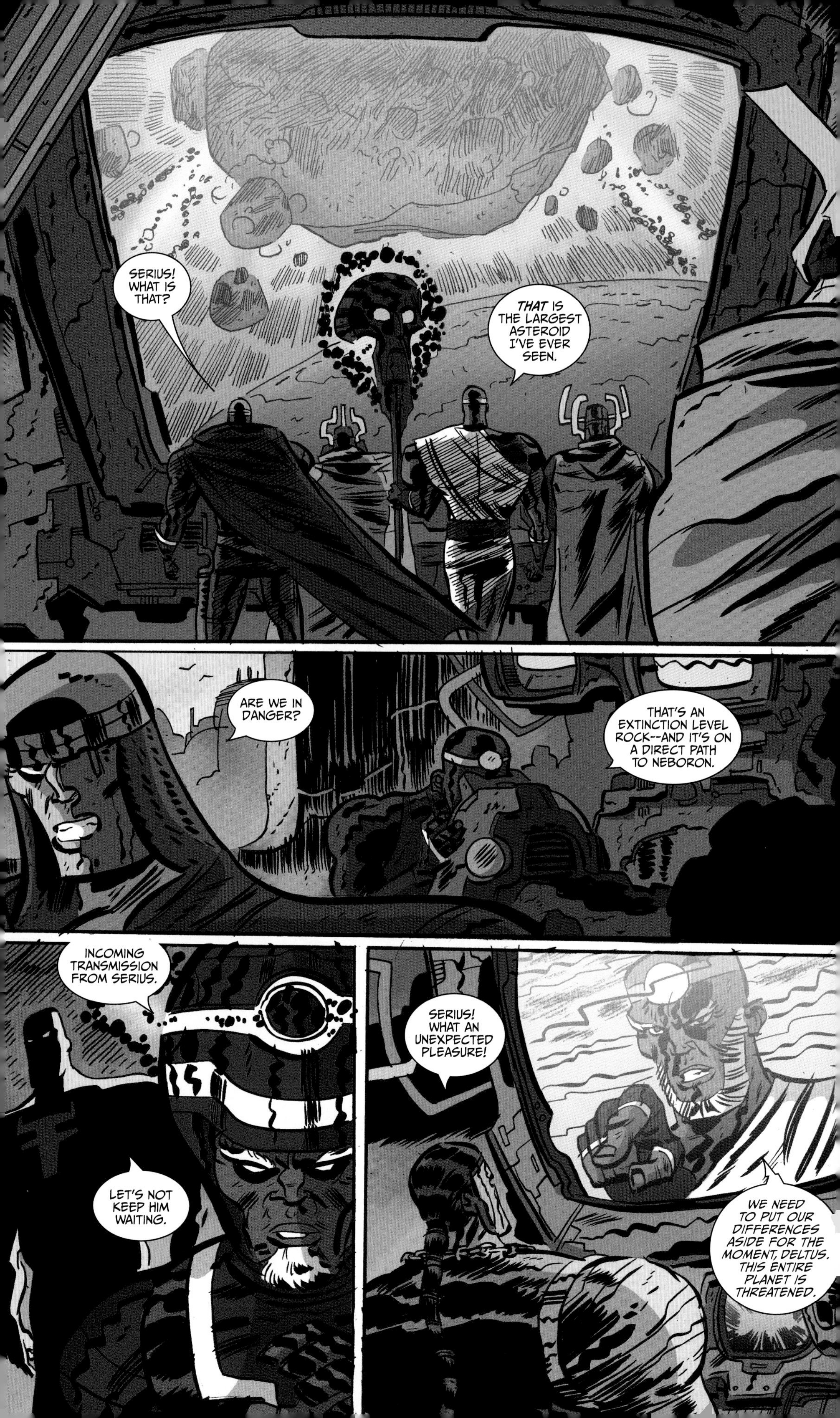
SERIUS! WHAT IS THAT?
THAT IS THE LARGEST ASTEROID I'VE EVER SEEN.
ARE WE IN DANGER?
THAT'S AN EXTINCTION LEVEL ROCK--AND IT'S ON A DIRECT PATH TO NEBORON.
INCOMING TRANSMISSION FROM SERIUS.
LET'S NOT KEEP HIM WAITING.
SERIUS! WHAT AN UNEXPECTED PLEASURE!
WE NEED TO PUT OUR DIFFERENCES ASIDE FOR THE MOMENT, DELTUS. THIS ENTIRE PLANET IS THREATENED.

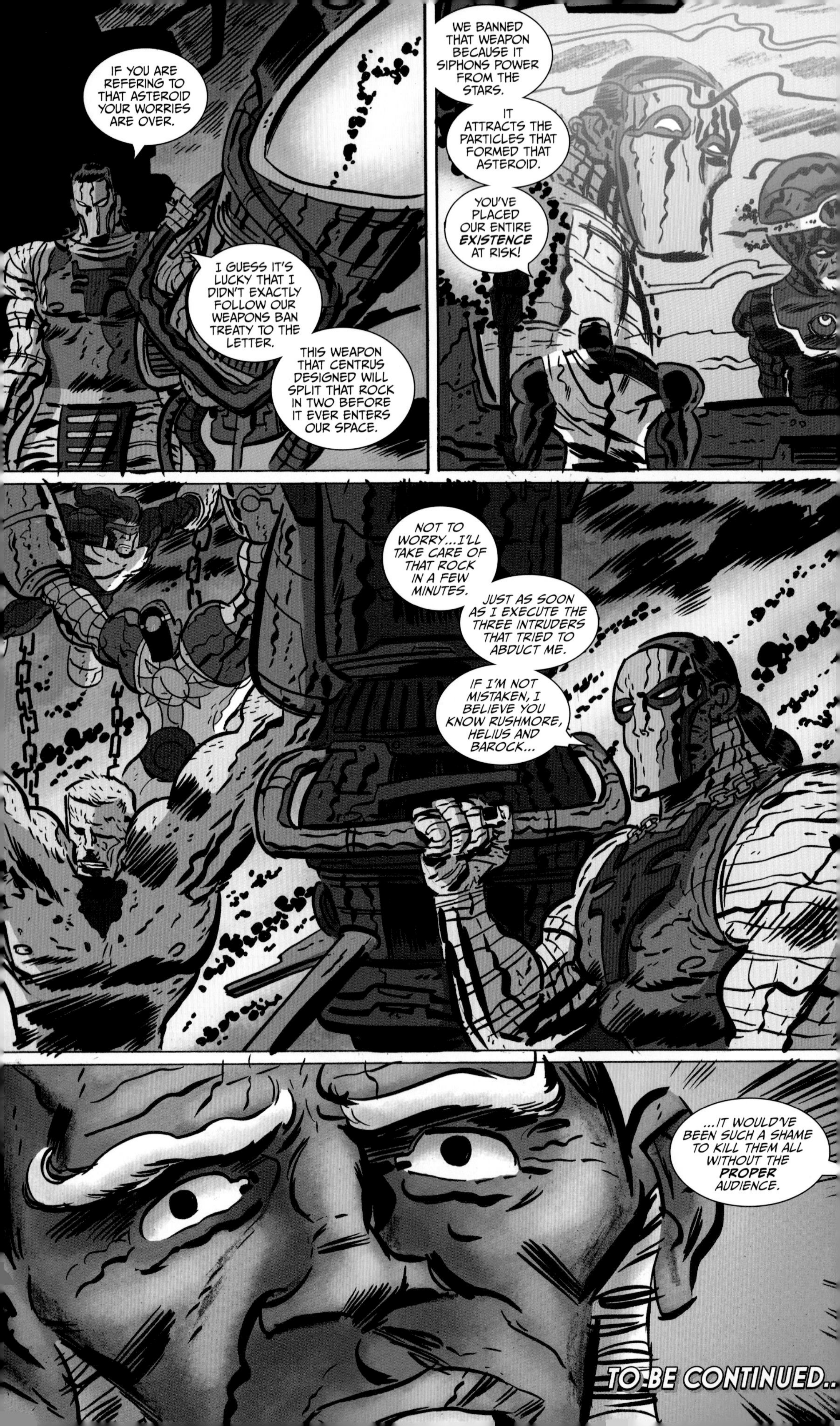
IF YOU ARE REFERING TO THAT ASTEROID YOUR WORRIES ARE OVER.
I GUESS IT'S LUCKY THAT I DIDN'T EXACTLY FOLLOW OUR WEAPONS BAN TREATY TO THE LETTER.
THIS WEAPON THAT CENTRUS DESIGNED WILL SPLIT THAT ROCK IN TWO BEFORE IT EVER ENTERS OUR SPACE.
WE BANNED THAT WEAPON BECAUSE IT SIPHONS POWER FROM THE STARS.
IT ATTRACTS THE PARTICLES THAT FORMED THAT ASTEROID.
YOU'VE PLACED OUR ENTIRE **EXISTENCE** AT RISK!
NOT TO WORRY...I'LL TAKE CARE OF THAT ROCK IN A FEW MINUTES.
JUST AS SOON AS I EXECUTE THE THREE INTRUDERS THAT TRIED TO ABDUCT ME.
IF I'M NOT MISTAKEN, I BELIEVE YOU KNOW RUSHMORE, HELIUS AND BAROCK...
...IT WOULD'VE BEEN SUCH A SHAME TO KILL THEM ALL WITHOUT THE **PROPER** AUDIENCE.
TO BE CONTINUED..

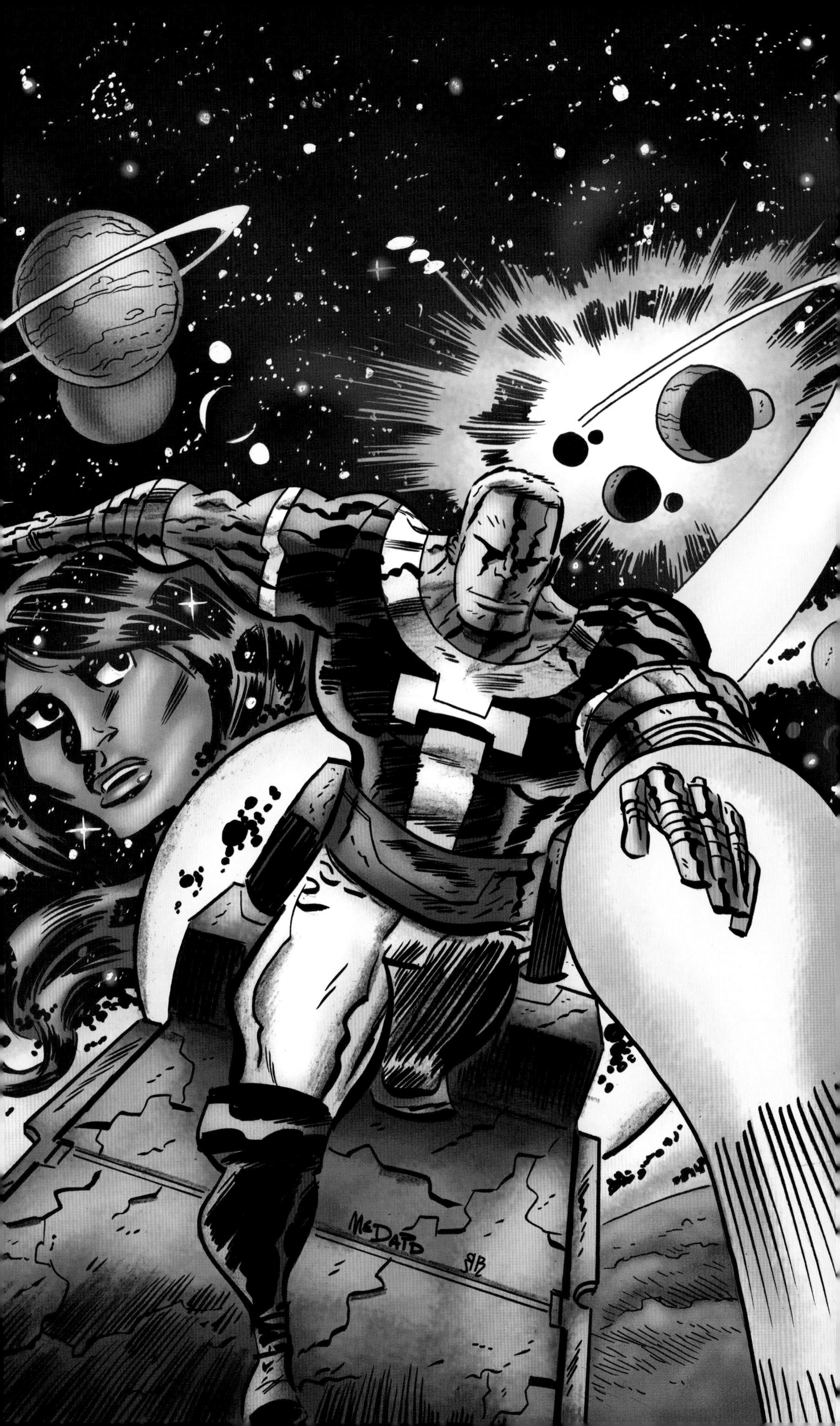
McDAID

CHAPTER FOUR

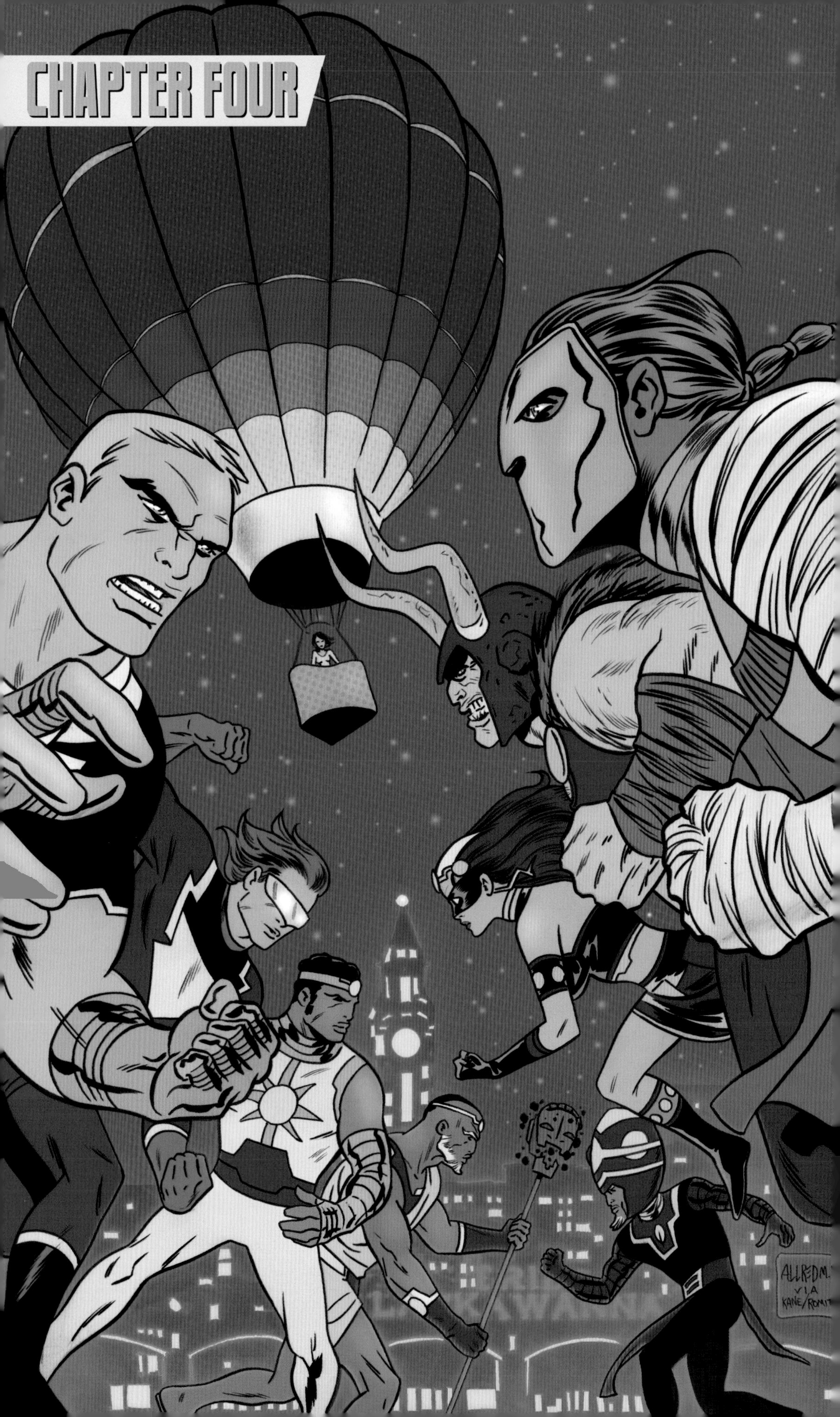

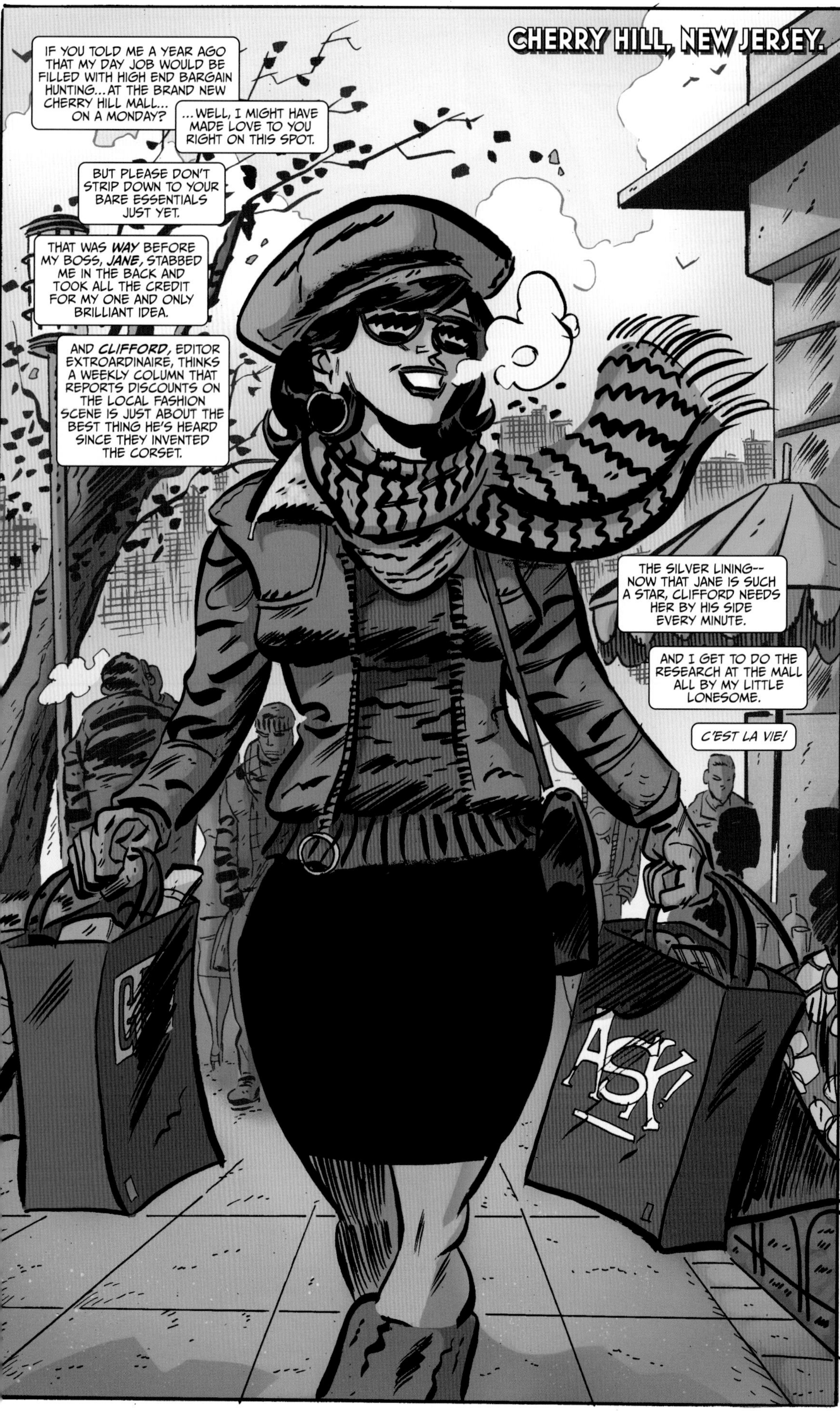
CHERRY HILL, NEW JERSEY.
IF YOU TOLD ME A YEAR AGO THAT MY DAY JOB WOULD BE FILLED WITH HIGH END BARGAIN HUNTING... AT THE BRAND NEW CHERRY HILL MALL... ON A MONDAY?
...WELL, I MIGHT HAVE MADE LOVE TO YOU RIGHT ON THIS SPOT.
BUT PLEASE DON'T STRIP DOWN TO YOUR BARE ESSENTIALS JUST YET.
THAT WAS *WAY* BEFORE MY BOSS, *JANE*, STABBED ME IN THE BACK AND TOOK ALL THE CREDIT FOR MY ONE AND ONLY BRILLIANT IDEA.
AND *CLIFFORD*, EDITOR EXTRAORDINAIRE, THINKS A WEEKLY COLUMN THAT REPORTS DISCOUNTS ON THE LOCAL FASHION SCENE IS JUST ABOUT THE BEST THING HE'S HEARD SINCE THEY INVENTED THE CORSET.
THE SILVER LINING-- NOW THAT JANE IS SUCH A STAR, CLIFFORD NEEDS HER BY HIS SIDE EVERY MINUTE.
AND I GET TO DO THE RESEARCH AT THE MALL ALL BY MY LITTLE LONESOME.
C'EST LA VIE!
ASK!

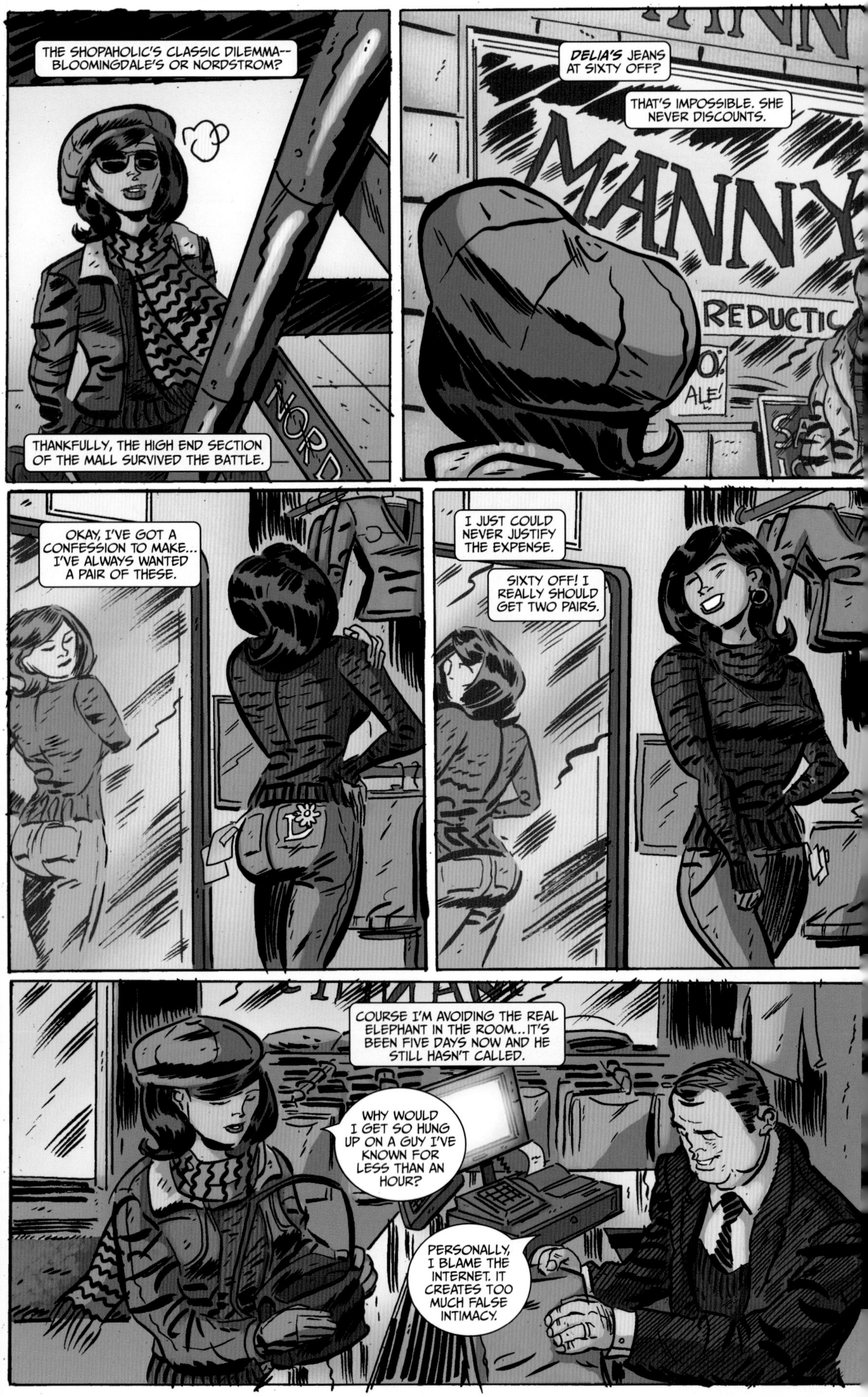
THE SHOPAHOLIC'S CLASSIC DILEMMA-- BLOOMINGDALE'S OR NORDSTROM?
THANKFULLY, THE HIGH END SECTION OF THE MALL SURVIVED THE BATTLE.
NORD
DELIA'S JEANS AT SIXTY OFF?
THAT'S IMPOSSIBLE. SHE NEVER DISCOUNTS.
MANNY
REDUCTIC
ALE!
OKAY, I'VE GOT A CONFESSION TO MAKE... I'VE ALWAYS WANTED A PAIR OF THESE.
I JUST COULD NEVER JUSTIFY THE EXPENSE.
SIXTY OFF! I REALLY SHOULD GET TWO PAIRS.
COURSE I'M AVOIDING THE REAL ELEPHANT IN THE ROOM...IT'S BEEN FIVE DAYS NOW AND HE STILL HASN'T CALLED.
WHY WOULD I GET SO HUNG UP ON A GUY I'VE KNOWN FOR LESS THAN AN HOUR?
PERSONALLY, I BLAME THE INTERNET. IT CREATES TOO MUCH FALSE INTIMACY.

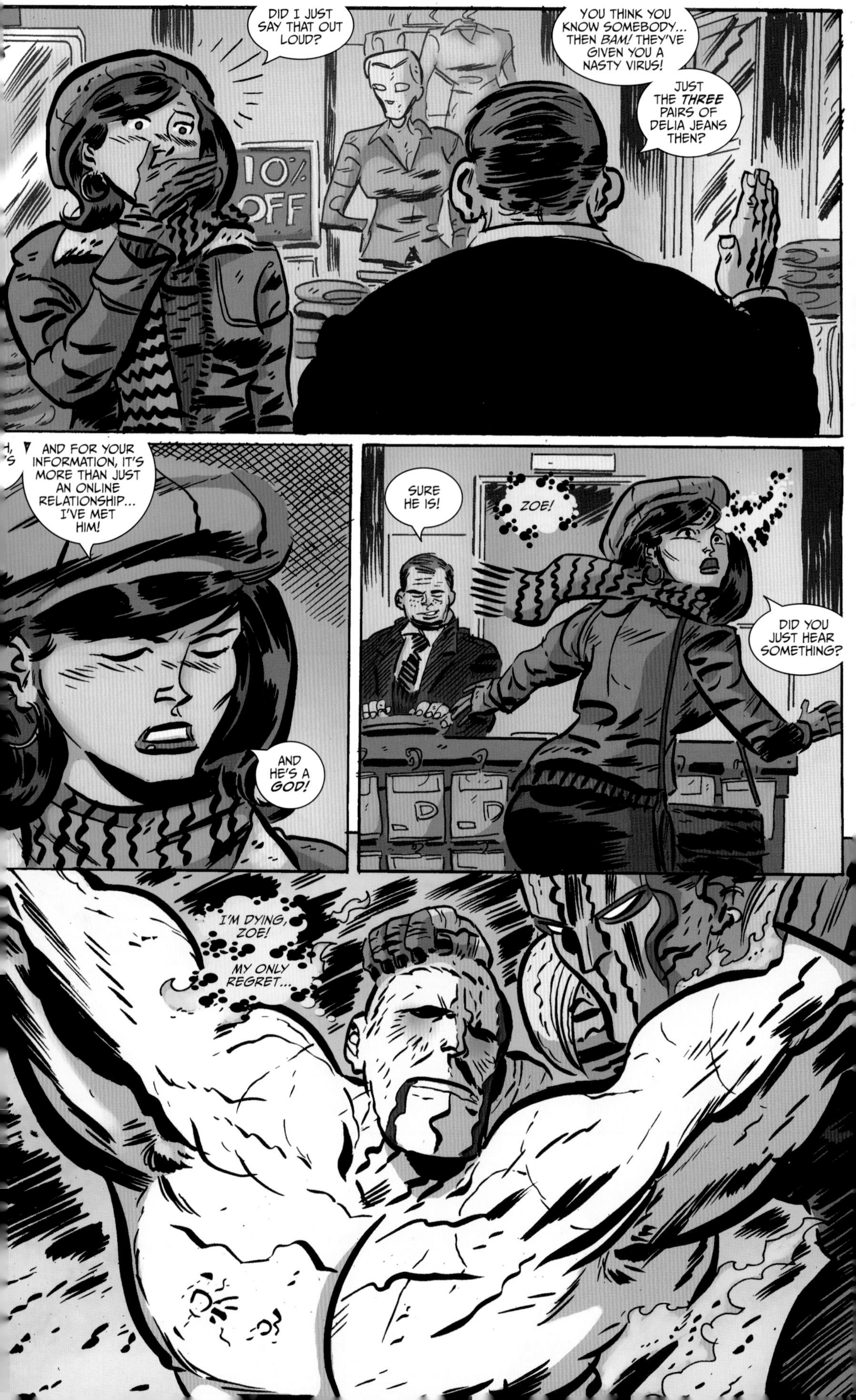
DID I JUST SAY THAT OUT LOUD?
YOU THINK YOU KNOW SOMEBODY... THEN BAM! THEY'VE GIVEN YOU A NASTY VIRUS!
JUST THE THREE PAIRS OF DELIA JEANS THEN?
10% OFF
AND FOR YOUR INFORMATION, IT'S MORE THAN JUST AN ONLINE RELATIONSHIP... I'VE MET HIM!
AND HE'S A GOD!
SURE HE IS!
ZOE!
DID YOU JUST HEAR SOMETHING?
I'M DYING, ZOE!
MY ONLY REGRET...

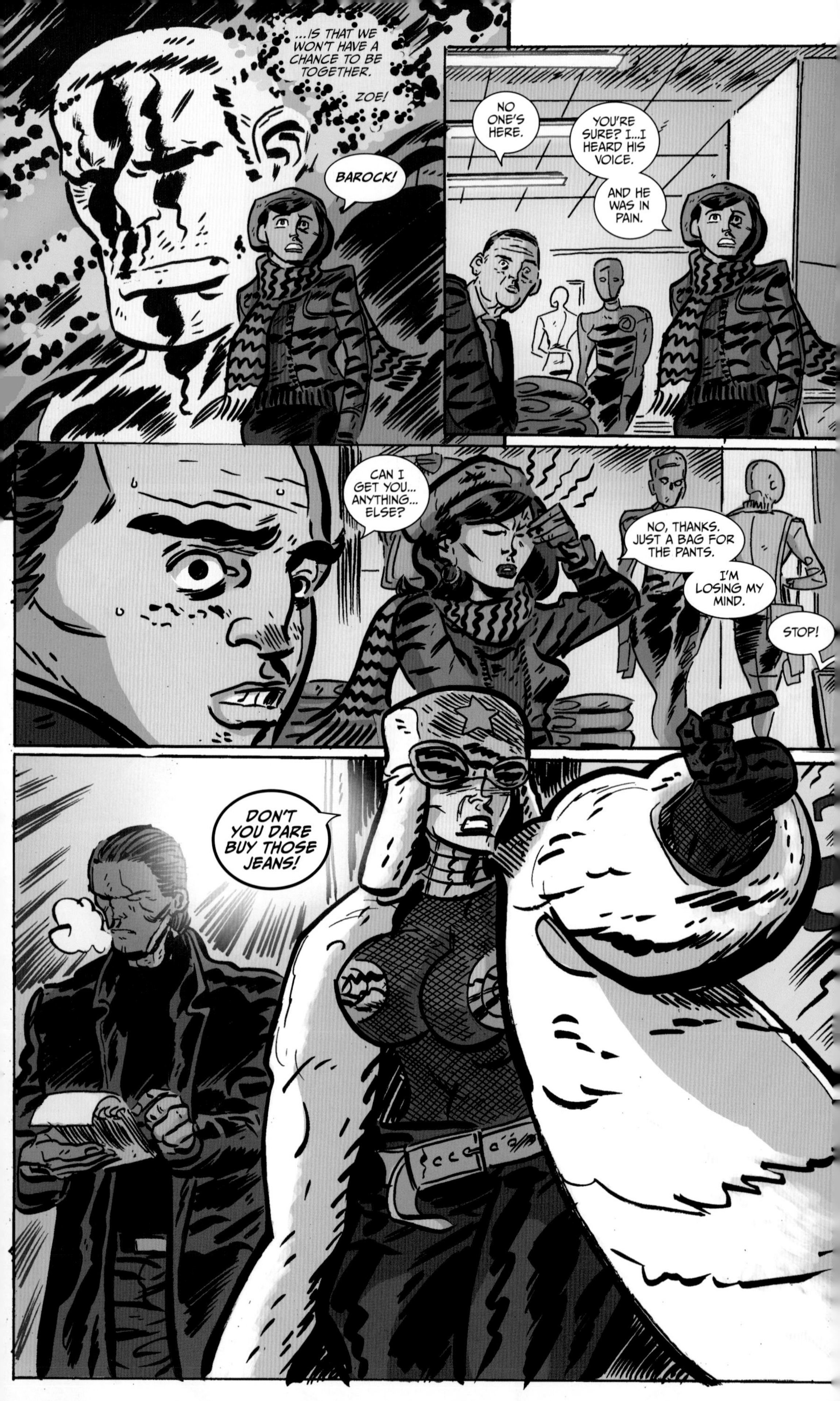
...IS THAT WE WON'T HAVE A CHANCE TO BE TOGETHER.
ZOE!
BAROCK!
NO ONE'S HERE.
YOU'RE SURE? I...I HEARD HIS VOICE.
AND HE WAS IN PAIN.
CAN I GET YOU... ANYTHING... ELSE?
NO, THANKS. JUST A BAG FOR THE PANTS.
I'M LOSING MY MIND.
STOP!
DON'T YOU DARE BUY THOSE JEANS!

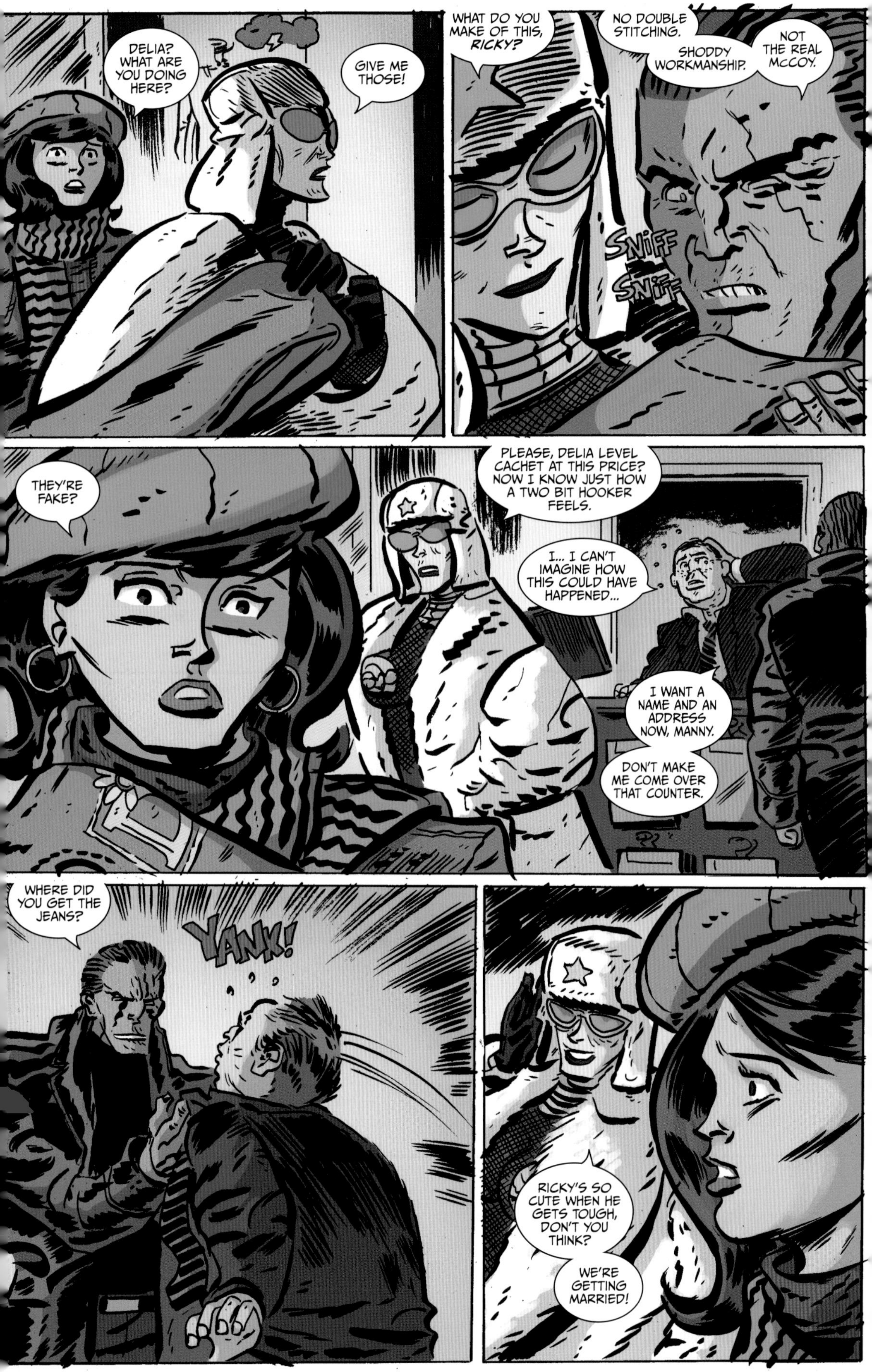
DELIA? WHAT ARE YOU DOING HERE?
GIVE ME THOSE!
WHAT DO YOU MAKE OF THIS, RICKY?
NO DOUBLE STITCHING.
SHODDY WORKMANSHIP.
NOT THE REAL McCOY.
SNIFF
SNIFF
THEY'RE FAKE?
PLEASE, DELIA LEVEL CACHET AT THIS PRICE? NOW I KNOW JUST HOW A TWO BIT HOOKER FEELS.
I... I CAN'T IMAGINE HOW THIS COULD HAVE HAPPENED...
I WANT A NAME AND AN ADDRESS NOW, MANNY.
DON'T MAKE ME COME OVER THAT COUNTER.
WHERE DID YOU GET THE JEANS?
YANK!
RICKY'S SO CUTE WHEN HE GETS TOUGH, DON'T YOU THINK?
WE'RE GETTING MARRIED!

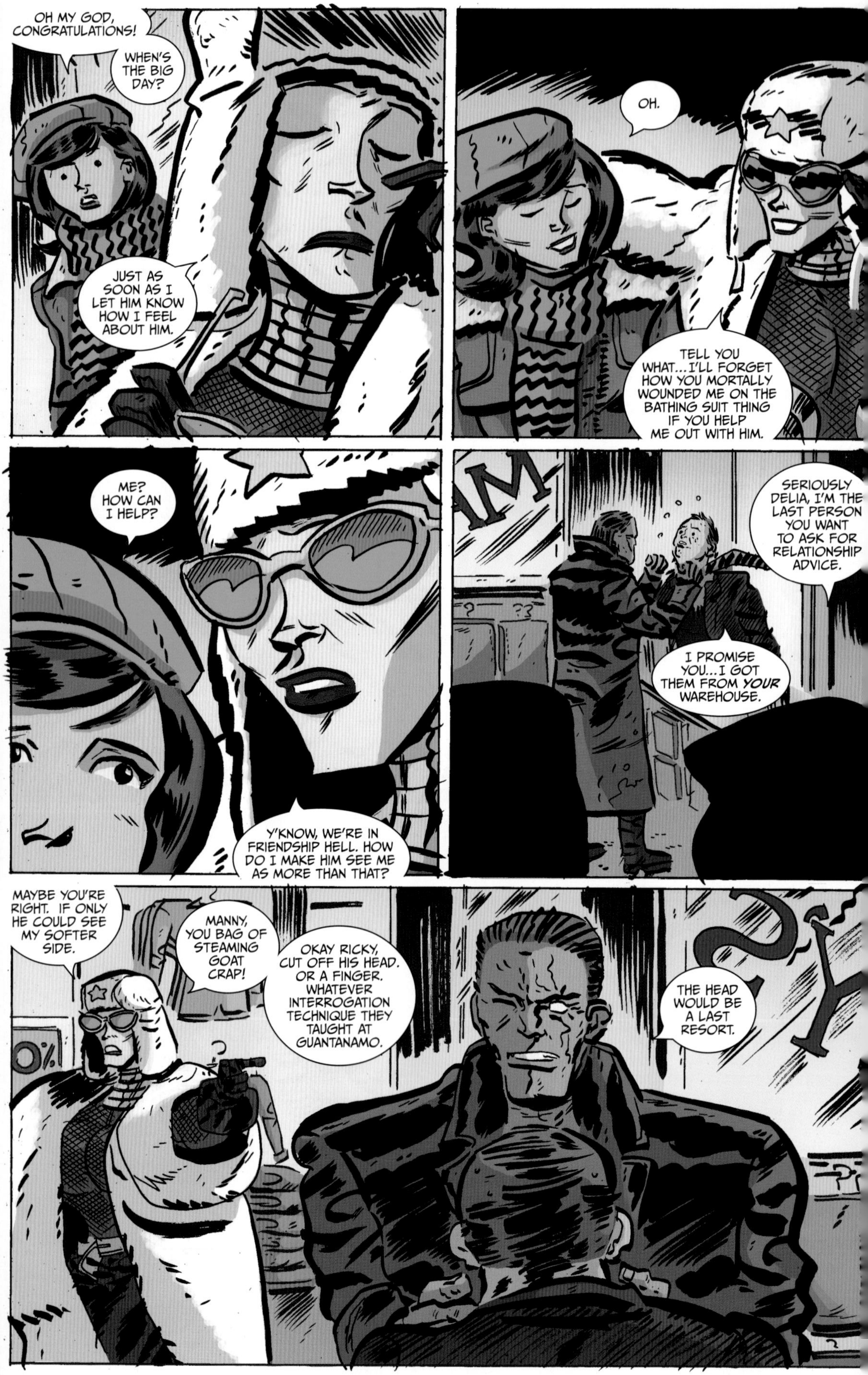
OH MY GOD, CONGRATULATIONS!
WHEN'S THE BIG DAY?
JUST AS SOON AS I LET HIM KNOW HOW I FEEL ABOUT HIM.
OH.
TELL YOU WHAT... I'LL FORGET HOW YOU MORTALLY WOUNDED ME ON THE BATHING SUIT THING IF YOU HELP ME OUT WITH HIM.
ME? HOW CAN I HELP?
Y'KNOW, WE'RE IN FRIENDSHIP HELL. HOW DO I MAKE HIM SEE ME AS MORE THAN THAT?
SERIOUSLY DELIA, I'M THE LAST PERSON YOU WANT TO ASK FOR RELATIONSHIP ADVICE.
I PROMISE YOU... I GOT THEM FROM *YOUR* WAREHOUSE.
MAYBE YOU'RE RIGHT. IF ONLY HE COULD SEE MY SOFTER SIDE.
MANNY, YOU BAG OF STEAMING GOAT CRAP!
OKAY RICKY, CUT OFF HIS HEAD. OR A FINGER. WHATEVER INTERROGATION TECHNIQUE THEY TAUGHT AT GUANTANAMO.
THE HEAD WOULD BE A LAST RESORT.

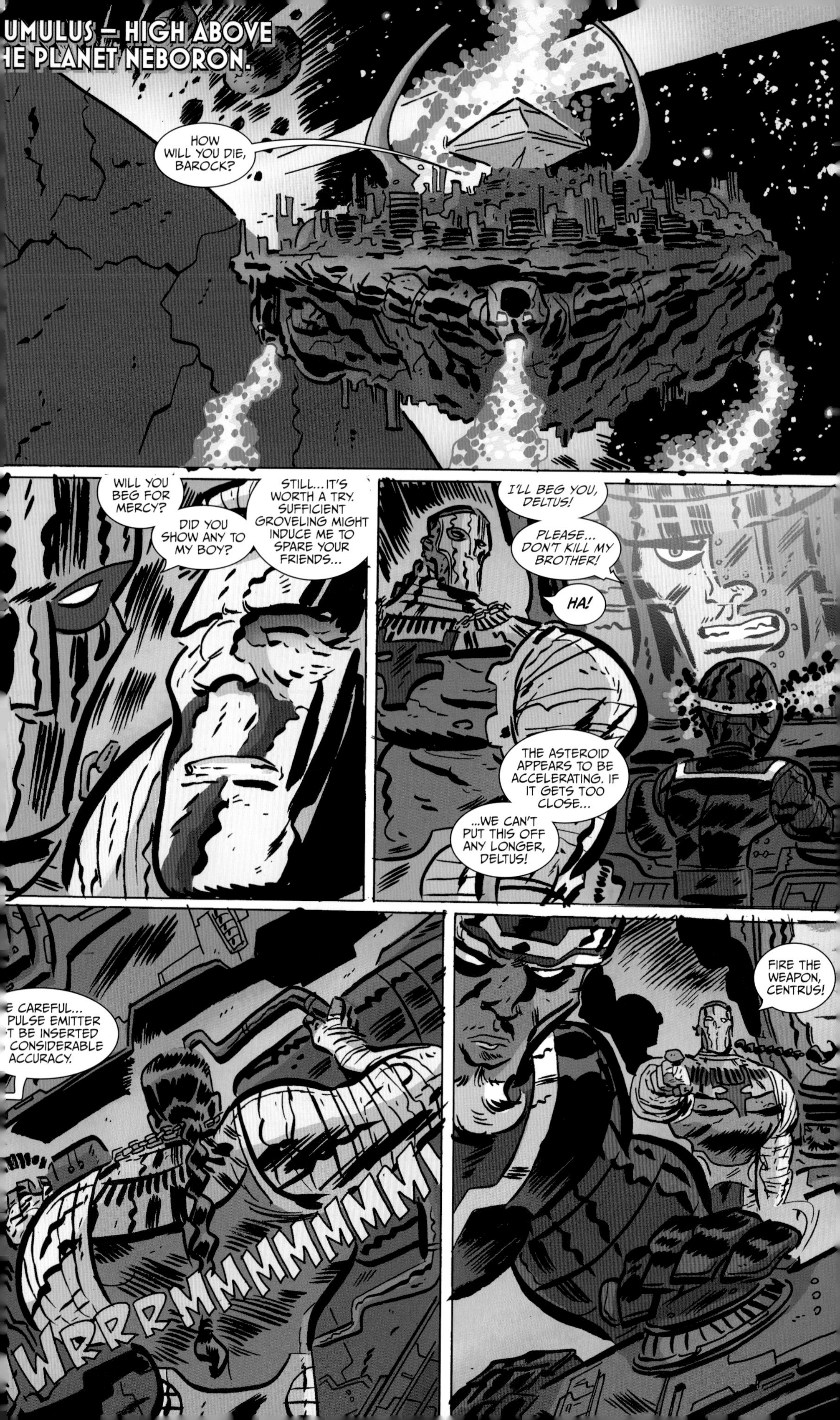
UMULUS — HIGH ABOVE
HE PLANET NEBORON.
HOW WILL YOU DIE, BAROCK?
WILL YOU BEG FOR MERCY?
DID YOU SHOW ANY TO MY BOY?
STILL... IT'S WORTH A TRY. SUFFICIENT GROVELING MIGHT INDUCE ME TO SPARE YOUR FRIENDS...
I'LL BEG YOU, DELTUS!
PLEASE... DON'T KILL MY BROTHER!
HA!
THE ASTEROID APPEARS TO BE ACCELERATING. IF IT GETS TOO CLOSE...
...WE CAN'T PUT THIS OFF ANY LONGER, DELTUS!
E CAREFUL... PULSE EMITTER T BE INSERTED CONSIDERABLE ACCURACY.
WRRRMMMMMMMMM
FIRE THE WEAPON, CENTRUS!

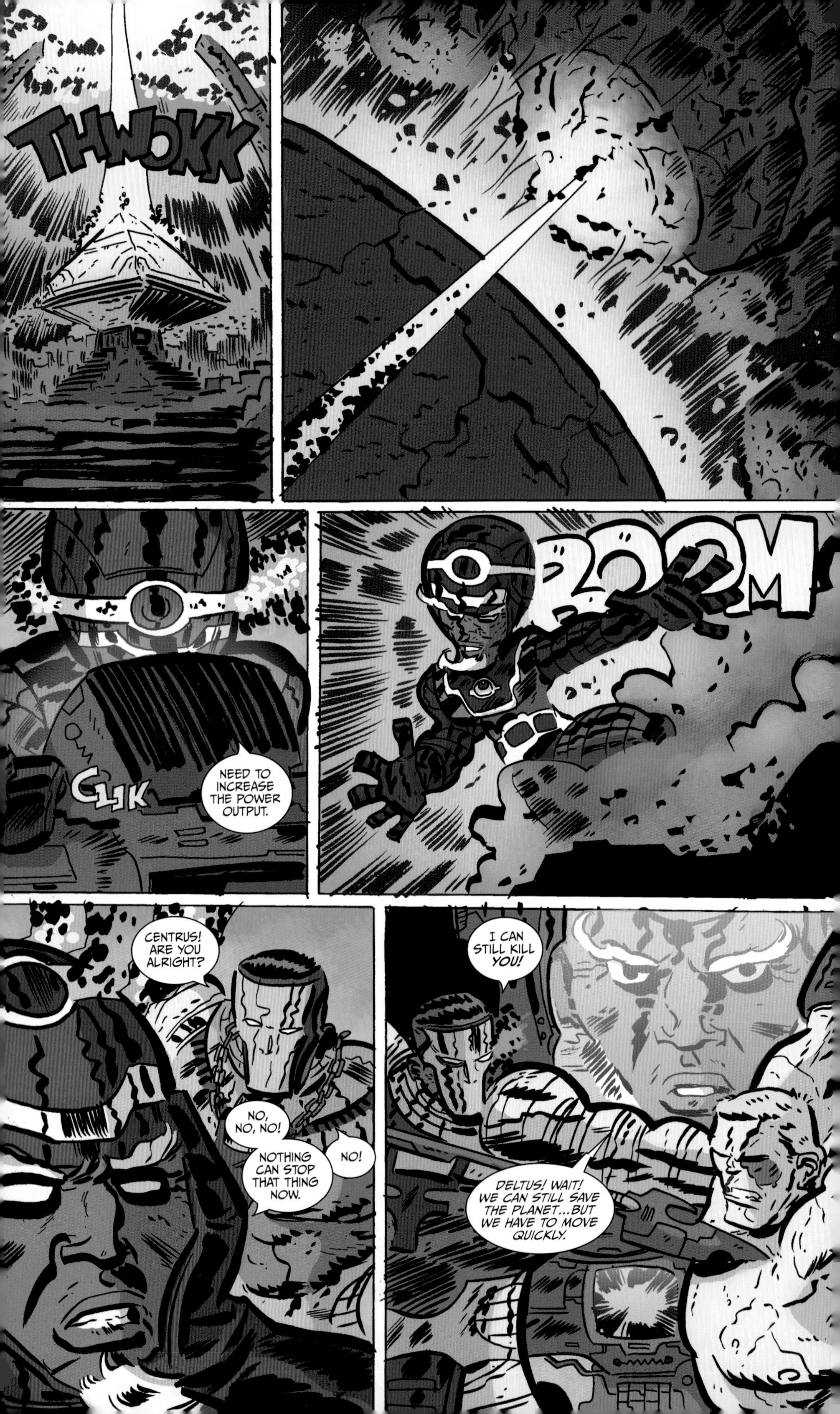
THWOKK
CLIK
NEED TO INCREASE THE POWER OUTPUT.
BOOM
CENTRUS! ARE YOU ALRIGHT?
NO, NO, NO!
NOTHING CAN STOP THAT THING NOW.
NO!
I CAN STILL KILL YOU!
DELTUS! WAIT! WE CAN STILL SAVE THE PLANET...BUT WE HAVE TO MOVE QUICKLY.

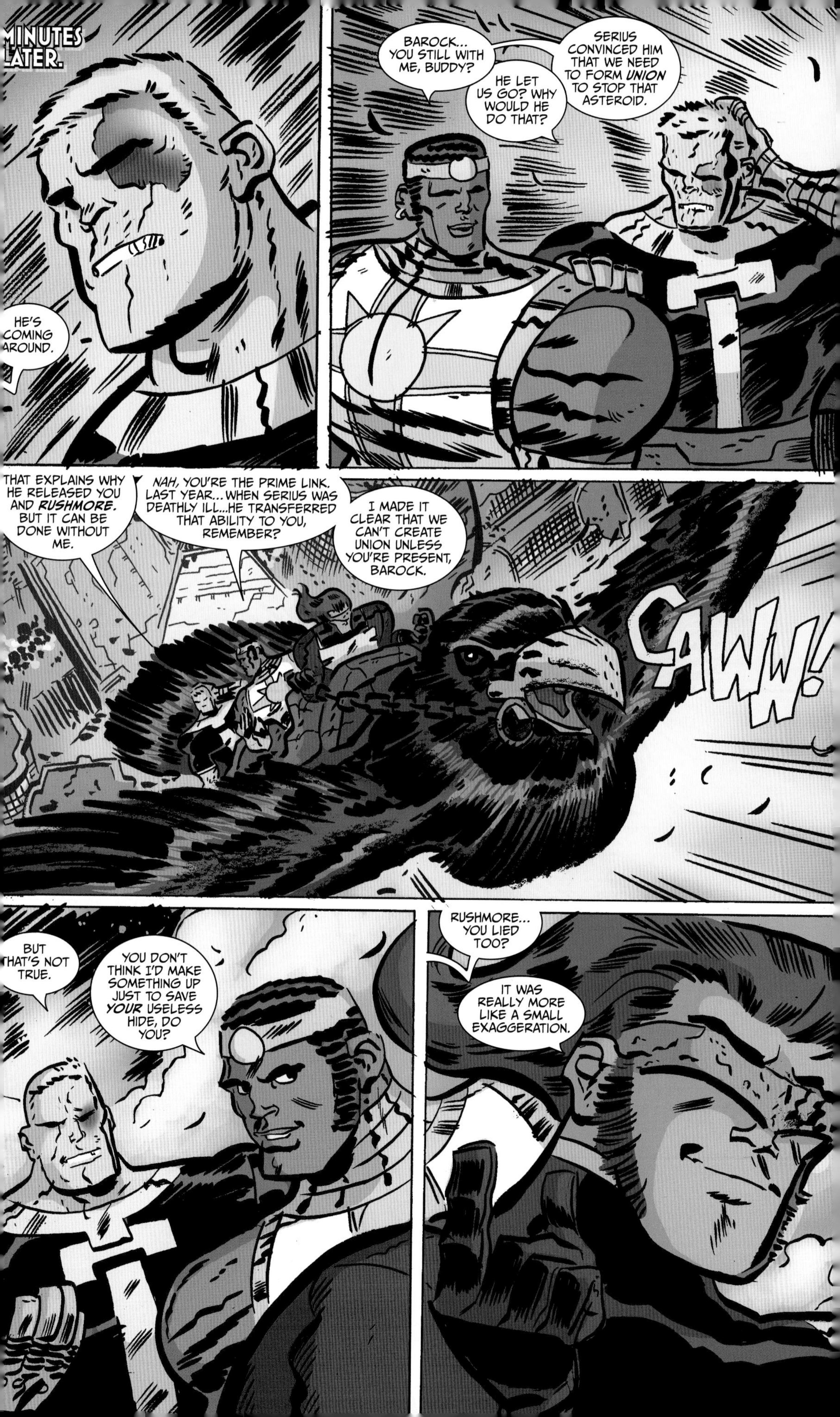
MINUTES LATER.
HE'S COMING AROUND.
BAROCK... YOU STILL WITH ME, BUDDY?
HE LET US GO? WHY WOULD HE DO THAT?
SERIUS CONVINCED HIM THAT WE NEED TO FORM *UNION* TO STOP THAT ASTEROID.
THAT EXPLAINS WHY HE RELEASED YOU AND ***RUSHMORE.*** BUT IT CAN BE DONE WITHOUT ME.
NAH, YOU'RE THE PRIME LINK. LAST YEAR... WHEN SERIUS WAS DEATHLY ILL... HE TRANSFERRED THAT ABILITY TO YOU, REMEMBER?
I MADE IT CLEAR THAT WE CAN'T CREATE UNION UNLESS YOU'RE PRESENT, BAROCK.
CAWW!
BUT THAT'S NOT TRUE.
YOU DON'T THINK I'D MAKE SOMETHING UP JUST TO SAVE ***YOUR*** USELESS HIDE, DO YOU?
RUSHMORE... YOU LIED TOO?
IT WAS REALLY MORE LIKE A SMALL EXAGGERATION.

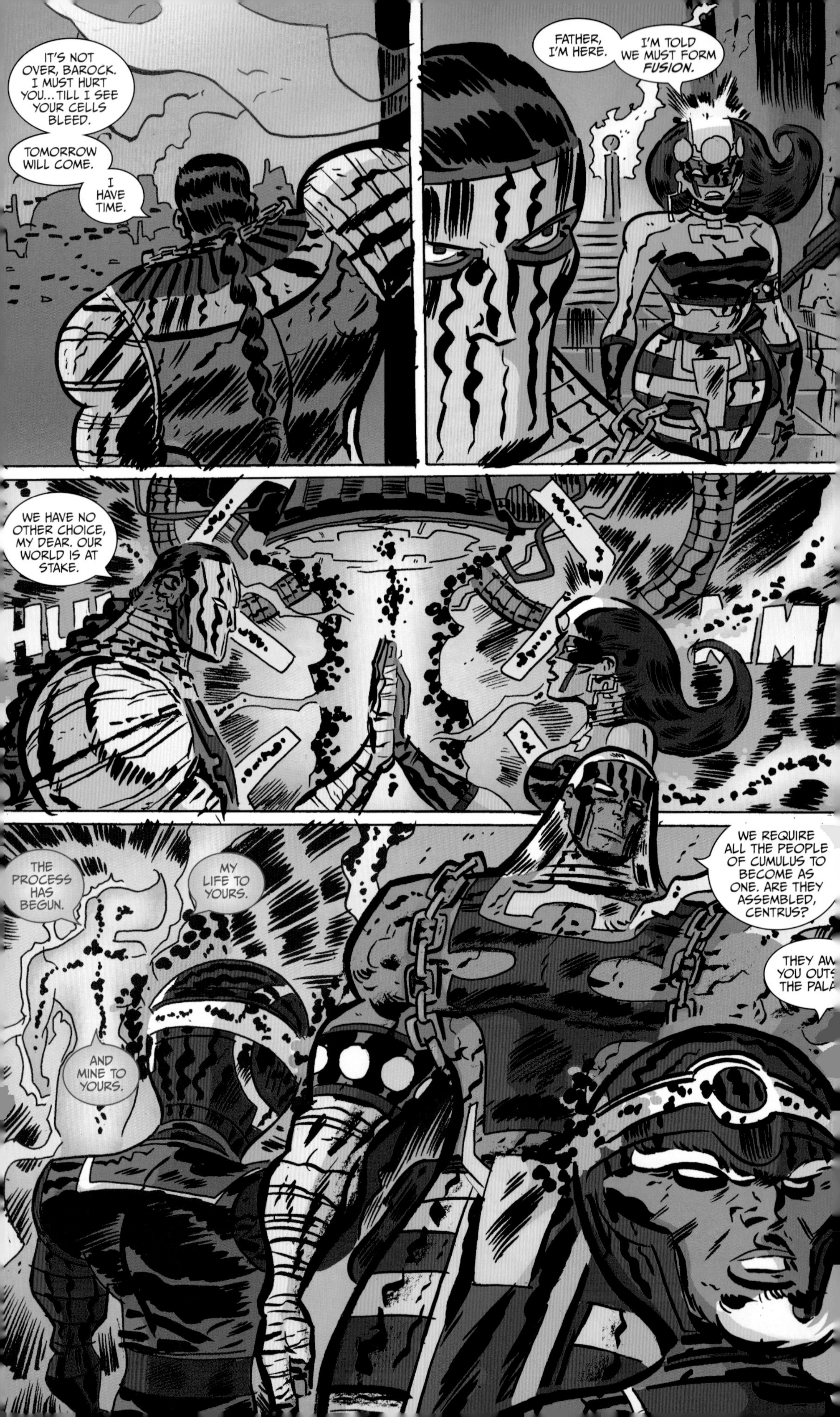
IT'S NOT OVER, BAROCK. I MUST HURT YOU...TILL I SEE YOUR CELLS BLEED.
TOMORROW WILL COME.
I HAVE TIME.
FATHER, I'M HERE.
I'M TOLD WE MUST FORM *FUSION.*
WE HAVE NO OTHER CHOICE, MY DEAR. OUR WORLD IS AT STAKE.
THE PROCESS HAS BEGUN.
MY LIFE TO YOURS.
AND MINE TO YOURS.
WE REQUIRE ALL THE PEOPLE OF CUMULUS TO BECOME AS ONE. ARE THEY ASSEMBLED, CENTRUS?
THEY AW
YOU OUTS
THE PALA

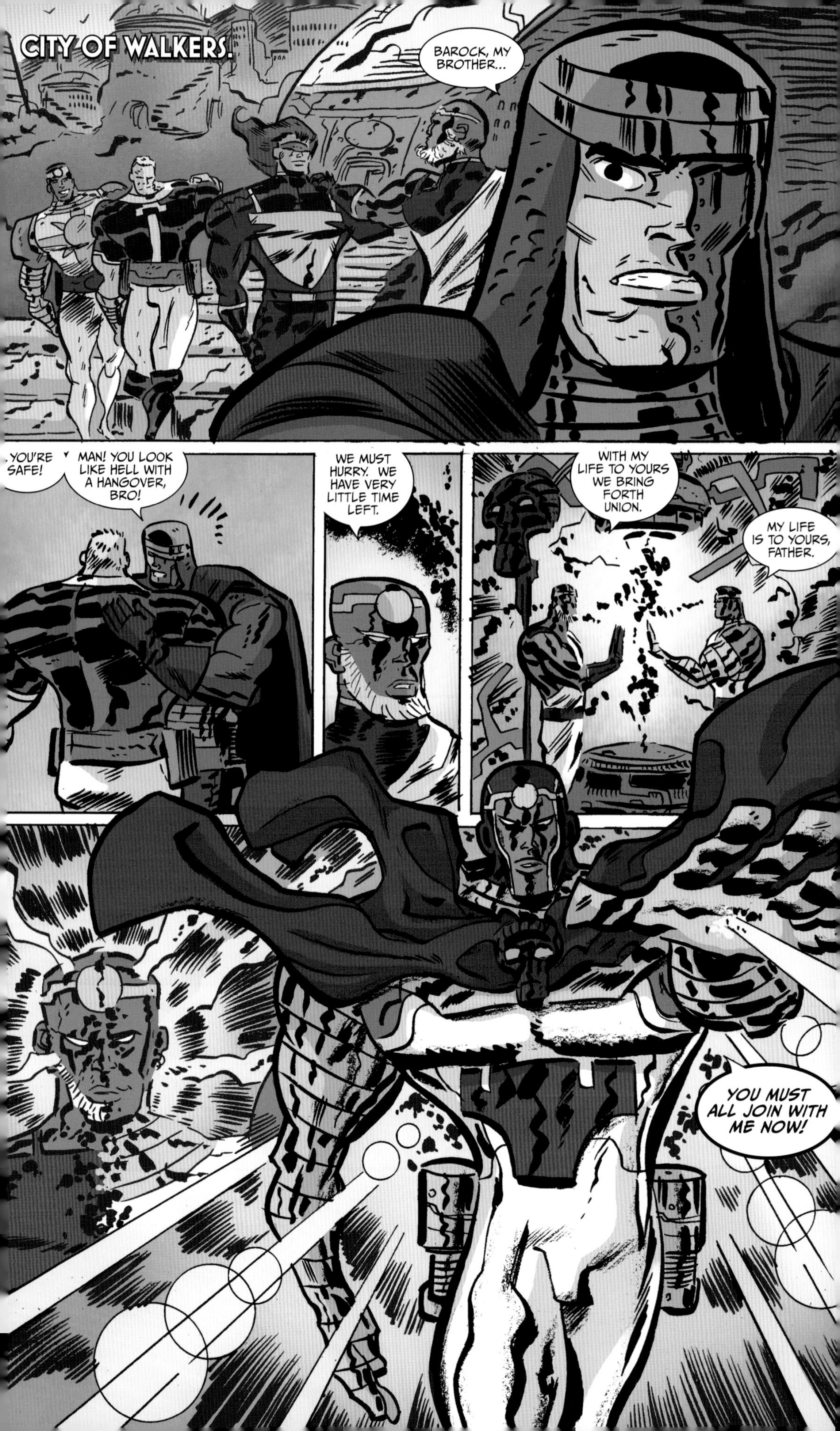
CITY OF WALKERS.
BAROCK, MY BROTHER...
YOU'RE SAFE!
MAN! YOU LOOK LIKE HELL WITH A HANGOVER, BRO!
WE MUST HURRY. WE HAVE VERY LITTLE TIME LEFT.
WITH MY LIFE TO YOURS WE BRING FORTH UNION.
MY LIFE IS TO YOURS, FATHER.
YOU MUST ALL JOIN WITH ME NOW!

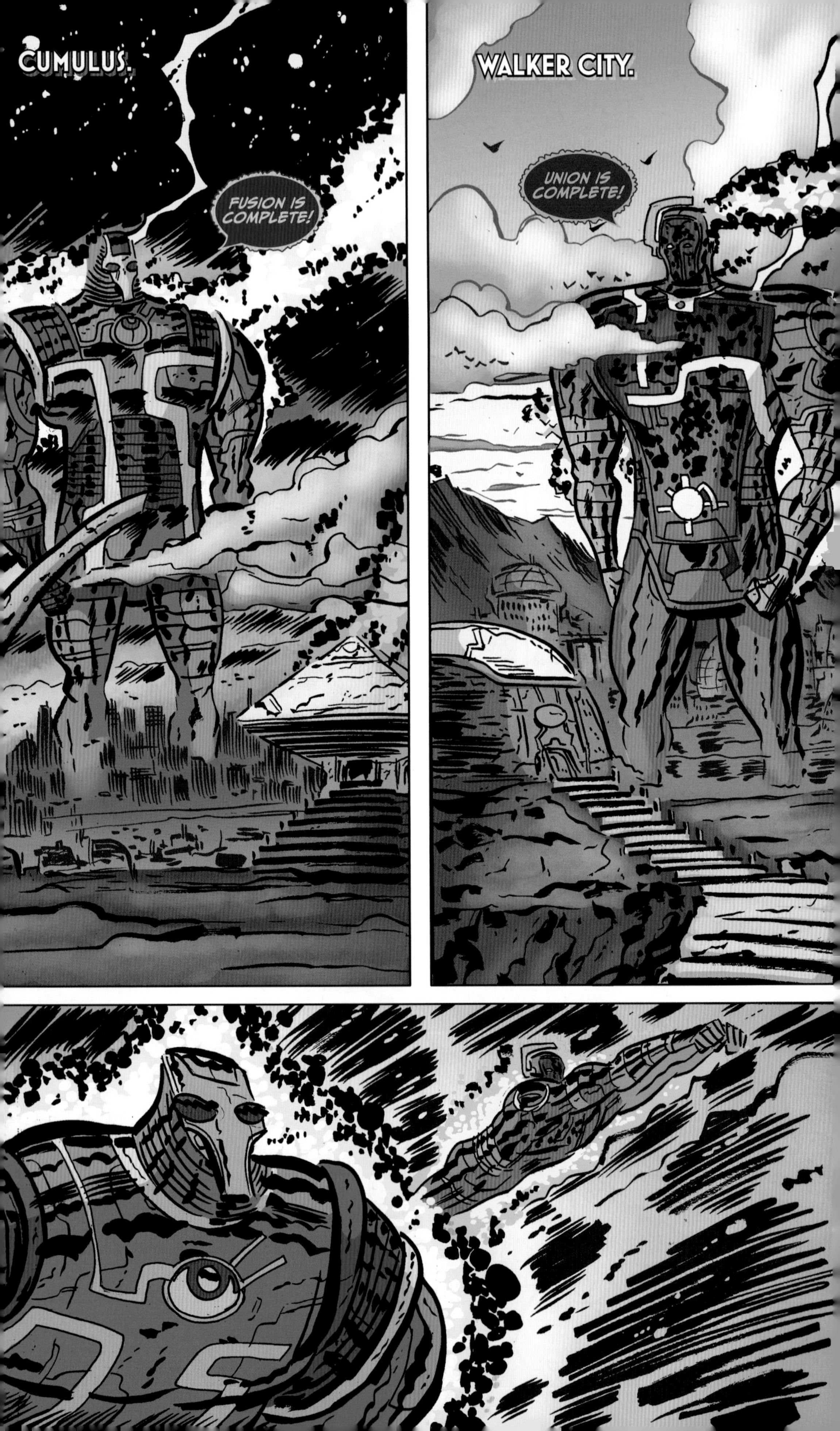
CUMULUS.
FUSION IS COMPLETE!
WALKER CITY.
UNION IS COMPLETE!

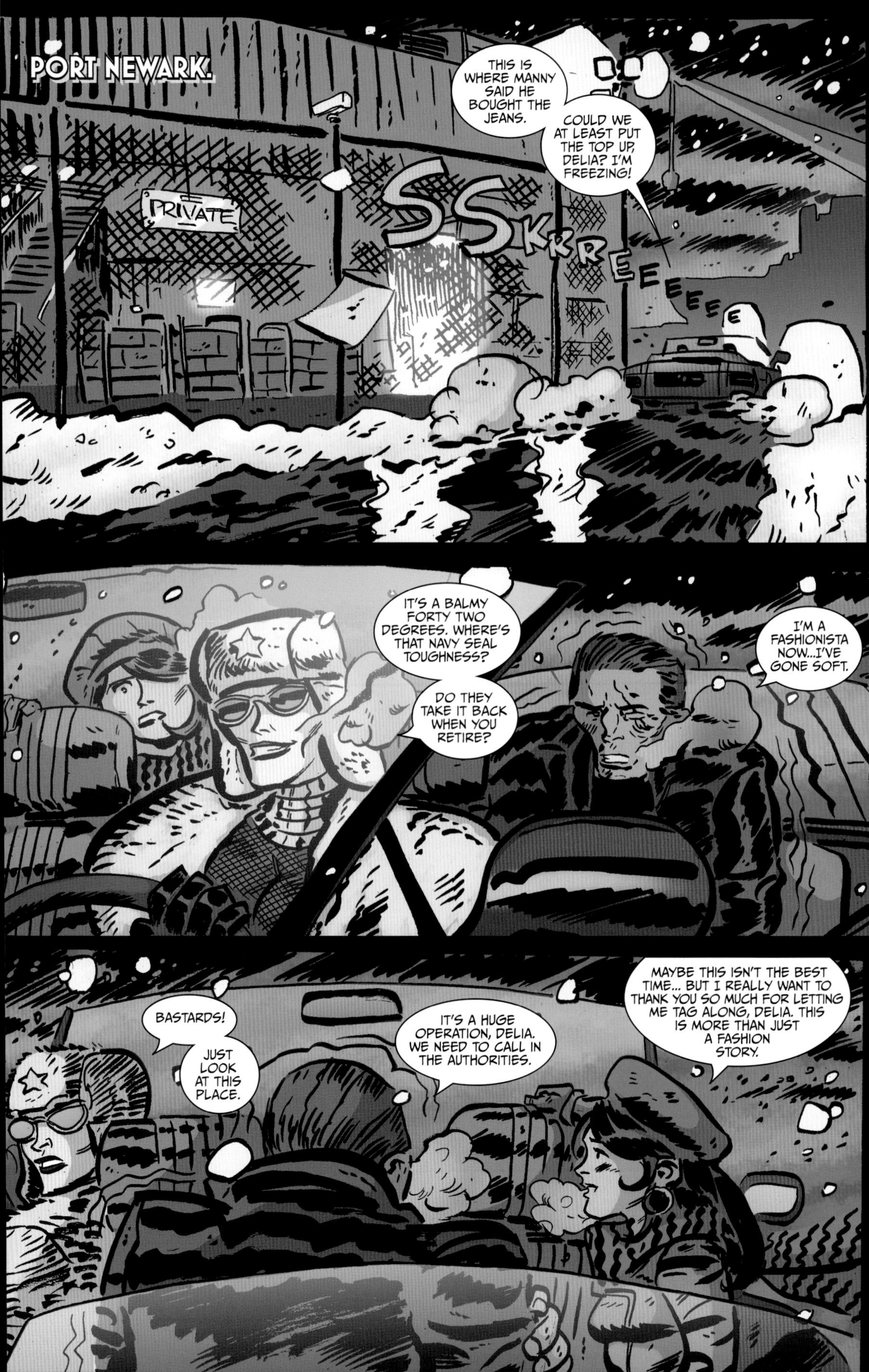
PORT NEWARK.
THIS IS WHERE MANNY SAID HE BOUGHT THE JEANS.
COULD WE AT LEAST PUT THE TOP UP, DELIA? I'M FREEZING!
PRIVATE
SSKKREEEEEE
IT'S A BALMY FORTY TWO DEGREES. WHERE'S THAT NAVY SEAL TOUGHNESS?
DO THEY TAKE IT BACK WHEN YOU RETIRE?
I'M A FASHIONISTA NOW...I'VE GONE SOFT.
BASTARDS!
JUST LOOK AT THIS PLACE.
IT'S A HUGE OPERATION, DELIA. WE NEED TO CALL IN THE AUTHORITIES.
MAYBE THIS ISN'T THE BEST TIME... BUT I REALLY WANT TO THANK YOU SO MUCH FOR LETTING ME TAG ALONG, DELIA. THIS IS MORE THAN JUST A FASHION STORY.

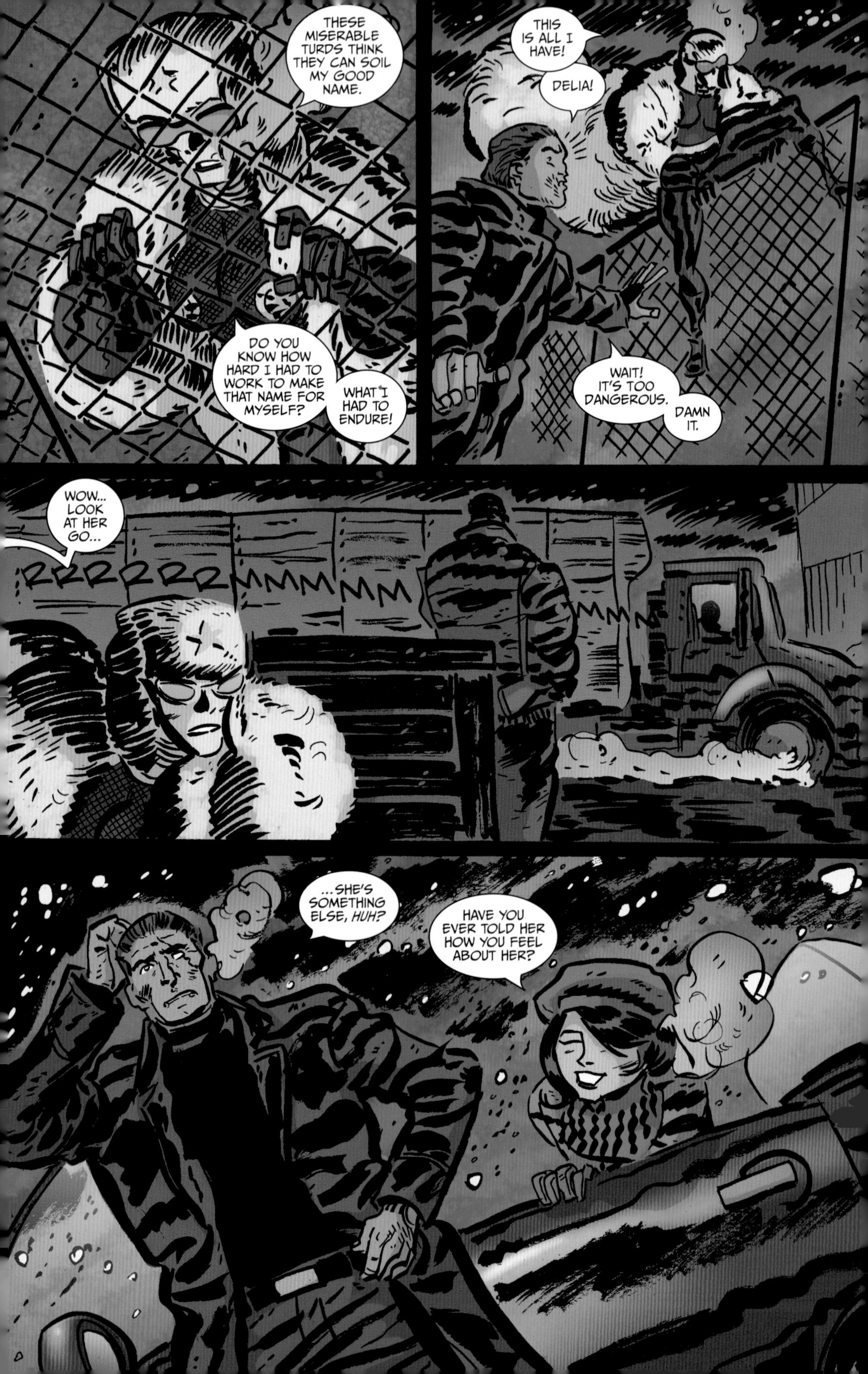
THESE MISERABLE TURDS THINK THEY CAN SOIL MY GOOD NAME.
DO YOU KNOW HOW HARD I HAD TO WORK TO MAKE THAT NAME FOR MYSELF?
WHAT I HAD TO ENDURE!
THIS IS ALL I HAVE!
DELIA!
WAIT! IT'S TOO DANGEROUS.
DAMN IT.
WOW... LOOK AT HER GO...
RRRRRRRMMMMMMM
MMMM
...SHE'S SOMETHING ELSE, *HUH?*
HAVE YOU EVER TOLD HER HOW YOU FEEL ABOUT HER?

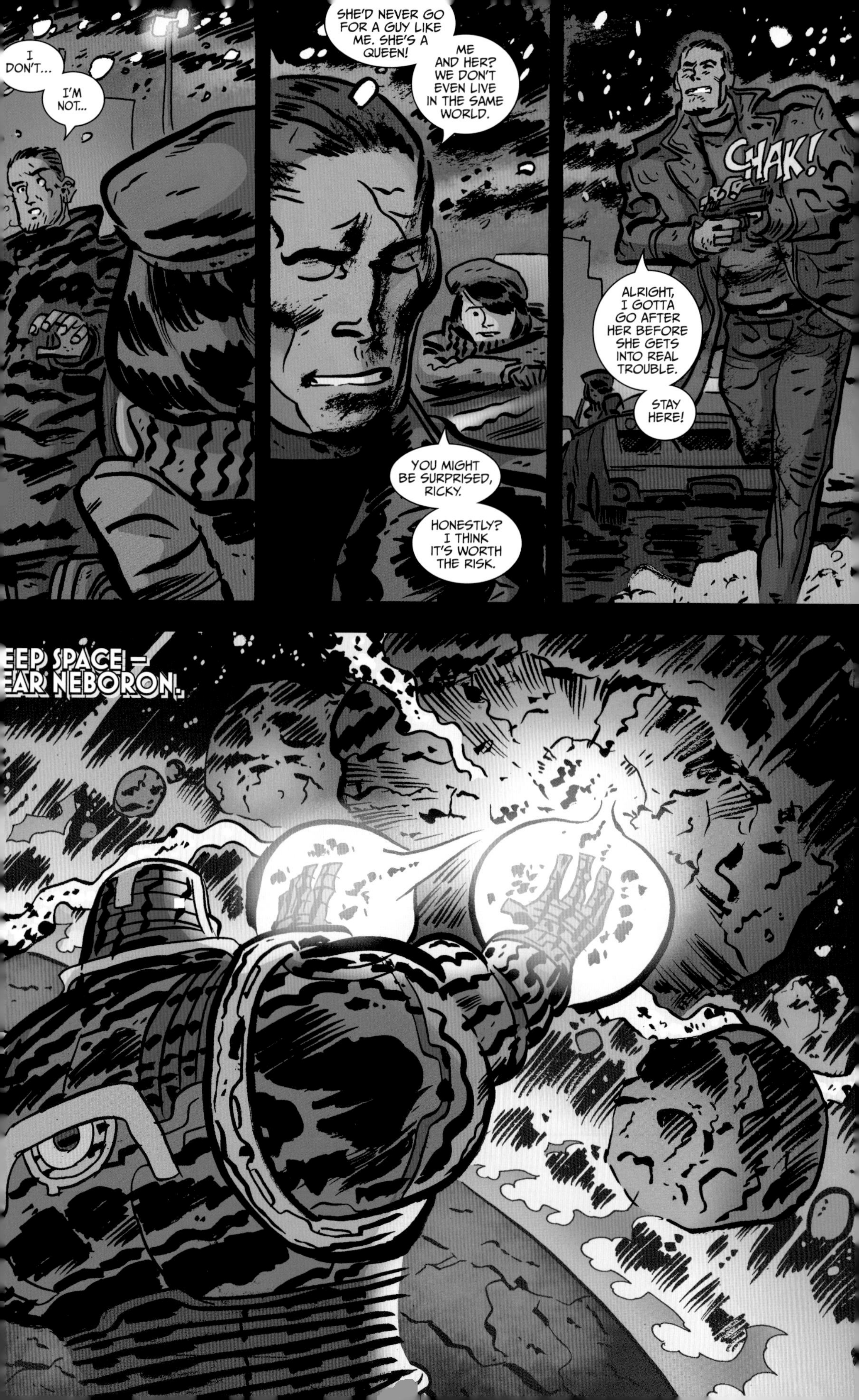

I DON'T...
I'M NOT...
SHE'D NEVER GO FOR A GUY LIKE ME. SHE'S A QUEEN!
ME AND HER? WE DON'T EVEN LIVE IN THE SAME WORLD.
YOU MIGHT BE SURPRISED, RICKY.
HONESTLY? I THINK IT'S WORTH THE RISK.
CHAK!
ALRIGHT, I GOTTA GO AFTER HER BEFORE SHE GETS INTO REAL TROUBLE.
STAY HERE!
EEP SPACE — EAR NEBORON.

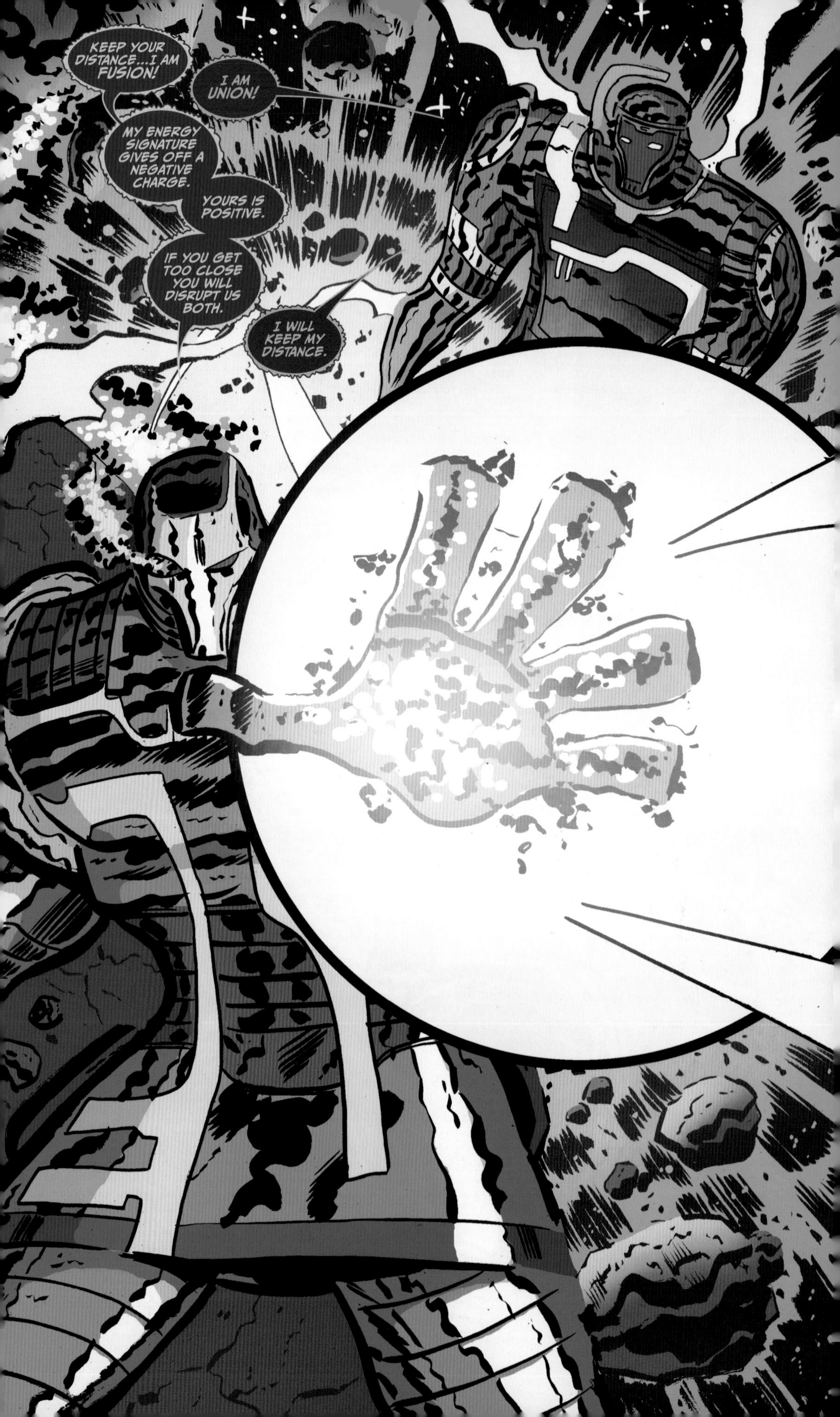
KEEP YOUR DISTANCE...I AM FUSION!
I AM UNION!
MY ENERGY SIGNATURE GIVES OFF A NEGATIVE CHARGE.
YOURS IS POSITIVE.
IF YOU GET TOO CLOSE YOU WILL DISRUPT US BOTH.
I WILL KEEP MY DISTANCE.

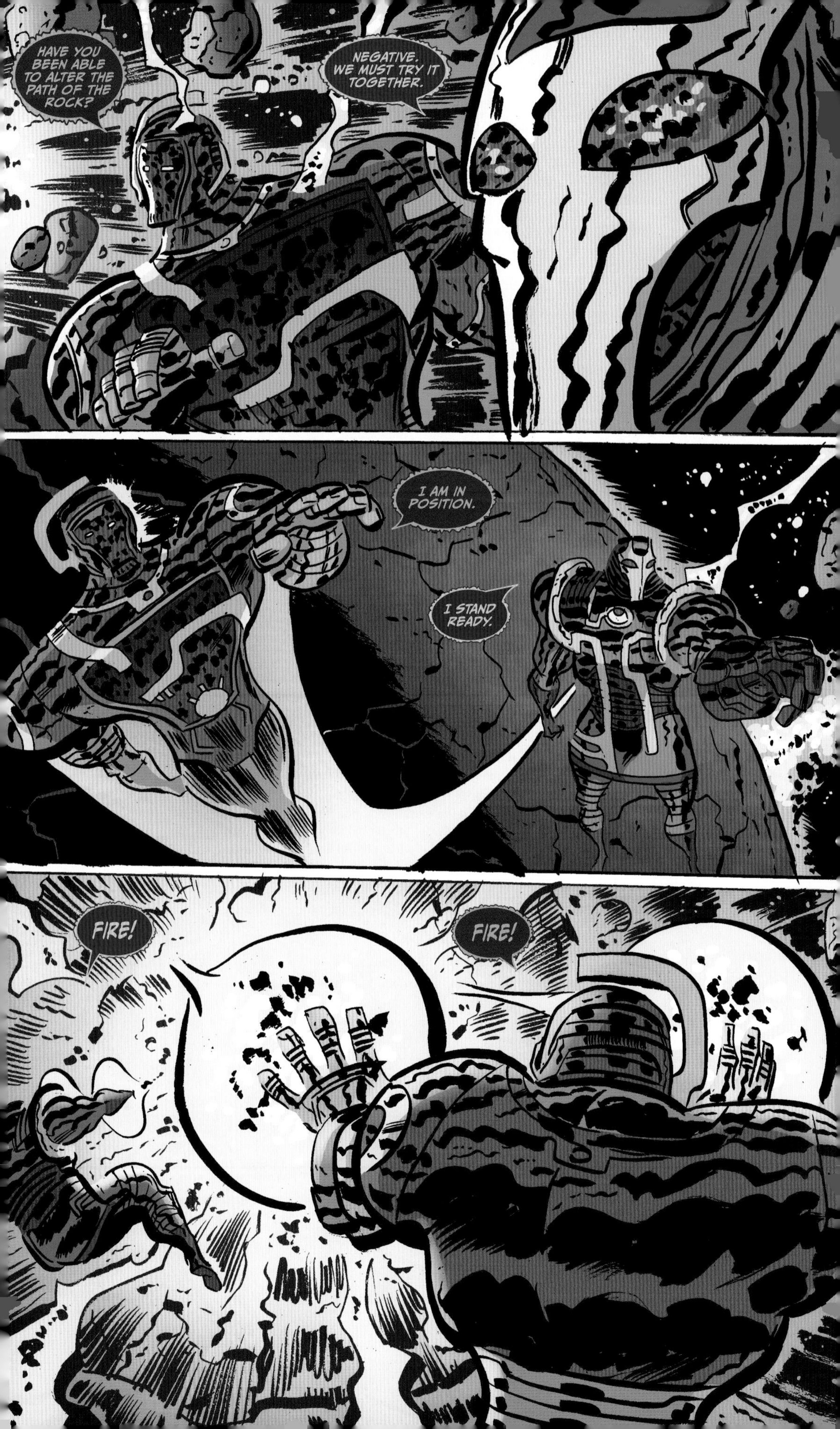
HAVE YOU BEEN ABLE TO ALTER THE PATH OF THE ROCK?
NEGATIVE. WE MUST TRY IT TOGETHER.
I AM IN POSITION.
I STAND READY.
FIRE!
FIRE!

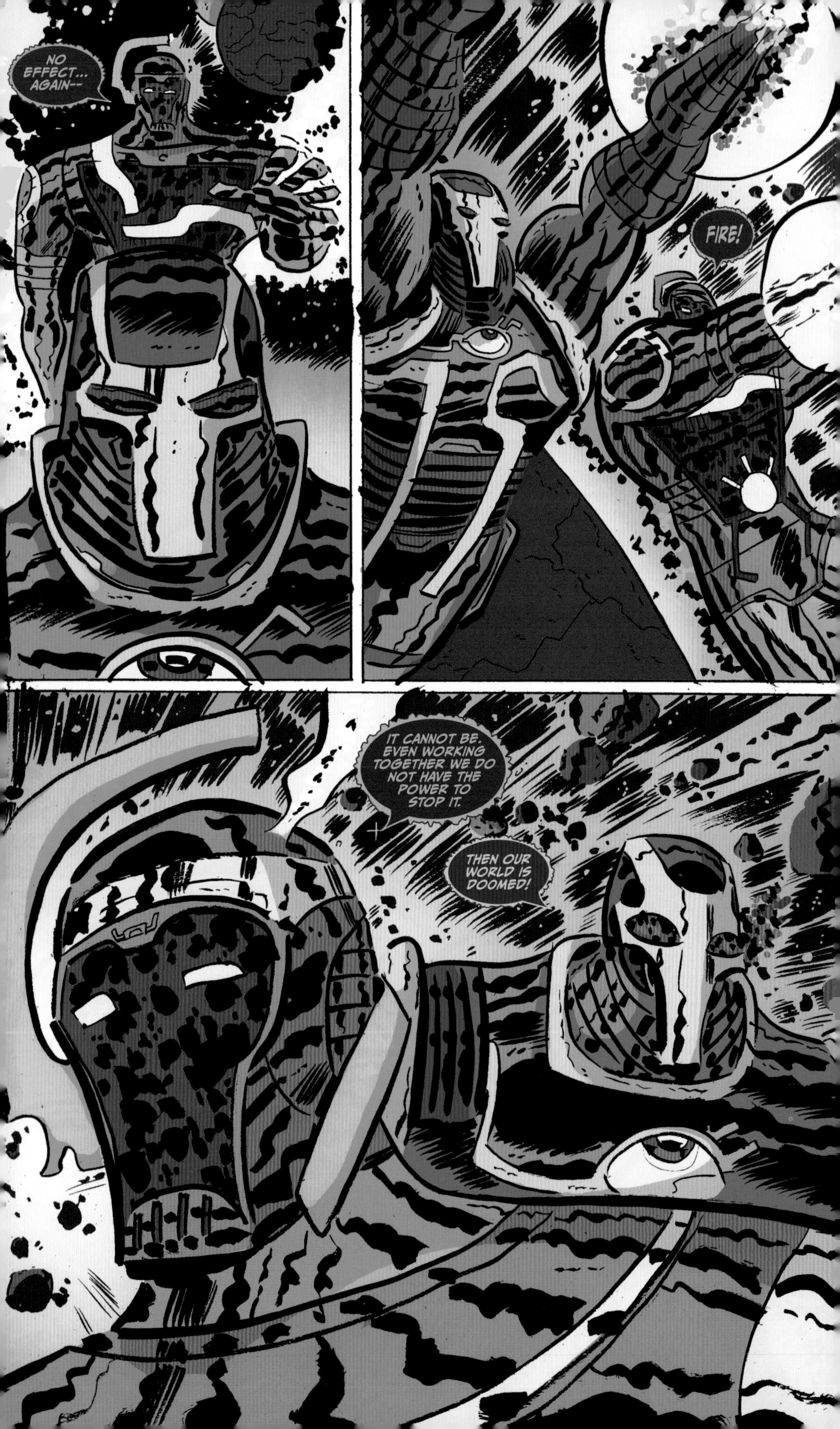
NO EFFECT... AGAIN--
FIRE!
IT CANNOT BE. EVEN WORKING TOGETHER WE DO NOT HAVE THE POWER TO STOP IT.
THEN OUR WORLD IS DOOMED!

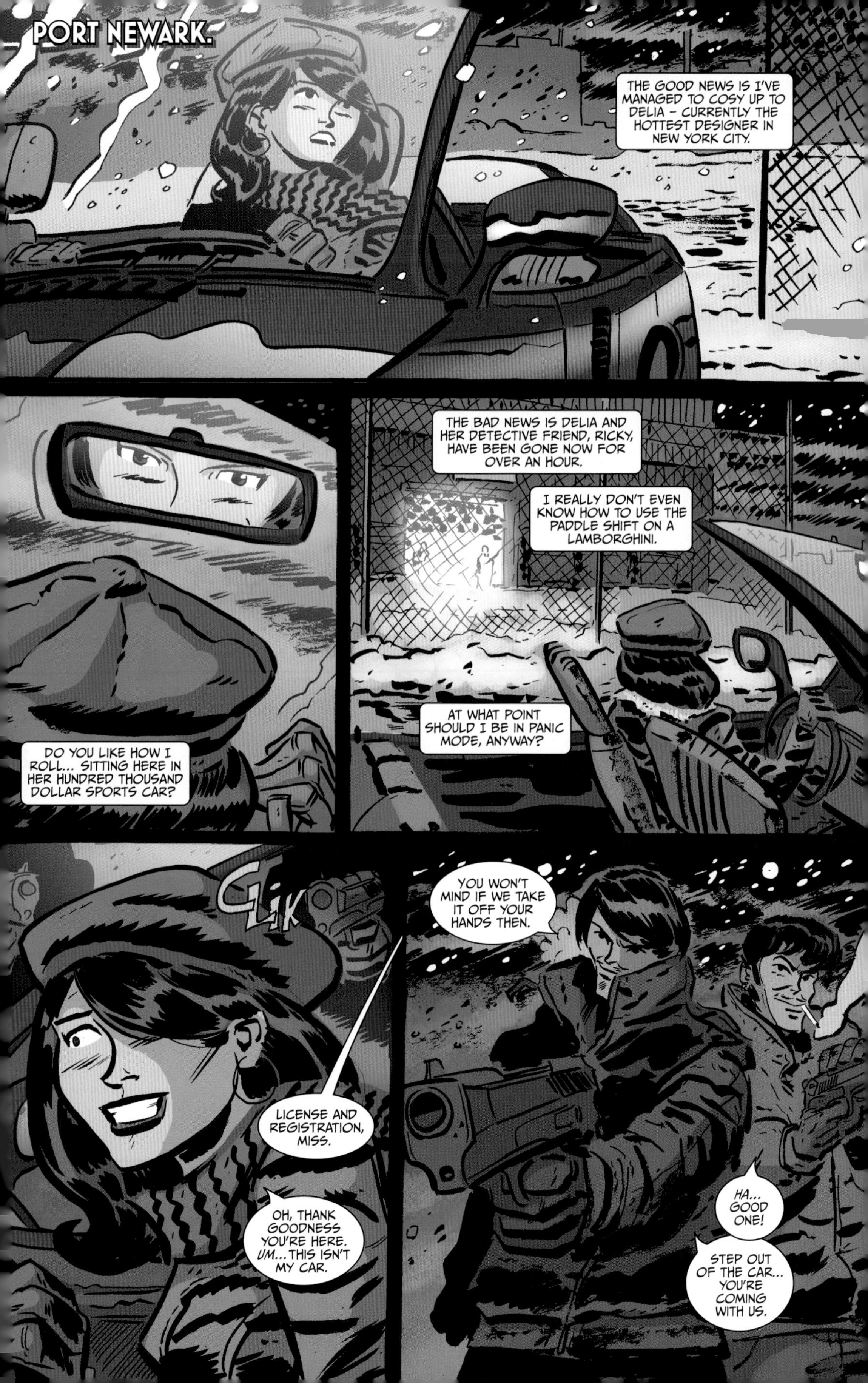
PORT NEWARK.
THE GOOD NEWS IS I'VE MANAGED TO COSY UP TO DELIA – CURRENTLY THE HOTTEST DESIGNER IN NEW YORK CITY.
DO YOU LIKE HOW I ROLL... SITTING HERE IN HER HUNDRED THOUSAND DOLLAR SPORTS CAR?
THE BAD NEWS IS DELIA AND HER DETECTIVE FRIEND, RICKY, HAVE BEEN GONE NOW FOR OVER AN HOUR.
I REALLY DON'T EVEN KNOW HOW TO USE THE PADDLE SHIFT ON A LAMBORGHINI.
AT WHAT POINT SHOULD I BE IN PANIC MODE, ANYWAY?
CLIK
LICENSE AND REGISTRATION, MISS.
OH, THANK GOODNESS YOU'RE HERE. UM... THIS ISN'T MY CAR.
YOU WON'T MIND IF WE TAKE IT OFF YOUR HANDS THEN.
HA... GOOD ONE!
STEP OUT OF THE CAR... YOU'RE COMING WITH US.

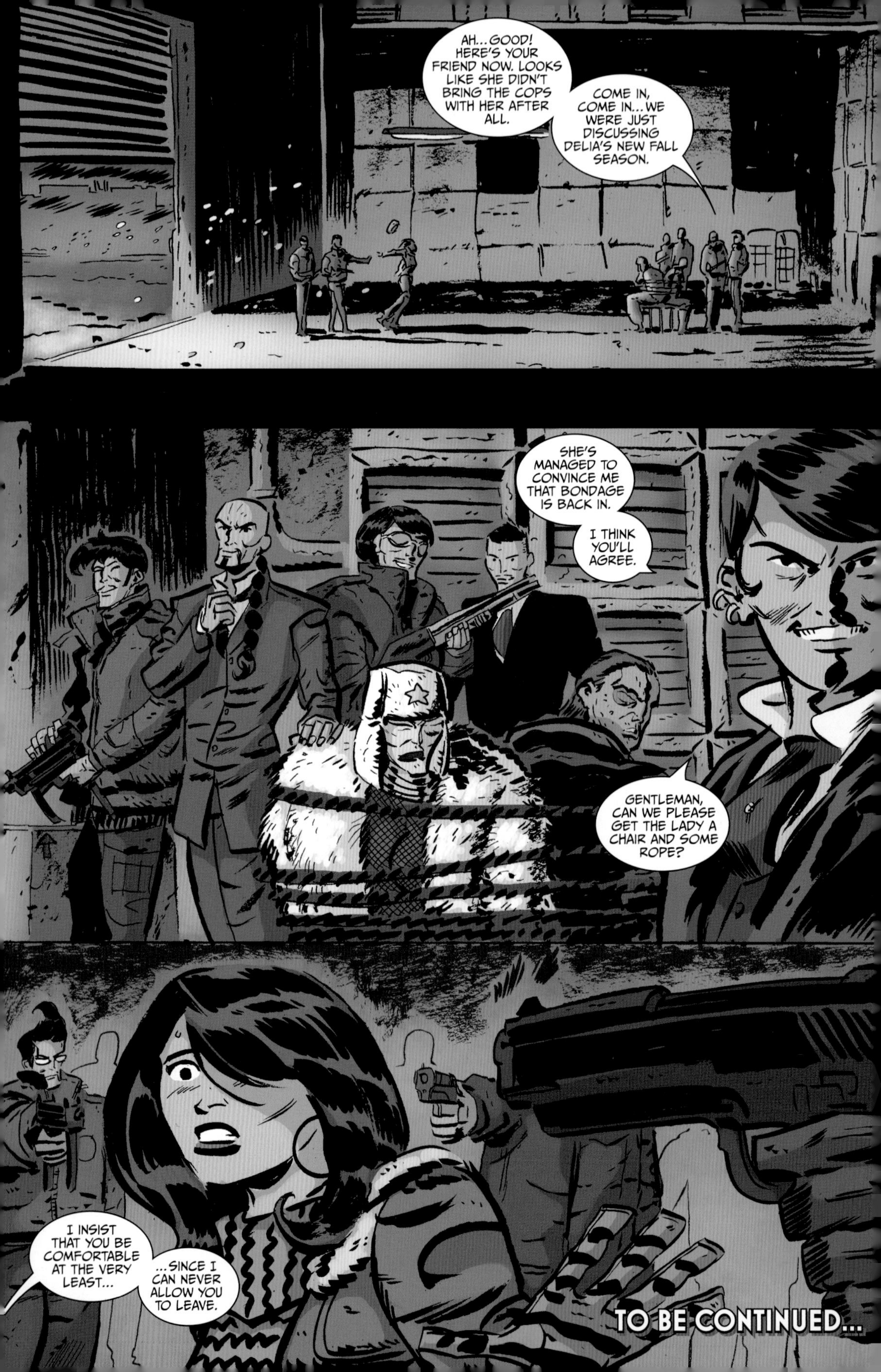
AH...GOOD! HERE'S YOUR FRIEND NOW. LOOKS LIKE SHE DIDN'T BRING THE COPS WITH HER AFTER ALL.
COME IN, COME IN...WE WERE JUST DISCUSSING DELIA'S NEW FALL SEASON.
SHE'S MANAGED TO CONVINCE ME THAT BONDAGE IS BACK IN.
I THINK YOU'LL AGREE.
GENTLEMAN, CAN WE PLEASE GET THE LADY A CHAIR AND SOME ROPE?
I INSIST THAT YOU BE COMFORTABLE AT THE VERY LEAST...
...SINCE I CAN NEVER ALLOW YOU TO LEAVE.
TO BE CONTINUED...

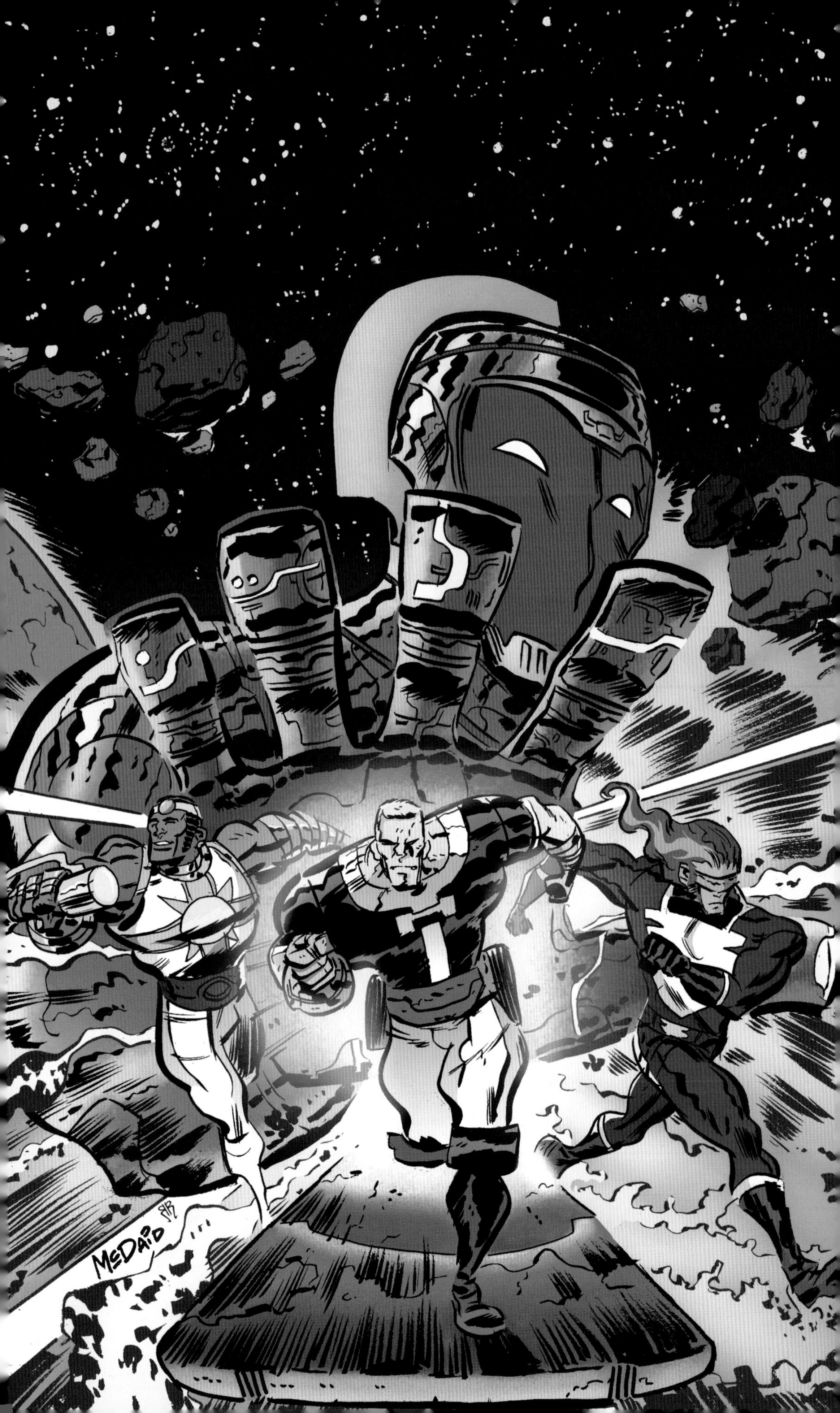
McDAID

CHAPTER FIVE

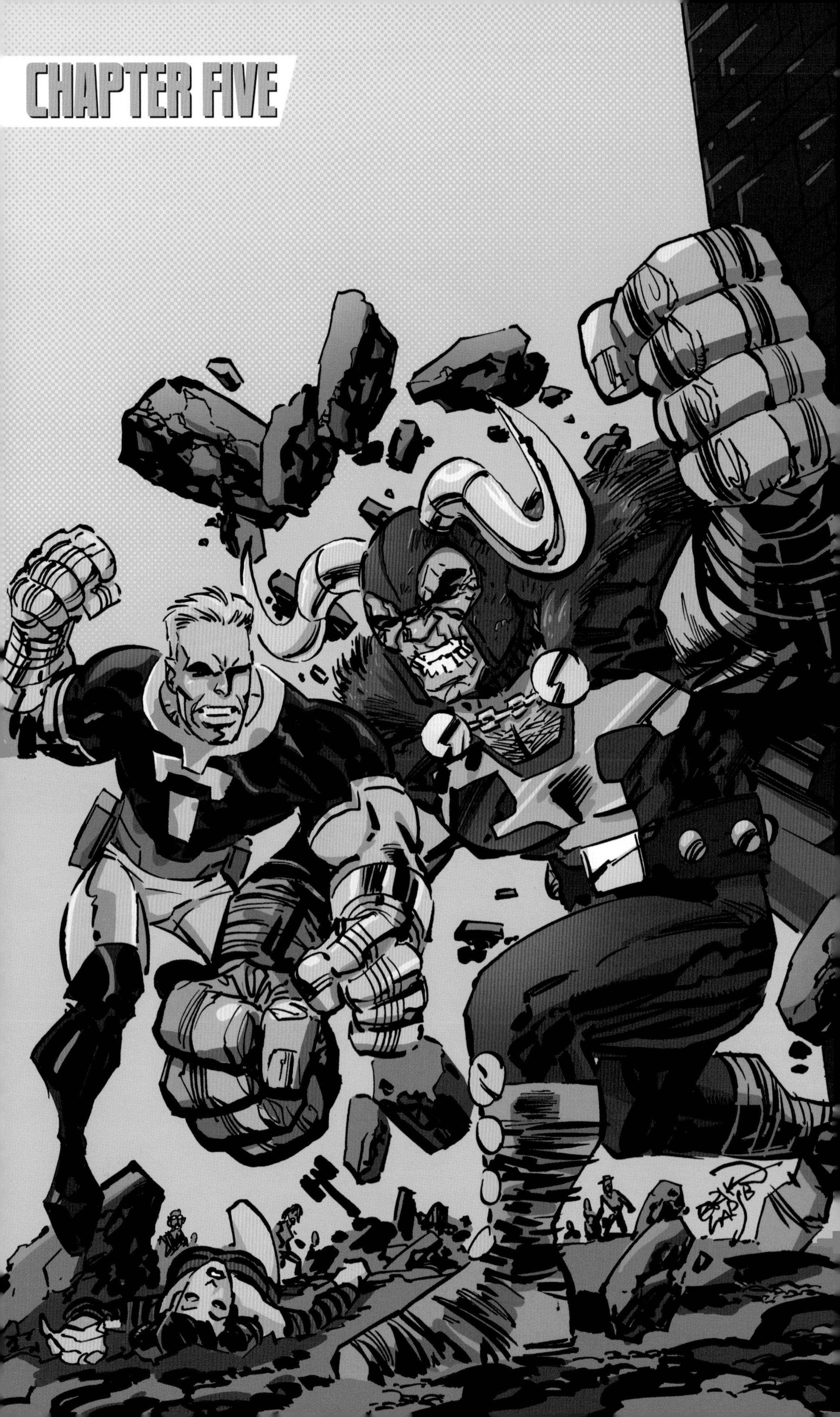

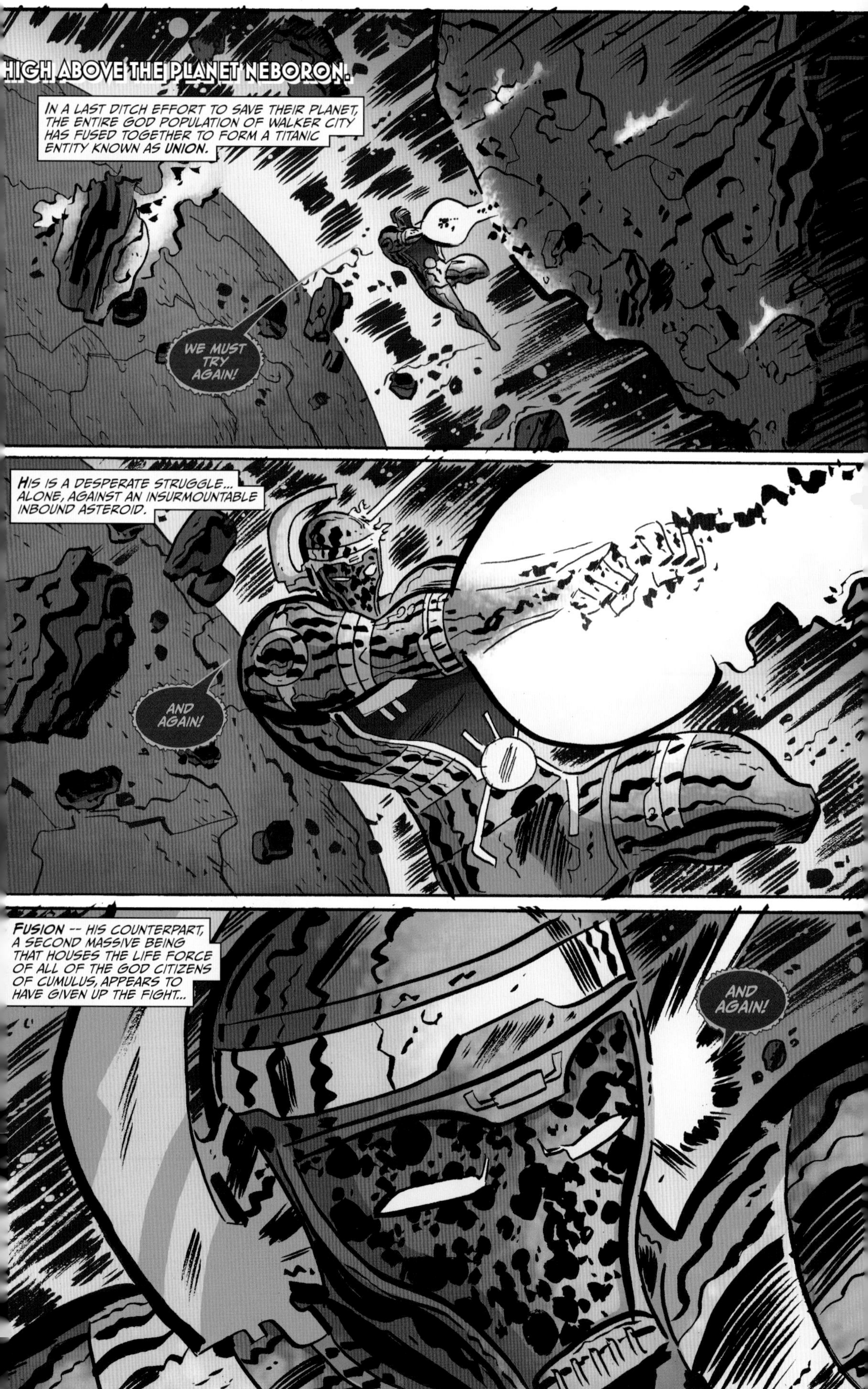

HIGH ABOVE THE PLANET NEBORON.
IN A LAST DITCH EFFORT TO SAVE THEIR PLANET, THE ENTIRE GOD POPULATION OF WALKER CITY HAS FUSED TOGETHER TO FORM A TITANIC ENTITY KNOWN AS UNION.
WE MUST TRY AGAIN!
HIS IS A DESPERATE STRUGGLE... ALONE, AGAINST AN INSURMOUNTABLE INBOUND ASTEROID.
AND AGAIN!
FUSION -- HIS COUNTERPART, A SECOND MASSIVE BEING THAT HOUSES THE LIFE FORCE OF ALL OF THE GOD CITIZENS OF CUMULUS, APPEARS TO HAVE GIVEN UP THE FIGHT...
AND AGAIN!

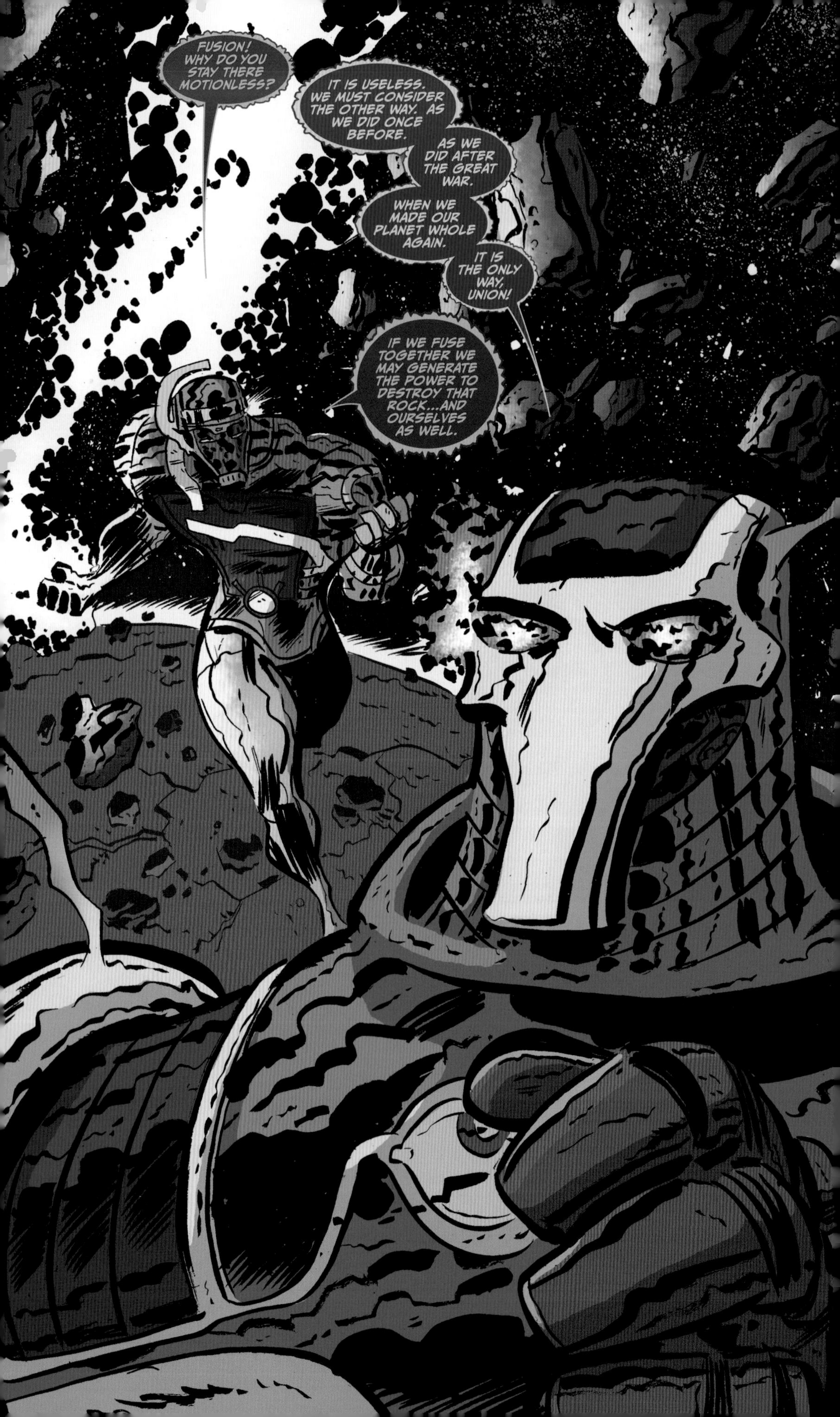
FUSION! WHY DO YOU STAY THERE MOTIONLESS?
IT IS USELESS. WE MUST CONSIDER THE OTHER WAY. AS WE DID ONCE BEFORE.
AS WE DID AFTER THE GREAT WAR.
WHEN WE MADE OUR PLANET WHOLE AGAIN.
IT IS THE ONLY WAY, UNION!
IF WE FUSE TOGETHER WE MAY GENERATE THE POWER TO DESTROY THAT ROCK...AND OURSELVES AS WELL.

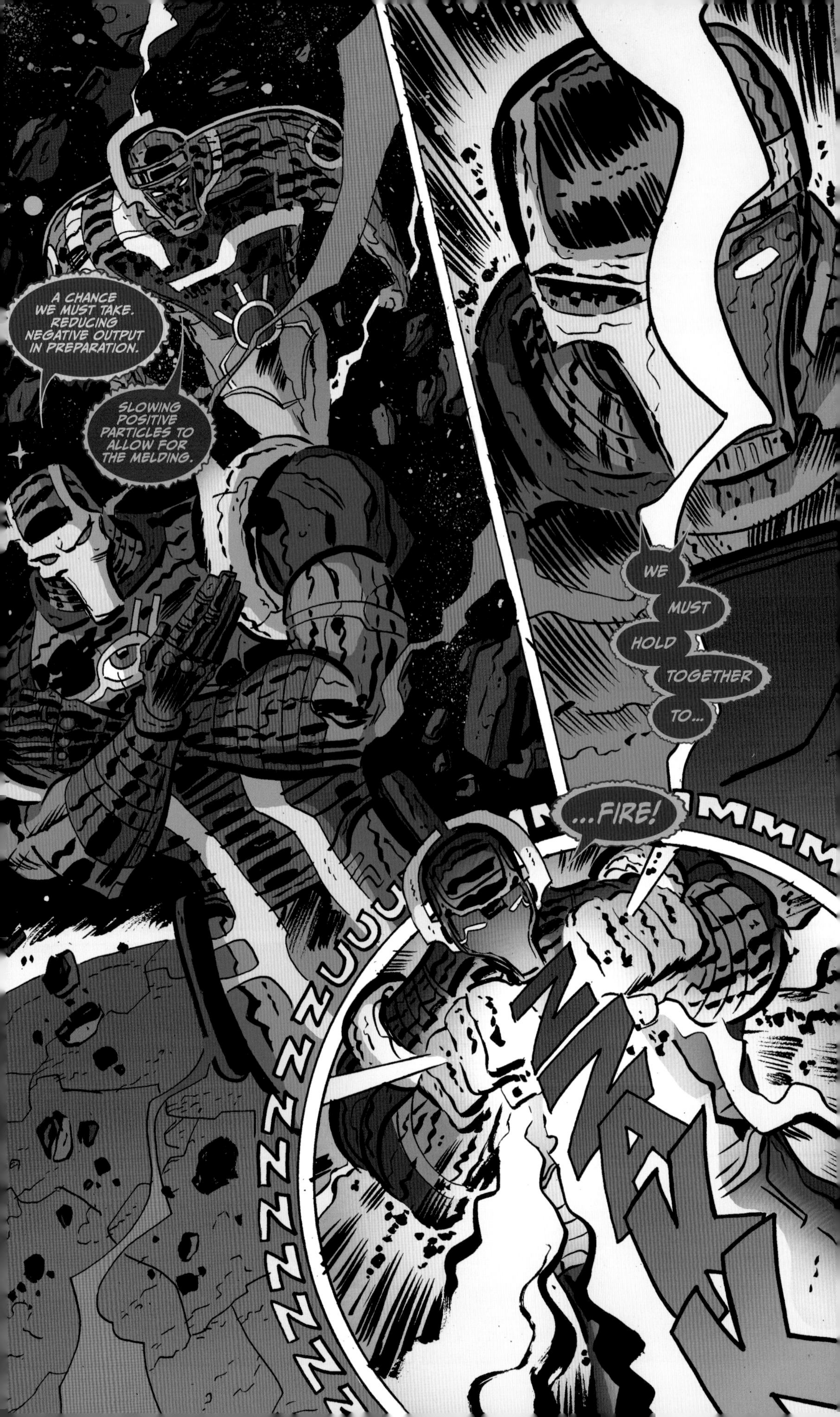
A CHANCE WE MUST TAKE. REDUCING NEGATIVE OUTPUT IN PREPARATION.
SLOWING POSITIVE PARTICLES TO ALLOW FOR THE MELDING.
WE MUST HOLD TOGETHER TO...
...FIRE!

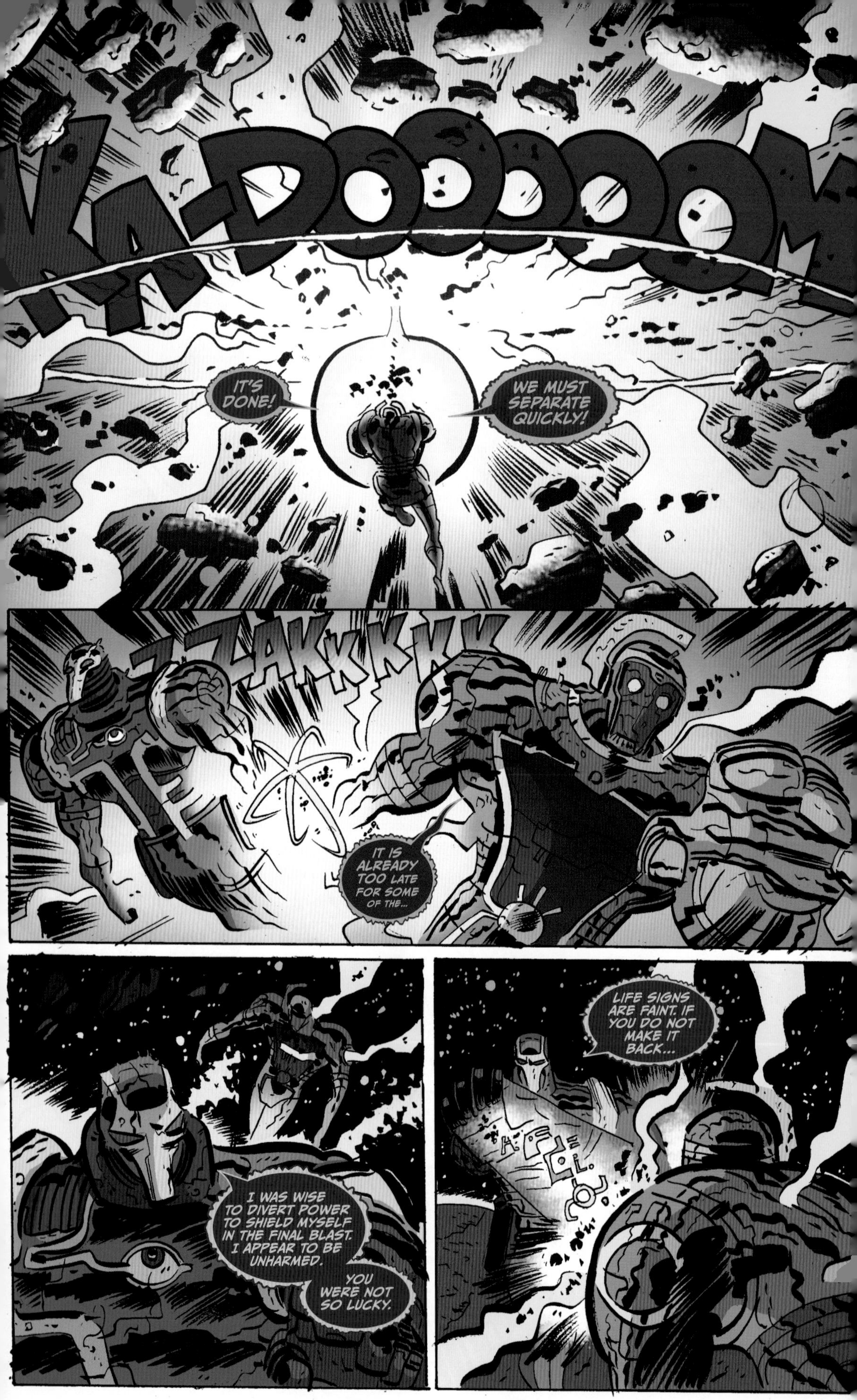
KA-DOOOOOOM
IT'S DONE!
WE MUST SEPARATE QUICKLY!
ZZAKKKKK
IT IS ALREADY TOO LATE FOR SOME OF THE...
I WAS WISE TO DIVERT POWER TO SHIELD MYSELF IN THE FINAL BLAST. I APPEAR TO BE UNHARMED.
YOU WERE NOT SO LUCKY.
LIFE SIGNS ARE FAINT. IF YOU DO NOT MAKE IT BACK...

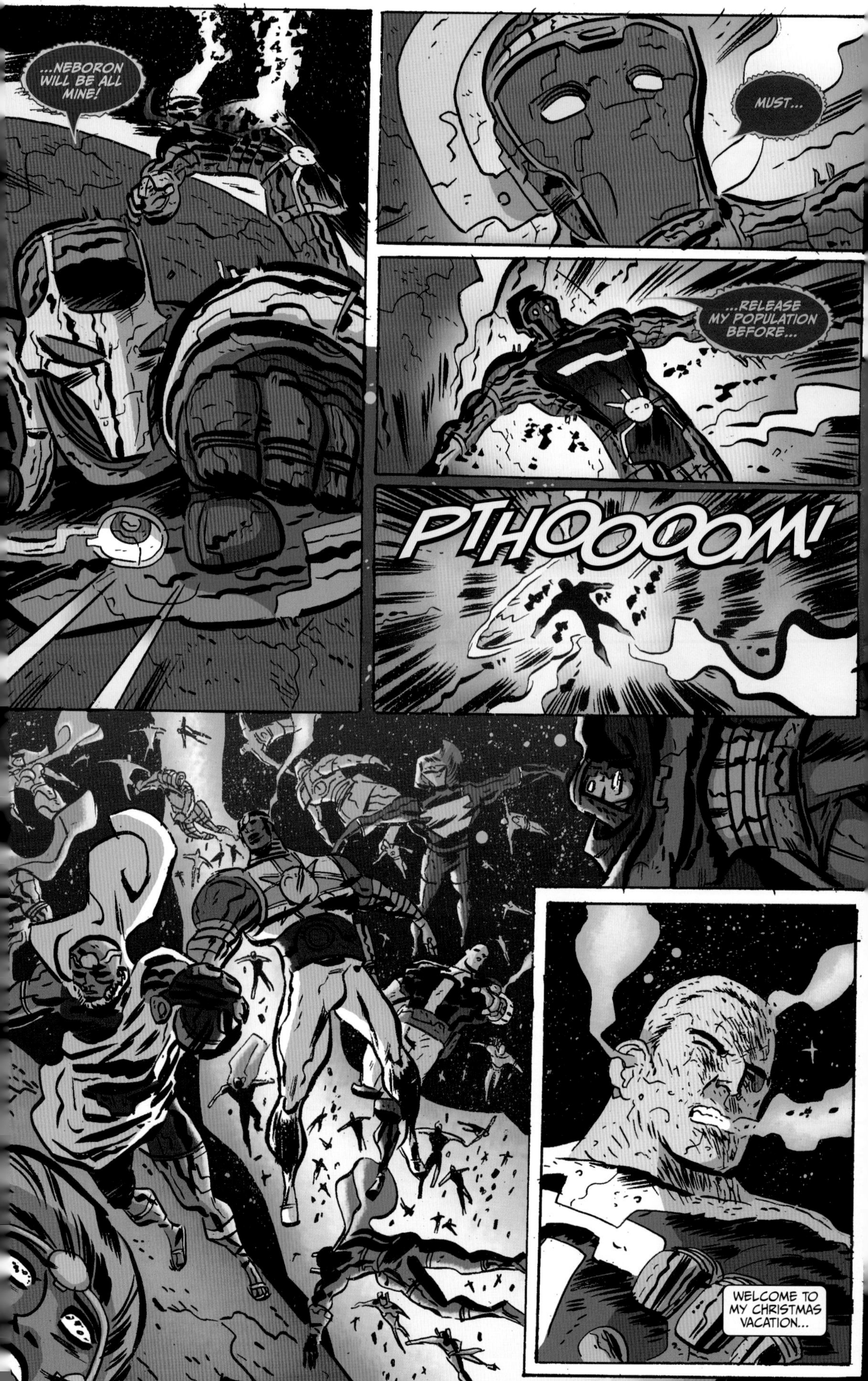
...NEBORON WILL BE ALL MINE!
MUST...
...RELEASE MY POPULATION BEFORE...
PTHOOOOOM!
WELCOME TO MY CHRISTMAS VACATION...

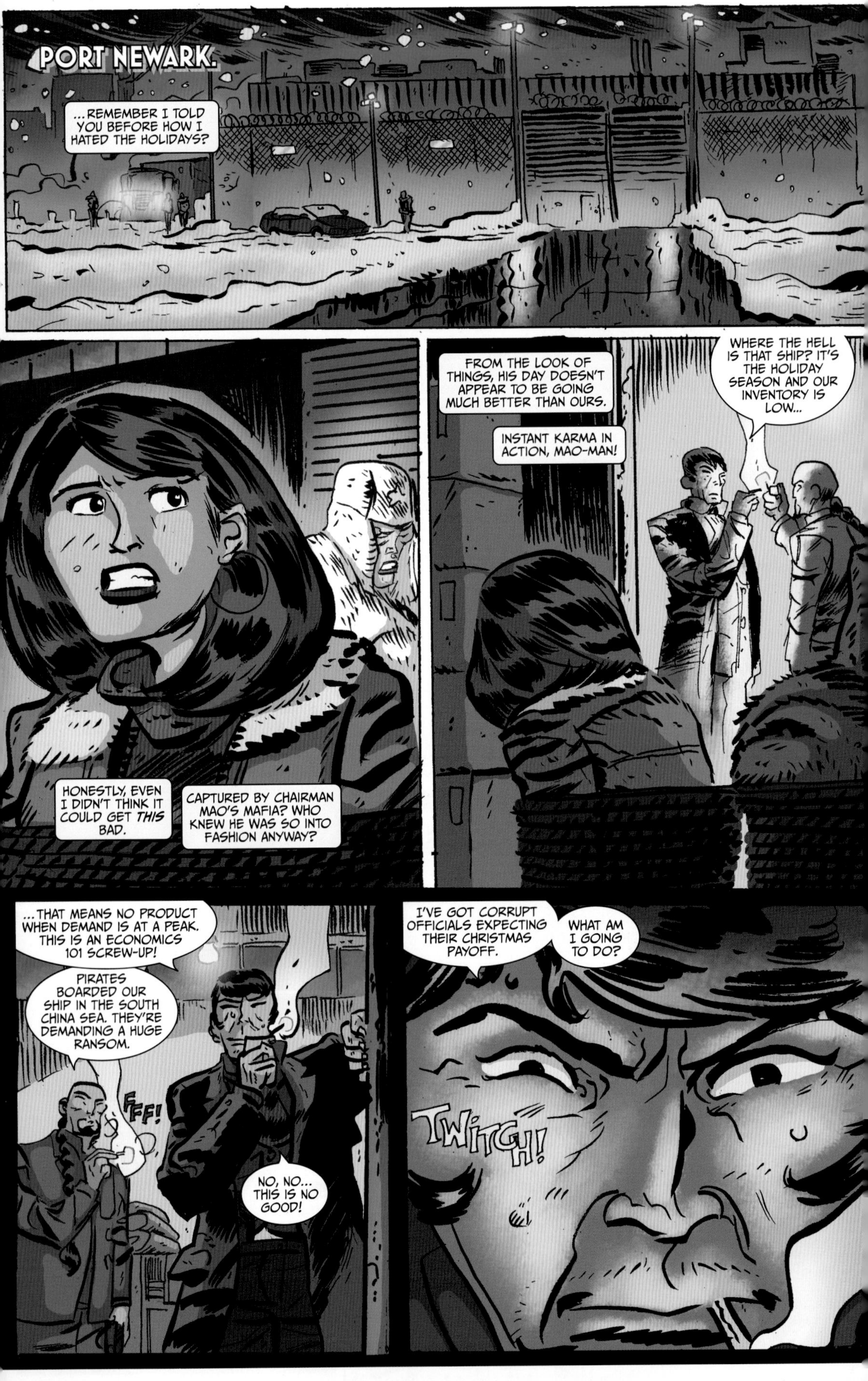
PORT NEWARK.
...REMEMBER I TOLD YOU BEFORE HOW I HATED THE HOLIDAYS?
HONESTLY, EVEN I DIDN'T THINK IT COULD GET *THIS* BAD.
CAPTURED BY CHAIRMAN MAO'S MAFIA? WHO KNEW HE WAS SO INTO FASHION ANYWAY?
FROM THE LOOK OF THINGS, HIS DAY DOESN'T APPEAR TO BE GOING MUCH BETTER THAN OURS.
INSTANT KARMA IN ACTION, MAO-MAN!
WHERE THE HELL IS THAT SHIP? IT'S THE HOLIDAY SEASON AND OUR INVENTORY IS LOW...
...THAT MEANS NO PRODUCT WHEN DEMAND IS AT A PEAK. THIS IS AN ECONOMICS 101 SCREW-UP!
PIRATES BOARDED OUR SHIP IN THE SOUTH CHINA SEA. THEY'RE DEMANDING A HUGE RANSOM.
FFFF!
NO, NO... THIS IS NO GOOD!
I'VE GOT CORRUPT OFFICIALS EXPECTING THEIR CHRISTMAS PAYOFF.
WHAT AM I GOING TO DO?
TWITCH!

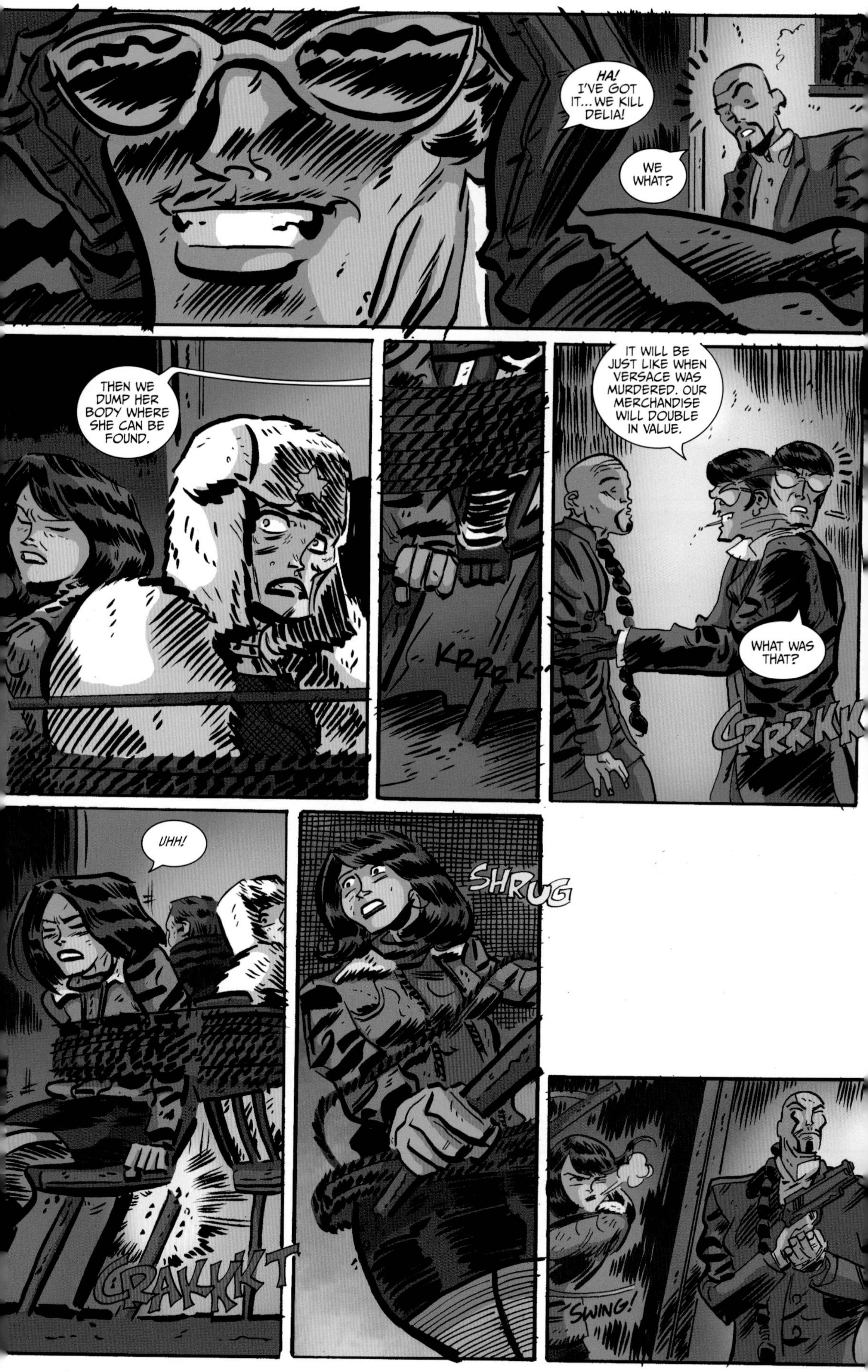
HA! I'VE GOT IT... WE KILL DELIA!
WE WHAT?
THEN WE DUMP HER BODY WHERE SHE CAN BE FOUND.
KRRRK...
IT WILL BE JUST LIKE WHEN VERSACE WAS MURDERED. OUR MERCHANDISE WILL DOUBLE IN VALUE.
WHAT WAS THAT?
CRRRKK
UHH!
CRAKKKT
SHRUG
SWING!

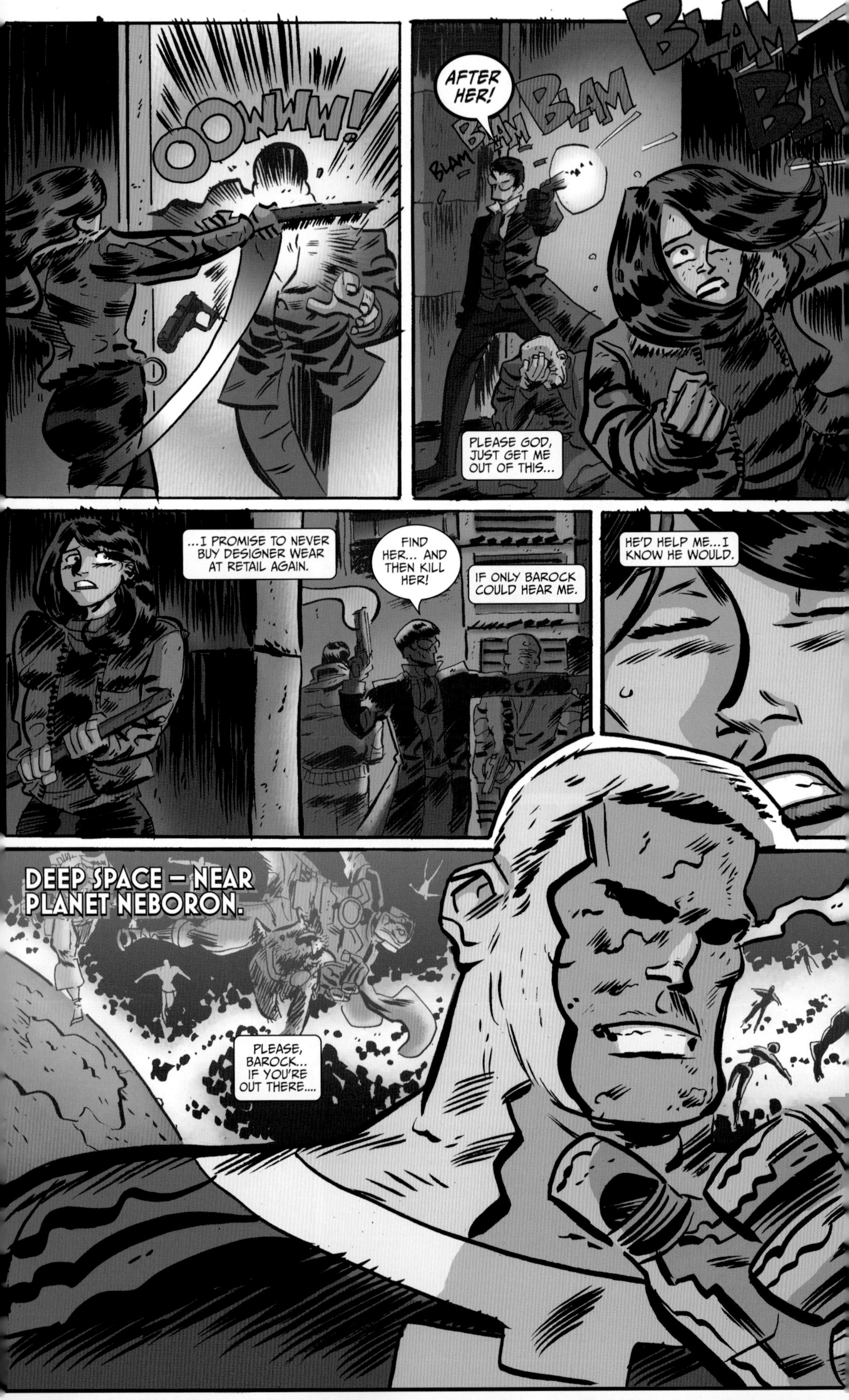
OOWWW!
AFTER HER!
BLAM BLAM BLAM BLAM
BLAM
PLEASE GOD, JUST GET ME OUT OF THIS...
...I PROMISE TO NEVER BUY DESIGNER WEAR AT RETAIL AGAIN.
FIND HER... AND THEN KILL HER!
IF ONLY BAROCK COULD HEAR ME.
HE'D HELP ME...I KNOW HE WOULD.
DEEP SPACE — NEAR PLANET NEBORON.
PLEASE, BAROCK... IF YOU'RE OUT THERE....

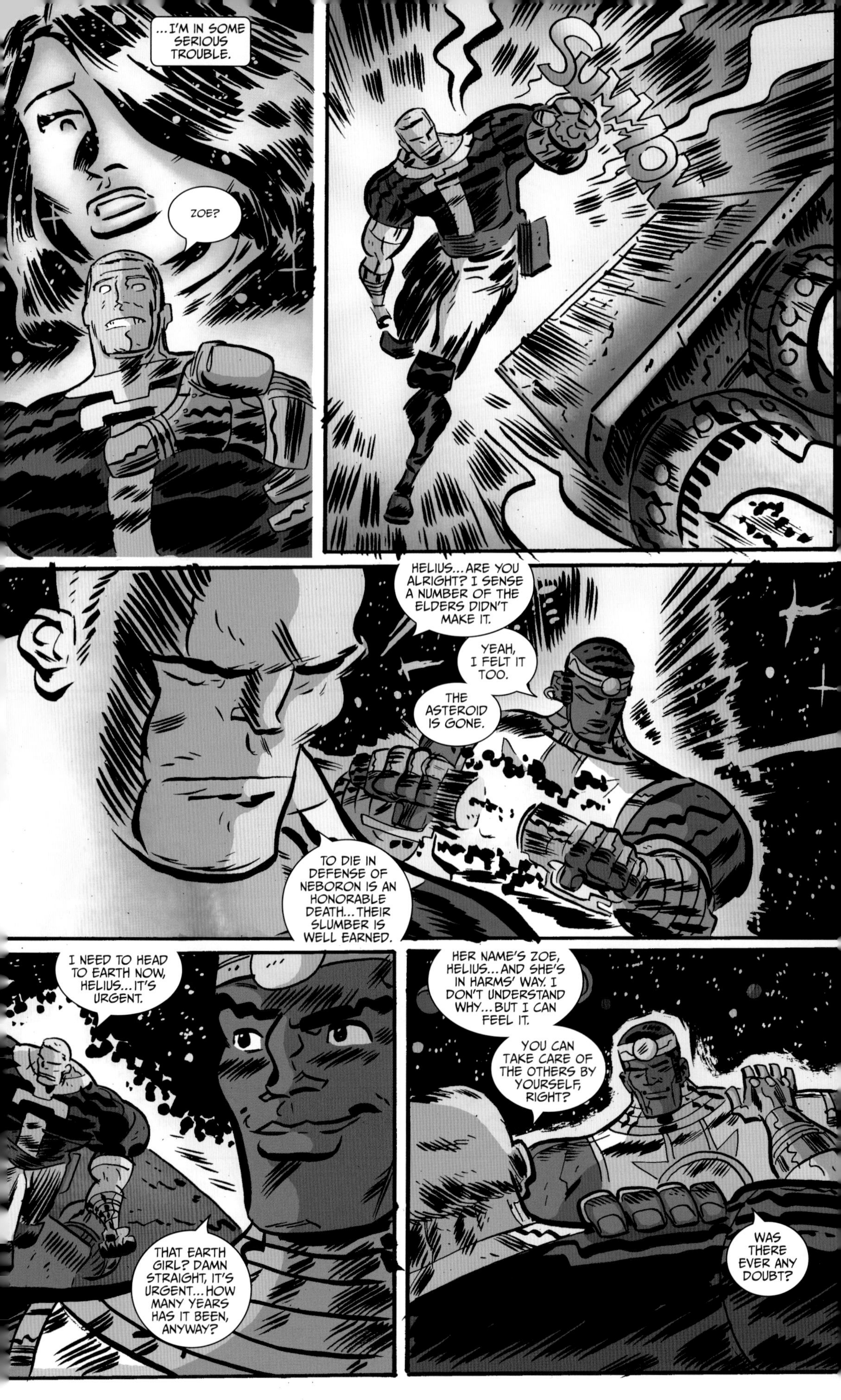

...I'M IN SOME SERIOUS TROUBLE.
ZOE?
HELIUS...ARE YOU ALRIGHT? I SENSE A NUMBER OF THE ELDERS DIDN'T MAKE IT.
YEAH, I FELT IT TOO.
THE ASTEROID IS GONE.
TO DIE IN DEFENSE OF NEBORON IS AN HONORABLE DEATH...THEIR SLUMBER IS WELL EARNED.
I NEED TO HEAD TO EARTH NOW, HELIUS...IT'S URGENT.
THAT EARTH GIRL? DAMN STRAIGHT, IT'S URGENT...HOW MANY YEARS HAS IT BEEN, ANYWAY?
HER NAME'S ZOE, HELIUS...AND SHE'S IN HARMS' WAY. I DON'T UNDERSTAND WHY...BUT I CAN FEEL IT.
YOU CAN TAKE CARE OF THE OTHERS BY YOURSELF, RIGHT?
WAS THERE EVER ANY DOUBT?

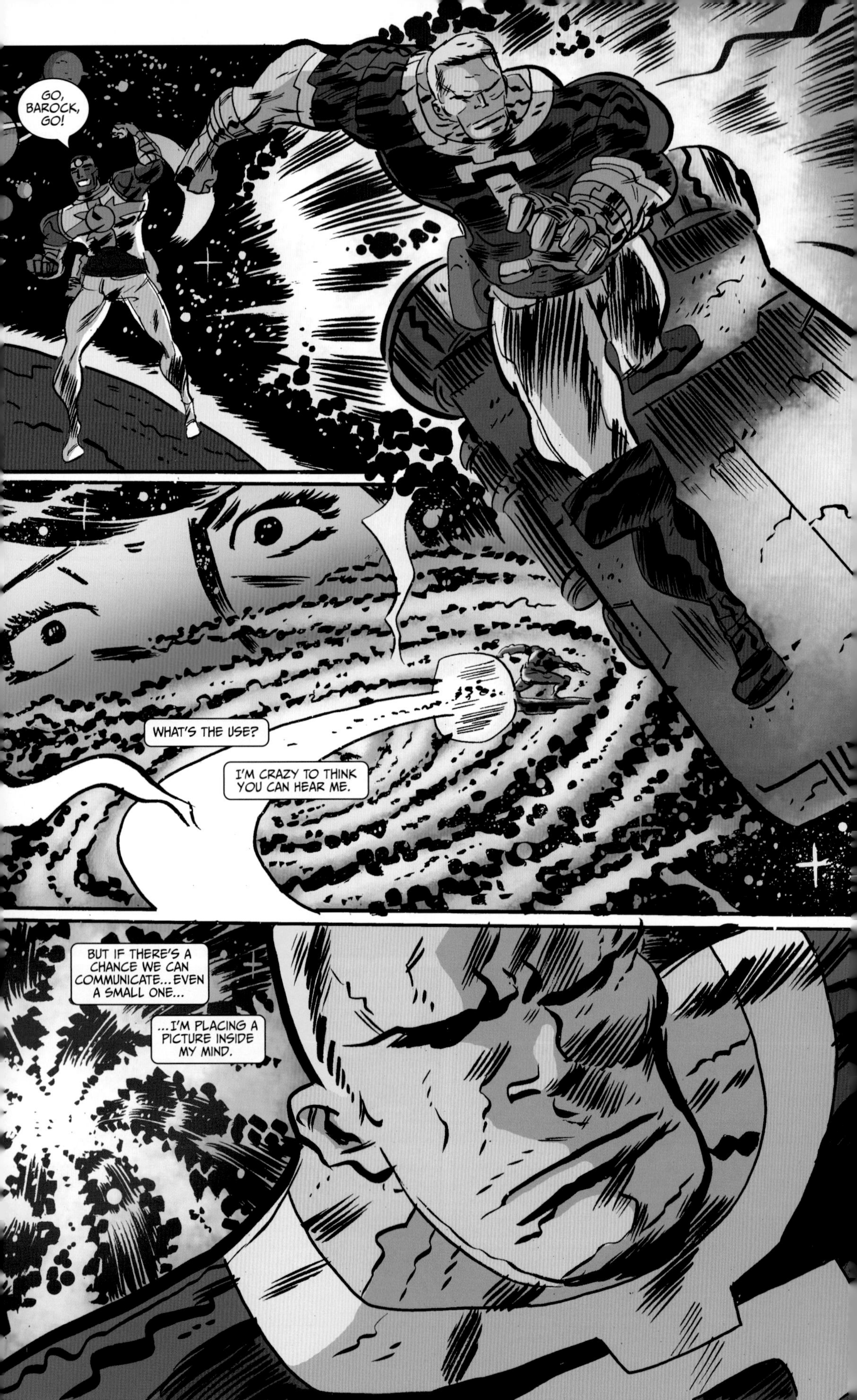
GO, BAROCK, GO!
WHAT'S THE USE?
I'M CRAZY TO THINK YOU CAN HEAR ME.
BUT IF THERE'S A CHANCE WE CAN COMMUNICATE...EVEN A SMALL ONE...
...I'M PLACING A PICTURE INSIDE MY MIND.

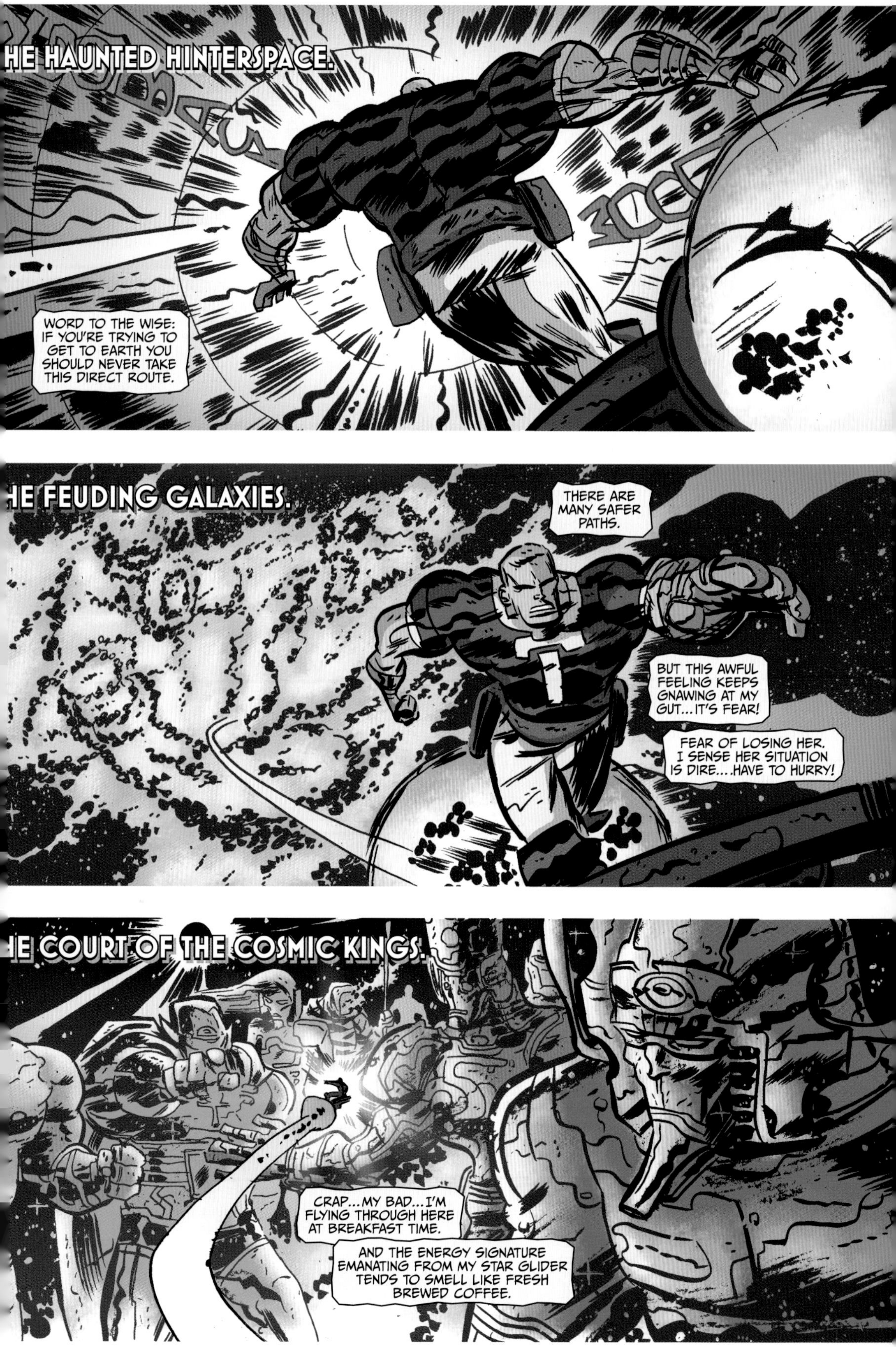
HE HAUNTED HINTERSPACE.
WORD TO THE WISE: IF YOU'RE TRYING TO GET TO EARTH YOU SHOULD NEVER TAKE THIS DIRECT ROUTE.
HE FEUDING GALAXIES.
THERE ARE MANY SAFER PATHS.
BUT THIS AWFUL FEELING KEEPS GNAWING AT MY GUT...IT'S FEAR!
FEAR OF LOSING HER. I SENSE HER SITUATION IS DIRE....HAVE TO HURRY!
HE COURT OF THE COSMIC KINGS.
CRAP...MY BAD...I'M FLYING THROUGH HERE AT BREAKFAST TIME.
AND THE ENERGY SIGNATURE EMANATING FROM MY STAR GLIDER TENDS TO SMELL LIKE FRESH BREWED COFFEE.

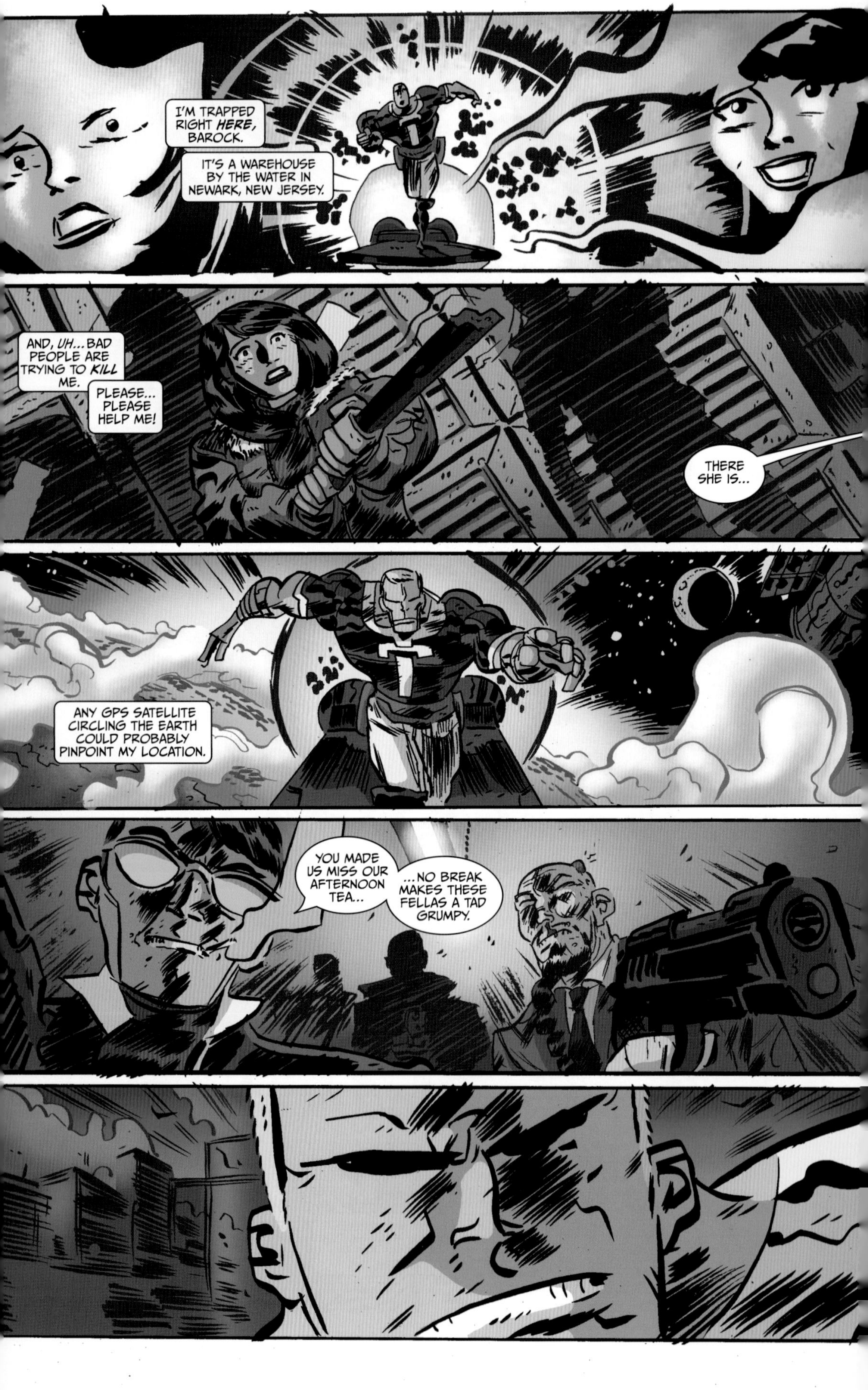
I'M TRAPPED RIGHT HERE, BAROCK.
IT'S A WAREHOUSE BY THE WATER IN NEWARK, NEW JERSEY.
AND, UH... BAD PEOPLE ARE TRYING TO KILL ME.
PLEASE... PLEASE HELP ME!
THERE SHE IS...
ANY GPS SATELLITE CIRCLING THE EARTH COULD PROBABLY PINPOINT MY LOCATION.
YOU MADE US MISS OUR AFTERNOON TEA...
...NO BREAK MAKES THESE FELLAS A TAD GRUMPY.

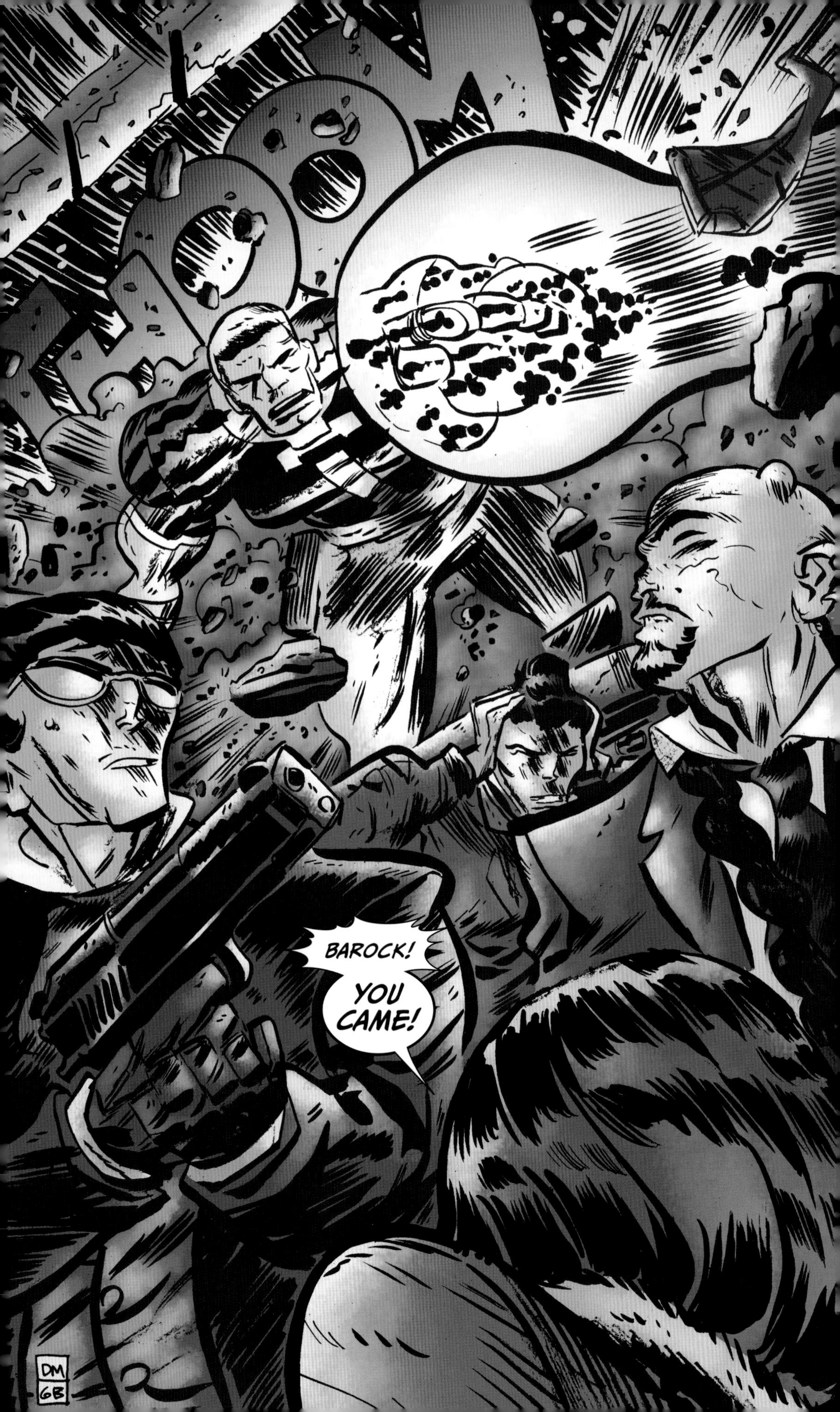
BAROCK!
YOU CAME!
DM
GB

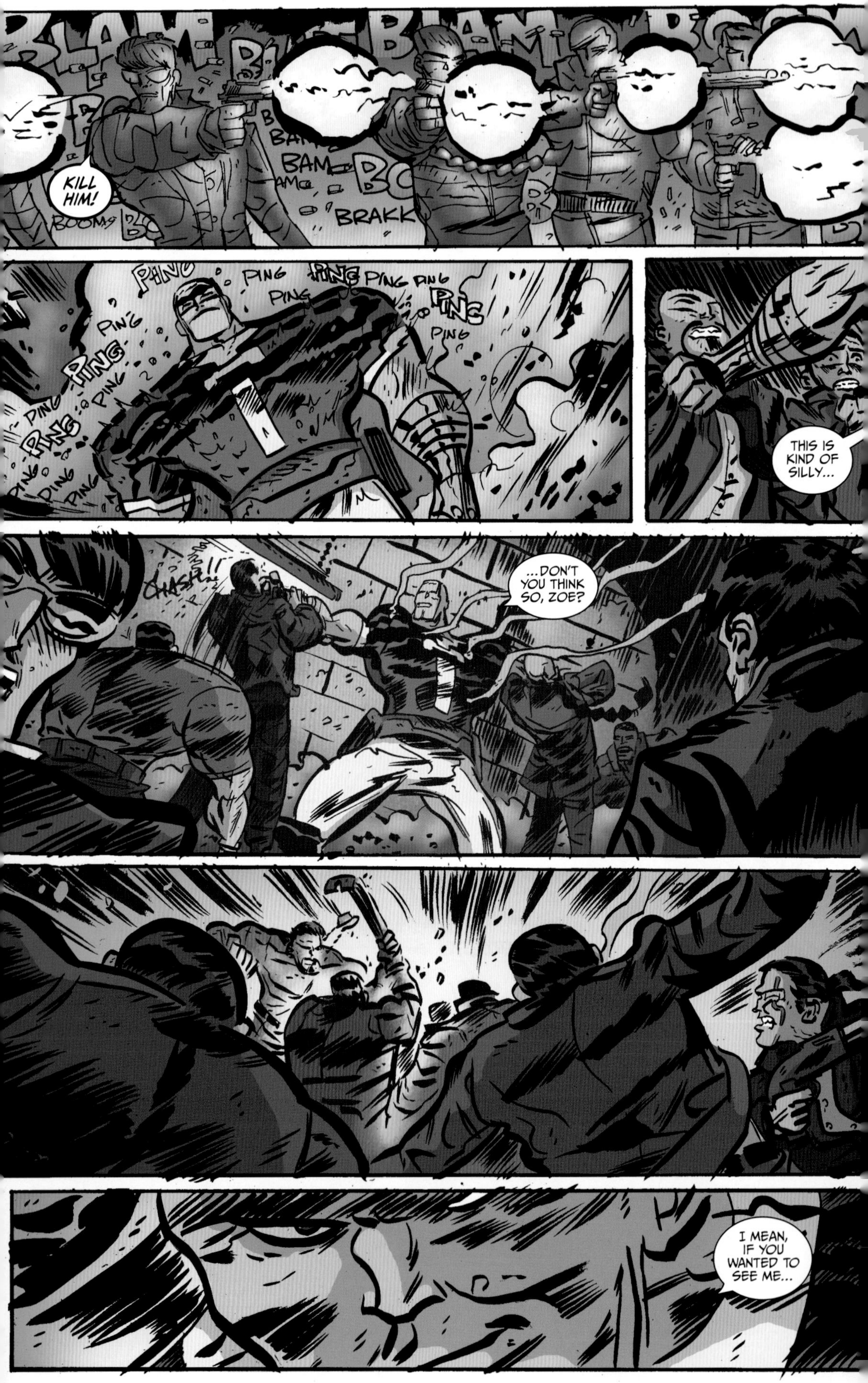
BLAM BLAM BOOM
BAM
BRAKK
KILL HIM!
PING PING PING
THIS IS KIND OF SILLY...
CHASH!!
...DON'T YOU THINK SO, ZOE?
I MEAN, IF YOU WANTED TO SEE ME...

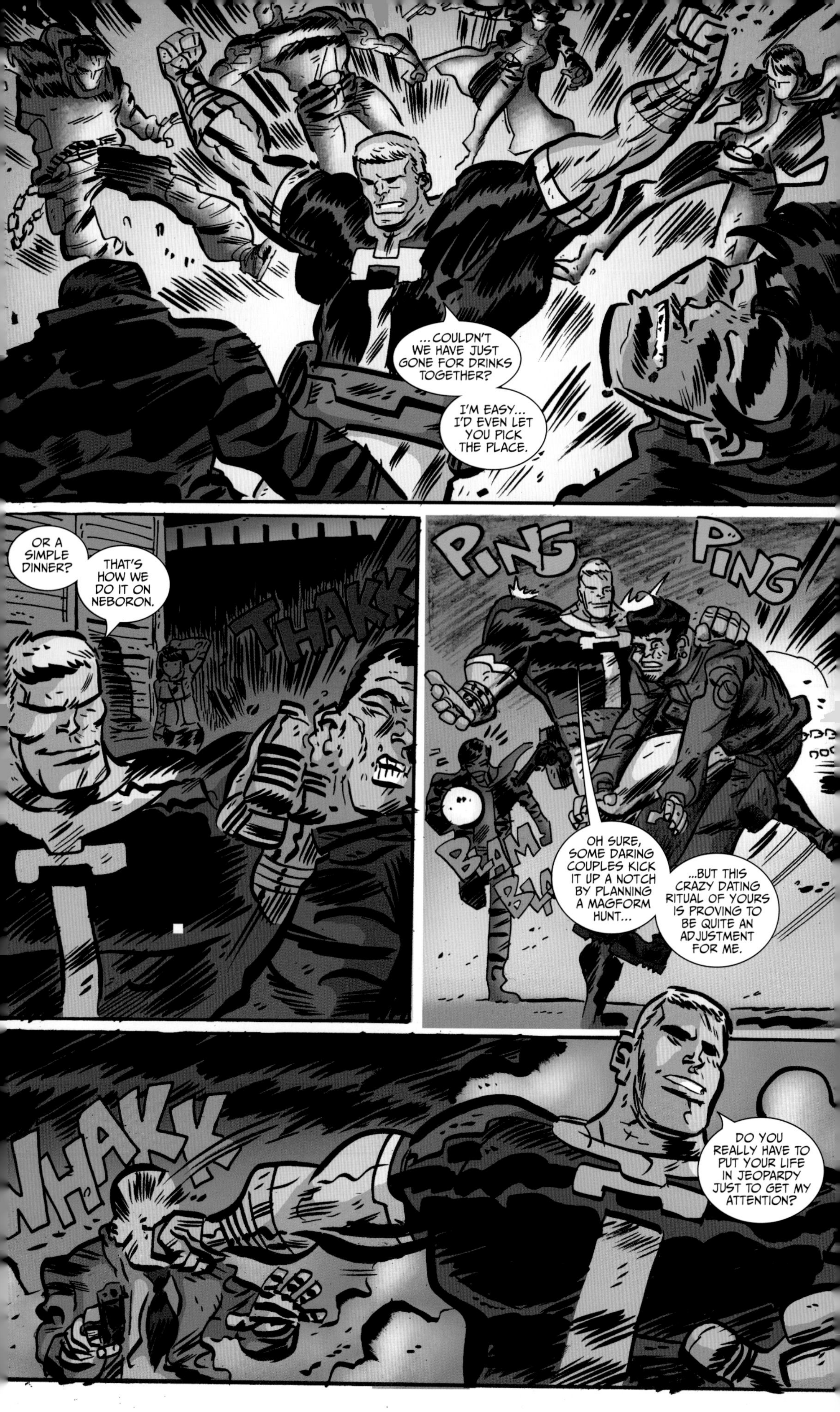
...COULDN'T WE HAVE JUST GONE FOR DRINKS TOGETHER?
I'M EASY... I'D EVEN LET YOU PICK THE PLACE.
OR A SIMPLE DINNER?
THAT'S HOW WE DO IT ON NEBORON.
THAKK
PING
PING
OH SURE, SOME DARING COUPLES KICK IT UP A NOTCH BY PLANNING A MAGFORM HUNT...
...BUT THIS CRAZY DATING RITUAL OF YOURS IS PROVING TO BE QUITE AN ADJUSTMENT FOR ME.
THAKK
DO YOU REALLY HAVE TO PUT YOUR LIFE IN JEOPARDY JUST TO GET MY ATTENTION?

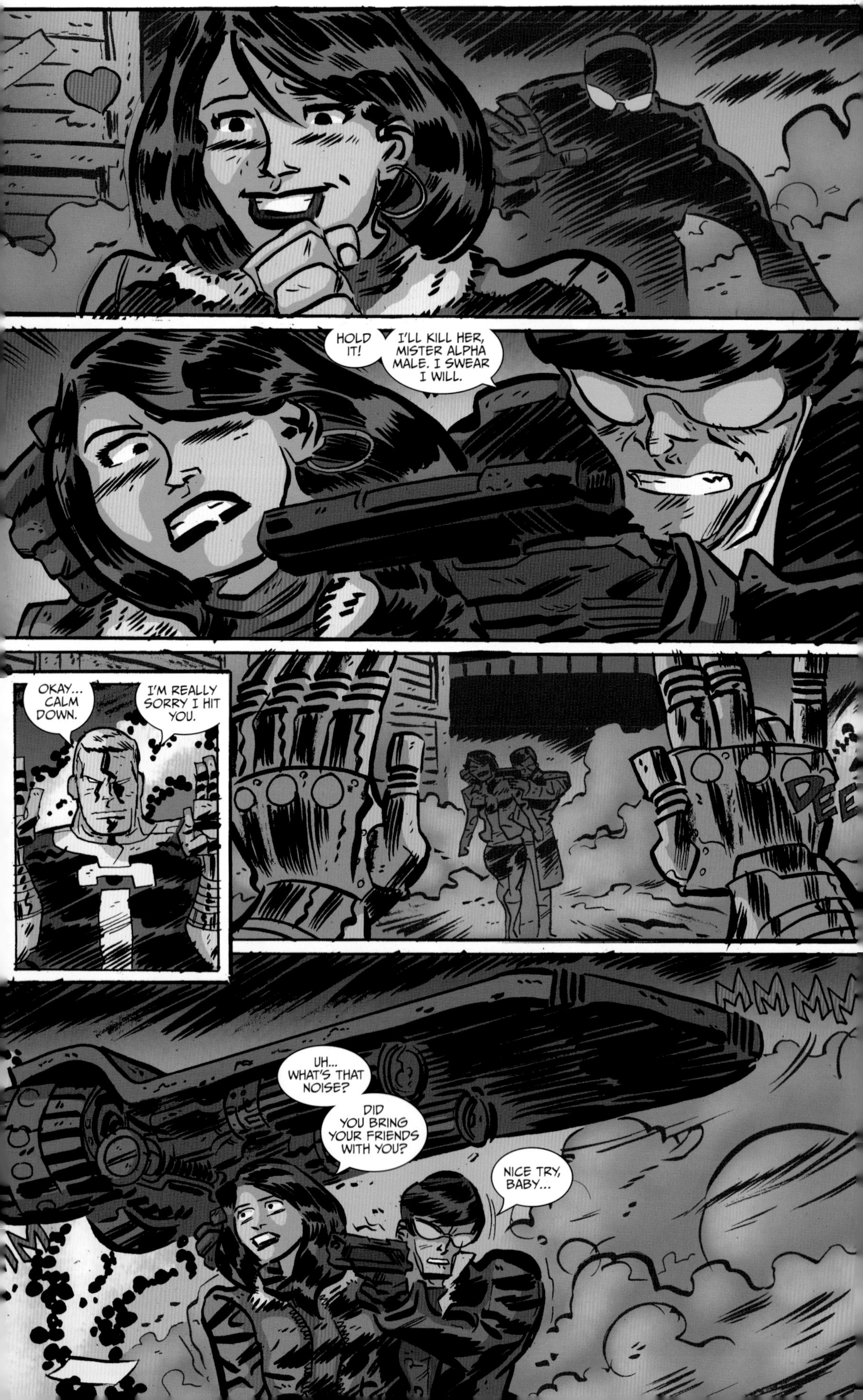

HOLD IT!
I'LL KILL HER, MISTER ALPHA MALE. I SWEAR I WILL.
OKAY... CALM DOWN.
I'M REALLY SORRY I HIT YOU.
DEE
MMMN
UH... WHAT'S THAT NOISE?
DID YOU BRING YOUR FRIENDS WITH YOU?
NICE TRY, BABY...

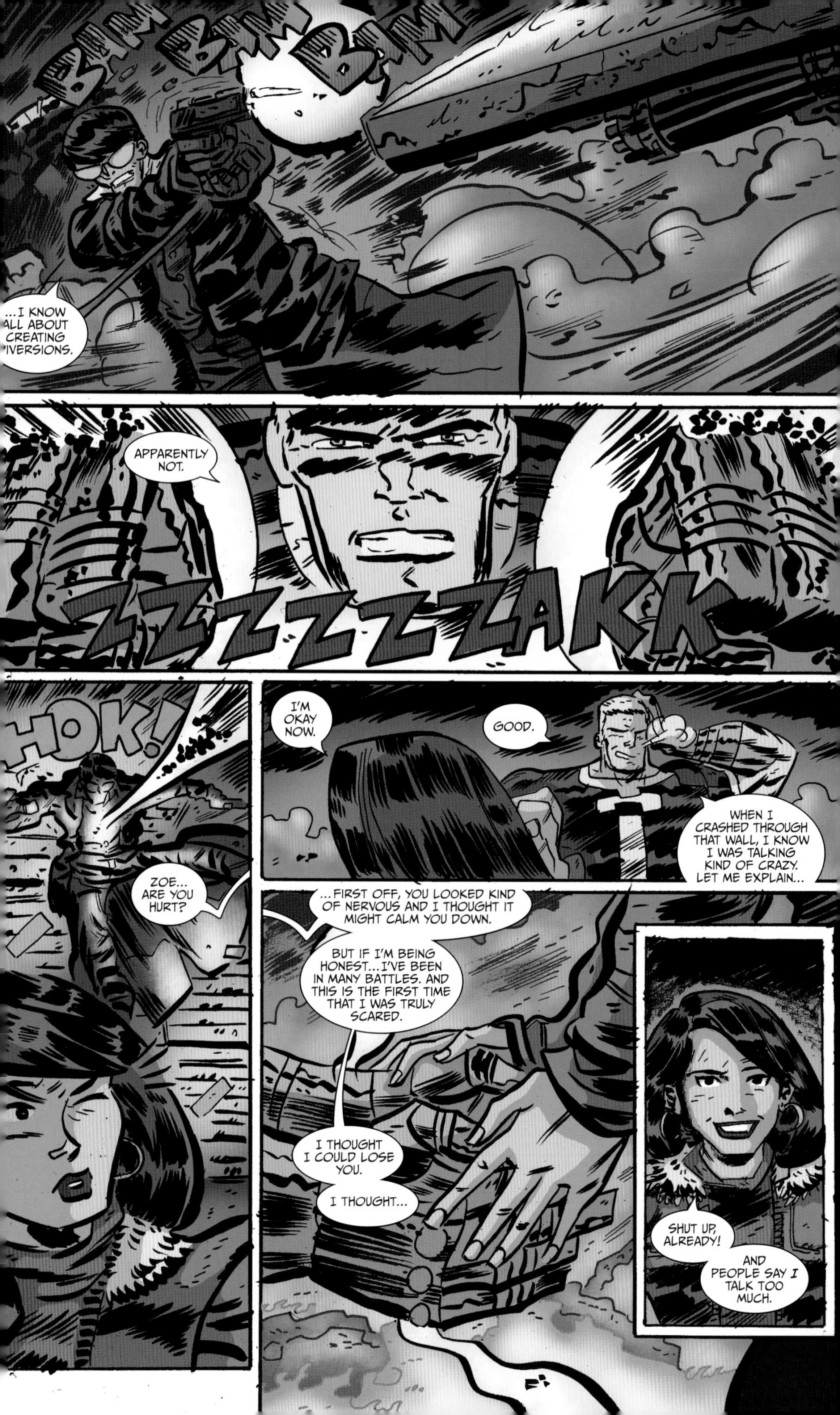
BIM BIM BIM
...I KNOW ALL ABOUT CREATING DIVERSIONS.
APPARENTLY NOT.
ZZZZZZAKK
HOK!
ZOE... ARE YOU HURT?
I'M OKAY NOW.
GOOD.
WHEN I CRASHED THROUGH THAT WALL, I KNOW I WAS TALKING KIND OF CRAZY. LET ME EXPLAIN...
...FIRST OFF, YOU LOOKED KIND OF NERVOUS AND I THOUGHT IT MIGHT CALM YOU DOWN.
BUT IF I'M BEING HONEST...I'VE BEEN IN MANY BATTLES. AND THIS IS THE FIRST TIME THAT I WAS TRULY SCARED.
I THOUGHT I COULD LOSE YOU.
I THOUGHT...
SHUT UP, ALREADY!
AND PEOPLE SAY I TALK TOO MUCH.

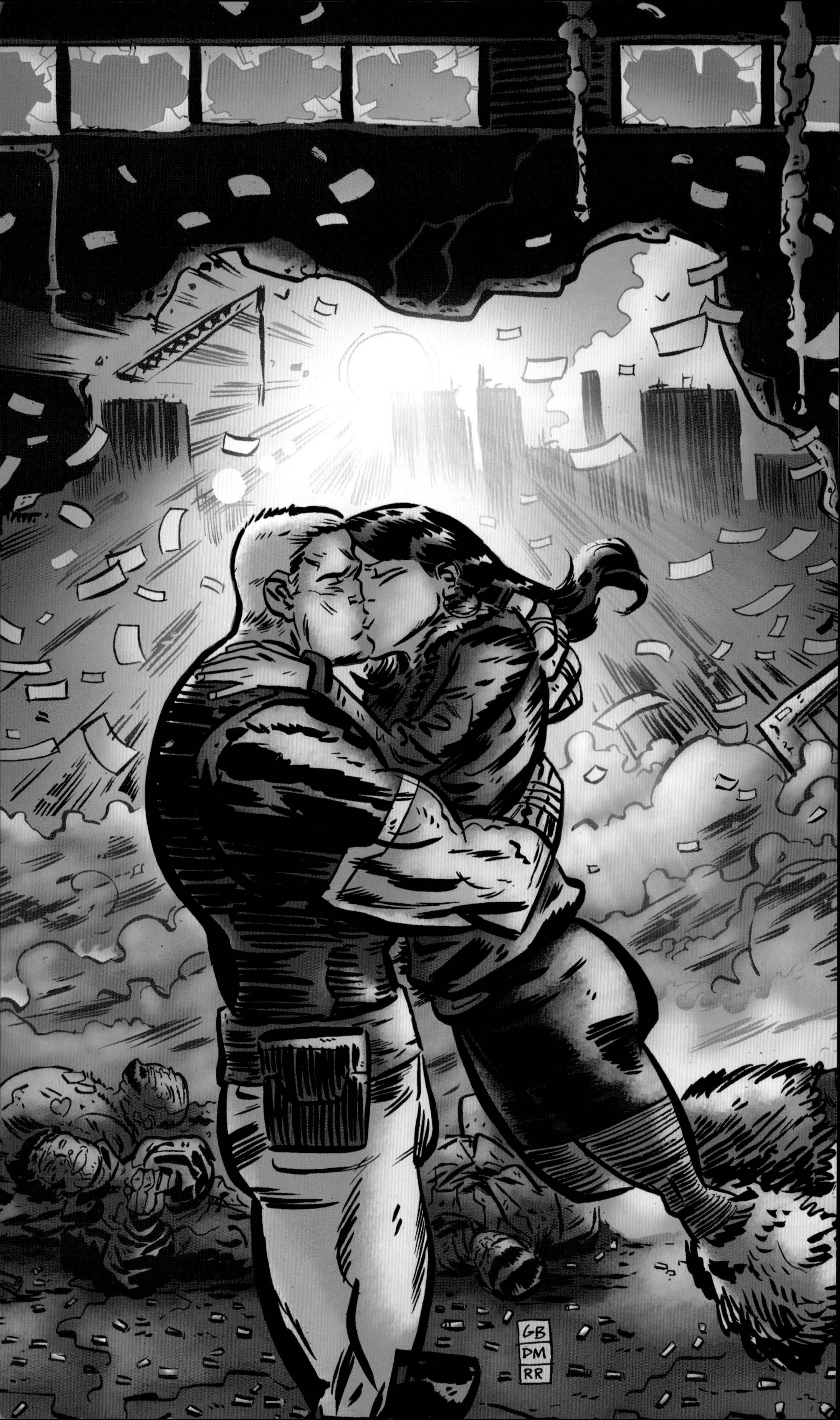
GB
DM
RR

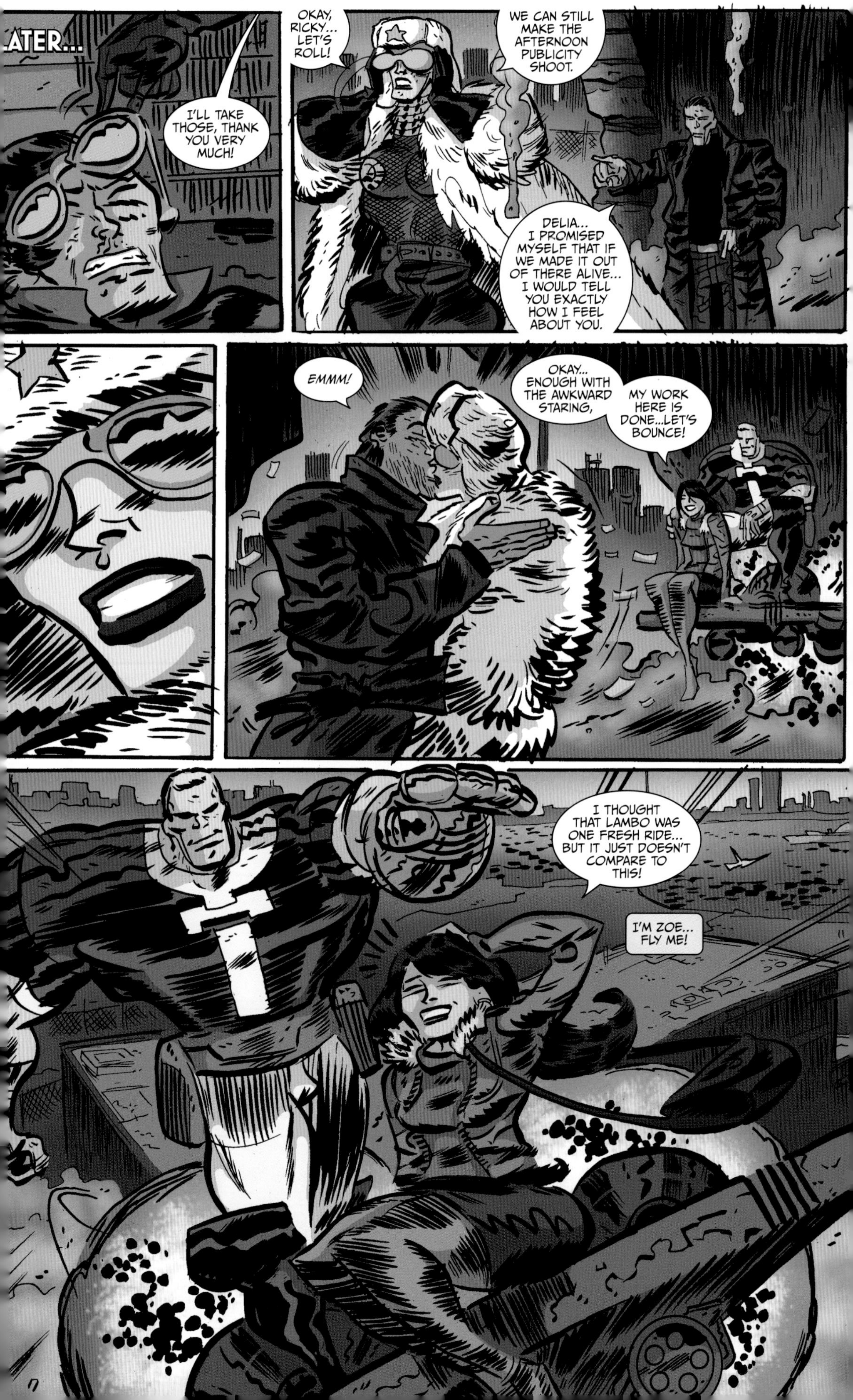
LATER...
I'LL TAKE THOSE, THANK YOU VERY MUCH!
OKAY, RICKY... LET'S ROLL!
WE CAN STILL MAKE THE AFTERNOON PUBLICITY SHOOT.
DELIA... I PROMISED MYSELF THAT IF WE MADE IT OUT OF THERE ALIVE... I WOULD TELL YOU EXACTLY HOW I FEEL ABOUT YOU.
EMMM!
OKAY... ENOUGH WITH THE AWKWARD STARING,
MY WORK HERE IS DONE...LET'S BOUNCE!
I THOUGHT THAT LAMBO WAS ONE FRESH RIDE... BUT IT JUST DOESN'T COMPARE TO THIS!
I'M ZOE... FLY ME!

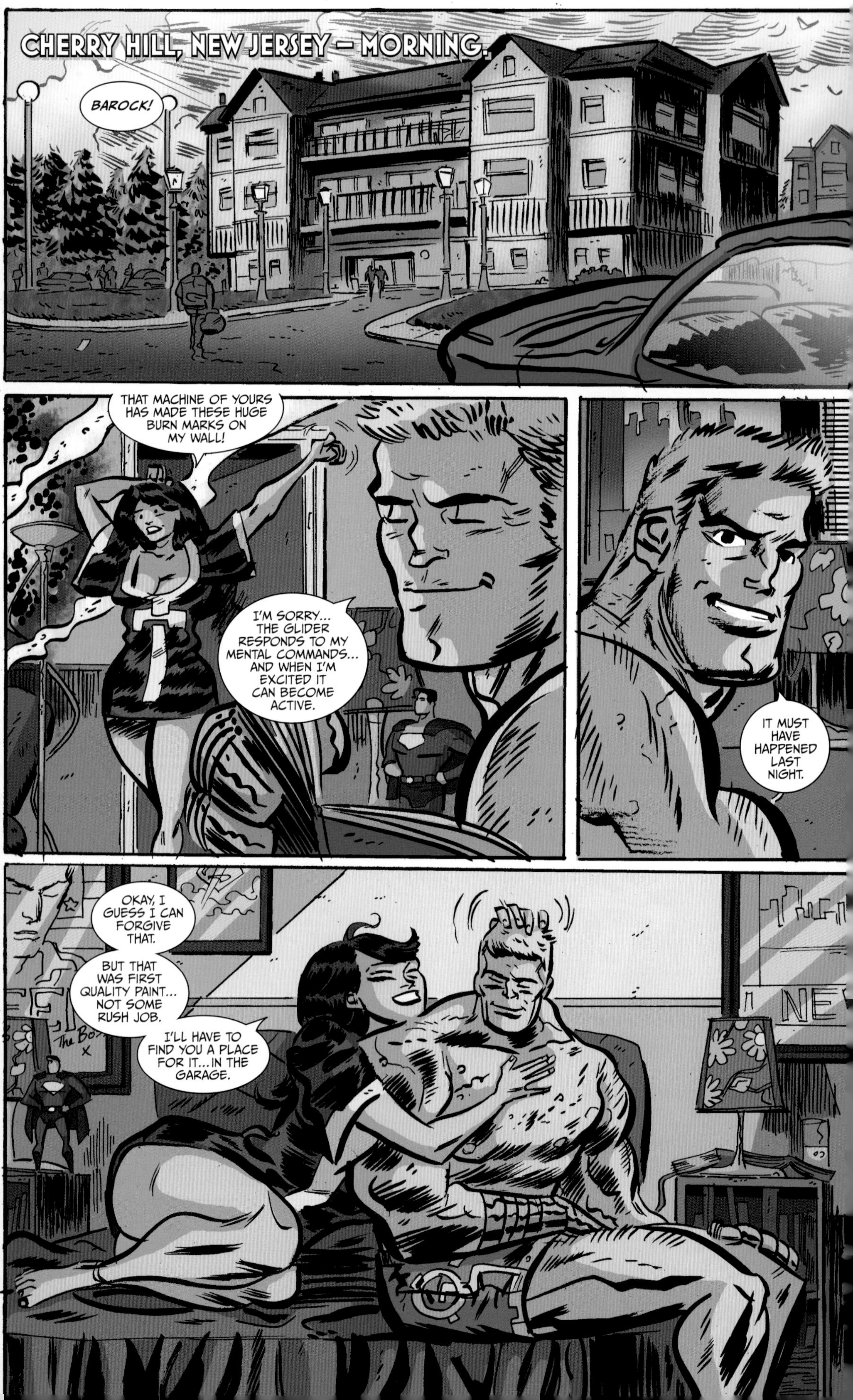
CHERRY HILL, NEW JERSEY – MORNING.
BAROCK!
THAT MACHINE OF YOURS HAS MADE THESE HUGE BURN MARKS ON MY WALL!
I'M SORRY... THE GLIDER RESPONDS TO MY MENTAL COMMANDS... AND WHEN I'M EXCITED IT CAN BECOME ACTIVE.
IT MUST HAVE HAPPENED LAST NIGHT.
OKAY, I GUESS I CAN FORGIVE THAT.
BUT THAT WAS FIRST QUALITY PAINT... NOT SOME RUSH JOB.
I'LL HAVE TO FIND YOU A PLACE FOR IT...IN THE GARAGE.

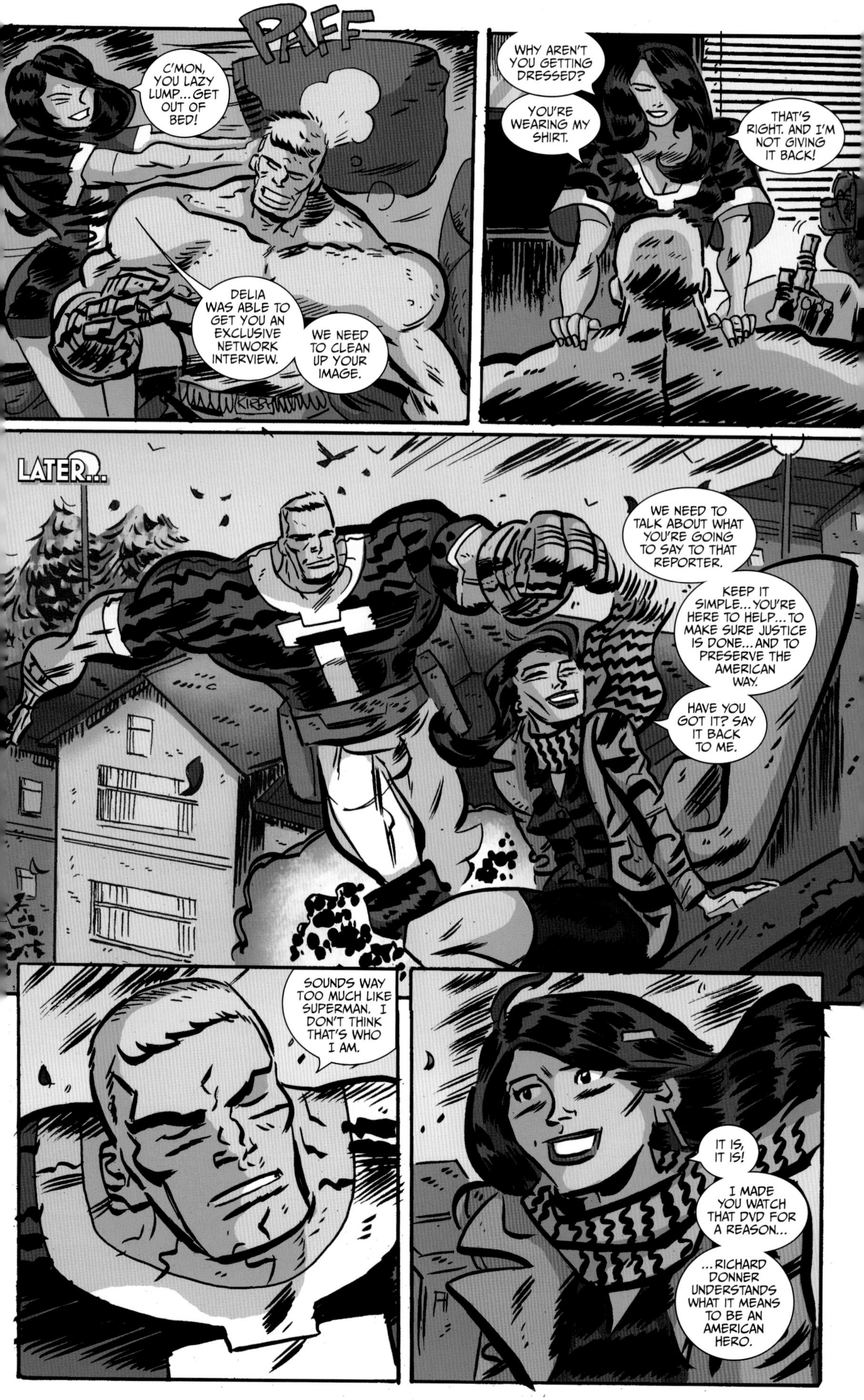
PAFF
C'MON, YOU LAZY LUMP...GET OUT OF BED!
DELIA WAS ABLE TO GET YOU AN EXCLUSIVE NETWORK INTERVIEW.
WE NEED TO CLEAN UP YOUR IMAGE.
WHY AREN'T YOU GETTING DRESSED?
YOU'RE WEARING MY SHIRT.
THAT'S RIGHT. AND I'M NOT GIVING IT BACK!
LATER...
WE NEED TO TALK ABOUT WHAT YOU'RE GOING TO SAY TO THAT REPORTER.
KEEP IT SIMPLE...YOU'RE HERE TO HELP...TO MAKE SURE JUSTICE IS DONE...AND TO PRESERVE THE AMERICAN WAY.
HAVE YOU GOT IT? SAY IT BACK TO ME.
SOUNDS WAY TOO MUCH LIKE SUPERMAN. I DON'T THINK THAT'S WHO I AM.
IT IS, IT IS!
I MADE YOU WATCH THAT DVD FOR A REASON...
...RICHARD DONNER UNDERSTANDS WHAT IT MEANS TO BE AN AMERICAN HERO.

ROCKEFELLER CENTER.

RICHARD WHO?

THE DIRECTOR... OF THE FILM WE SAW.

LOOK, ZOE... DON'T WORRY. I KNOW WHAT I'M GOING TO SAY.

I'M STANDING HERE BESIDE BAROCK – WHO CLAIMS TO BE A GOD FROM THE PLANET NEBORON. BAROCK WAS INVOLVED IN THAT MASSIVE DESTRUCTION TWO WEEKS AGO AT THE BRAND NEW CHERRY HILL SHOPPING MALL IN NEW JERSEY.

THIS REPORTER HAS BEEN INFORMED HOWEVER THAT HIS PURPOSE HERE IS IN FACT BENEVOLENT. HE HAS BEEN SENT HERE TO HELP US.

IS THIS TRUE, BAROCK? IS THAT WHY YOU'RE HERE?

NO... NOT EXACTLY.

I'VE RECENTLY STUDIED YOUR EARTH MYTHS – HOW A HERO FROM ANOTHER PLANET COMES TO FIGHT FOR TRUTH, JUSTICE AND THE AMERICAN WAY...

...BUT I DIDN'T COME HERE FOR THAT.

I'M HERE FOR SOMET[H]... MUCH MOR... IMPORTANT...

LIVE   "BAROCK"   NY-1

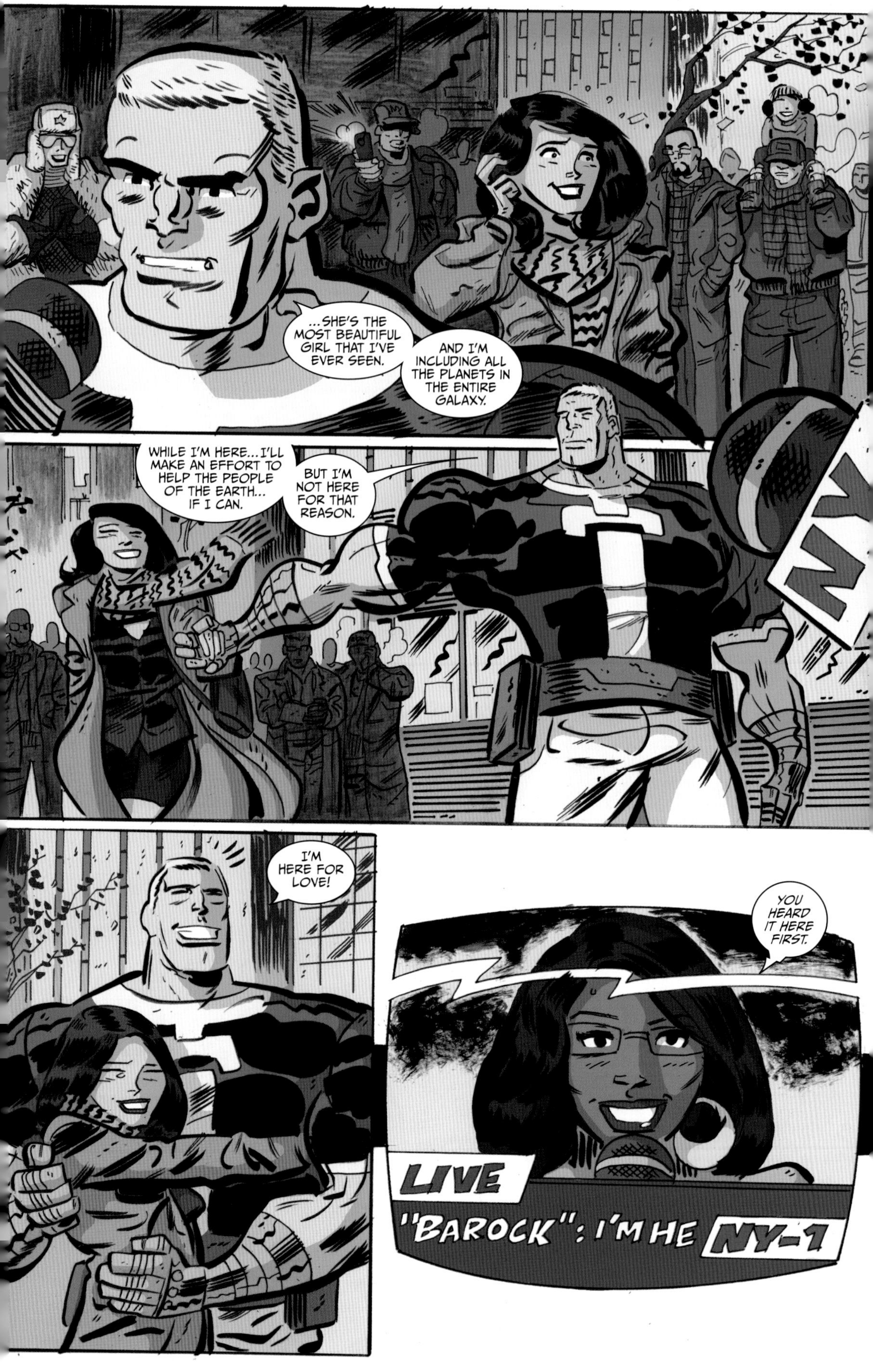
...SHE'S THE MOST BEAUTIFUL GIRL THAT I'VE EVER SEEN.
AND I'M INCLUDING ALL THE PLANETS IN THE ENTIRE GALAXY.
WHILE I'M HERE...I'LL MAKE AN EFFORT TO HELP THE PEOPLE OF THE EARTH... IF I CAN.
BUT I'M NOT HERE FOR THAT REASON.
NY
I'M HERE FOR LOVE!
YOU HEARD IT HERE FIRST.
LIVE
"BAROCK": I'M HE
NY-1

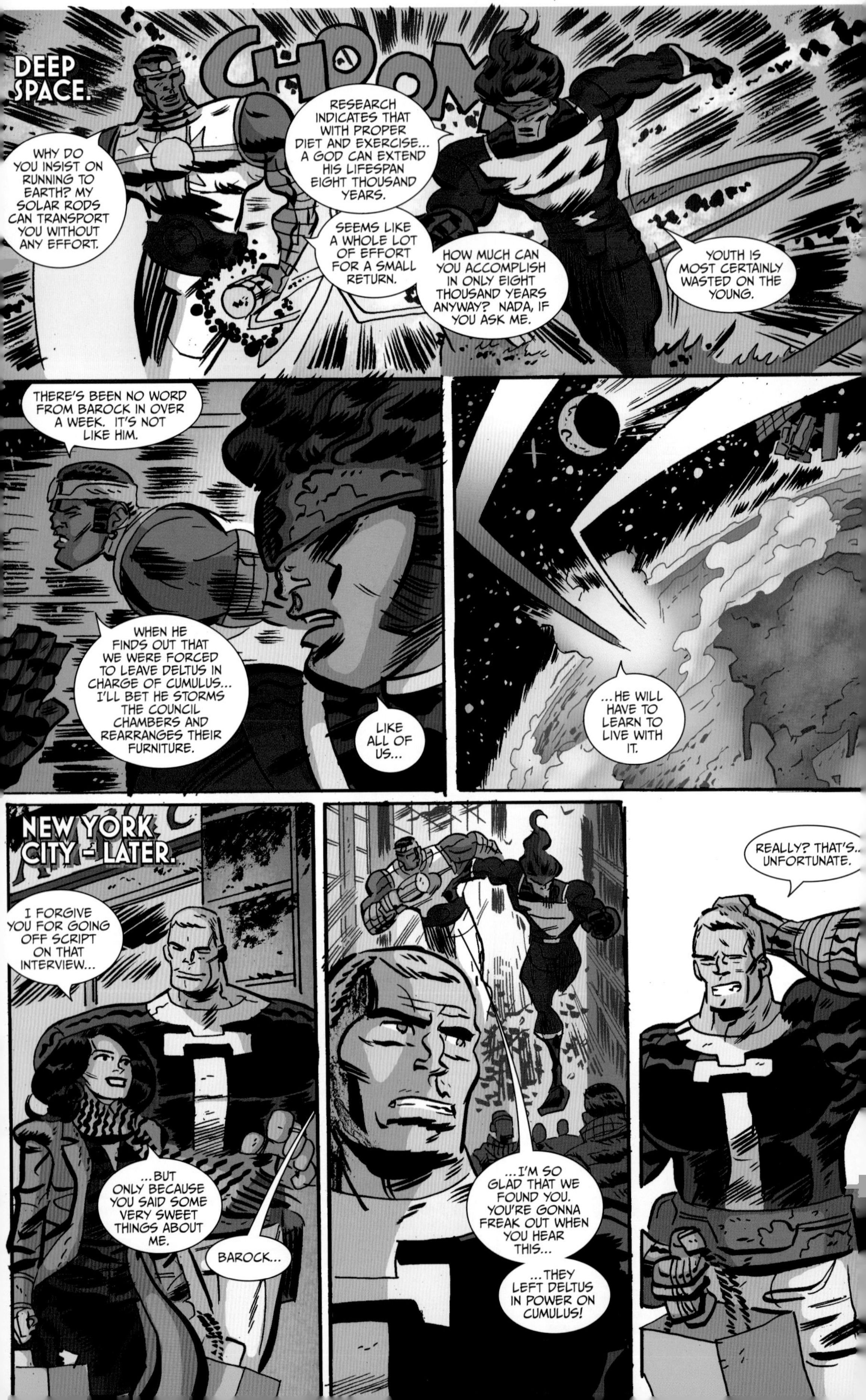
DEEP SPACE.
CHOOM
WHY DO YOU INSIST ON RUNNING TO EARTH? MY SOLAR RODS CAN TRANSPORT YOU WITHOUT ANY EFFORT.
RESEARCH INDICATES THAT WITH PROPER DIET AND EXERCISE... A GOD CAN EXTEND HIS LIFESPAN EIGHT THOUSAND YEARS.
SEEMS LIKE A WHOLE LOT OF EFFORT FOR A SMALL RETURN.
HOW MUCH CAN YOU ACCOMPLISH IN ONLY EIGHT THOUSAND YEARS ANYWAY? NADA, IF YOU ASK ME.
YOUTH IS MOST CERTAINLY WASTED ON THE YOUNG.
THERE'S BEEN NO WORD FROM BAROCK IN OVER A WEEK. IT'S NOT LIKE HIM.
WHEN HE FINDS OUT THAT WE WERE FORCED TO LEAVE DELTUS IN CHARGE OF CUMULUS... I'LL BET HE STORMS THE COUNCIL CHAMBERS AND REARRANGES THEIR FURNITURE.
LIKE ALL OF US...
...HE WILL HAVE TO LEARN TO LIVE WITH IT.
NEW YORK CITY - LATER.
I FORGIVE YOU FOR GOING OFF SCRIPT ON THAT INTERVIEW...
...BUT ONLY BECAUSE YOU SAID SOME VERY SWEET THINGS ABOUT ME.
BAROCK...
...I'M SO GLAD THAT WE FOUND YOU. YOU'RE GONNA FREAK OUT WHEN YOU HEAR THIS...
...THEY LEFT DELTUS IN POWER ON CUMULUS!
REALLY? THAT'S... UNFORTUNATE.

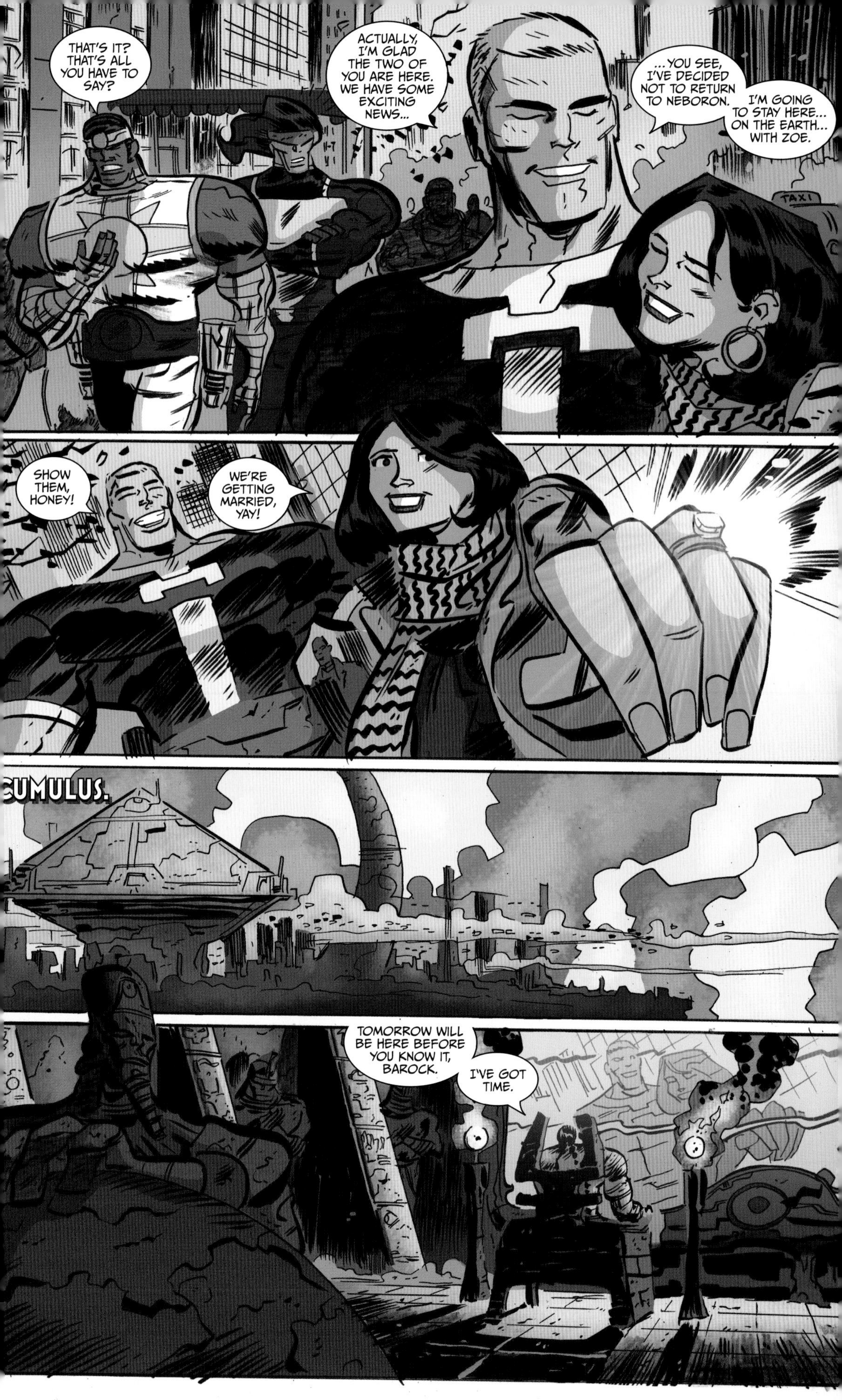
THAT'S IT? THAT'S ALL YOU HAVE TO SAY?
ACTUALLY, I'M GLAD THE TWO OF YOU ARE HERE. WE HAVE SOME EXCITING NEWS...
...YOU SEE, I'VE DECIDED NOT TO RETURN TO NEBORON.
I'M GOING TO STAY HERE... ON THE EARTH... WITH ZOE.
TAXI
SHOW THEM, HONEY!
WE'RE GETTING MARRIED, YAY!
CUMULUS.
TOMORROW WILL BE HERE BEFORE YOU KNOW IT, BAROCK.
I'VE GOT TIME.

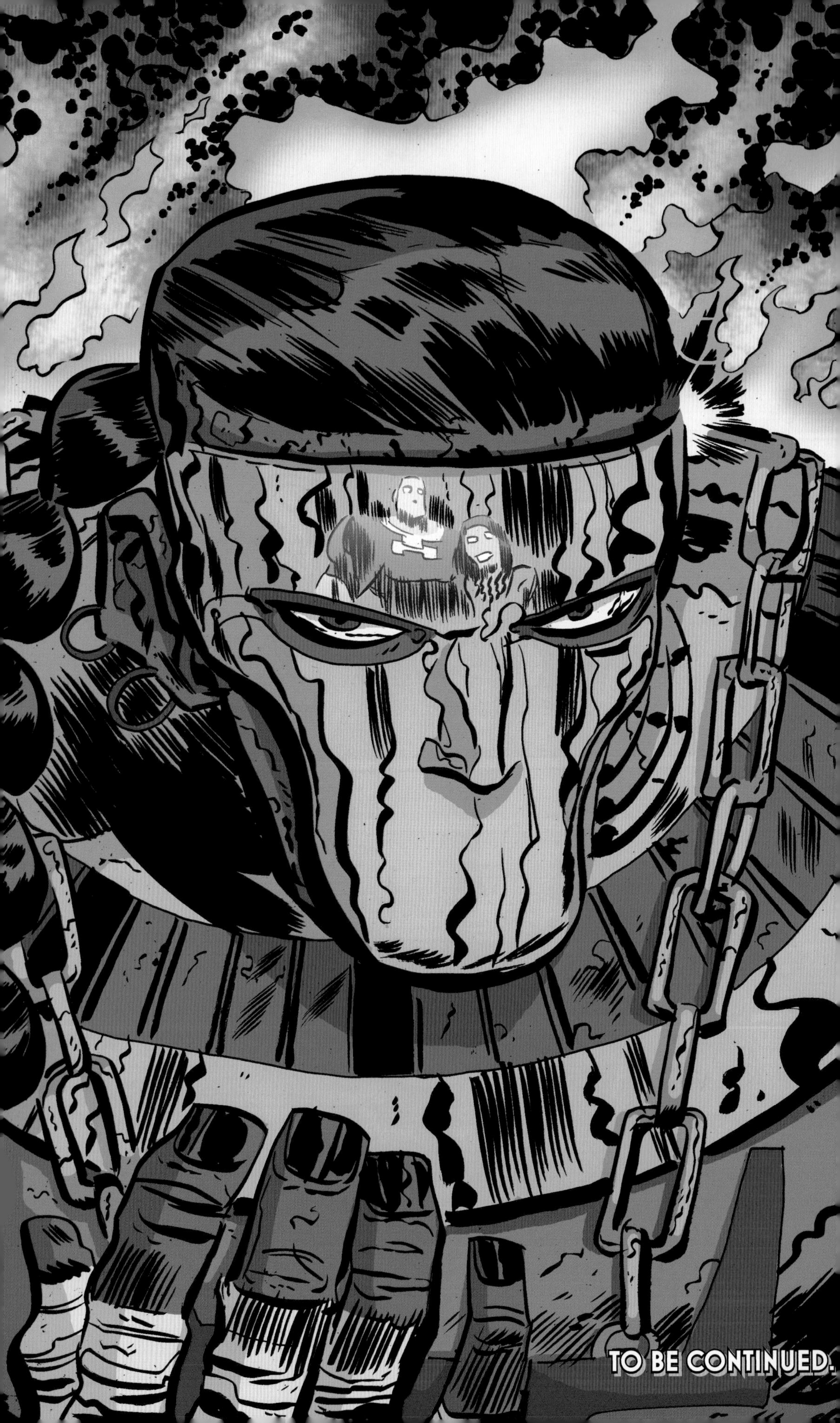
TO BE CONTINUED.

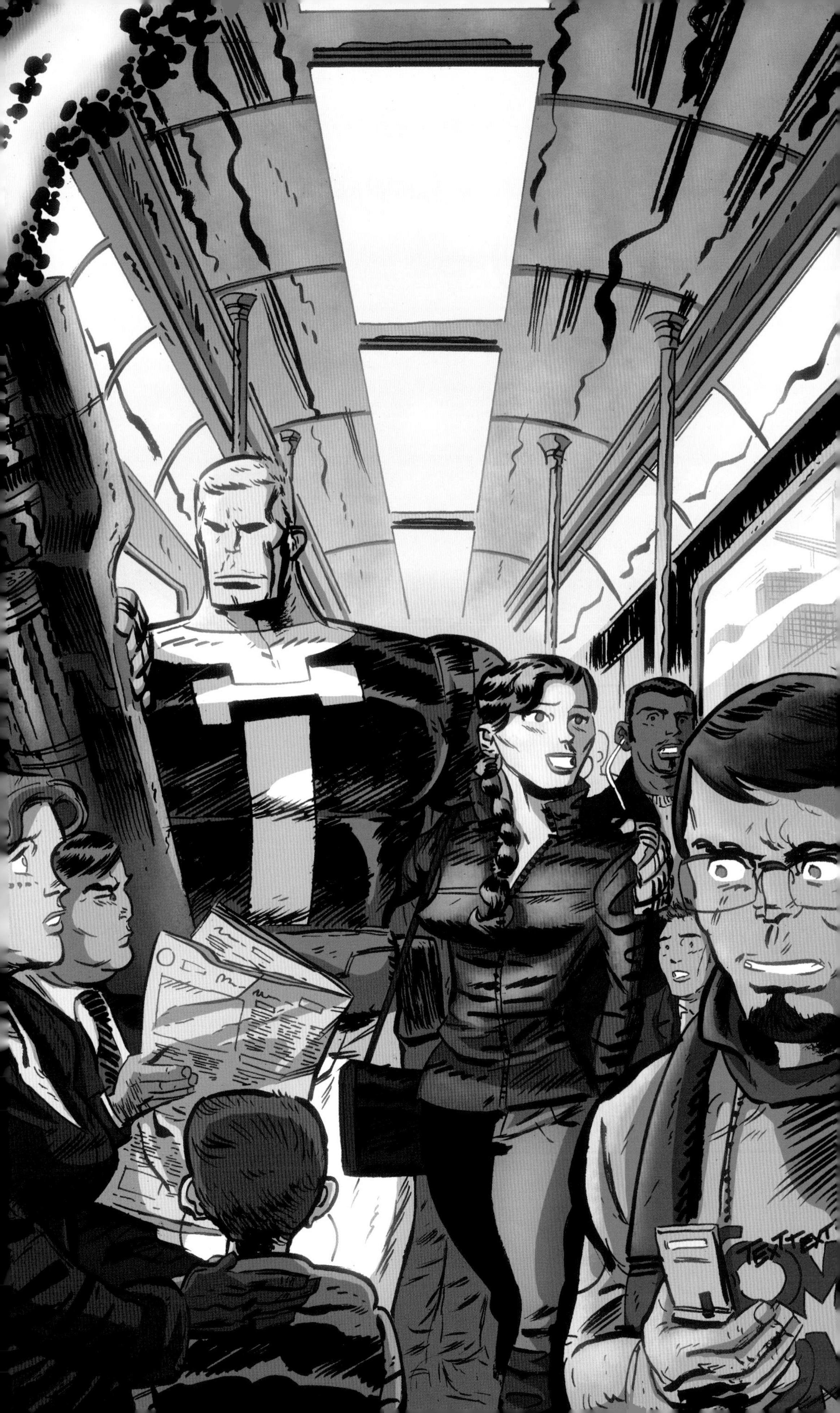
TEXT-TEXT

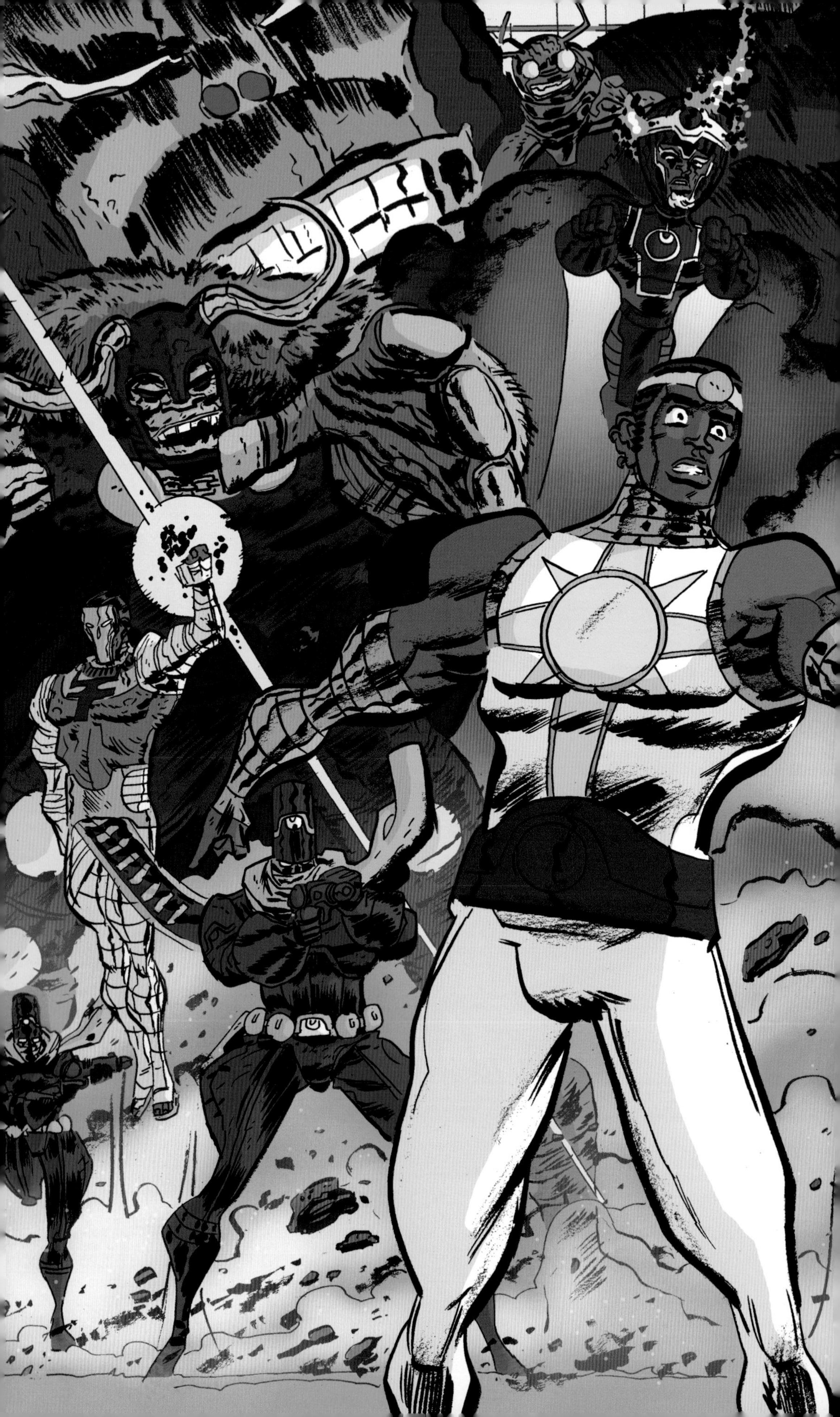

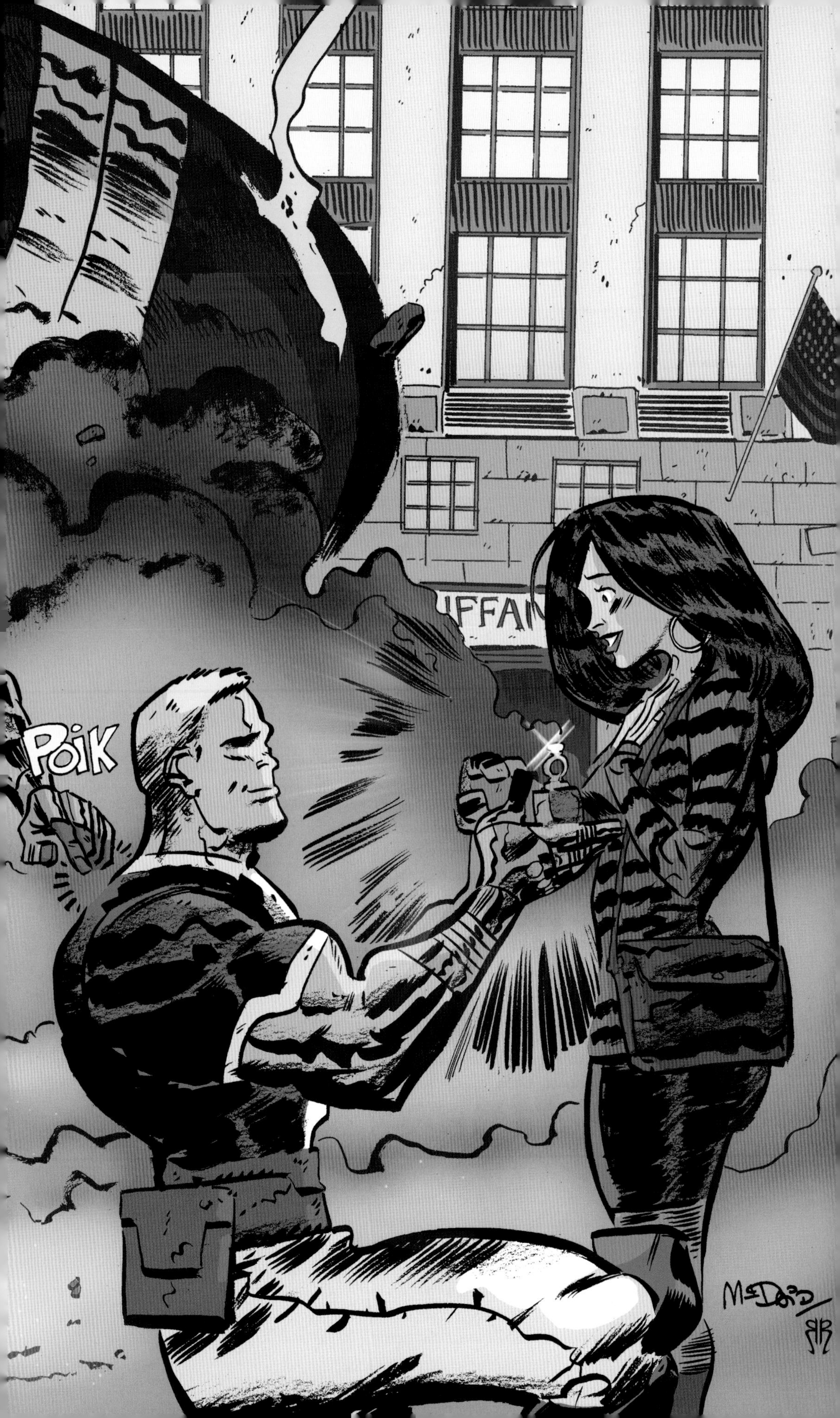
POIK

JERSEY GODS EXTRAS

DM: Hello everyone, I'm Dan McDaid, and I'm the artist-in-residence on Jersey Gods. Over the next few pages, I'll be showing off some never-before-seen design sketches and thumbnails, and Glen and I will be filling the space between pictures with a load of old rubbish about... well, pretty much whatever comes to mind. So sit back, remove your trousers and enjoy!

GB: Glen Brunswick, here. I think I should point out, Dan, that some of us over here in the colonies like to read with our pants on. Okay... I'm going to kiss up to Dan a little bit now and tell you all what an amazing artist I think he is. It's unfortunate that I have to do this in print, 'cause he almost certainly will hold it against me.

DM: Yeah, I pretty much will. Sorry about that.

GB: Dan can draw anything — from huge alien cities to small intimate moments between two characters. He's going to be a major force in the comic book industry. I was just lucky to nab him for Jersey Gods first. But the thing that's really exciting for me is seeing his evolution as a comic artist right before my eyes. I thought the job he did on our first issue was fantastic, and then my jaw dropped as he just got better and better with each subsequent issue. In this art section you can see where he began and just how far he's come. And the good news for me is this is only the beginning of the three year story arc we have planned out for all of you. It's going to be quite a ride!

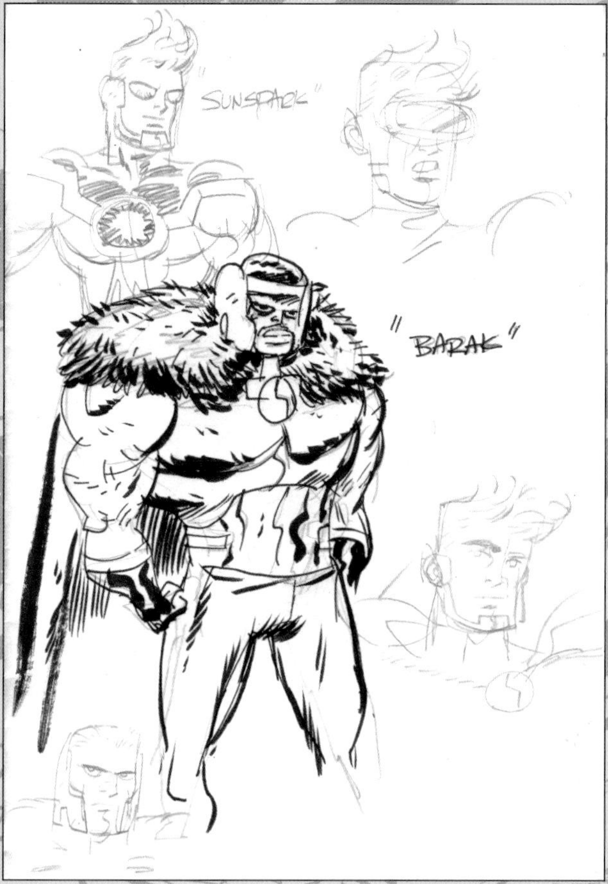
"SUNSPARK"
"BARAK"

DM: This, believe it or not is Barock (or Barak, as he was back then). This design was a bit of a false-step during the inception of the book: too thuggish, too inhuman, too "hulking". More of a villain than a hero. Behind him we can some early designs for Helius (or Sun-spark as he was back then). None of this stuck, though you can see hints at how Barock would work out from that corner left pic.

GB: We changed his name because Obama beat Hillary Clinton who was supposed to make history and be the nominee. The problem is we changed it to a name that is spelled differently but still sounds like our President's name. My feeling is if we wait him out, Obama will change his name before we have to change our character. We can wait... he's only going to be President another seven years tops, right?

DM: Right. Only problem is, I hear he's changing his name to Helius.

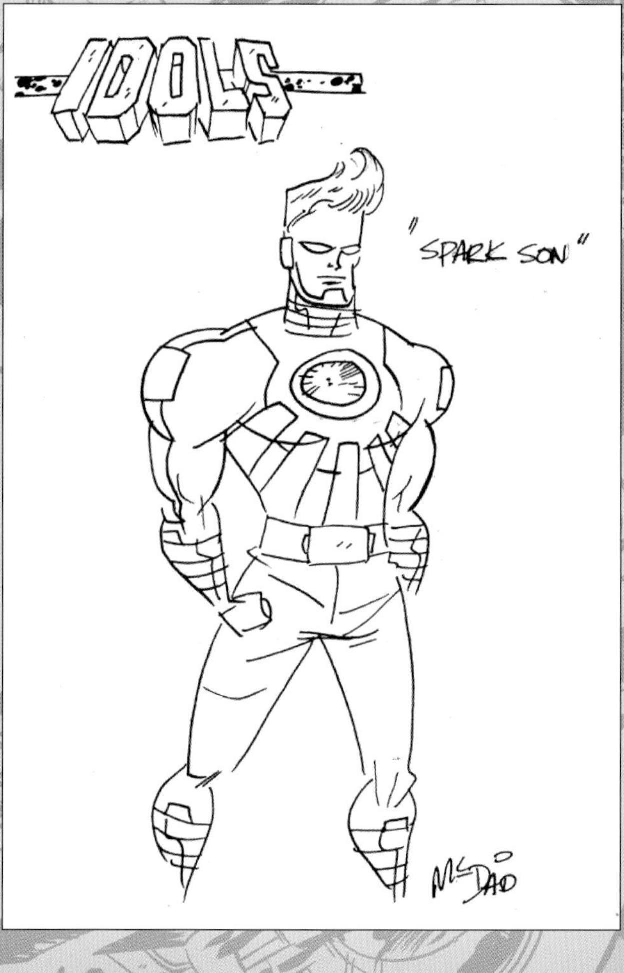
IDOLS
"SPARK SON"

DM: Very early Helius.

GB: What's up with that name? Spark Son? Would that make him the son of Spark?

DM: That was the plan. But who is Spark...?

IDOLS

BARRAC

FEROCIOUS FIGHTER, QUICK TEMPER,
LACKING IN SOCIAL GRACES. FIERCELY
LOYAL, UTTERLY DEPENDABLE,
INCREDIBLE STRATEGIST

UGLY AND SCARRED, BUT CHARISMATIC.
I THOUGHT WE COULD STEAL A LITTLE
GIMMICK FROM THE GOON AND VERY,
VERY RARELY SHOW HIS EYES -
MOSTLY HIDDEN BY HIS BROW.
RARELY SMILES AND WHEN HE
DOES... THAT MEANS THE WORST
SORT OF TROUBLE.

WEARS A HELM AND FURRED CLOAK
INTO BATTLE. THESE ITEMS SMELL OF
CANNON-FIRE AND MUSK.

DM: OK, now we're getting there. Still a couple of bum notes - too much fur, which contradicted Glen's "high-tech" vision for these characters, and the helmet didn't make it through...

GB: This was the first sketch that you showed me and I dug it. I knew we were on the same page with our hero. Exciting stuff from the very beginning.

DM: He's got a good face now, and has a cool "Thor-by-way-of-The-Goon" quality. Yeah, we're pretty much there. From here on in I just found ways to simplify him.

DM: And here's Helius! Bar some extra bells and whistles, this is pretty much the final iteration of this character. He originally had puffy sleeves - which I still like! Glen wasn't so keen...

GB: What super-hero worth his salt has puffy sleeves?

DM: Batman would look fabulous with puffy sleeves. And a tiara for that matter. Tiaras for men are gonna be massive in 2010 - you read it here first.

GB: I think I told you to make him look like Sidney Poitier. I wanted him handsome and cool. He's one of my favourite characters to write.

DM: One of my favourites to draw as well. Where Barock is hunched and heavy, Helius just kind of struts around the page. He's a sexy guy. And I'm always looking for ways to emphasise his package. And Barock's for that matter. I may have a problem...

GB: You're just repressed. I saw "Remains of the Day."

DM. Did you know what was going on? I know — it's a tough film. LOTTA talking.

SOLAR RODS CONTAIN THE POWER OF THE STARS, AND WHEN STRUCK TOGETHER CAN CAUSE THE NOVA FLASH"!

"HELIUS"
MK 3

McDAID

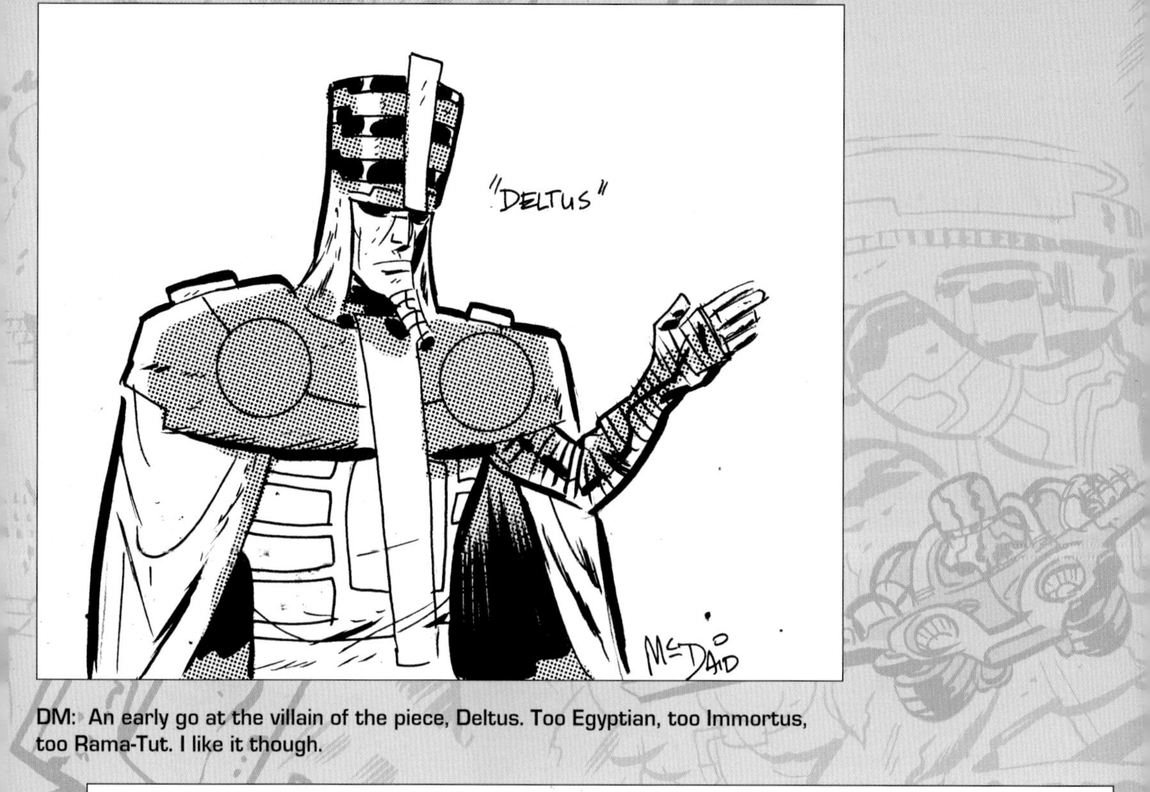
"DELTUS"
McDAID

DM: An early go at the villain of the piece, Deltus. Too Egyptian, too Immortus, too Rama-Tut. I like it though.

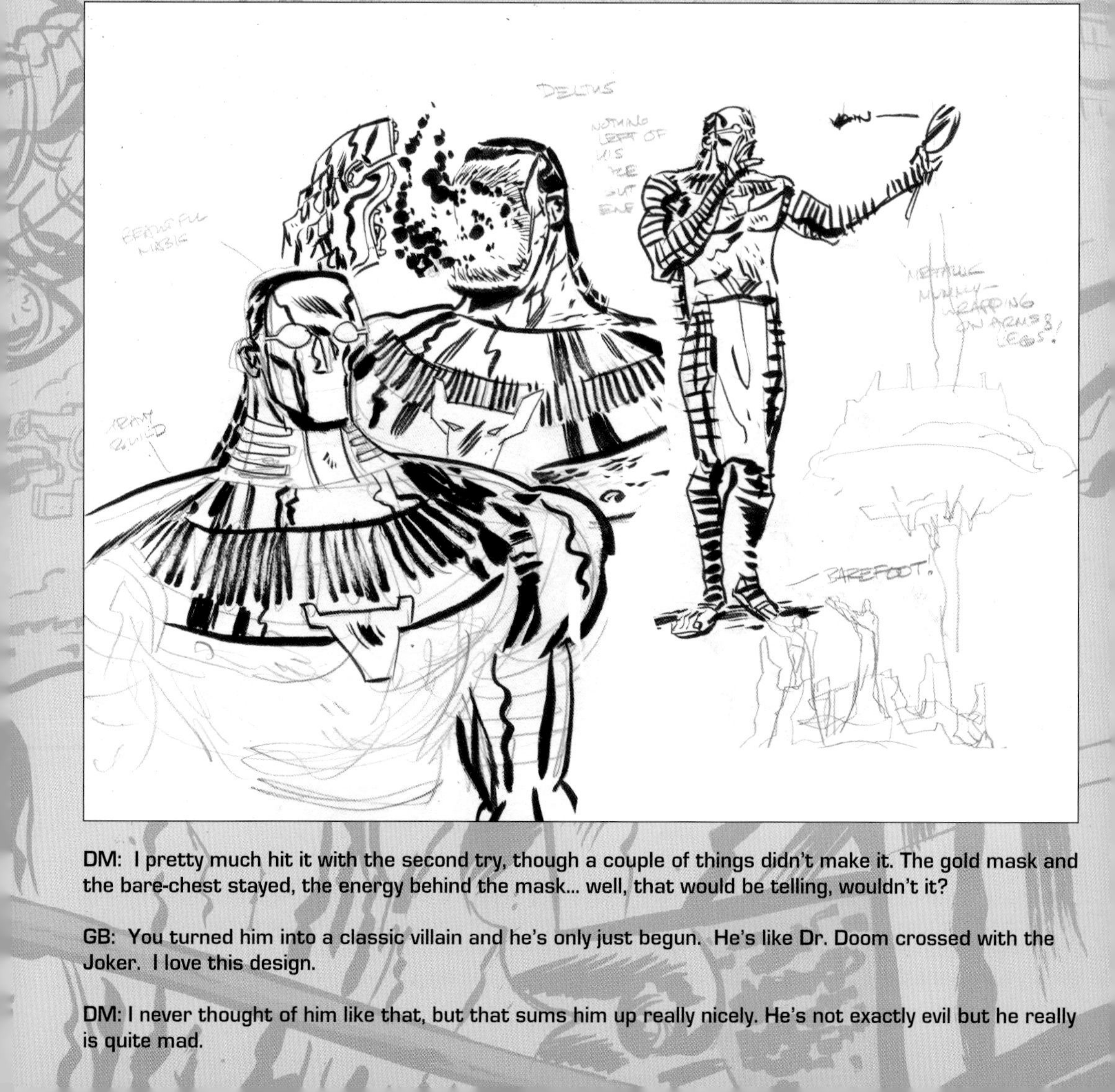
DELTUS
BAREFOOT!

DM: I pretty much hit it with the second try, though a couple of things didn't make it. The gold mask and the bare-chest stayed, the energy behind the mask... well, that would be telling, wouldn't it?

GB: You turned him into a classic villain and he's only just begun. He's like Dr. Doom crossed with the Joker. I love this design.

DM: I never thought of him like that, but that sums him up really nicely. He's not exactly evil but he really is quite mad.

DM: Hey, it's Zoe! I had a clear idea of how Zoe would look right from the start. She's a cross between a friend of mine and erstwhile BBC TV presenter Christine Bleakley. Bet Glen didn't know that...!

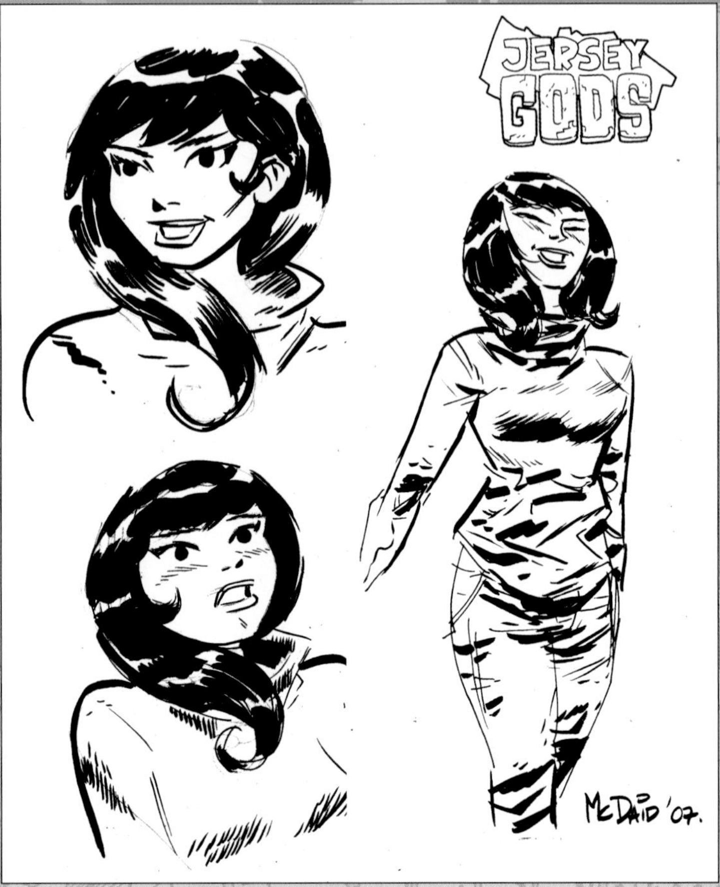
JERSEY GODS
McDAID '07.

GB: I loved the design for Zoe immediately.

DM: I did get her spectacularly wrong to begin with though. For the first two issues in fact. And that's all I'm saying about that!

GB: You mean you don't want to talk about how you thought I was a racist for the first two issues but you were willing to work with me anyway? I wanted Zoe to be a Jewish American Princess, but I referred to her as a JAP in the outline. I didn't realize that someone from across the pond would see that as a person of Japanese ethnicity. You're right, it's embarrassing. Let's not talk about it.

DM: I didn't realise until I phoned Glen one day and said something like "so... are both her parents Japanese?" And there was this stunned silence. And I pretty much thought that was it, and he would get in someone less daft. Luckily, that hasn't proven to be the case.

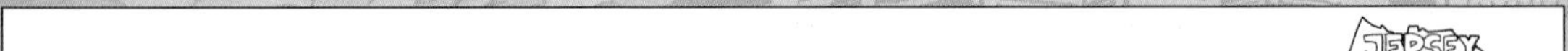
JERSEY GODS
"MINOG"
McDAID '07
RUSHMORE"
JERSEY GODS
McDAID
"CENTRUS"
McDAID '07

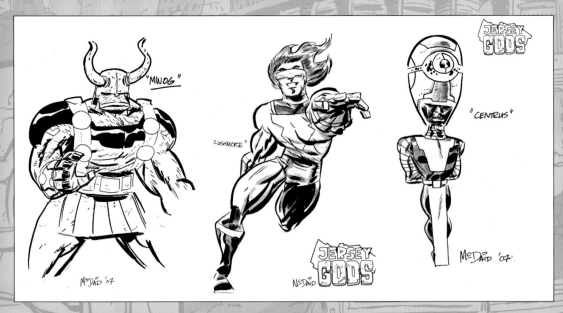

DM: Minog, Rushmore and Centrus. With Minog, we knew we wanted a heavy hitter for Barock to fight in issues one and two, and who better than a minotaur? Rushmore appeared fully-formed in my mind, though Glen cleverly tweaked him from the usual grinning speedster to more of a Spock-like figure. And with Centrus, we've got the anti-Spock — a devious, brilliant, morally ambiguous lackey.

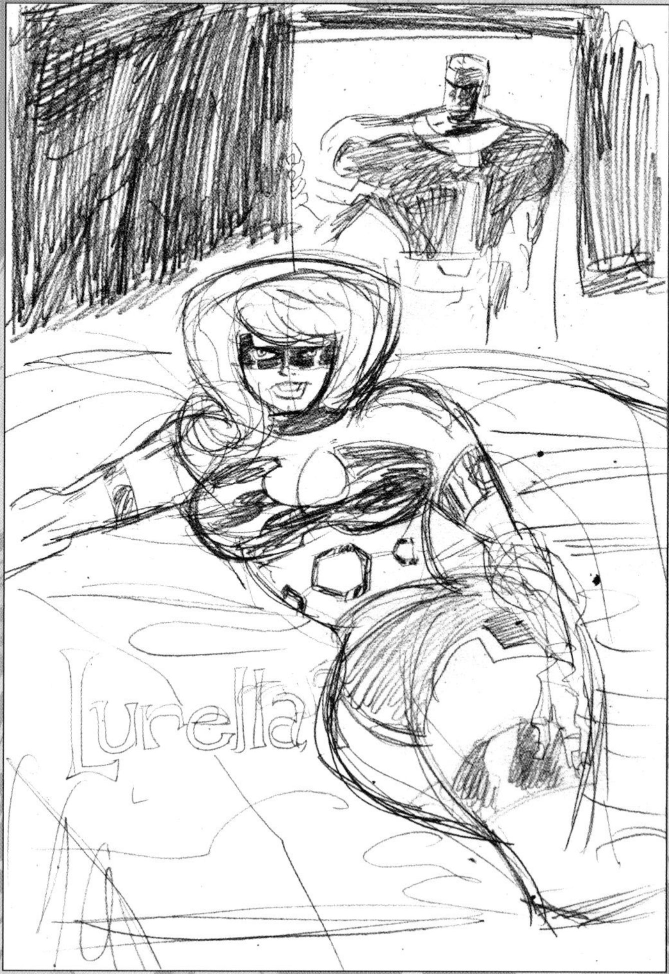
Lurella

DM: This is Lurella, in an early, sultry pose. She was definitely a lot slyer and sexier before she made it to the page. Now she's yer classic flame-haired warrior woman with a mad-on/crush for Barock... and I adore her. Easily one of my favourite characters to draw, and I love that she almost, but never quite consummates her combative relationship with Barock. I'm hoping we'll see more of that frustration in subsequent instalments — it's funny!

DM: An early go at a bit of Neboron tech. My reasoning was that everything on Cumulus would be sleek and new and all of the Walker City tech would be hewn from stone. Remnants of that idea can still be seen (though Cumulus is a lot shabbier than I had originally envisioned... more like a knackered, corruped Utopia).

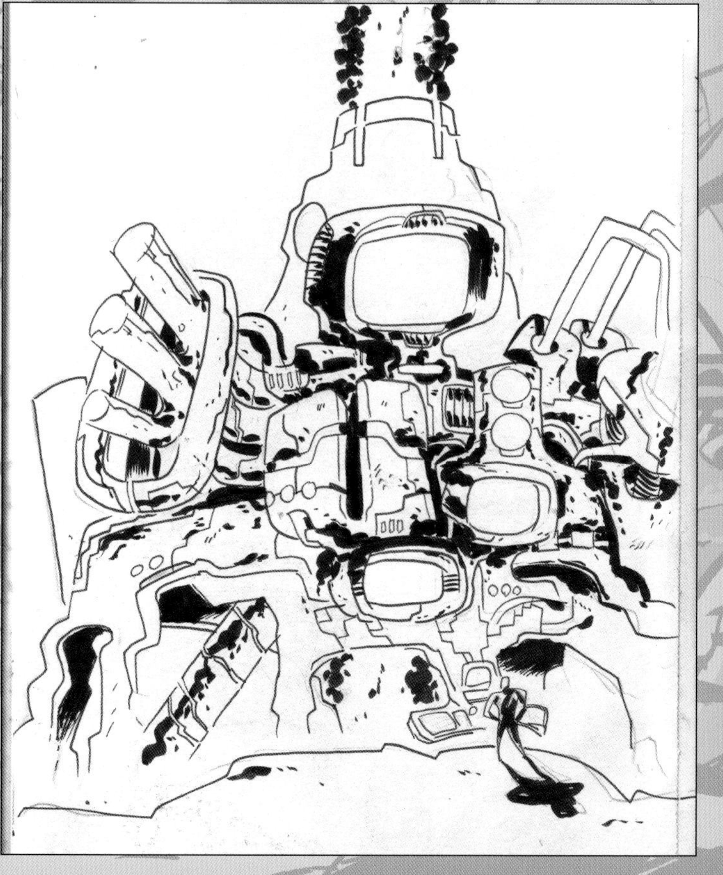

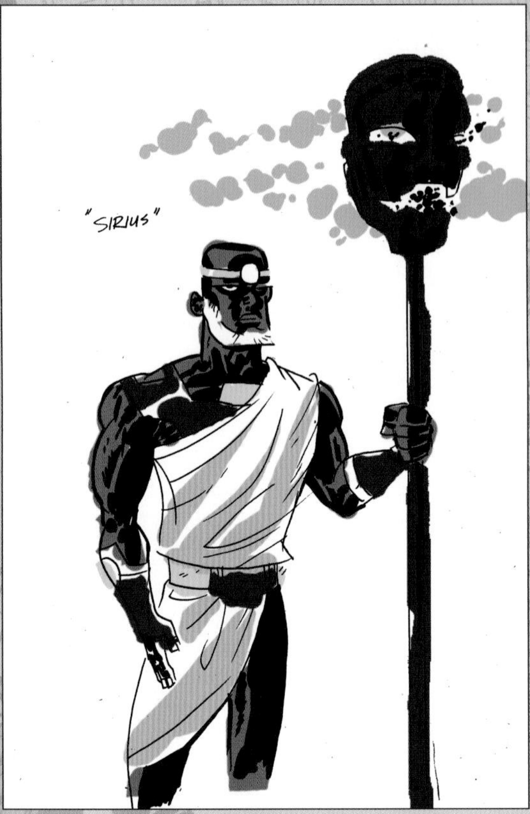
"SIRIUS"

DM: The leader of the heroes, Serius. This guy has a fairly involved backstory that I'd love to get into someday (his name is kind of a clue). This was one of the colour guides I prepared for our stunning colorist Rachelle Rosenberg. Let's hear it for Rachelle!

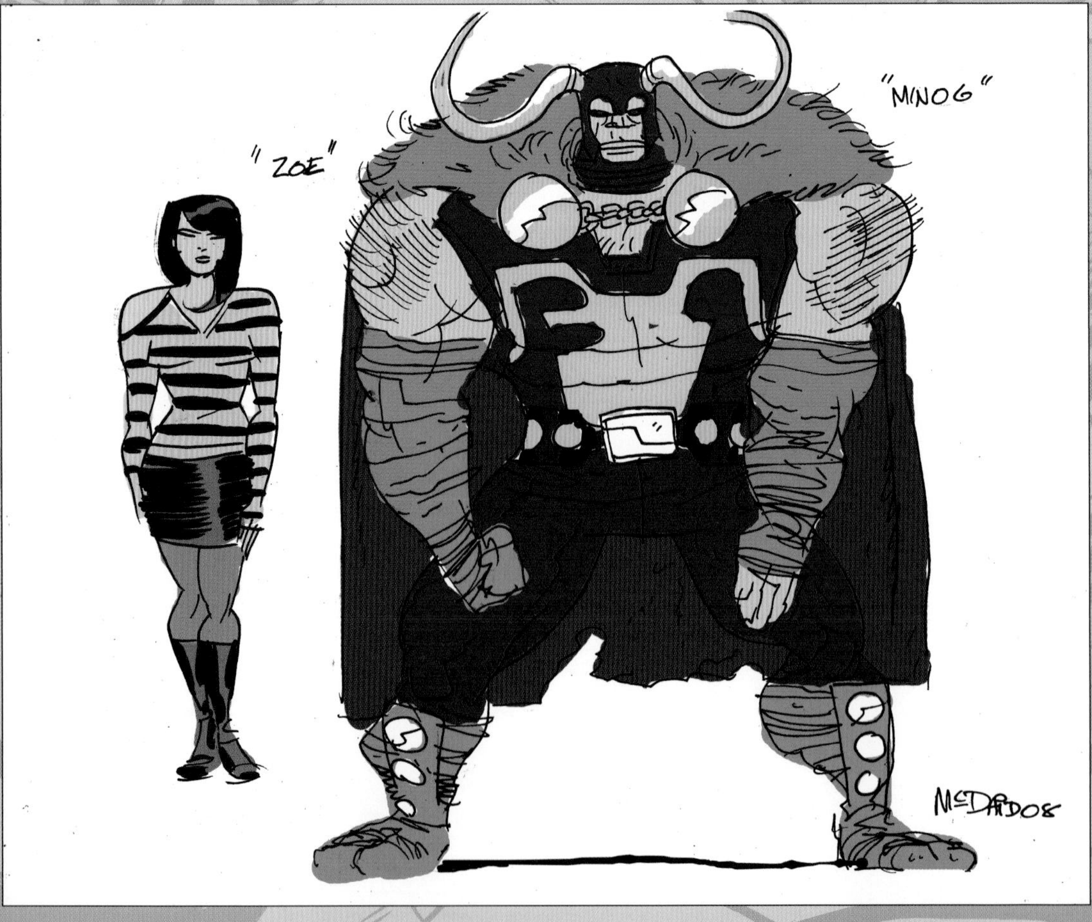
"ZOE"
"MINOG"
McDaid 08

DM: Zoe and Minog. I wanted to create an iconic look for Zoe, a distinctive top and hairstyle. Minog is just one big, ugly bastard.

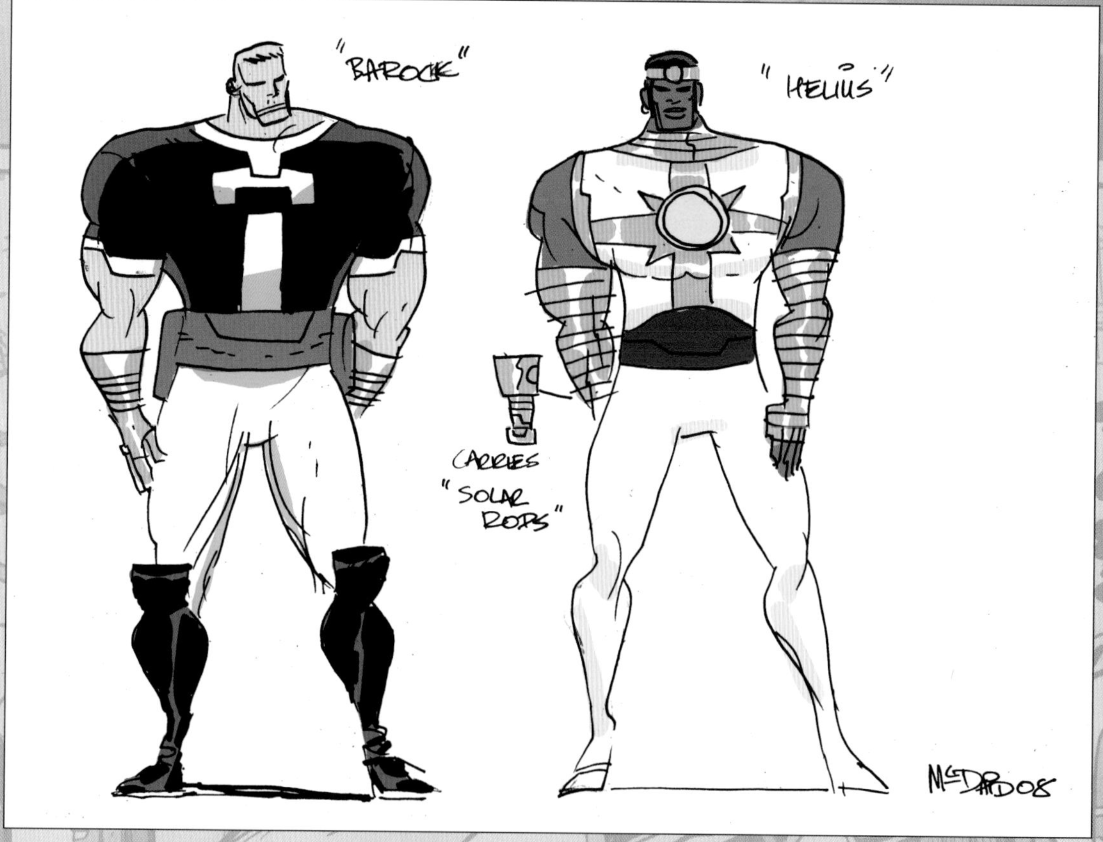
"BAROCK"
"HELIUS"
CARRIES
"SOLAR
RODS"
McDANIEL 08

DM: Barock and Helius. Don't they look like action figures? Hasbro, call us!

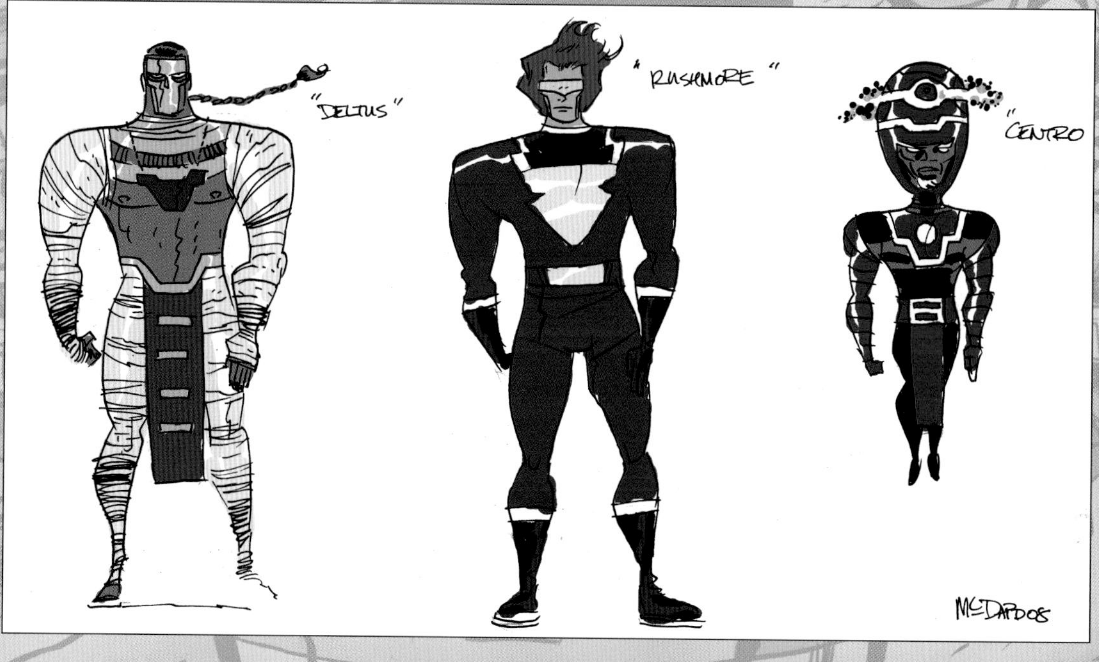
"DELTUS"
"RUSHMORE"
"CENTRO

DM: Deltus, Rushmore and Centris.

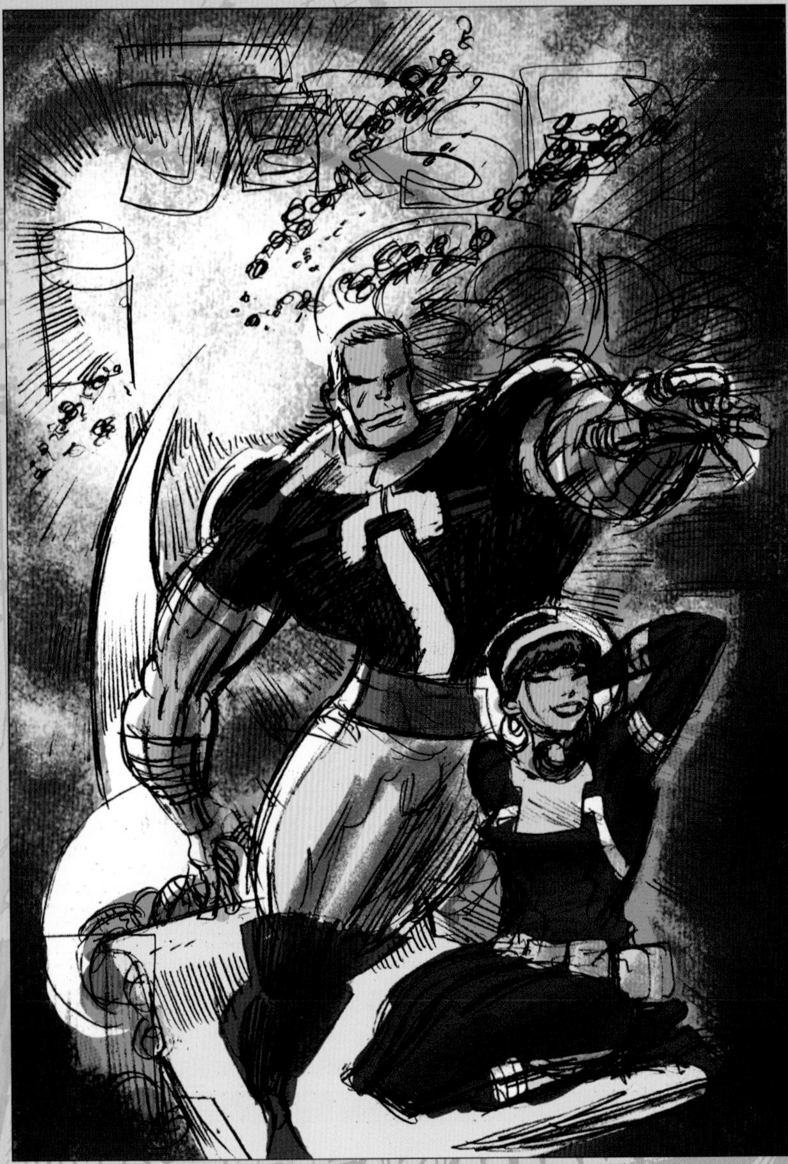

DM: An early cover rough for the issue one cover. Among Glen's many talents is his eye for a bad-ass cover: pretty much every cover for the first arc (even the non-variant, superstar covers) was conjured in the gloomy recesses of Glen's skull. With this one, he asked for a Wally Wood style space suit for Zoe, and a cool Silver Surfer-style pose for Barock.

GB: I love this prelim — his left hand extended in a Kirby Surfer pose. One day I'm going to have to convince you to take another crack at this.

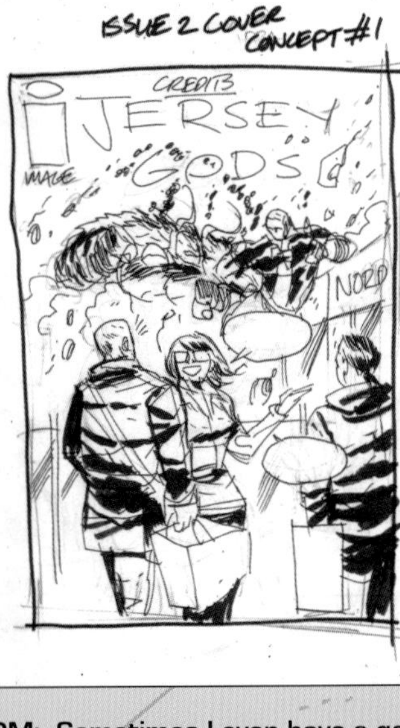
ISSUE 2 COVER CONCEPT #1
CREDITS
JERSEY
GODS
IMAGE

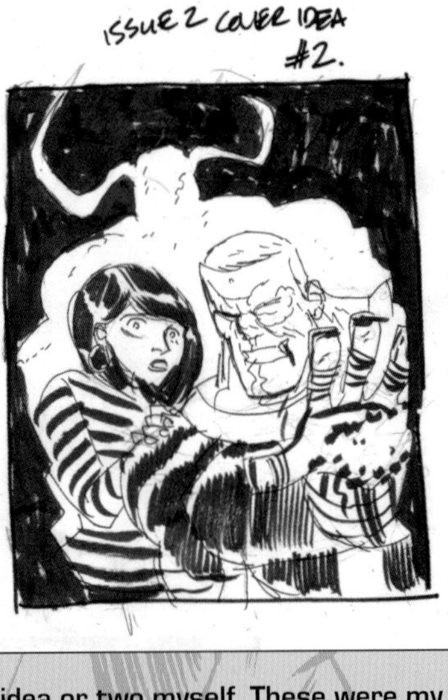
ISSUE 2 COVER IDEA #2.

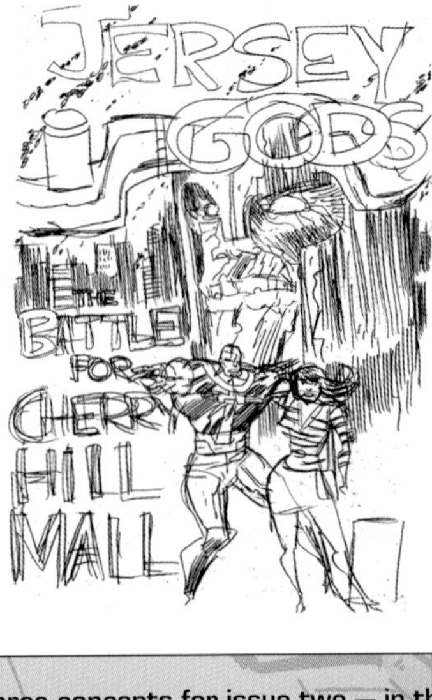
JERSEY
GODS
THE BATTLE FOR
CHERRY
HILL
MALL

DM: Sometimes I even have a good idea or two myself. These were my three concepts for issue two — in the end we went with number one.

GB: Number two was really strong as well. We're going to have to do something like that down the line.

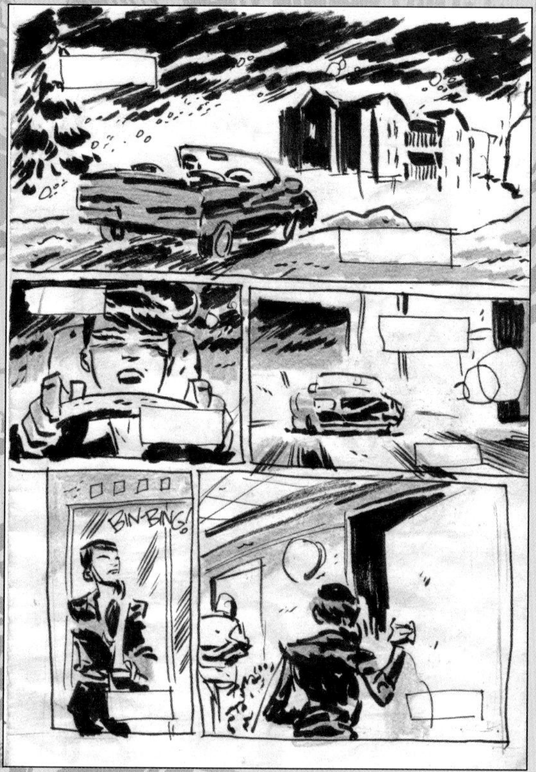
BIN-BING!

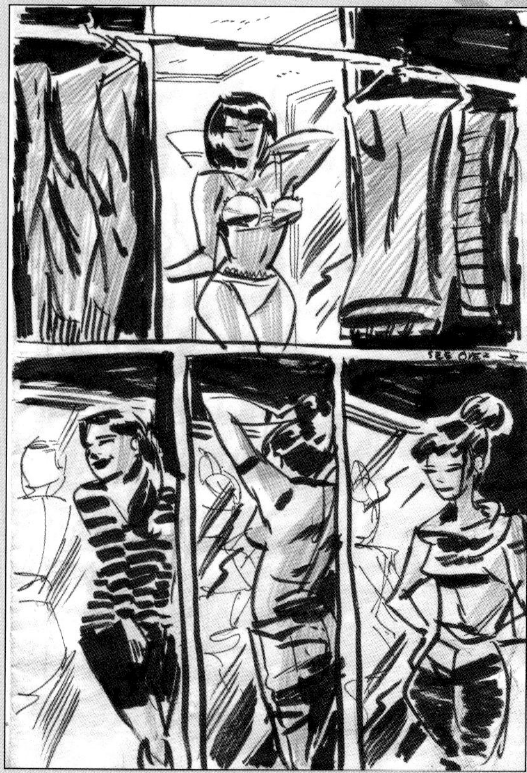

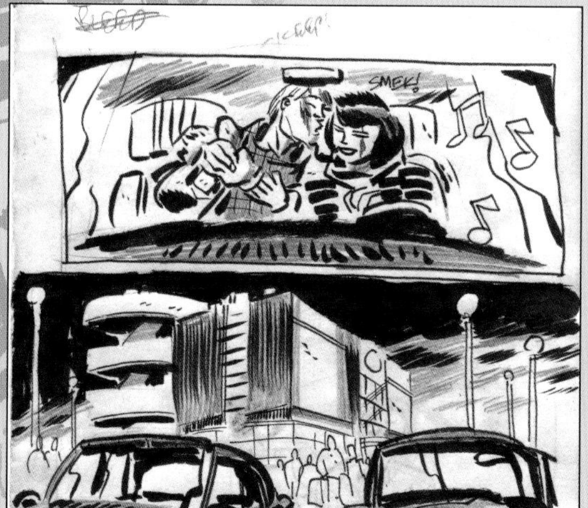
SMEK!

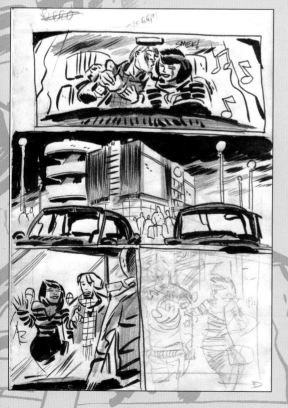

DM: Here's where the story begins — Zoe driving home through the snow, choosing something sexy to wear... then heading to the mall for a fateful meeting with beings from another world.

DM: Of course for me, this is really where the story begins. We were fortunate enough to be invited to participate in Popgun Volume Two, and elected to come up with a couple of neat, one-page shorts to "tease" the idea. Glen's scripts were "ROCK GOD" and "TURNPIKE", each riffing on some unique aspect of Jersey livin' (specifically the Springsteen connection and that enormous road. You Americans!). My first proper JG job, this is (it probably shows)!

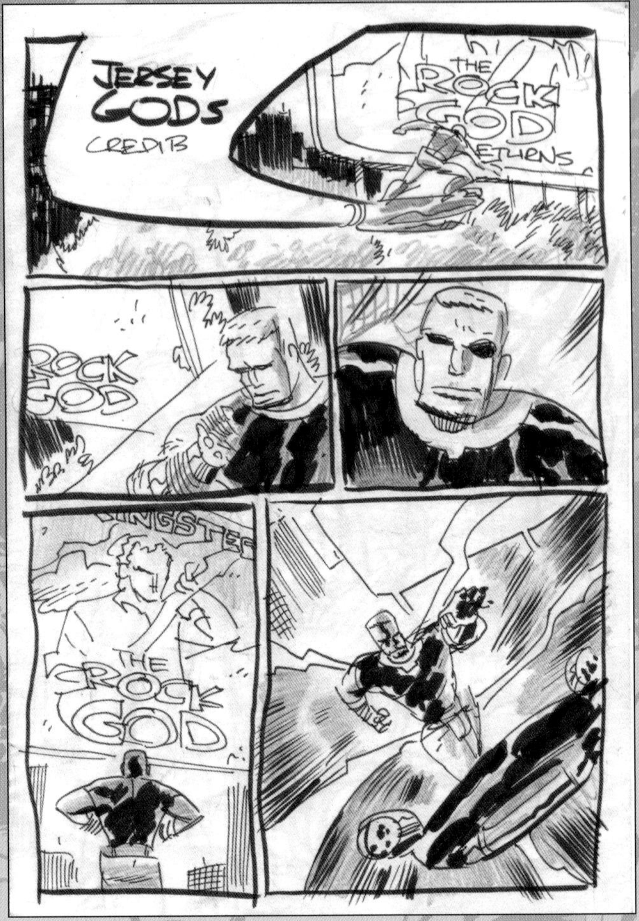
JERSEY GODS
CREDITS
THE ROCK GOD RETURNS
ROCK GOD
THE ROCK GOD

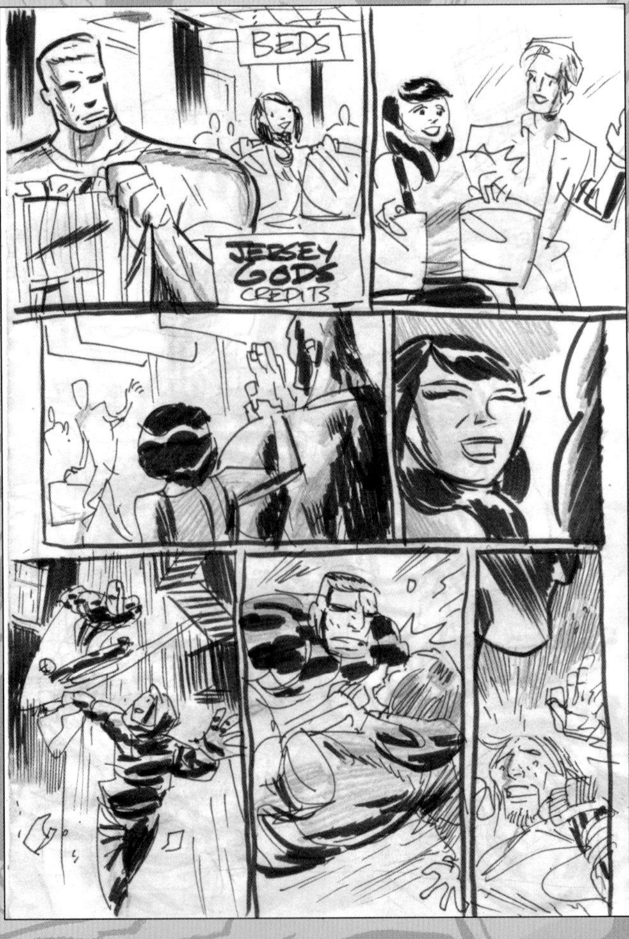
BEDS
JERSEY GODS
CREDITS

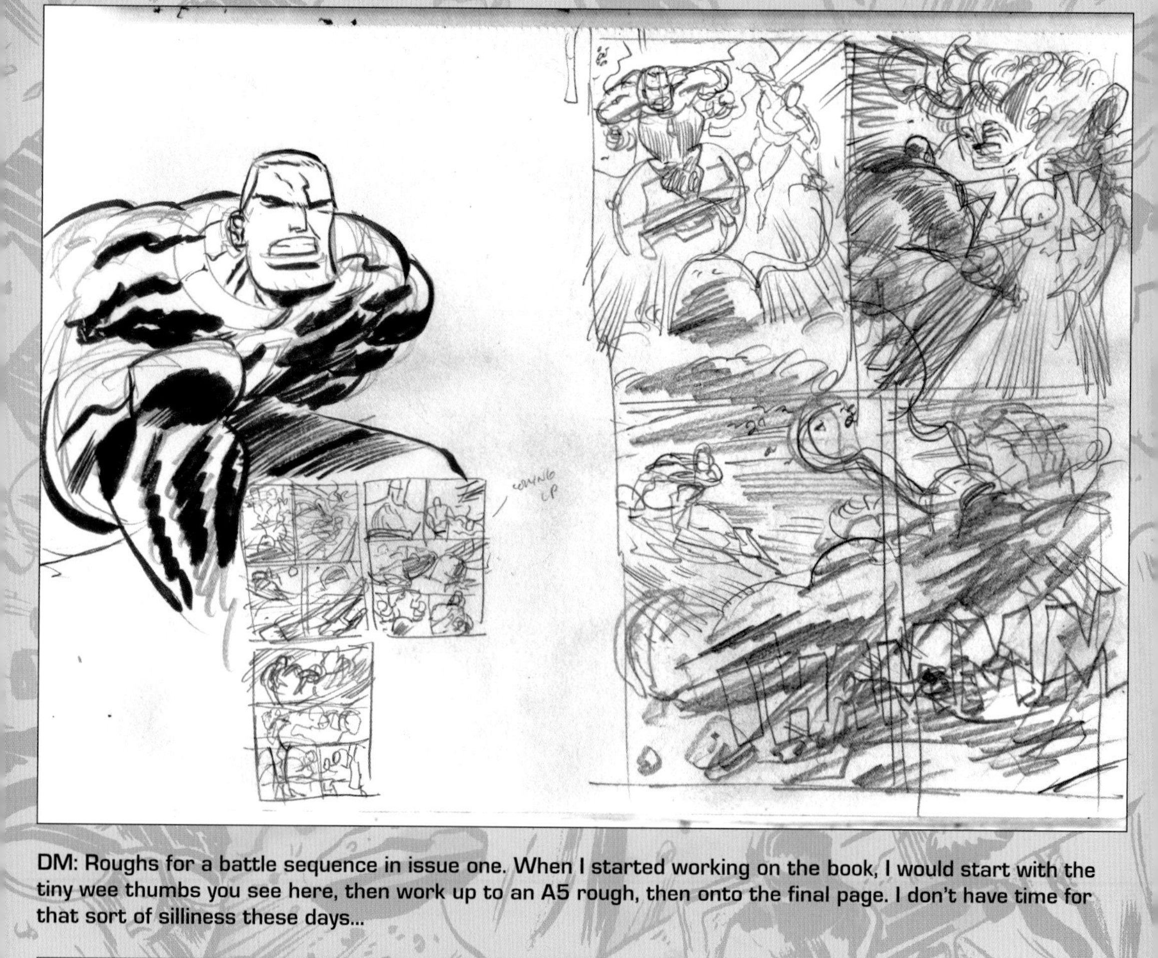

DM: Roughs for a battle sequence in issue one. When I started working on the book, I would start with the tiny wee thumbs you see here, then work up to an A5 rough, then onto the final page. I don't have time for that sort of silliness these days...

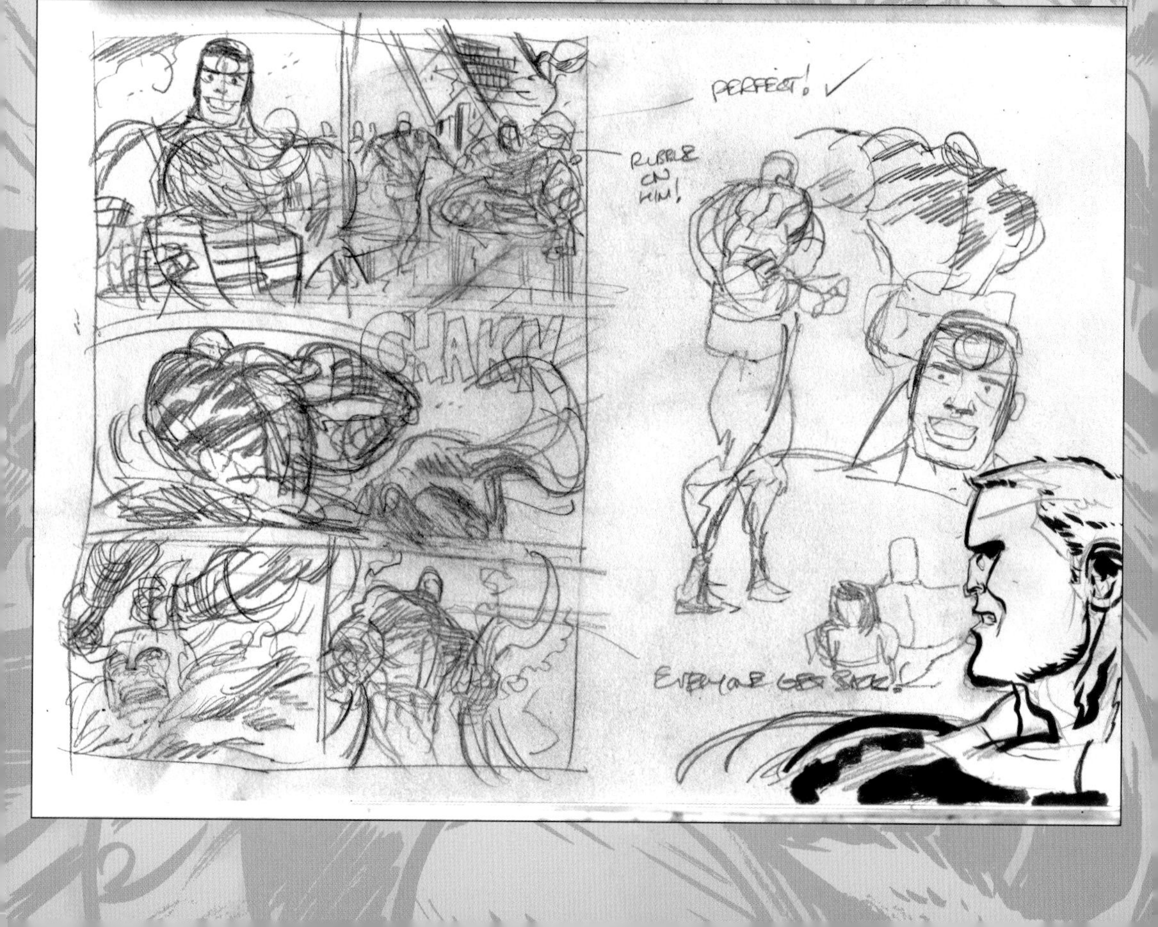
PERFECT!
RUBBLE ON HIM!
EVERYONE GET BACK!

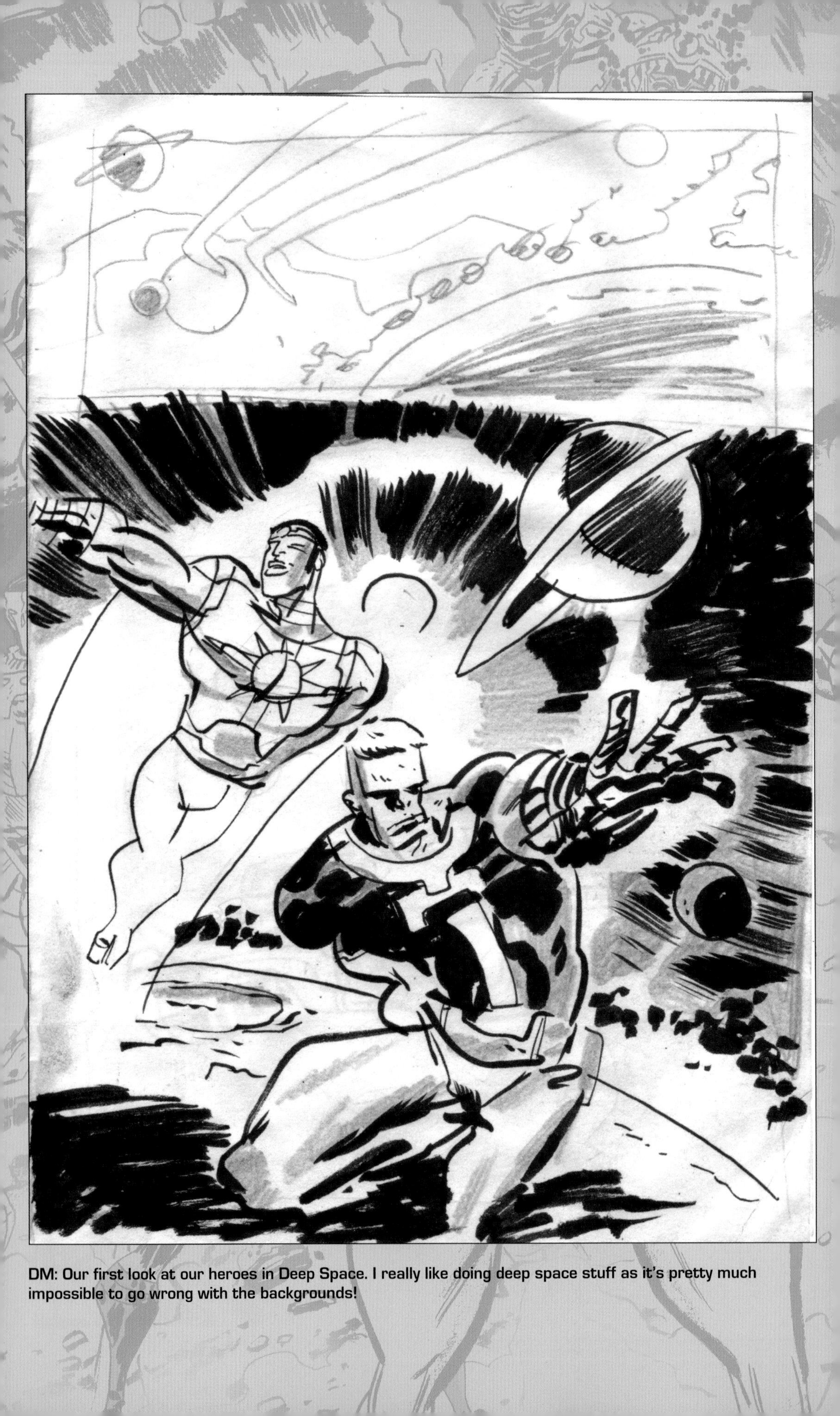

DM: Our first look at our heroes in Deep Space. I really like doing deep space stuff as it's pretty much impossible to go wrong with the backgrounds!

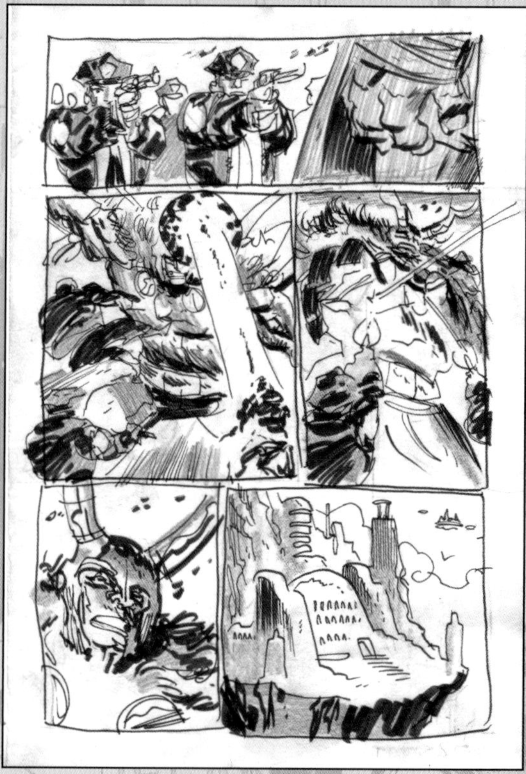

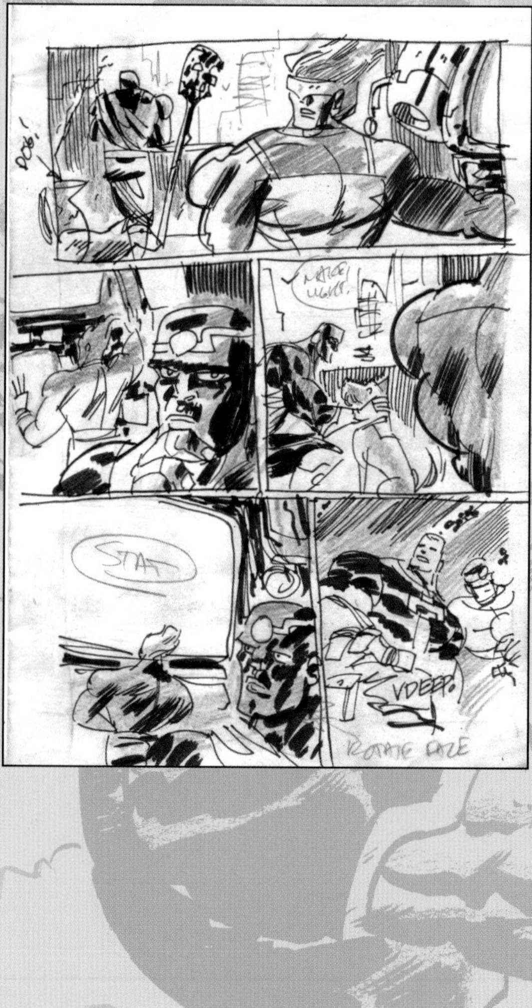

DM: Another sequence from issue one — and a glimpse into a bit of Neboron realpolitik. Serius dispatches Helius and Barock to Earth, where the God of War must face his deadliest enemy...

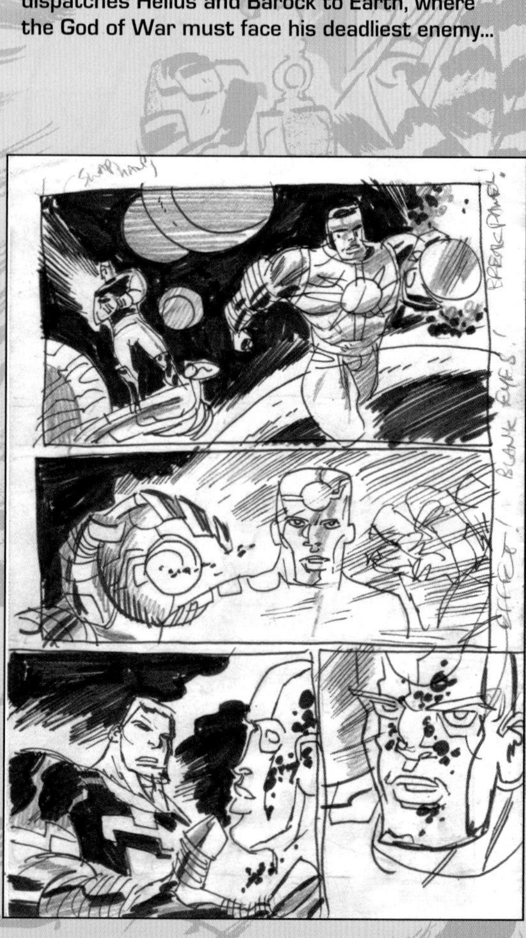

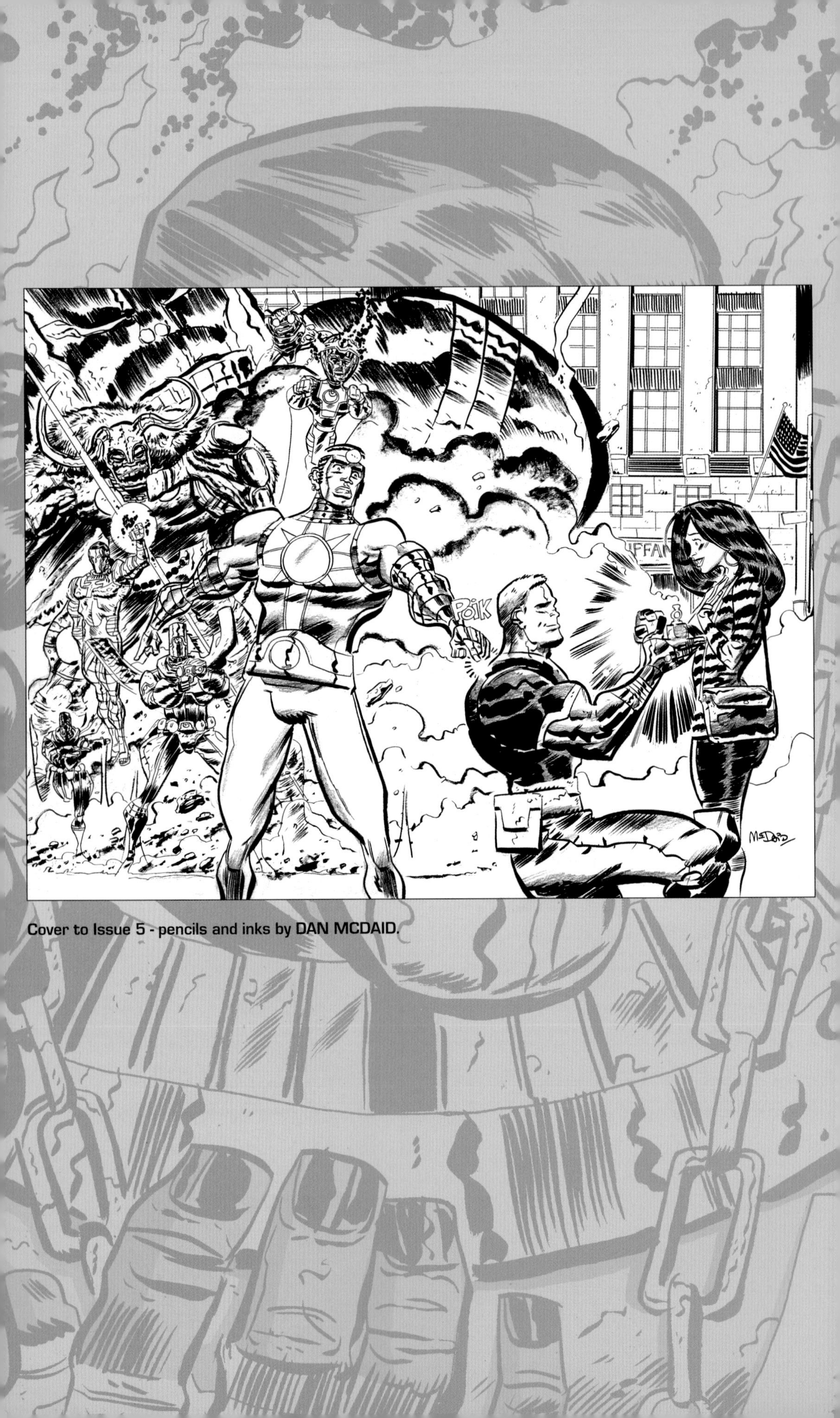
POIK

Cover to Issue 5 - pencils and inks by DAN MCDAID.